IBM Db2 11.1 Certification Guide

Explore techniques to master database programming and administration tasks in IBM Db2

Mohankumar Saraswatipura
Robert (Kent) Collins

BIRMINGHAM - MUMBAI

IBM Db2 11.1 Certification Guide

Commissioning Editor: Amey Varangaonkar
Acquisition Editor: Divya Poojari
Content Development Editor: Eisha Dsouza
Technical Editor: Ishita Vora
Copy Editors: Safis Editing, Vikrant Phadkay
Project Coordinator: Shweta Birwatkar
Proofreader: Safis Editing
Indexer: Priyanka Dhadke
Graphics: Jisha Chirayil
Production Coordinator: Nilesh Mohite

First published: June 2018
Production reference: 1270618

Published by Packt Publishing Ltd.
Livery Place
35 Livery Street
Birmingham
B3 2PB, UK.

ISBN 978-1-78862-691-0

www.packtpub.com

mapt.io

Mapt is an online digital library that gives you full access to over 5,000 books and videos, as well as industry leading tools to help you plan your personal development and advance your career. For more information, please visit our website.

Why subscribe?

- Spend less time learning and more time coding with practical eBooks and Videos from over 4,000 industry professionals

- Improve your learning with Skill Plans built especially for you

- Get a free eBook or video every month

- Mapt is fully searchable

- Copy and paste, print, and bookmark content

PacktPub.com

Did you know that Packt offers eBook versions of every book published, with PDF and ePub files available? You can upgrade to the eBook version at www.PacktPub.com and as a print book customer, you are entitled to a discount on the eBook copy. Get in touch with us at service@packtpub.com for more details.

At www.PacktPub.com, you can also read a collection of free technical articles, sign up for a range of free newsletters, and receive exclusive discounts and offers on Packt books and eBooks.

Foreword

It is my pleasure and honor to introduce this book's authors, Mohankumar "Mohan" Saraswatipura and Robert "Kent" Collins. Since the late 1990s, my work and life's mission has been to help grow, nurture, and support the community around IBM® Db2® databases. Through presenting at the International Db2 User Group, helping worldwide Db2 customers and clients, and producing the ever-popular edutainment webinar series The Db2Night Show™, I have come to know the best of the best in the Db2 industry. You are about to learn from, and enjoy, an excellent book written by two of the brightest minds in the Db2 world.

I first noticed Mohan in 2013 when he participated in "Db2's GOT TALENT" on The Db2Night Show. His presentations were brilliant, polished, professional, and helpful, and ultimately he won first place in this worldwide competition. I met him in person at IDUG's 25th Anniversary in Orlando later that year and was further impressed by his professionalism, articulate communication, and enthusiastic and polite demeanor. In recent years, Mohan also authored a DB2 9.7 Advanced Application Developer Cookbook, co-authored the DB2 10.1 and 10.5 Administration Certification Study Guide, and presented at IDUG several times. He has been a repeat popular guest on The Db2Night Show many times and has published several popular magazine articles. Seriously, we should all worry about his health—it seems this man never sleeps, or, if he does, his life revolves around Db2 24x7.

I first met Kent when IBM was launching DB2 V10.5 with "BLU" columnar capabilities at the Almaden Research Center. If you're an IBM groupie like many, Kent's face might be more familiar to you because IBM has featured him at many of their roadshow events for emerging technologies. He has been featured as a "talking head" during keynotes at IBM IOD conferences, the Pure System Launch event in Boston, IBM Tech and Customer Briefings, and more. He has authored many TCP style documents on pre-release versions of Db2 that showcase new features, functionality, and Db2 performance breakthroughs. And like Mohan, Kent also co-authored the DB2 10.1 and 10.5 Administration Certification Study Guide. He has presented at several IBM and IDUG conferences, and he's been our guest many times on The Db2Night Show. Frankly, when it comes to IBM Db2 pureScale, I think Kent is absolutely on the top shelf, with very few peers if any.

As a key executive at a Db2 Performance Tools company, I've long believed that it is critically important for people to first understand what is important to monitor, how to do it, and how to interpret and react to the Db2 performance data. Once people have this foundational understanding, then they can make smart choices about the processes and tools that they will use to automate analysis. This is why I've taught technical sessions at IDUG every year since 1996, and it's also one of the reasons that I think you are going to love this book. Mohan and Kent have a gift for explaining the complex; making it simple; and leading with examples, samples, and illustrations. After you read Chapter 5 on monitoring Db2 activity and try out many of the sample monitoring SQLs provided, you'll be torn between keeping this book at your desk and under your pillow. Maybe you should buy a second copy!

Finally, and not surprisingly, both Mohan and Kent have been awarded IBM Champion status from 2010 to 2018 (current). Because of their deep knowledge of and love for IBM Db2, their many devoted contributions to the worldwide Db2 community, and their professional, helpful demeanor, I recently nominated both Mohan and Kent to become IBM Db2 GOLD Consultants. I hope you enjoy this book and learn a lot from it, and that someday you might be blessed with the opportunity to meet these Db2 professionals in person at an IDUG conference, have the ability to work alongside them professionally, or both!

With kindest regards,

Scott Hayes

President and Founder of DBI Software, IBM Db2 GOLD Consultant, and IBM Champion

Contributors

About the authors

Mohankumar Saraswatipura is a database solutions architect focusing on IBM Db2, Linux, Unix, Windows, and SAP HANA solutions. He is an IBM Champion (2010-2018) and a DB2's Got Talent 2013 winner. He is also a frequent speaker at the DB2Night Show and IDUG North America conferences. He has written dozens of technical papers for IBM developerWorks, Data Magazine, and the DB2 10.1/10.5 certification guide. He holds a Master's of technology in computer science and an executive MBA from IIM Calcutta.

Robert (Kent) Collins, the founder of Shiloh Consulting, is currently a database solutions architect at BNSF Railway. He is an IBM Champion (2010–2018) and a frequent speaker at the DB2Night Show, IDUG North America, and IBM Insight conferences. Kent has worked continually with Db2 since its introduction to the market in 1984, amassing a wealth of knowledge and experience. He graduated from University of Texas in Dallas with majors in mathematics and computer science.

About the reviewers

Colin A. Chapman has worked for 30+ years as an IT professional in a broad range of technical roles. His experience covers mainframe operations, application design and development, systems programming, and database design and administration. More recently, he has specialized in Db2 on Linux, Unix, and Windows platforms. He has a broad range of in-depth Db2 skills, particularly in areas such as large partitioned databases, clustering, high availability, cross-platform replication, performance, recovery, security, and complex problem diagnostics.

Corina Munsch has 25+ years of software design and development experience. She has developed applications in C++, Java, and Groovy/Grails. She has experience with both Oracle and Db2 databases. She is currently a senior consulting application developer.

Lan Pham has worked for over 27 years as an IT professional in a broad range of product development roles within IBM Toronto Lab (especially Db2) for over 24 years. More recently, he worked on Db2 pureScale kernel development. He holds a Bachelor of Science degree in electrical engineering from University of Western Ontario.

Packt is searching for authors like you

If you're interested in becoming an author for Packt, please visit `authors.packtpub.com` and apply today. We have worked with thousands of developers and tech professionals, just like you, to help them share their insight with the global tech community. You can make a general application, apply for a specific hot topic that we are recruiting an author for, or submit your own idea.

Table of Contents

Preface

IBM Db2 is a Relational Database Management System (RDBMS) that helps users to store, analyze, and retrieve their data efficiently. This guide will help you understand Db2 v11.1 DBA certification topics. It covers more than 50 step-by-step procedures for DBAs, all of Db2 v11.1's new features, and its benefits in the real world. This book can also be used to enhance your Db2 skill set.

Who this book is for

This guide is an excellent choice for database administrators, architects, and application developers who are keen to obtain a certification in Db2. Basic understanding of Db2 is expected in order to get the most out of this guide.

What this book covers

Chapter 1, *Introduction to the Db2 Certification Path*, covers the certification exam and how to register for it.

Chapter 2, *Db2 Server Management*, is about building and configuring Db2 instances and databases. It also covers topics on autonomic computing, which will help you to manage your database optimally.

Chapter 3, *Physical Design*, covers all the Db2 database design aspects for DBAs.

Chapter 4, *Implementing Business Rules*, explains business implementation rules through Db2 constraints.

Chapter 5, *Monitoring Db2 Activity*, covers all Db2 monitoring aspects for DBAs and architects.

Chapter 6, *Db2 Utilities*, explains all Db2 utilities and their uses.

Chapter 7, *High Availability*, covers all Db2 high availability and disaster recovery features, including pureScale.

Chapter 8, *Db2 Security*, explains all Db2 security features and their implementation methods.

To get the most out of this book

Download and install IBM Db2 v11.1 Developer Community Edition from `https://www.ibm.com/account/reg/us-en/signup?formid=urx-19888` and follow the instructions in the chapters. This certification guide gives you easy access to the invaluable learning techniques. Try out every single command and statement to experience the techniques.

Download the color images

We also provide a PDF file that has color images of the screenshots/diagrams used in this book. You can download it here: `http://www.packtpub.com/sites/default/files/downloads/Bookname_ColorImages.pdf`.

Conventions used

There are a number of text conventions used throughout this book.

`CodeInText`: Indicates code words in text, database table names, folder names, filenames, file extensions, pathnames, dummy URLs, user input, and Twitter handles. Here is an example: "Mount the downloaded `WebStorm-10*.dmg` disk image file as another disk in your system."

A block of code is set as follows:

```
html, body, #map {
 height: 100%;
 margin: 0;
 padding: 0
}
```

When we wish to draw your attention to a particular part of a code block, the relevant lines or items are set in bold:

```
[default]
exten => s,1,Dial(Zap/1|30)
exten => s,2,Voicemail(u100)
exten => s,102,Voicemail(b100)
exten => i,1,Voicemail(s0)
```

Any command-line input or output is written as follows:

```
$ mkdir css
$ cd css
```

Bold: Indicates a new term, an important word, or words that you see onscreen. For example, words in menus or dialog boxes appear in the text like this. Here is an example: "Select **System info** from the **Administration** panel."

Warnings or important notes appear like this.

Tips and tricks appear like this.

Get in touch

Feedback from our readers is always welcome.

General feedback: Email `feedback@packtpub.com` and mention the book title in the subject of your message. If you have questions about any aspect of this book, please email us at `questions@packtpub.com`.

Errata: Although we have taken every care to ensure the accuracy of our content, mistakes do happen. If you have found a mistake in this book, we would be grateful if you would report this to us. Please visit `www.packtpub.com/submit-errata`, selecting your book, clicking on the Errata Submission Form link, and entering the details.

Piracy: If you come across any illegal copies of our works in any form on the Internet, we would be grateful if you would provide us with the location address or website name. Please contact us at `copyright@packtpub.com` with a link to the material.

If you are interested in becoming an author: If there is a topic that you have expertise in and you are interested in either writing or contributing to a book, please visit `authors.packtpub.com`.

Reviews

Please leave a review. Once you have read and used this book, why not leave a review on the site that you purchased it from? Potential readers can then see and use your unbiased opinion to make purchase decisions, we at Packt can understand what you think about our products, and our authors can see your feedback on their book. Thank you!

For more information about Packt, please visit `packtpub.com`.

1

Introduction to the Db2 Certification Path

This certification guide is designed for IT professionals who plan to take the IBM Certified Database Administrator–Db2 11.1 for Linux, Unix, and Windows exam C2090-600. Using this certification study guide, you will learn how to do the following:

- Configure and manage Db2 v11.1 servers, instances, and databases
- Implement Db2 BLU Acceleration databases
- Create and implement database objects
- Implement business rules using constraints
- Implement high availability and disaster recovery solutions
- Monitor and troubleshoot at instance and database levels
- Implement security at instance, database, and objects levels

This certification study guide is designed to provide the Db2 professional with the information required to successfully obtain C2090-600 certification. Each chapter contains topics covered in the exam, plus valuable insights into each topic, along with sample exam questions and detailed answers.

Db2 11.1 Certification track

IBM offers one Certification track in Db2 for Linux, Unix, and Windows, essentially covering the fundamentals of intermediate level DBA concepts. The diagram that follows shows the database administration track and the prerequisites required to obtain the DBA certification:

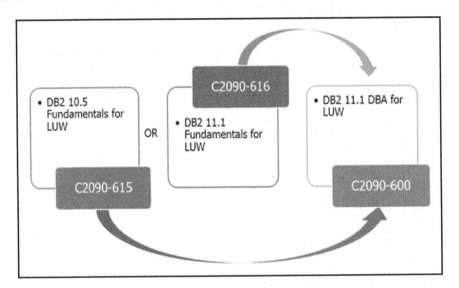

Db2 v11.1 Certification track

Db2 10.5 Fundamentals for LUW–Exam C2090-615

C2090-615 is an entry-level exam for Db2 users who are familiar with the fundamental concepts of Db2 10.5 for Linux, Unix, and Windows. This exam covers the following topics:

- Knowledge of Db2 product packing, including the editions and supported features
- Knowledge of database workloads, such as **Online Transactional Processing (OLTP)**, data warehouse, and **Hybrid Transactional/Analytical Processing (HTAP)** and which Db2 products must be installed to support the desired workload

- Knowledge of Db2 10.5 BLU Acceleration and implementation steps
- Knowledge of Oracle compatibility features and the application enablement process
- Knowledge of data and database security overall including authorities, privileges, **Row and Column Access Control (RCAC)**, and **Label-Based Access Control (LBAC)**
- Knowledge of trusted context and its uses
- Knowledge of different types of tables available within Db2, such as **multi-dimensional clustering (MDC)**, **insert time clustering (ITC)**, **range clustered table (RCT)**, **materialized query table (MQT)**, and range partitioned and temporal tables
- Knowledge of **Structured Query Language (SQL)** statements such as SELECT, INSERT, UPDATE, and DELETE
- Knowledge of **Data Control Language (DCL)** statements such as COMMIT, ROLLBACK, AUTOCOMMIT, and SAVEPOINT
- Knowledge of using SQL stored procedures, **user-defined functions (UDF)**, and triggers
- Knowledge of SQL compatibility enhancements made in Db2 10.5 such as extended rows and excluding NULL keys from indexes
- Knowledge of **Extensible Markup Language (XML)** data retrieval and manipulation using XQuery and XPath expressions
- Knowledge of isolation levels and locking behaviors

Db2 11.1 Fundamentals for LUW–Exam C2090-616

This is an entry-level exam for Db2 users on the fundamental concepts of Db2 11.1 for Linux, Unix, and Windows. This exam covers the following topics:

- Knowledge of Db2 product packing, including the editions and supported features
- Knowledge of database workloads such as OLTP, data warehouse, and HTAP and which Db2 products must be installed to support the desired workload
- Knowledge of Db2 BLU Acceleration and implementation steps
- Knowledge of Db2 pureScale architecture and its benefits

- Knowledge of federation support to link the objects between Db2 databases and other database vendor products
- Knowledge of Oracle and Neteeza compatibility features and the application enablement process
- Knowledge of data and database security overall including authorities, privileges, RCAC, and LBAC
- Knowledge of trusted context and its uses
- Knowledge of different types of tables available within Db2 such as MDC, ITC, RCT, MQT, and range partitioned and temporal tables
- Knowledge of SQL statements such as SELECT, INSERT, UPDATE, and DELETE
- Knowledge of DCL statements such as COMMIT, ROLLBACK , AUTOCOMMIT and SAVEPOINT
- Knowledge of using SQL stored procedures, UDF, and triggers
- Knowledge of SQL compatibility enhancements made in Db2 11.1, such as BINARY and VARBINARY data type support, regular expression support in scalar functions, OLAP extension specifications, including NTH_VALUE, CUME_DIST, PERCENT_RANK, the OFFSET clause in SELECT to skip the number of rows, support for outer joins using the outer join operator (+), new built-in aggregate and scalar functions, new data types, and new synonyms
- Knowledge of OLAP specification functions, such as CUME_DIST(), PERCENT_RANK(), RANK(), DENSE_RANK(), and NTILE(), and the business use cases for each
- Knowledge of XML data retrieval and manipulation using XQuery and XPath expressions
- Knowledge of isolation levels and locking behaviors

Db2 11.1 DBA for LUW–Exam C2090-600

This certification is intended for experienced Db2 users who have the knowledge necessary to perform the regular day-to-day administration of Db2 11.1 instances and databases on Linux, UNIX, and Windows. This exam covers the following topics:

- Ability to install, configure, and manage Db2 servers, instances, and databases
- Knowledge about System Managed, Database Managed, and Automatic Storage table spaces

- Ability to create and manage storage groups based on frequency of data access, acceptable access time, volatility of data, and application business requirements
- Knowledge of Db2 autonomic features such as the **self-tuning memory manager (STMM)**, automatic maintenance, and the configuration advisor
- Knowledge of IBM **Data Server Manager (DSM)** including the editions and its monitoring capabilities
- Ability to design, create, and manage databases using Db2 11.1 BLU Acceleration
- Knowledge of Db2 11.1 pureScale enhancements such as support for HADR sync and near sync data synchronization modes, unified workload balancing, **geographically dispersed Db2 pureScale cluster (GDPC)** support, ease of pureScale cluster health check commands, and GPFS replication support
- Ability to create, manage, and alter database objects
- Ability to implement table, index compression, and backup compression
- Knowledge of SQL compatibility enhancements made in Db2 11.1
- Knowledge of partitioning capabilities available within Db2 including range partitioning, database partitioning, or **Massively Parallel Processing (MPP)**
- Ability to create and modify constraints between tables and to enforce constraint checking using the `SET INTEGRITY` command
- Ability to use the Db2 administrative views and table functions, along with event monitors and `db2pd` command options to monitor the health of the database
- Knowledge of the dsmtop command and its capabilities
- Ability to capture and analyze Db2 explain information for any specific SQL statement and/or workload
- Ability to use Export, Import, Load, and Ingest data movement utilities
- Ability to use the `REORGCHK`, `REORG`, `REBIND`, `RUNSTATS`, `FLUSH PACKAGE CACHE`, `ADMIN_CMD()`, `db2look`, and `db2move` commands
- Ability to back up and recover the database at the database and table space level
- Ability to implement **High Availability and Disaster Recovery (HADR)** in multiple standby environments and to perform HADR takeover with zero or minimal data loss
- Ability to implement and maintain a Db2 pureScale cluster
- Ability to protect data and the database objects against unauthorized access or modification

- Ability to implement RCAC and LBAC to protect sensitive data
- Knowledge of data encryption at rest and in transit using Db2 native encryption and **Secured Socket Layer** (**SSL**) features
- Ability to implement a database audit facility to monitor and record sensitive data access and/or modification

To acquire the IBM Certified Database Administrator–Db2 11.1 for Linux, Unix, and Windows (C2090-600: IBM Db2 11.1 DBA for LUW), candidates must hold either IBM Certified Database Associate–Db2 10.5 Fundamentals for LUW (C2090-615) or the IBM Certified Database Associate–Db2 11.1 Fundamentals for LUW (C2090-616) certification.

Preparing for the C2090-600 certification exam

This certification study guide prepares you for every exam objective with necessary sample questions to ensure that you have the skills and knowledge necessary to take the exam. The Db2 11.1 DBA certification exam questions are categorized into seven units and the percentage of each unit is as listed in the following table. Understanding the percentage of each unit will help you to focus on important concepts and areas:

Unit	Topic	Percentage Coverage
1	Server Management	15
2	Physical Design	22
3	Implementing Business Rules	10
4	Monitoring Db2 Activity	12
5	Utilities	13
6	High Availability	13
7	Security	15

Db2 v11.1 Certification unit percentage split

Registering for the C2090-600 certification exam

Once you are confident and ready to take the certification exam, contact Pearson VUE—an IBM-authorized testing vendor—via `www.pearsonvue.com/ibm` and register for the exam. You must make arrangements to take a certification exam at least 24 hours in advance and be ready with the following information:

- Your name (name as you want it to appear on the certification).
- An identification number (if you have taken IBM certification exams before, this is the number assigned to you at the time of the exam; if you don't have one, the testing vendor will create a new one for you).
- Primary contact information.
- Email address.
- Contact number.
- Certification exam number such as C2090-600.
- The testing center where you would like to take the certification exam.
- The date when you would like to take the certification exam.

For more information about this exam, visit IBM Professional Certification Program at `http://www-03.ibm.com/certify/certs/08002109.shtml`.

Summary

The objective of this chapter was to acquaint you with the certification examinations path available for Db2 v11.1, the certification examination pattern, and the certification examination registration process.

Db2 Server Management 2

This chapter covers the steps to configure and manage Db2 servers, instances, and databases. You will learn how to create and efficiently manage the database storage groups. You will also learn how to use many of the Db2 autonomic computing features to improve database availability and performance. You will learn how to use the Db2 **workload manager (WLM)** and its functionalities to efficiently meet the service-level agreements in the environment. By the end of the chapter, you will also be able to use the **data server manager (DSM)** to administer, monitor, and manage the Db2 database server. After the completion of this chapter, you will be able to demonstrate the ability to:

- Create and manage Db2 instances and databases
- View and modify the Db2 registry variables
- View and modify the Db2 database manager configuration parameters
- View and modify the Db2 database configuration parameters
- Use Db2 autonomic computing features, including the **self-tuning memory manager (STMM)**, data compression, automatic maintenance, the configuration advisor, and utility throttling
- Create and modify storage groups
- Use Db2 WLM to effectively manage the Db2 server
- Use IBM DSM to administer the Db2 database server

Working with Db2 instances

A Db2 instance is an environment responsible for managing system resources and the databases that fall under their control. Basically, an instance is made up of a set of processes, threads, and memory areas. The following diagram illustrates the relationship between a Db2 server, its instances, and its associated databases:

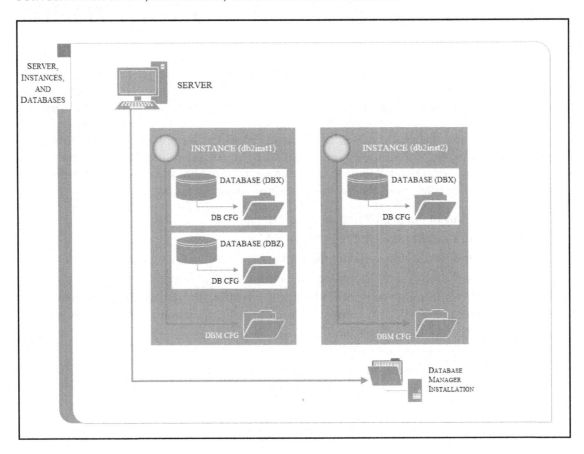

Relationship between server, instances, and databases

The server is at the highest level in the hierarchy, and you can have multiple Db2 versions installed on a given server. It is recommended that you check the system requirements for IBM Db2 for Linux, Unix, and Windows installations at https://www-01.ibm.com/support/docview.wss?uid=swg27038033.

Instances are second in the hierarchy and are responsible for managing the system resources required to run the database. You can create multiple instances on a server, providing a unique database environment for each instance. In the example shown in the figure above, there are two instances, db2inst1 and db2inst2, which provide an environment to run a different set of databases of the same or different versions. Once an instance is created, the instance directory stores all information that pertains to a database instance. Each instance contains:

- The **database manager configuration (DBM CFG)** file
- The system database directory
- The node directory
- The node configuration file, called db2nodes.cfg
- Other files, which contain troubleshooting information

Databases occupy the third level in the hierarchy and are responsible for managing the storage, modification, and retrieval of data. When a database is first created, the database directory stores all information that pertains to a database. Each database contains:

- The **database configuration (DB CFG)** file
- The system catalog tables and associated objects, including storage groups, table spaces, buffer pools, and containers
- Allocation of the database recovery log, sometimes known as the transaction log

Db2 provides a number of commands for creating and managing instances. The following table shows the system commands that can be executed directly from a regular Unix shell. In order to invoke the CLP on Windows, execute and run db2cmd. On Unix servers, log in to the server as an instance owner and start a command line session:

Command	Purpose	Command Path
db2icrt	Creates a new instance	Unix: DB2DIR/instance Windows: DB2PATHbin
db2idrop	Removes an existing instance	Unix: DB2DIR/instance Windows: DB2PATHbin
db2ilist	Lists all of the instances that have been defined within one installation	Unix: DB2DIR/instance Windows: DB2PATHbin
db2level	Shows the version and service level of the installed Db2 product for the current instance	~/sqllib/bin/db2level

db2ckupgrade	Verifies that one or more databases are ready to be upgraded to a newer version of Db2	Unix: DB2DIR/bin of the newly installed DB2 version Windows: db2WindowsUtilities from the product CD
db2iupgrade	Upgrades an existing instance to a newer version of Db2	Unix: DB2DIR/instance Windows: DB2PATHbin
db2iupdt	Updates an instance to a higher Fix Pack level within a release, converts an instance from non-pureScale to pureScale, or changes the topology of a Db2 pureScale instance	Unix: DB2DIR/instance Windows: DB2PATHbin
db2start	Starts the database manager for the current instance	Unix: ~/sqllib/adm/
db2stop	Stops the database manager for the current instance	Unix: ~/sqllib/adm/

Db2 instance management commands

Creating an instance

The db2icrt command creates a Db2 instance in the home directory of the instance owner. It creates the SQLLIB subdirectory and DBM CFG parameters, with the default settings.

The syntax for the command in the Unix environment is as follows:

```
db2icrt -u <FencedUserID> <InstanceName>
```

In the preceding command, the following applies:

- FencedUserID: Identifies the name of the user ID under which fenced user-defined functions and fenced stored procedures will run
- InstanceName: Identifies the name of the instance, which is also the name of the user in the operating system

If you want to create an instance named `db2inst1` using the fenced username `db2fenc1`, you can do so by executing the command `db2icrt` as the root user from the Db2 installation instance directory, also called the `DB2DIR/instance` directory:

```
cd /opt/ibm/db2/V11.1/instance
db2icrt -u db2fenc1 db2inst1
```

Dropping an instance

The `db2idrop` command drops an existing Db2 instance and removes the `SQLLIB` subdirectory and DBM CFG parameter file. However, this command can only be run when the instance is stopped and is inactive.

The syntax for the command is as follows:

```
db2idrop <InstanceName>
```

In the preceding command, the following applies:

- `InstanceName`: Identifies the name of the instance intended to be dropped

If you want to drop an instance named `db2inst1`, execute the command `db2idrop` as the root user from the `DB2DIR/instance` directory:

```
db2idrop db2inst1
```

Listing instances

The `db2ilist` command lists all of the instances that have been defined within one installation, and the syntax for the command is as follows:

```
db2ilist
```

If you want to list all of the instances for the Db2 `v11.1` installation, you can do so by executing the command `db2ilist` as an instance owner:

```
db2ilist

-- Output of db2ilist would look something like:

db2inst1
db2inst2
```

Displaying the Db2 service level

The db2level command shows the current version and service level of the installed Db2 product for the current instance.

In Db2, what do mod pack and Fix Pack mean?
This is Db2's four-part product signature, of the format VV, RR, MM, FF where:

- VV - Version number

- RR - Release number

- MM - Modification number

- FF - Fix Pack number

For example, in db2levelDB21085I, the instance or installation (instance name, where applicable: db2inst1) uses 64 bits and Db2 code release SQL11013, with level identifier 0204010F. Informational tokens are Db2 v11.1.3.3, s1708150100, DYN1708150100AMD64, and Fix Pack 3. The product is installed at /opt/ibm/db2/V11.1. Here, the Db2 version is 11, the release number is 1, and the modification number is 3, with Fix Pack 3. Until Db2 11.1.1.1, the modification value was always 0 (zero), and starting with Db2 11.1.1.1, the modification number (MM) will be updated in Fix Packs that contain new functionalities.

Verifying the database's readiness for upgrading

The db2ckupgrade command verifies that a database is ready for an upgrade, and the syntax for the command is as follows:**db2ckupgrade <DatabaseName> -l <UpgradeCheckLog>**

In the preceding command, the following applies:

- UpgradeCheckLog: Identifies a log file to write a list of errors and warning messages generated for the scanned database.

- DatabaseName: Identifies the name of the database intended to be upgraded:

```
db2ckupgrade SAMPLE -l upgradecheck.log
```

If you want to check the readiness of database SAMPLE to upgrade from Db2 10.5 to Db2 11.1, you can do so by executing the command db2ckupgrade as the instance owner of the database SAMPLE from the DB2DIR/bin directory, where DB2DIR is the location of the newer Db2 version installation:

```
db2ckupgrade SAMPLE -l upgradecheck.log
```

Upgrading a database instance

The db2iupgrade command upgrades the database instance from an older version to a newer version.

The syntax for the command is as follows:

```
db2iupgrade <InstanceName>
```

In the preceding command, the following applies:

- InstanceName: Identifies the name of the instance intended to be upgraded

    If you want to upgrade an instance named db2inst1 from Db2 10.5 to Db2 11.1, you can do so by executing the command db2iupgrade as the root user from the DB2DIR/instance directory of Db2 11.1:

```
db2iupgrade db2inst1
```

Starting and stopping an instance

The db2start command starts the database manager background processes associated with a particular instance. The syntax for this command is as follows:

```
db2start
```

The syntax could also be:

```
START [DATABASE MANAGER | DB MANAGER | DBM]
```

If you want to start the database manager for the db2inst1, execute the following command:

```
db2start
```

You can also execute the following:

```
db2 "START DATABASE MANAGER"
```

The db2stop command stops the database manager processes for a particular instance. The syntax for this command is as follows:

```
db2stop
```

You can also use:

```
STOP [DATABASE MANAGER | DB MANAGER | DBM] <FORCE>
```

If you want to start the database manager for the db2inst1, execute the following command:

```
db2stop
```

You can also execute the following:

```
db2 "STOP DATABASE MANAGER"
```

Attaching and detaching to an instance

The ATTACH command attaches a user or an application to an instance. The basic syntax for this command is as follows:

```
ATTACH TO [InstanceName] USER [UserID] USING [Password]
```

In the preceding command, the following applies:

- InstanceName: Identifies the name of the instance to make an attachment
- UserID: Identifies the user under whom the instance will attach
- Password: Identifies the password for the user under whom the instance will attach

If you want to attach to an instance db2inst1 using the user db2admin, the command will look as follows:

```
db2 "ATTACH TO db2inst1 USER db2admin USING MyPassw0rd"
   Instance Attachment Information
Instance server        = DB2/LINUXX8664 11.1.3.3
Authorization ID       = DB2ADMIN
Local instance alias   = DB2INST1
```

The DETACH command detaches a user or an application from the earlier attached Db2 instance. If you want to detach from instance db2inst1, issue the following command:

```
db2 "DETACH"
```

Quiescing an instance

The QUIESCE command forces all users off of an instance or a specific database. You can still perform database administrative tasks while the instance or the database is in quiesced mode. To reactivate the instance and restore the database to the regular operational mode, use the UNQUIESCE command. Note that the users with SYSADM, SYSMAINT, and SYSCTRL authority will continue to have access to the instance, and the users with SYSADM and DBADM authority will continue to have access to the database while instance and databases are quiesced.

The basic syntax to QUIESCE an instance is as follows:

```
QUIESCE INSTANCE [InstanceName]
[RESTRICTED ACCESS]
[IMMEDIATE | DEFER <WITH TIMEOUT [Minutes]
<FORCE CONNECTIONS>
```

In the preceding command, the following applies:

- InstanceName: Identifies the name of the instance to be placed in restricted mode

```
db2 "QUIESCE INSTANCE db2inst1 RESTRICTED ACCESS IMMEDIATE FORCE
CONNECTIONS"
```

The basic syntax to QUIESCE a database is as follows:

```
QUIESCE DATABASE [IMMEDIATE | DEFER <WITH TIMEOUT [Minutes]
<FORCE CONNECTIONS>
db2 "CONNECT TO sample"
   Database Connection Information
 Database server        = DB2/LINUXX8664 11.1.3.3
 SQL authorization ID   = DB2INST1
 Local database alias   = SAMPLE
db2 "QUIESCE DATABASE IMMEDIATE FORCE CONNECTIONS"
```

Once the maintenance is complete, you can you use the `UNQUIESCE` command to return the database from a restricted access mode to a regular operational mode. You can do so by executing the `UNQUIESCE` command, as shown:

```
db2 "UNQUIESCE INSTANCE db2inst1"
db2 "UNQUIESCE DATABASE"
```

Configuring the Db2 system environment

The Db2 database environment contains a number of operating system environment variables and Db2-specific profile registry variables that are used to manage, monitor, and control the behavior of the Db2 system.

Environment variables are set at the operating system level using standard operating system commands, such as `set` on a Windows operating system and `export` on a UNIX operating system. Examples are shown here:

```
set DB2INSTANCE=db2inst1 [On Windows]
export DB2INSTANCE=db2inst1 [On UNIX]
```

The Db2 profile registry settings are categorized as:

- **Db2 global-level profile registry**: All server-wide environment variable settings reside in this registry, and these settings are applicable to all of the instances that pertain to a particular version of Db2.
- **Db2 instance-level profile registry**: The environment variable settings for a particular instance are stored in this registry. The values defined in this profile registry override any corresponding settings in the global-level profile registry.
- **Db2 instance node-level profile registry**: The environment variable settings that are specific to a node in a **Massively Parallel Processing** (**MPP**) (also called a **Database Partitioning Feature** (**DPF**)) database environment are stored in this registry. The values defined in this profile registry override any corresponding settings in the global-level and instance-level profile registries.
- **DB2 user-level profile registry**: The environment variable settings that are specific to each user are stored in this registry, and they takes higher precedence over other profile registry settings.

The following table shows the order in which Db2 resolves the registry settings and the environment variables when configuring the system:

Profile Registry	Precedence	Location on Linux and UNIX platform
Environment Variables	1	For Bourne or korn shell: `instance_home/sqllib/db2profile` For C shell: `instance_home/sqllib/db2cshrc`
User Level	2	Not applicable
Instance Node Level	3	`$INSTHOME/sqllib/nodes` Filename: `<nodenumber>.env`
Instance Level	4	`$INSTHOME/sqllib/profile.env`
Global Level	5	For root installations: `/var/db2/global.reg` For non-root installations: `home_directory/sqllib/global.reg`

DB2 profile registry precedence and registry location

Listing and modifying the global registry

The `db2greg` command can be used to list and modify the global registry settings. The physical global registry file is located at `/var/db2/global.reg` in a root Db2 installation, and at `$HOME/sqllib/global.reg` in a non-root Db2 installation. The command output for a root installation would look like this:

```
db2greg -dump
    S,TSA,4.1.0.3,/opt/IBM/tsamp,DG_NOT_ALLOWED,DB2_INSTALLED,0,0,-
,1496866184,0
    S,RSCT,3.2.1.2,/usr/sbin/rsct,DG_NOT_ALLOWED,DB2_INSTALLED,0,0,-
,1496866184,0
    S,DB2,11.1.3.3,/opt/ibm/db2/V11.1,,,3,0,,1503867003,0
    V,DB2GPRF,DB2SYSTEM,vmlxeiml001.system.lab,/opt/ibm/db2/V11.1,
I,DB2,11.1.3.3,db2inst1,/db/home/db2inst1/sqllib,,1,0,/opt/ibm/db2/V11.1,,
I,DB2,11.1.3.3,db2inst2,/db/home/db2inst2/sqllib,,1,0,/opt/ibm/db2/V11.1,,
```

As you can see in the preceding command output, the global registry consists of three record types:

- **Service (S)**: This records product level information, such as version and installation path, for each copy of Db2 installed on the server
- **Instance (I)**: This records instance level information, such as instance name, instance path, version, installation path, and the auto restart flag, for each instance on the server
- **Variables (V)**: This records global-level registry variables and values

The db2set system command can be used to display, set, or modify the Db2 profile registry settings. The syntax for this command is as follows:

```
db2set [registry variable = [value]]
       [-g | -i instance [member-number | db-partition-number]]
          [-all]
       [-null]
       [-r [instance] [member-number]]
       [-l | -lr]
       [-v]
```

In the preceding command, the following applies:

- registry variable: Identifies the registry variable whose value is to be displayed, set, or modified.
- value: Identifies the value to be assigned to a variable. If no value is supplied, it will unset the registry variable.
- instance: Identifies the instance profile with which to associate the specified registry variable.
- member-number: Identifies the member number of the instance within the Db2 pureScale setup to apply the registry changes to.
- db-partition-number: Identifies the node number of the instance within the MPP setup to apply the registry changes to.

The following table describes the options available with the db2set command:

db2set Command option	Description
-g	Indicates that the global profile registry is to be displayed, set, or modified

-i	Indicates that instance profile registries are to be displayed, set, or modified
-all	Indicates that all of the registry variables are to be displayed: [-e All environment variables [-n] All node-level registry variables [-i] All instance-level profile registry variables [-g] All global-level profile registry variables
-null	Indicates that the value of the variable at a specified registry level is to be set to NULL
-r	Indicates that the profile registry for a given instance is to be reset to factory settings
-l	Indicates that all of the instance profile are to be listed
-lr	Indicates that all of the supported registry variables are to be listed
-v	Indicates that the command is to be executed in verbose mode

The db2set command options

The following command will list all of the registry settings:

```
db2set -all
[i] DB2TCP_CLIENT_KEEPALIVE_TIMEOUT=15
[i] DB2_PMODEL_SETTINGS=MAX_BACKGROUND_SYSAPPS:500
[i] DB2_BINSORT=YES
[i] DB2_PRED_FACTORIZE=YES
[i] DB2MEMDISCLAIM=YES
[i] DB2ENVLIST=EXTSHM
[i] DB2COMM=TCPIP
[i] DB2_PARALLEL_IO=*
[i] DB2AUTOSTART=NO
[g] DB2SYSTEM=vmlxeiml001.system.lab
```

To set a registry variable at an instance level, such as db2inst1, the command would look as follows; however, the instance name is not necessary if you are logged on as the instance owner:

```
db2set -i db2inst1 DB2_AVOID_LOCK_ESCALATION=ON
db2set -all | grep -i DB2_AVOID_LOCK_ESCALATION
[i] DB2_AVOID_LOCK_ESCALATION=ON
```

To set a registry variable at the global level, execute the following command with a root privilege:

```
. /db/home/db2inst1/sqllib/db2profile
db2set -g DB2COMM=TCPIP,SSL
db2set -all | grep DB2COMM
[g] DB2COMM=TCPIP,SSL
```

To unset a registry variable, the command would look as follows:

```
db2set -all | grep DB2AUTOSTART
[i] DB2AUTOSTART=ON
db2set DB2AUTOSTART=
db2set -all | grep DB2AUTOSTART
```

Aggregate registry variables

An aggregate registry variable is a group of several registry variables, such as a configuration, that is identified by one registry variable name. The purpose of an aggregated registry variable is to ease registry configuration for broad operational objectives.

In Db2 11.1, the only valid aggregate registry variable is DB2_WORKLOAD, and the valid values for this variable are:

- ANALYTICS: Column-organized BLU-specific workload setting
- 1C: 1C application-specific workload setting
- CM: Content manager-specific workload setting
- COGNOS_CS: Cognos content server-specific workload setting
- FILENET_CM: FileNet content manager-specific workload setting
- INFOR_ERP_LN: Infor **enterprise resource planning (ERP)** Baan-specific workload setting
- MAXIMO: Maximo-specific workload setting
- MDM: Master data management-specific workload setting
- SAP: SAP application-specific workload setting
- TPM: Tivoli provisioning manager-specific workload setting
- WAS: WebSphere application server-specific workload setting
- WC: WebSphere commerce-specific workload setting
- WP: WebSphere portal-specific workload setting

If you want to set the aggregated registry variable DB2_WORKLOAD to support the SAP application workload, you can do so by executing the following command:

```
db2set DB2_WORKLOAD=SAP

db2set -all | grep -i DB2_WORKLOAD
[i] DB2_ONLINERECOVERY_WITH_UR_ACCESS=FALSE [DB2_WORKLOAD]
[i] DB2_PARALLEL_ACS=YES [DB2_WORKLOAD]
[i] DB2_TRANSCHEMA_EXCLUDE_STATS=TRUE [DB2_WORKLOAD]
[i] DB2_USE_FAST_LOG_PREALLOCATION=TRUE [DB2_WORKLOAD]
[i] DB2_CDE_STMTCACHING=YES [DB2_WORKLOAD]
[i] DB2_INDEX_PCTFREE_DEFAULT=0 [DB2_WORKLOAD]
[i] DB2_SKIP_VIEWRECREATE_SAP=TRUE [DB2_WORKLOAD]
[i] DB2_BLOCKING_WITHHOLD_LOBLOCATOR=NO [DB2_WORKLOAD]
[i] DB2_AGENT_CACHING_FMP=OFF [DB2_WORKLOAD]
[i] DB2_TRUST_MDC_BLOCK_FULL_HINT=YES [DB2_WORKLOAD]
[i] DB2_CREATE_INDEX_COLLECT_STATS=YES [DB2_WORKLOAD]
[i] DB2_ATS_ENABLE=YES [DB2_WORKLOAD]
[i] DB2_RESTRICT_DDF=YES [DB2_WORKLOAD]
[i] DB2_DUMP_SECTION_ENV=YES [DB2_WORKLOAD]
[i] DB2_WORKLOAD=SAP
[i] DB2_TRUNCATE_REUSESTORAGE=IMPORT,LOAD [DB2_WORKLOAD]
[i] DB2_MDC_ROLLOUT=DEFER [DB2_WORKLOAD]
[i] DB2_ATM_CMD_LINE_ARGS=-include-manual-tables [DB2_WORKLOAD]
[i] DB2_VIEW_REOPT_VALUES=YES [DB2_WORKLOAD]
[i] DB2_OBJECT_TABLE_ENTRIES=65532 [DB2_WORKLOAD]
[i] DB2_IMPLICIT_UNICODE=YES [DB2_WORKLOAD]
[i] DB2_BCKP_PAGE_VERIFICATION=TRUE [DB2_WORKLOAD]
[i] DB2_BCKP_INCLUDE_LOGS_WARNING=YES [DB2_WORKLOAD]
[i] DB2_RUNTIME_DEBUG_FLAGS=TOLERANT_FLOAT,DISABLE_BLANK_TOLERANCE
[DB2_WORKLOAD]
[i] DB2STMM=APPLY_HEURISTICS:YES,GLOBAL_BENEFIT_SEGMENT_UNIQUE:YES
[DB2_WORKLOAD]
[i] DB2_INLIST_TO_NLJN=YES [DB2_WORKLOAD]
[i] DB2_MINIMIZE_LISTPREFETCH=YES [DB2_WORKLOAD]
[i]
DB2_REDUCED_OPTIMIZATION=4,INDEX,JOIN,NO_TQ_FACT,NO_HSJN_BUILD_FACT
,STARJN_CARD_SKEW,NO_SORT_MGJOIN,REDUCE_LOCKING,CART OFF,CAP OFF
[DB2_WORKLOAD]
[i] DB2NOTIFYVERBOSE=YES [DB2_WORKLOAD]
[i] DB2_INTERESTING_KEYS=YES [DB2_WORKLOAD]
[i] DB2_EXTENDED_OPTIMIZATION=GY_DELAY_EXPAND
1000,NO_NLJN_SPLIT_BUFFER [DB2_WORKLOAD]
[i]
DB2COMPOPT=VOLATILETSF,WORKLOADSAP,BLU_SAP_MEMTBL,LOTO1,BREAK_VIEWC
SE,REPL_UNLIMITED [DB2_WORKLOAD]
[i] DB2COMM=TCPIP [DB2_WORKLOAD]
```

To view all of the registry variables that are implicitly set by the preceding aggregated registry setting command, you can execute the db2set command with the -gd option:

```
db2set -gd DB2_WORKLOAD=SAP
DB2_REDUCED_OPTIMIZATION=4,INDEX,JOIN,NO_TQ_FACT,NO_HSJN_BUILD_FACT
,STARJN_CARD_SKEW,NO_SORT_MGJOIN,REDUCE_LOCKING,CART OFF,CAP OFF
DB2_MINIMIZE_LISTPREFETCH=YES
DB2_INLIST_TO_NLJN=YES
.....
.....
DB2_AVOID_LOCK_ESCALATION=TRUE

You can SYSPROC.ENV_GET_REG_VARIABLES table function to retrieve
the registry settings:
SELECT SUBSTR (REG_VAR_NAME, 1, 20) as REG_VAR_NAME,
SUBSTR (REG_VAR_VALUE, 1, 20) as REG_VAR_VALUE_IN_MEM,
IS_AGGREGATE FROM TABLE (ENV_GET_REG_VARIABLES (-1)) AS T1;
```

Configuring Db2 instances and databases

Along with registry variables, Db2 also uses a set of **database manager configuration (DBM)** and database configuration (DB) parameters to control how system resources are allocated and managed to optimally run the database engine. Let's look at the DBM and DB configuration parameters in detail.

The Db2 database manager configuration

When you create an instance, a corresponding DBM file called db2systm is created in the $HOME/sqllib directory. You can display and modify the content of the DBM file for a particular instance by executing the GET DBM CFG command.

The basic syntax for the command to display the DBM configuration file is as follows:

```
GET [DATABASE MANAGER | DB MANAGER | DBM]
[CONFIGURATION | CONFIG | CFG] <SHOW DETAIL>
```

If you want to display the settings of the database manager configuration for the instance db2inst1, you can do so by executing the following commands:

```
db2 "ATTACH TO db2inst1"

Instance Attachment Information
```

```
Instance server        = DB2/LINUXX8664 11.1.3.3
Authorization ID       = DB2INST1
Local instance alias   = DB2INST1

db2 "GET DBM CFG SHOW DETAIL"

           Database Manager Configuration

      Node type = Enterprise Server Edition with local and remote
clients

 Description      Parameter    Current Value        Delayed Value
 -------------------------------------------------------------------
 ------------------------------------------------------
 Database manager configuration release level          = 0x1400
Max number of concurrently active databases   (NUMDB)  = 32
32
 Federated Database System Support       (FEDERATED)   = NO
NO
 Transaction processor monitor name      (TP_MON_NAME) =
...
Keystore type         (KEYSTORE_TYPE)           = NONE     NONE
 Keystore location     (KEYSTORE_LOCATION) =
```

There are two other ways to display the DBM configuration parameters, by using either the SYSIBMADM.DBMCFG administrative view or SYSPROC.DBM_GET_CFG table functions:

```
SELECT NAME,
SUBSTR (VALUE, 1, 20) AS VALUE,
SUBSTR (DEFERRED_VALUE, 1, 20) AS DEFERRED_VALUE,
SUBSTR (DEFERRED_VALUE_FLAGS, 1, 10) AS DEFERRED_VALUE_FLAGS,
SUBSTR (DATATYPE, 1, 10) AS DATATYPE FROM SYSIBMADM.DBMCFG;

SELECT NAME,
SUBSTR (VALUE, 1, 20) AS VALUE,
SUBSTR (DEFERRED_VALUE, 1, 20) AS DEFERRED_VALUE,
SUBSTR (DEFERRED_VALUE_FLAGS, 1, 10) AS DEFERRED_VALUE_FLAGS,
SUBSTR (DATATYPE, 1, 10) AS DATATYPE FROM
TABLE (SYSPROC.DBM_GET_CFG ());
```

The basic syntax for the command to modify the DBM configuration file is:

```
UPDATE [DATABASE MANAGER | DB MANAGER | DBM]
[CONFIGURATION | CONFIG | CFG]
USING    [[Paramter] [Value] |
      [Paramter] [Value] AUTOMATIC |
      [Parameter] AUTOMATIC ...]
<IMMEDIATE | DEFERRED>
```

In the preceding command, the following applies:

- `Parameter`: Identifies one or more Db2 DBM configuration parameter whose values are to be modified
- `Value`: Identifies the new value to be assigned to the Db2 DBM configuration parameter

If the `AUTOMATIC` keyword is specified as the value for a particular instance parameter, Db2 will automatically adjust the parameter based on the current system resources and the workload requirements.

You can also update certain parameters instantaneously by attaching to the instance; for example, to set the `DIAGLEVEL` to a higher value to troubleshoot an issue, you can execute the following commands:

```
db2 "ATTACH TO db2inst1"

    Instance Attachment Information

 Instance server        = DB2/LINUXX8664 11.1.3.3
 Authorization ID       = DB2INST1
 Local instance alias   = DB2INST1

db2 "UPDATE DBM CFG USING DIAGLEVEL 4 IMMEDIATE"
```

It is necessary to `ATTACH` to the instance to modify any online configurable DBM CFG with an immediate effect or to use the `SHOW DETAIL` option within the `GET DBM CFG` command (without having to restart the database instance).

If you want to reset all of the DBM CFG settings to a default factory setting, you can do so by executing the following command:

```
db2 "RESET DBM CFG"
```

The following table shows the DBM parameters in Db2 v11.1, with a short description for each:

Parameter	Description
agent_stack_sz	Agent stack size configuration parameter. This parameter determines the memory that is allocated by Db2 for each agent thread stack.
aslheapsz	Application support layer heap size configuration parameter. The application support layer heap represents a communication buffer between the local application and its associated agent. This buffer is allocated as shared memory by each database manager agent that is started.
audit_buf_sz	Audit buffer size configuration parameter. This parameter specifies the size of the buffers used when you audit the Db2 instance.
authentication	Authentication type configuration parameter. This parameter specifies and determines how and where authentication of a user takes place.
catalog_noauth	Cataloging allowed without authority configuration parameter. This parameter specifies whether users are able to catalog and uncatalog databases and nodes, or DCS and ODBC directories, without SYSADM authority.
clnt_krb_plugin	Client Kerberos plugin configuration parameter. This parameter specifies the name of the default Kerberos plugin library to be used for client-side authentication and local authorization.
clnt_pw_plugin	Client userid-password plugin configuration parameter. This parameter specifies the name of the userid-password plugin library to be used for client-side authentication and local authorization.
cluster_mgr	Cluster manager name configuration parameter. This parameter enables the database manager to communicate incremental cluster configuration changes to the specified cluster manager.
comm_bandwidth	Communications bandwidth configuration parameter. This parameter helps the query optimizer determine access paths by indicating the bandwidth between database partition servers.

`conn_elapse`	Connection elapse time configuration parameter. This parameter specifies the number of seconds within which a network connection is to be established between Db2 members.
`cpuspeed`	CPU speed configuration parameter. This parameter reflects the CPU speed of the machine(s) the database is installed on.
`dft_account_str`	Default charge-back account configuration parameter. This parameter acts as the default suffix of accounting identifiers.
`dft_mon_bufpool`	Database system buffer pool monitor switch configuration parameter. This parameter allows you to enable or disable the buffer pool monitor capability.
`dft_mon_lock`	Database system lock monitor switch configuration parameter. This parameter allows you to enable or disable the lock monitor capability.
`dft_mon_sort`	Database system sort monitor switch configuration parameter. This parameter allows you to enable or disable the sort operation monitor capability.
`dft_mon_stmt`	Database system statement monitor switch configuration parameter. This parameter allows you to enable or disable the statement monitor capability.
`dft_mon_table`	Database system table monitor switch configuration parameter. This parameter allows you to enable or disable the table monitor capability.
`dft_mon_timestamp`	Database system timestamp monitor switch configuration parameter. This parameter allows you to enable or disable the timestamp information monitor capability.
`dft_mon_uow`	Database system unit of work monitor switch configuration parameter. This parameter allows you to enable or disable the unit of work monitor capability.
`dftdbpath`	Default database path configuration parameter. This parameter contains the default file path used to create databases under the database manager. If no path is specified when a database is created, the database is created under the path specified by the this parameter.
`diaglevel`	Diagnostic error capture level configuration parameter. This parameter specifies the types of diagnostic errors that will be recorded in the `db2diag` log file.

diagpath	Diagnostic data directory path configuration parameter. This parameter allows you to specify the fully qualified primary path for Db2 diagnostic information.
dir_cache	Directory cache support configuration parameter. This parameter determines whether the database, node, and DCS directory files will be cached in memory.
discover	Discovery mode configuration parameter. You can use this parameter to determine what kind of discovery requests, if any, the client can make.
discover_inst	Discover server instance configuration parameter. You can use this parameter to specify whether this instance can be detected by Db2 discovery.
fcm_num_buffers	Number of FCM buffers configuration parameter. You can use this parameter to specify the number of 4 KB buffers that are used for internal communications, referred to as messages, both among and within database servers.
fed_noauth	Bypass federated authentication configuration parameter. This parameter determines whether federated authentication will be bypassed at the instance.
federated	Federated database system support configuration parameter. This parameter enables or disables support for applications submitting distributed requests for data managed by data sources (such as the Db2, SQL Server, and Oracle).
fenced_pool	Maximum number of fenced processes configuration parameter. This parameter represents the number of threads cached in each db2fmp process for threaded db2fmp processes (processes serving thread-safe stored procedures and UDFs). For non-threaded db2fmp processes, this parameter represents the number of processes cached.
group_plugin	Group plugin configuration parameter. This parameter specifies the name of the group plugin library.
indexrec	Index re-creation time configuration parameter. This parameter indicates when the database manager attempts to rebuild invalid indexes, and whether or not any index build is redone during roll-forward or **high availability disaster recovery (HADR)** log replay on the standby database.

`instance_memory`	Instance memory configuration parameter. This parameter specifies the maximum amount of memory that can be allocated for a database partition if you are using Db2 database products with memory usage restrictions or if you set it to a specific value. Otherwise, the `AUTOMATIC` setting allows instance memory to grow as needed.
`rstrt_light_mem`	Restart light memory configuration parameter. This parameter specifies the maximum amount of memory that is allocated and reserved on a host for restart light recovery purposes. The amount is a percentage of the `instance_memory` configuration parameter.
`intra_parallel`	Enable intra-partition parallelism configuration parameter. This parameter specifies whether or not the database connections will use intra-partition query parallelism by default.
`java_heap_sz`	Maximum Java interpreter heap size configuration parameter. You can use this parameter to determine the maximum size of the heap that is used by the Java interpreter started to service Java Db2 stored procedures and UDFs.
`jdk_path`	Software Developer's Kit for Java installation path DAS configuration parameter. This parameter specifies the directory under which the **Software Developer's Kit (SDK)** for Java, to be used for running Db2 administration server functions, is installed.
`keepfenced`	Keep fenced process configuration parameter. This parameter indicates if a fenced mode process is kept after a fenced mode routine call is complete. Fenced mode processes are created as separate system entities in order to isolate user-written fenced mode code from the database manager agent process. This parameter is only applicable on database servers.
`local_gssplugin`	GSS API plugin used for local instance level authorization configuration parameter. This parameter specifies the name of the default GSS API plugin library to be used for instance-level local authorization when the value of the authentication database manager configuration parameter is set to `GSSPLUGIN` or `GSS_SERVER_ENCRYPT`.
`max_connections`	Maximum number of client connections configuration parameter. This parameter indicates the maximum number of client connections allowed per member.

`max_connretries`	Node connection retries configuration parameter. This parameter specifies the maximum number of times an attempt will be made to establish a network connection between two Db2 members.
`max_coordagents`	Maximum number of coordinating agents configuration parameter. You can use this parameter to limit the number of coordinating agents.
`max_querydegree`	Maximum query degree of parallelism configuration parameter. This parameter specifies the maximum degree of intra-partition parallelism that is used for any SQL statement executing on this instance of the database manager. An SQL statement will not use more than this number of parallel operations within a database partition when the statement is executed.
`max_time_diff`	Maximum time difference between members configuration parameter. This parameter specifies the maximum time difference that is permitted between members in a Db2 pureScale or in a Db2 MPP environment that are listed in the node configuration file.
`mon_heap_sz`	Database system monitor heap size configuration parameter. This parameter determines the amount of memory, in pages, to allocate for database system monitor data. Memory is allocated from the monitor heap when database monitoring activities are performed. Monitoring activities include turning on monitor switches, resetting monitor data, activating an event monitor, or sending monitor events to an active event monitor.
`notifylevel`	Notify level configuration parameter. This parameter specifies the type of administration notification messages that are written to the administration notification log.
`num_initagents`	Initial number of agents in pool configuration parameter. You can use this parameter to determine the initial number of idle agents that are created in the agent pool when the `db2start` command is issued.
`num_initfenced`	Initial number of fenced processes configuration parameter. This parameter indicates the initial number of non-threaded, idle db2fmp processes that are created in the db2fmp pool at `START DBM` time.
`num_poolagents`	Agent pool size configuration parameter. This parameter sets the maximum size of the idle agent pool.

numdb	Maximum number of concurrently active databases in an instance configuration parameter. This parameter specifies the number of local databases that can be concurrently active in a Db2 database instance.
resync_interval	Transaction resync interval configuration parameter. This parameter specifies the time interval, in seconds, for which a **transaction manager (TM)**, **resource manager (RM)**, or **sync point manager (SPM)** should retry the recovery of any outstanding in-doubt transactions found in the TM, the RM, or the SPM.
rqrioblk	Client I/O block size configuration parameter. This parameter specifies the block size at the Data Server Runtime Client when a blocking cursor is opened.
sheapthres	Sort heap threshold configuration parameter. This parameter represents a threshold on the total amount of private sort memory reservation available to sort-heap based operations on a member. Any sort memory reservation requests above this threshold might be reduced.
spm_log_file_sz	Sync point manager log file size configuration parameter. This parameter identifies the **sync point manager (SPM)** log file size in 4 KB pages.
spm_log_path	Sync point manager log file path configuration parameter. This parameter specifies the directory where the SPM logs are written.
spm_max_resync	Sync point manager resync agent limit configuration parameter. This parameter identifies the number of agents that can simultaneously perform resync operations.
spm_name	Sync point manager name configuration parameter. This parameter identifies the name of the SPM instance to the database manager.
srvcon_auth	Authentication type for incoming connections at the server configuration parameter. This parameter specifies how and where user authentication is to take place when handling incoming connections at the server; it is used to override the current authentication type.

`srvcon_gssplugin_list`	List of GSS API plugins for incoming connections at the server configuration parameter. This parameter specifies the GSS API plugin libraries that are supported by the database server. It handles incoming connections at the server when the `srvcon_auth` configuration parameter is specified as `KERBEROS`, `KRB_SERVER_ENCRYPT`, `GSSPLUGIN` or `GSS_SERVER_ENCRYPT`, or when `srvcon_auth` is not specified, and authentication is specified as `KERBEROS`, `KRB_SERVER_ENCRYPT`, `GSSPLUGIN`, or `GSS_SERVER_ENCRYPT`.
`srv_plugin_mode`	Server plugin mode configuration parameter. This parameter specifies whether plugins are to run in fenced mode or unfenced mode. Unfenced mode is the only supported mode.
`srvcon_pw_plugin`	`Userid-password` plugin for incoming connections at the server configuration parameter. This parameter specifies the name of the default `userid-password` plugin library to be used for server-side authentication. It handles incoming connections at the server when the `srvcon_auth` parameter is specified as `CLIENT`, `SERVER`, `SERVER_ENCRYPT`, `DATA_ENCRYPT`, or `DATA_ENCRYPT_CMP`, or when `srvcon_auth` is not specified, and authentication is specified as `CLIENT`, `SERVER`, `SERVER_ENCRYPT`, `DATA_ENCRYPT`, or `DATA_ENCRYPT_CMP`.
`start_stop_time`	Start and stop timeout configuration parameter. This parameter specifies the time, in minutes, within which all database partition servers must respond to a `START DBM` or a `STOP DBM` command. It is also used as the timeout value during `ADD DBPARTITIONNUM` and `DROP DBPARTITIONNUM` operations.
`svcename`	TCP/IP service name configuration parameter. This parameter contains the name of the TCP/IP port which a database server will use to await communications from remote client nodes. This name must be reserved for use by the database manager.
`tm_database`	Transaction manager database name configuration parameter. This parameter identifies the name of the TM database for each Db2 instance.

tp_mon_name	Transaction processor monitor name configuration parameter. This parameter identifies the name of the TP monitor product being used.
trust_allclnts	Trust all clients configuration parameter. This parameter and trust_clntauth are used to determine where users are validated to the database environment.
trust_clntauth	Trusted client authentication configuration parameter. This parameter specifies whether a trusted client is authenticated by the server or the client when the client provides a user ID and password combination for a connection. This parameter (and trust_allclnts) is only active if the authentication parameter is set to CLIENT. If a user ID and password are not provided, the client is assumed to have validated the user, and no further validation is performed by the server.
util_impact_lim	Instance impact policy configuration parameter. This parameter allows the **database administrator** (**DBA**) to limit the performance degradation of a throttled utility on the workload.
nodetype	Instance node type configuration parameter. This parameter specifies the type of instance (the type of database manager) created by Db2 products installed on your machine.
release	Configuration file release level configuration parameter. This parameter specifies the release level of the configuration file.
federated_async	Maximum asynchronous TQs per query configuration parameter. This parameter determines the maximum number of **asynchrony table queues** (**ATQs**) in the access plan that the federated server supports. The mechanism of ATQs does not work in Db2 pureScale environments.
alternate_auth_enc	Alternate encryption algorithm for incoming connections to the server configuration parameter. This configuration parameter specifies the alternate encryption algorithm used to encrypt the user IDs and passwords submitted to a Db2 database server for authentication. Specifically, this parameter affects the encryption algorithm when the authentication method negotiated between the Db2 client and the Db2 database server is SERVER_ENCRYPT.

`ssl_cipherspecs`	Supported cipher specifications at the server configuration parameter. This configuration parameter specifies the cipher suites that the server allows for incoming connection requests when using the SSL protocol.
`ssl_clnt_keydb`	SSL key file path for outbound SSL connections using the client configuration parameter. This configuration parameter specifies the key file to be used for SSL connection at the client side.
`ssl_clnt_stash`	SSL stash file path for outbound SSL connections using the client configuration parameter. This configuration parameter specifies the fully qualified file path of the stash file to be used for SSL connections at the client side.
`ssl_svcename`	SSL service name configuration parameter. This configuration parameter specifies the name of the port that a database server uses to await communications from remote client nodes using SSL protocol.
`ssl_svr_keydb`	SSL key file path for incoming SSL connections using the server configuration parameter. This configuration parameter specifies the key file to be used for SSL setup at the server side.
`ssl_svr_label`	Label in the key file for incoming SSL connections using the server configuration parameter. This configuration parameter specifies a label of the personal certificate of the server in the key database.
`ssl_svr_stash`	SSL stash file path for incoming SSL connections using the server configuration parameter. This configuration parameter specifies a fully qualified file path of the stash file to be used for SSL setup at server side.
`ssl_versions`	Supported SSL versions using the server configuration parameter. This configuration parameter specifies **Secure Sockets Layer (SSL)** and **Transport Layer Security (TLS)** versions that the server supports for incoming connection requests.
`sysadm_group`	System administration authority group name configuration parameter. This parameter defines the group name with SYSADM authority for the database manager instance.

`sysctrl_group`	System control authority group name configuration parameter. This parameter defines the group name with **system control (SYSCTRL)** authority. SYSCTRL has privileges that allow operations to affect system resources, but does not allow direct access to data.
`sysmaint_group`	System maintenance authority group name configuration parameter. This parameter defines the group name with **system maintenance (SYSMAINT)** authority.
`sysmon_group`	System monitor authority group name configuration parameter. This parameter defines the group name with **system monitor (SYSMON)** authority.
`cf_num_workers`	Number of worker threads configuration parameter. The `cf_num_workers` parameter specifies the total number of worker threads on the cluster **caching facility (CF)**. Worker threads are distributed among the communication adapter ports to balance the number of worker threads servicing requests on each interface.
`cf_mem_sz`	CF memory configuration parameter. This parameter controls the total memory that is used by the cluster CF.
`fcm_num_channels`	Number of FCM channels configuration parameter. This parameter specifies the number of FCM channels for each database partition.
`diagsize`	Rotating diagnostic and administration notification logs configuration parameter. This parameter helps to control the maximum sizes of the diagnostic log and administration notification log files.
`alt_diagpath`	Alternate diagnostic data directory path configuration parameter. This parameter allows you to specify the fully qualified alternate path for Db2 diagnostic information that is used when the primary diagnostic data path, that is, `diagpath`, is unavailable.
`cf_diaglevel`	Diagnostic error capture level configuration parameter for the CF. This parameter specifies the types of diagnostic errors that will be recorded in the `cfdiag*.log` files.
`cf_diagpath`	Diagnostic data directory path configuration parameter for the CF. This parameter allows you to specify the fully qualified path for the diagnostic information file for the CF.

`cf_num_conns`	Number of CF connections per member per CF configuration parameter. This parameter controls the initial size of the cluster CF connection pool.
`comm_exit_list`	Communication exit library list configuration parameter. This parameter specifies the list of communication exit libraries that the database manager uses. A communication exit library is a dynamically loaded library that vendor applications use to examine communication buffers and the database manager runtime environment.
`wlm_dispatcher`	Workload management dispatcher configuration parameter. This parameter enables YES or disables NO for the Db2 workload management dispatcher. By default, an enabled dispatcher allows the setting of the CPU limits.
`wlm_disp_concur`	Workload manager dispatcher thread concurrency configuration parameter. This parameter specifies how the Db2 WLM dispatcher sets the thread concurrency level. You can also manually set the thread concurrency level to a fixed value.
`wlm_disp_cpu_shares`	Workload manager dispatcher CPU shares configuration parameter. This parameter enables (**YES**) or disables (**NO**) the control of CPU shares by the Db2 WLM dispatcher. By default, an enabled WLM dispatcher only controls CPU limits.
`wlm_disp_min_util`	Workload manager dispatcher minimum CPU utilization configuration parameter. This parameter specifies the minimum amount of CPU utilization that is necessary for a service class to be included in the Db2 WLM managed sharing of CPU resources.
`fcm_parallelism`	Internode communication parallelism configuration parameter. This parameter specifies the degree of parallelism that is used for communication (both control messages and data flow) between members within a Db2 instance. This parameter determines the number of sender and receiver fast communication manager conduit pairs. By default, an instance has only one pair: one sender and one receiver, which handle all communication to and from other members in the instance.
`cur_eff_arch_lvl`	Current effective architecture level configuration parameter. This parameter displays the **current effective architecture level (CEAL)** at which the instance is operating.

cur_eff_code_lvl	Current effective code level configuration parameter. This parameter displays the CECL at which the instance is operating.
cf_transport_method	Network transport method configuration parameter. In Db2 pureScale environments, the cf_transport_method configuration parameter controls what method is used for communication between Db2 members and the cluster CF.
keystore_location	Keystore location configuration parameter. This parameter specifies the location of the keystore that is used to store encryption keys or remote storage account credentials.
keystore_type	Keystore type configuration parameter. This parameter specifies the type of keystore that is used to store encryption keys or remote storage account credentials.
fcm_buffer_size	Inter-member buffer size configuration parameter. This parameter specifies the size of the **Fast Communications Manager (FCM)** buffer. The FCM buffer is used to send work units between members (especially within MPP and pureScale setup) within a Db2 instance.

The Db2 database manager instance configuration parameters (Source: IBM Db2 v11.1.0 Knowledge Center
at https://www.ibm.com/support/knowledgecenter/en/SSEPGG_11.1.0/com.ibm.db2.luw.welcome.doc/doc/welcome.html)

What if the SYSADM_GROUP database configuration parameter is set to NULL?

If the SYSADM_GROUP database manager configuration parameter is set to NULL, then the following listed users automatically get SYSADM authority to the instance:

- Windows:
    - Members of the local administrators group.
    - Members of the administrators group in the domain controller, if DB2_GRP_LOOKUP is not set or is set to DOMAIN.
    - Members of the DB2ADMNS group if the extended security feature is enabled. The location of the DB2ADMNS group was decided during installation.
    - The LocalSystem account.

- UNIX:
    - Primary group of the Db2 instance owner

The Db2 database configuration

When you create a database, a corresponding DB configuration file called SQLDBCONF is created at the location ~NODExxxx/SQLyyyy, where xxxx is the database partition number and yyyy is the database token. You can display the content of the DB file for a particular database by connecting to the database and executing the GET DB CFG command.

The basic syntax for the command to display the DB configuration file is:

```
GET [DATABASE | DB] [CONFIGURATION | CONFIG | CFG]
FOR [DatabaseAlias] <SHOW DETAIL>
```

In the preceding command, the following applies:

- DatabaseAlias: Identifies the alias assigned to the database for which to display the configuration information

If you want to display the database configuration settings for the database SAMPLE, you can do so by executing the following commands:

```
db2 "CONNECT TO sample"
   Database Connection Information
Database server        = DB2/LINUXX8664 11.1.3.3
SQL authorization ID   = DB2INST1
Local database alias   = SAMPLE
db2 "GET DB CFG SHOW DETAIL"
      Database configuration for Database sample
Description                                        Parameter   Current
Value            Delayed Value
-----------------------------------------------------------------------
Database configuration release level                        = 0x1400
Database release level                                      = 0x1400
...
...
CPU share behavior (hard/soft)      (WLM_CPU_SHARE_MODE) = HARD
HARD
   Maximum allowable CPU utilization (%)   (WLM_CPU_LIMIT) = 0
0
```

Two other ways to display the DB configuration parameters are by using the SYSIBMADM.DBCFG administrative view and the SYSPROC.DB_GET_CFG table function:

```
SELECT NAME,
SUBSTR (VALUE, 1, 20) AS VALUE,
SUBSTR (DEFERRED_VALUE, 1, 20) AS DEFERRED_VALUE,
SUBSTR (DEFERRED_VALUE_FLAGS, 1, 10) AS DEFERRED_VALUE_FLAGS, SUBSTR
(DATATYPE, 1, 10) AS DATATYPE,
DBPARTITIONNUM, MEMBER FROM SYSIBMADM.DBCFG;
SELECT NAME,
SUBSTR (VALUE, 1, 20) AS VALUE,
SUBSTR (DEFERRED_VALUE, 1, 20) AS DEFERRED_VALUE,
SUBSTR (DEFERRED_VALUE_FLAGS, 1, 10) AS DEFERRED_VALUE_FLAGS, SUBSTR
(DATATYPE, 1, 10) AS DATATYPE,
DBPARTITIONNUM, MEMBER FROM TABLE (SYSPROC.DB_GET_CFG ());
```

The basic syntax for the command to modify the DB configuration file is:

```
UPDATE [DATABASE | DB]
[CONFIGURATION | CONFIG | CFG]
FOR [DatabaseAlias]
USING    [[Paramter] [Value] |
      [Paramter] [Value] AUTOMATIC |
      [Parameter] AUTOMATIC ...]
<IMMEDIATE | DEFERRED>
```

In the preceding command, the following applies:

- `DatabaseAlias`: Identifies the alias assigned to the database for which to modify the configuration information
- `Parameter`: Identifies one or more DB configuration parameters whose values are to be modified
- `Value`: Identifies the new value to be assigned to the DB configuration parameter

If the `AUTOMATIC` keyword is specified as the value for a particular database parameter, Db2 will automatically adjust the parameter based on the current system resources and the workload requirements.

You can also update certain database configuration parameters instantaneously; for example, to update the `LOCKLIST` database configuration parameter to a higher value instantaneously to avoid the lock escalation problem, you can execute the following commands:

```
db2 "CONENCT TO sample"
   Database Connection Information
 Database server        = DB2/LINUXX8664 11.1.3.3
 SQL authorization ID   = DB2INST1
 Local database alias   = SAMPLE
db2 "UPDATE DB CFG FOR sample USING LOCKLIST 14336 IMMEDIATE"
```

It is necessary to CONNECT to the instance to modify any online configurable DB CFG with immediate effect or to use the **SHOW DETAIL** option of the GET DB CFG command (without having to deactivate and reactivate the database).

If you want to reset all of the DB CFG settings to a default factory setting, you can do so by executing the following command:

```
db2 "RESET DB CFG FOR sample"
```

The following table shows the DB parameters in Db2 v11.1, with a short description of each:

Parameter	Description
applheapsz	Application heap size configuration parameter. The applheapsz configuration parameter refers to the total amount of application memory that can be consumed by the entire application.
archretrydelay	Archive retry delay on error configuration parameter. This parameter specifies the number of seconds to wait after a failed archive attempt before trying to archive the log file again.

`auto_del_rec_obj`	Automated deletion of recovery objects configuration parameter. This parameter specifies whether database log files, backup images, and load copy images should be deleted when their associated recovery history file entry is pruned.
`auto_maint`	Automatic maintenance configuration parameter. This parameter is the parent of all of the other automatic maintenance database configuration parameters (`auto_db_backup`, `auto_tbl_maint`, `auto_runstats`, `auto_stmt_stats`, `auto_stats_views`, `auto_reorg`, and `auto_sampling`).
`auto_db_backup`	Automatic maintenance configuration parameter. This parameter specifies whether the database backup should be automatically backed up.
`auto_tbl_maint`	Automatic maintenance configuration parameter. This parameter specifies whether the table maintenance should automatically run.
`auto_runstats`	Automatic maintenance configuration parameter. This parameter specifies whether the statistics update should automatically run.
`auto_stmt_stats`	Automatic maintenance configuration parameter. This parameter specifies whether the **real-time statistics** (**RTS**) feature is enabled to collect statistics at compilation time.
`auto_stats_views`	Automatic maintenance configuration parameter. This parameter specifies whether automatic statistic collection of statistical views is enabled.
`auto_sampling`	Automatic maintenance configuration parameter. This parameter specifies whether automatic sampling for all background statistic collections is enabled.
`auto_reorg`	Automatic maintenance configuration parameter. This parameter specifies whether automatic table and index reorganization is enabled for the database.
`autorestart`	Auto-restart enable configuration parameter. The auto-restart configuration parameter determines if the database manager automatically initiates crash recovery when a user connects to a database that had previously terminated abnormally. If the auto-restart configuration parameter is not set, the user must issue an explicit restart database command before they can connect to the database.

auto_reval	Automatic revalidation and invalidation configuration parameter. This configuration parameter controls the revalidation and invalidation semantics.
avg_appls	Average number of active applications configuration parameter. This parameter is used by the query optimizer to help estimate how much buffer pool space will be available at runtime for the access plan chosen.
blk_log_dsk_ful	Block on log disk full configuration parameter. This parameter can be set to prevent disk full errors from being generated when the Db2 database system cannot create a new log file in the active log path.
blocknonlogged	Block creation of tables that allow non-logged activity configuration parameter. This parameter specifies whether the database manager will allow tables to have the NOT LOGGED or NOT LOGGED INITIALLY attributes activated.
catalogcache_sz	Catalog cache size configuration parameter. This parameter specifies the maximum space, in pages, that the catalog cache can use from the database heap.
chngpgs_thresh	Changed pages threshold configuration parameter. This parameter specifies the level (percentage) of changed pages at which the asynchronous page cleaners will be started, if they are not currently active.
database_memory	Database shared memory size configuration parameter. The database memory configuration parameter specifies the size of the database memory set. The database memory size counts towards any instance memory limit in effect. The setting must be large enough to accommodate the following configurable memory pools: buffer pools, the database heap, the locklist, the utility heap, the package cache, the catalog cache, the shared sort heap, and an additional minimum overflow area of five percent.
dbheap	Database heap configuration parameter. You can use this parameter to limit the maximum amount of memory allocated for the database heap. Additional memory is automatically added for critical memory requirements.
dft_degree	Default degree configuration parameter. This parameter specifies the default value for the CURRENT DEGREE special register and the DEGREE bind option.

`dft_extent_sz`	Default extent size of table spaces configuration parameter. This parameter sets the default extent size of table spaces.
`dft_loadrec_ses`	Default number of load recovery sessions configuration parameter. This parameter specifies the default number of sessions that will be used during the recovery of a table load.
`dft_mttb_types`	Default maintained table types for optimization configuration parameter. This parameter specifies the default value for the CURRENT MAINTAINED TABLE TYPES FOR OPTIMIZATION special register. The value of this register determines what types of refresh deferred materialized query tables will be used during query optimization.
`dft_prefetch_sz`	Default pre-fetch size configuration parameter. This parameter sets the default pre-fetch size of table spaces.
`dft_queryopt`	Default query optimization class configuration parameter. The query optimization class is used to direct the optimizer to use different degrees of optimization when compiling SQL and XQuery queries. This parameter provides additional flexibility by setting the default query optimization class used when neither the SET CURRENT QUERY OPTIMIZATION statement nor the QUERYOPT option on the BIND command are used.
`dft_refresh_age`	Default refresh age configuration parameter. This parameter specifies the default value for the CURRENT REFRESH AGE special register.
`dft_sqlmathwarn`	Continue upon arithmetic exceptions configuration parameter. This parameter sets the value that determines the handling of arithmetic errors, such as division by zero, and retrieval conversion errors during SQL statement execution.
`discover_db`	Discover database configuration parameter. You can use this parameter to prevent information about a database from being returned to a client when a discovery request is received at the server.
`dlchktime`	Time interval for checking deadlock configuration parameter. This parameter defines the frequency at which the database manager checks for deadlocks among all of the applications connected to a database.

`failarchpath`	Failover log archive path configuration parameter. This parameter specifies a path to which the Db2 database system will try to archive log files if the log files cannot be archived to either the primary or the secondary (if set) archive destinations because of a media problem affecting those destinations. This specified path must reference a disk.
`hadr_local_host`	HADR local host name configuration parameter. This parameter specifies the local host for high availability disaster recovery (HADR) TCP communication.
`hadr_local_svc`	HADR local service name configuration parameter. This parameter specifies the TCP service name or port number for which the local HADR process accepts connections.
`hadr_remote_host`	HADR remote hostname configuration parameter. This parameter specifies the TCP/IP hostname or IP address of the remote HADR database server.
`hadr_remote_inst`	HADR instance name of the remote server configuration parameter. This parameter specifies the instance name of the remote server. HADR also checks whether a remote database requesting a connection belongs to the declared remote instance.
`hadr_remote_svc`	HADR remote service name configuration parameter. This parameter specifies the TCP service name or port number that will be used by the remote HADR database server.
`hadr_syncmode`	HADR synchronization mode for log writes in peer state configuration parameter. This parameter specifies the synchronization mode, which determines how log writes on the primary are synchronized with log writes on the standby when the systems are in peer state.
`hadr_timeout`	HADR timeout value configuration parameter. This parameter specifies the time (in seconds) that the HADR process waits before considering a communication attempt to have failed.
`hadr_peer_window`	HADR peer window configuration parameter. When you set `hadr_peer_window` to a non-zero time value, then a HADR primary-standby database pair continues to behave as though still in peer state, for the configured amount of time, if the primary database loses connection with the standby database. This helps to ensure data consistency.

`indexrec`	Index recreation time configuration parameter. This parameter indicates when the database manager attempts to rebuild invalid indexes, and whether or not any index build is redone during roll-forward or HADR log replay on the standby database.
`locklist`	Maximum storage for lock list configuration parameter. This parameter indicates the amount of storage that is allocated to the lock list. There is one lock list per database, and it contains the locks held by all applications concurrently connected to the database.
`locktimeout`	Lock timeout configuration parameter. This parameter specifies the number of seconds that an application will wait to obtain a lock, helping to avoid global deadlocks for applications.
`logarchmeth1`	Primary log archive method configuration parameter. You can use this parameter to specify the media type of the primary destination for logs that are archived from the current log path.
`logarchmeth2`	Secondary log archive method configuration parameter. This parameter specifies the media type of the secondary destination for logs that are archived from either the current log path or the mirror log path.
`logarchopt1`	Primary log archive options configuration parameter. This parameter specifies the options field for the primary destination for archived logs (if required).
`logarchopt2`	Secondary log archive options configuration parameter. This parameter specifies the options field for the secondary destination for archived logs (if required).
`logbufsz`	Log buffer size configuration parameter. This parameter allows you to specify the amount of the database heap (defined by the `dbheap` parameter) to use as a buffer for log records before writing these records to disk.
`logfilsiz`	Size of log files configuration parameter. This parameter defines the size of each primary and secondary log file. The size of these log files limits the number of log records that can be written to them before they become full and a new log file is required.
`alt_collate`	Alternate collating sequence configuration parameter. This parameter specifies the collating sequence that is to be used for Unicode tables in a non-Unicode database.

logindexbuild	Log index pages created configuration parameter. This parameter specifies whether index creation, recreation, or reorganization operations are logged so that indexes can be reconstructed during Db2 roll-forward operations or HADR log replay procedures.
logprimary	Number of primary log files configuration parameter. This parameter allows you to specify the number of primary log files to be pre-allocated. The primary log files establish a fixed amount of storage allocated to the recovery log files.
logsecond	Number of secondary log files configuration parameter. This parameter specifies the number of secondary log files that are created and used for recovery log files. The secondary log files are created only as needed.
max_log	Maximum log per transaction configuration parameter. This parameter specifies if there is a limit to the percentage of the primary log space that a transaction can consume, and what that limit is.
maxappls	Maximum number of active applications configuration parameter. This parameter specifies the maximum number of concurrent applications that can be connected (both local and remote) to a database. Since each application that attaches to a database causes some private memory to be allocated, allowing a larger number of concurrent applications will potentially use more memory.
maxfilop	Maximum database files open per database. This parameter specifies the maximum number of file handles that can be open per database. Each active application is counted towards the value specified by maxfilop.
maxlocks	Maximum percent of lock list before escalation of the configuration parameter. This parameter defines a percentage of the lock list held by an application that must be filled before the database manager performs lock escalation.
min_dec_div_3	Decimal division scale to three configuration parameter. This parameter is provided as a quick way to enable a change to computation of the scale for decimal division in SQL.
mirrorlogpath	Mirror log path configuration parameter. This parameter specifies a string of up to 242 bytes for the mirror log path. The string must point to a fully qualified path name.

`newlogpath`	Change the database log path configuration parameter. This parameter allows you to specify a string of up to 242 bytes to change the location where the log files are stored.
`num_db_backups`	Number of database backups configuration parameter. This parameter specifies the number of full database backups to retain for a database.
`num_freqvalues`	Number of frequent values retained configuration parameter. This parameter allows you to specify the number of "most frequent values" that will be collected when the `WITH DISTRIBUTION` option is specified in the `RUNSTATS` command.
`num_iocleaners`	Number of asynchronous page cleaners configuration parameter. This parameter allows you to specify the number of asynchronous page cleaners for a database.
`num_ioservers`	Number of I/O server configurations parameter. This parameter specifies the number of I/O servers for a database. No more than this number of I/Os for pre-fetching and utilities can be in progress for a database at any time.
`num_log_span`	Number log span configuration parameter. This parameter specifies whether there is a limit to how many log files one transaction can span, and what that limit is.
`num_quantiles`	Number of quantiles for columns configuration parameter. This parameter controls the number of quantiles that will be collected when the `WITH DISTRIBUTION` option is specified on the `RUNSTATS` command.
`numarchretry`	Number of retries on the error configuration parameter. This parameter specifies the number of attempts that Db2 must make to archive a log file to the primary or the secondary archive directory before trying to archive log files to the failover directory.
`overflowlogpath`	Overflow log path configuration parameter. The `overflowlogpath` parameter specifies a location for Db2 databases to find log files needed for a roll-forward operation, as well as where to store active log files retrieved from the archive.
`pckcachesz`	Package cache size configuration parameter. This parameter is allocated out of the database shared memory and is used for the caching of sections for static and dynamic SQL and XQuery statements on a database.

`rec_his_retentn`	Recovery history retention period configuration parameter. This parameter specifies the number of days that historical information on backups is retained.
`self_tuning_mem`	Self-tuning memory configuration parameter. This parameter determines whether the memory tuner will dynamically distribute available memory resources, as required, between memory consumers that are enabled for self-tuning.
`seqdetect`	Sequential detection and read-ahead flag configuration parameter. This parameter controls whether the database manager is allowed to perform sequential detection or read-ahead prefetching during I/O activity.
`sheapthres_shr`	Sort heap threshold for shared sort configuration parameter. This parameter represents a soft limit on the total amount of shared sort memory reservation available to sort heap-based operations.
`sortheap`	Sort heap size configuration parameter. This parameter defines the maximum number of private or shared memory pages that an operation that requires sort heap memory allocates.
`stat_heap_sz`	Statistics heap size configuration parameter. This parameter indicates the maximum size of the heap used in collecting statistics using the RUNSTATS command.
`stmtheap`	Statement heap size configuration parameter. This parameter specifies the limit of the heap statement, which is used as a work space for the SQL or XQuery compiler during compilation of an SQL or XQuery statement.
`trackmod`	Track modified pages enable configuration parameter. This parameter specifies whether the database manager will track database modifications so that the backup utility can detect which subsets of the database pages must be examined by an incremental backup and potentially included in the backup image.
`tsm_mgmtclass`	**Tivoli storage manager** (TSM) management class configuration parameter. The TSM management class determines how the TSM server manages the backup versions of the objects being backed up.
`tsm_nodename`	TSM node name configuration parameter. This parameter is used to override the default setting for the node name associated with the TSM product.

tsm_owner	TSM owner name configuration parameter. This parameter is used to override the default setting for the owner associated with the TSM product.
tsm_password	TSM password configuration parameter. This parameter is used to override the default setting for the password associated with the TSM product.
util_heap_sz	Utility heap size configuration parameter. This parameter guides the amount of memory that is allocated by the database utilities.
vendoropt	Vendor options configuration parameter. This parameter specifies additional parameters that Db2 might need to use to communicate with storage systems during backup, restore, or load copy operations.
backup_pending	Backup pending indicator configuration parameter. The backup_pending parameter indicates whether you need to do a full backup of the database before accessing it.
codepage	Code page for the database configuration parameter. This parameter shows the code page that was used to create the database. The codepage parameter is derived based on the codeset parameter.
codeset	Codeset for the database configuration parameter. This parameter shows the codeset that was used to create the database. codeset is used by the database manager to determine codepage parameter values.
collate_info	Collating information configuration parameter. This parameter determines the database's collating sequence.
country	Database territory code configuration parameter. This parameter shows the territory code used to create the database.
database_consistent	Database is consistent configuration parameter. This parameter indicates whether the database is in a consistent state.
database_level	Database release level configuration parameter. This parameter indicates the release level of the database manager which can use the database.
hadr_db_role	HADR database role configuration parameter. This parameter indicates the current role of a database, whether the database is online or offline.

log_retain_status	Log retain status indicator configuration parameter. If the logarchmeth1 database configuration parameter is set to logretain, then the log retain status parameter will show a value of RECOVERY; otherwise, it will show a value of NO.
loghead	First active log file configuration parameter. This parameter contains the name of the log file that is currently active.
logpath	Location of log files configuration parameter. This parameter contains the current path being used for logging purposes.
multipage_alloc	Multipage file allocation enabled configuration parameter. Multipage file allocation is used to improve insert performance. It applies to SMS table spaces only. If enabled, all SMS table spaces are affected: there is no selection possible for individual SMS table spaces.
pagesize	Database default page size. This parameter contains the value that was used as the default page size when the database was created. Possible values are: "4 096, 8 192, 16 384 and 32 768". When a buffer pool or table space is created in that database, the same default page size applies.
release	Configuration file release level configuration parameter. This parameter specifies the release level of the configuration file.
restore_pending	Restore pending configuration parameter. This parameter states whether a RESTORE PENDING status exists in the database.
rollfwd_pending	Roll forward pending indicator configuration parameter. This parameter informs you whether or not a roll-forward recovery is required, and where it is required.
territory	Database territory configuration parameter. This parameter shows the territory used to create the database. The territory is used by the database manager when processing data that is territory sensitive.
user_exit_status	User exit status indicator configuration parameter. If set to YES, the user_exit_status parameter indicates that the database manager is enabled for roll-forward recovery and that the database archives and retrieves log files based on the values set by either the logarchmeth1 parameter or the logarchmeth2 parameter.

db_mem_thresh	Database memory threshold configuration parameter. This parameter represents the maximum percentage of committed, but currently unused, database shared memory that the database manager will allow before starting to release committed pages of memory back to the operating system.
enable_xmlchar	Enable conversion to XML configuration parameter. This parameter determines whether XMLPARSE operations can be performed on non-BIT DATA CHAR (or CHAR-type) expressions in an SQL statement.
restrict_access	Database has restricted access configuration parameter. This parameter indicates whether the database was created using the restrictive set of default actions. In other words, if it was created with the RESTRICTIVE clause in the CREATE DATABASE command.
appl_memory	Application memory configuration parameter. The appl_memory configuration parameter specifies the size of the application memory set. The application memory size counts towards any instance_memory limit in effect.
wlm_collect_int	WLM collection interval configuration parameter. This parameter specifies a collect and reset interval, in minutes, for WLM statistics.
decflt_rounding	Decimal floating point rounding configuration parameter. This parameter specifies the rounding mode for **decimal floating point (DECFLOAT)** values. The rounding mode affects decimal floating-point operations in the server, and in LOAD command operations.
number_compat	Number compatibility database configuration parameter. This parameter indicates whether the compatibility semantics associated with the NUMBER data type are applied to the connected database.
varchar2_compat	VARCHAR2 compatibility database configuration parameter. This parameter indicates whether the compatibility semantics associated with the VARCHAR2 and NVARCHAR2 data types are applied to the connected database.
date_compat	Date compatibility database configuration parameter. This parameter indicates whether the DATE compatibility semantics associated with the TIMESTAMP (0) data type are applied to the connected database.

cur_commit	Currently committed configuration parameter. This parameter controls the behavior of **cursor stability (CS)** scans.
smtp_server	SMTP server database configuration parameter. This parameter identifies a **simple mail transfer protocol (SMTP)** server. This SMTP server transmits email sent by the UTL_MAIL built-in module.
mon_req_metrics	Monitoring request metrics configuration parameter. This parameter controls the collection of request metrics on the entire database and affects requests executing in any Db2 service classes.
mon_act_metrics	Monitoring activity metrics configuration parameter. This parameter controls the collection of activity metrics on the entire database and affects activities submitted by connections associated with any Db2 workload definitions.
mon_obj_metrics	Monitoring object metrics configuration parameter. This parameter controls the collection of data object metrics on an entire database.
mon_uow_data	Monitoring unit of work events configuration parameter. This parameter specifies whether information about a unit of work, also referred to as a transaction, is sent to the active unit of work event monitors when the unit of work is completed. It is a parent parameter to the mon_uow_execlist and mon_uow_pkglist configuration parameters.
mon_locktimeout	Monitoring lock timeout configuration parameter. This parameter controls the generation of lock timeout events at the database level for the lock event monitor and affects all Db2 workload definitions.
mon_deadlock	Monitoring deadlock configuration parameter. This parameter controls the generation of deadlock events at the database level for the lock event monitor.
mon_lockwait	Monitoring lock wait configuration parameter. This parameter controls the generation of lock wait events at the database level for the lock event monitor.
mon_lw_thresh	Monitoring lock wait threshold configuration parameter. This parameter controls the amount of time spent in lock wait before an event for mon_lockwait is generated.

`mon_pkglist_sz`	Monitoring package list size configuration parameter. This parameter controls the maximum number of entries that can appear in the package listing per unit of work as captured by the unit of work event monitor.
`mon_lck_msg_lvl`	Monitoring lock event notification messages configuration parameter. This parameter controls the logging of messages to the administration notification log when lock timeout, deadlock, and lock escalation events occur.
`sql_ccflags`	Conditional compilation flags configuration parameter. This parameter contains a list of conditional compilation values for use in the conditional compilation of selected SQL statements.
`stmt_conc`	Statement concentrator configuration parameter. This configuration parameter sets the default statement concentrator behavior.
`section_actuals`	Section actuals configuration parameter. Section actuals are runtime statistics that are measured during section execution. This parameter enables the collection of section actuals, such that the statistics can be viewed when an event monitor is subsequently created.
`cf_catchup_trgt`	Target for catch-up time of secondary cluster caching facility configuration parameter. This configuration parameter determines the target time, in minutes, for completing the catch up to bring a newly added or newly restarted cluster caching facility into peer state with an existing primary cluster caching facility.
`cf_db_mem_sz`	Database memory configuration parameter. This parameter controls the total memory limit for the cluster CF, for this database.
`cf_gbp_sz`	Group buffer pool configuration parameter. This parameter determines the memory size used by the cluster CF, for **group buffer pool** (GBP) usage for this database.
`cf_lock_sz`	CF Lock manager configuration parameter. This parameter determines the memory size used by the CF for locking the usage for this database.
`cf_sca_sz`	**Shared Communication Area** (SCA) configuration parameter. This **SCA** configuration parameter determines the memory size used by the SCA in the cluster caching facility (CF). The SCA is a per database entity and contains database-wide control block information for tables, indexes, table spaces, and catalogs.

`dec_to_char_fmt`	Decimal to character function configuration parameter. This parameter is used to control the result of the CHAR scalar function and the CAST specification for converting decimals to character values.
`systime_period_adj`	Adjust temporal SYSTEM_TIME period database configuration parameter. This database configuration parameter specifies what action to take when a history row for a system period temporal table is generated with an end timestamp that is less than the begin timestamp.
`suspend_io`	Database I/O operations state configuration parameter. This parameter shows whether the I/O write operations for a database are suspended or are being suspended.
`mon_uow_pkglist`	Monitoring unit of work events with package list configuration parameter. This parameter controls the generation of units of work events, with package listing information included. This is done at the database level for the unit of work event monitor. The `mon_uow_pkglist` database configuration parameter is a child parameter of the `mon_uow_data` database configuration parameter.
`mon_uow_execlist`	Monitoring unit of work events with executable list configuration parameter. This parameter controls the generation of unit of work events, with executable ID listing information included. This is done at the database level for the unit of work event monitor. The `mon_uow_execlist` database configuration parameter is a child parameter of the `mon_uow_data` database configuration parameter.
`connect_proc`	Connect procedure name database configuration parameter. This database configuration parameter allows you to input or update a two-part connect procedure name that will be executed every time an application connects to the database.
`log_ddl_stmts`	Log DDL statements database configuration parameter. This parameter specifies that extra information regarding DDL statements will be written to the log.
`log_appl_info`	Application information log record database configuration parameter. This parameter specifies that the application information log record is written at the start of each update transaction.

dft_schemas_dcc	Default data capture on new schemas configuration parameter. This parameter allows the control of default settings for DATA CAPTURE CHANGES on newly created schemas, for replication purposes.
hadr_target_list	HADR target list database configuration parameter. This parameter specifies a list of target host:port pairs that represent HADR standby databases. You must set the hadr_target_list parameter to enable multiple standby databases or to set up HADR in a Db2 pureScale environment.
hadr_spool_limit	HADR log spool limit configuration parameter. This parameter determines the maximum amount of log data that is allowed to be spooled to the disk on HADR standby.
hadr_replay_delay	HADR replay delay configuration parameter. This parameter specifies the number of seconds that must pass from the time that a transaction is committed on the primary database to the time that the transaction is committed on the standby database.
logarchcompr1	Primary archived log file compression configuration parameter. This parameter specifies whether the log files written to the primary archive destination for logs are compressed.
logarchcompr2	Secondary archived log file compression configuration parameter. This parameter specifies whether the log files written to the secondary archive destination for logs are compressed.
dft_table_org	Default table organization. This parameter specifies whether a user table is created as a column-organized table or a row-organized table if you do not specify the ORGANIZE BY COLUMN or the ORGANIZE BY ROW clause for the CREATE TABLE statement.
mon_rtn_execlist	Monitoring routine executable list configuration parameter. This parameter controls the monitoring of statements executed by routines. This is done at the database level and takes effect for any routine invocation within the database.
mon_rtn_data	Monitoring routine capture configuration parameter. The mon_rtn_data configuration parameter controls the capture of routine invocations. It is a parent parameter to the mon_rtn_execlist configuration parameter.
string_units	Default string units configuration parameter. This parameter specifies the default string units that are used when defining character data types and graphic data types in Unicode databases.

nchar_mapping	National character mapping configuration parameter. This parameter determines the data type mapping for national character string data types in Unicode databases.
extended_row_sz	Extended row size configuration parameter. You can use the extended_row_sz configuration parameter to control whether or not a table definition can exceed the maximum row length of a page.
opt_direct_wrkld	Optimize directed workload configuration parameter. This database configuration parameter enables or disables explicit hierarchical locking (EHL). It affects the entire Db2 pureScale instance.
page_age_trgt_mcr	Page age target member crash recovery configuration parameter. This configuration parameter specifies the target duration (in seconds) for changed pages to be kept in the local buffer pool before they are persisted to table space storage or, for Db2 pureScale instances, to table space storage or to the group buffer pool.
page_age_trgt_gcr	Page age target group crash recovery configuration parameter. This configuration parameter specifies the target duration (in seconds) for changed pages to be kept in the group buffer pool before the pages are persisted to the disk or the caching facility. This parameter applies only to Db2 pureScale instances.
encrlib	Encryption library configuration parameter. The encrlib configuration parameter enables the automatic encryption of backups.
encropts	Encryption options configuration parameter. The encropts configuration parameter specifies a string of options for the automatic encryption of backups. Use the encropt parameter in tandem with the encrlib parameter.
encrypted_database	Database encryption state configuration parameter. This parameter indicates whether the database is encrypted. It is set when the database is created and cannot be changed.
pl_stack_trace	SQL PL and PL/SQL error stack logging configuration parameter. Starting from Db2 Version 10.5 Fix Pack 7, this parameter determines whether error stack logging is enabled or disabled for SQL PL and PL/SQL routines.

`hadr_ssl_label`	Label name in the key file for SSL communication between HADR primary and standby instances configuration parameter. This configuration parameter specifies the label of the SSL certificate, which encrypts communication between primary and standby HADR instances in the key database.
`wlm_agent_load_trgt`	WLM agent load target configuration parameter. This parameter is reserved for future use and cannot be modified to anything other than the default value. When set to AUTOMATIC, an appropriate value will be set automatically, based on the number of physical cores.
`wlm_admission_ctrl`	WLM admission control configuration parameter. This parameter is reserved for future use and cannot be modified to anything other than the default value.
`wlm_cpu_shares`	WLM CPU shares configuration parameter. This parameter specifies the number of shares of CPU resources allocated for work in a database.
`wlm_cpu_share_mode`	WLM CPU share mode configuration parameter. Db2 workload management can manage CPU resources by using shares-based entitlements that are assigned to a database. The number of CPU shares that are assigned can be specified by using the `WLM_CPU_SHARES` configuration parameter. This parameter specifies the type of share.
`wlm_cpu_limit`	WLM CPU limit configuration parameter. This parameter specifies the fixed amount of CPU that can be consumed by work that is running on a database.

The Db2 database configuration parameters (Source: IBM Db2 v11.1.0 Knowledge Center at https://www.ibm.com/support/knowledgecenter/en/SSEPGG_11.1.0/com.ibm.db2.luw.welcome.doc/doc/welcome.html.)

DB2 autonomic computing features

In today's dynamic world, we need databases that are self-configurable and self-optimizable, based on changes in workload characteristics. Db2 comes with a rich set of autonomic computing features to appropriately sense and respond to many situations, and to optimize the database for the best possible performance and use of available resources.

The following table, provides a summary of Db2 autonomic computing features, and a short description of each:

Autonomic Feature	Description
Self-tuning memory	Simplifies the memory configuration management across various configuration parameters and buffer pools.
Automatic storage	Simplifies storage management across all of the table spaces within the database. The database manager takes responsibility for creating and managing (expanding/shrinking) the containers, as and when required.
Data compression	Reduces the storage use by compressing the data at table (regular and temporary table objects), index, and backup image level.
Automatic database backup	Simplifies database backup management by providing an effective backup policy.
Automatic index and table maintenance	Simplifies index and table maintenance by determining the fragmentation level and automatically performing the `REORG` operation on the identified objects.
Automatic statistics collection	Simplifies the statistics collection process by automatically collecting statistics during statement compilation time via the real-time statistics (RTS) `auto_stmt_stats` database configuration parameter and automatically running `RUNSTATS` in the background via the `auto_runstats` database configuration parameter.
Configuration advisor	Designed to provide recommendations or make changes to the configuration settings, based on specific information provided to improve system performance or availability.
Utility throttling	Designed to regulate the performance impact of maintenance utilities such as `RUNSTATS`; backup can run during business hours without impacting application performance.

The Db2 autonomic computing features

Self-Tuning Memory Manager (STMM)

The following database memory-related configuration parameters are tuned automatically when the STMM future is enabled via the `self_tuning_mem` database configuration parameter:

- `database_memory`: This parameter specifies the amount of shared memory that is reserved for the database shared memory region. When you set this parameter to `AUTOMATIC`, the initial memory requirement is calculated based on the underlying configuration settings:

- `Buffer pools`: Amount of memory allocated to cache a table's index and data pages, as they are read from the disk, to be selected or modified.
- `dbheap`: Amount of memory used to fulfil the global database memory requirements.
- `locklist`: Amount of memory allocated to store the lock attributes.
- `util_heap_sz`: Amount of memory allocated to the database utilities.
- `pckcachesz`: Amount of memory allocated to cache sections of static SQL, dynamic SQL, and XQuery statements.
- `catalogcache_sz`: Amount of memory of the `dbheap` allocated to cache the catalog information.
- `sheapthres_shr`: Amount of memory allocated to serve shared sorts.
- `* Overflow area`: The percentage of memory that can be controlled via the `DB2_MEM_TUNING_RANGE` registry variable, to manage the volatile memory requirement.

- `maxlocks`: Percentage of the lock list that can be consumed by an application before the database manager performs lock escalation.
- `pckcachesz`: Amount of memory allocated to buffer the sections of static SQL, dynamic SQL, and XQuery statements.
- `sheapthres_shr`: Amount of memory allocated to shared sort operations. Self-tuning of the `sheapthres_shr` parameter is not supported when a database is created with the registry setting `DB2_WORKLOAD=ANALYTICS` (BLU accelerated column-organized tables).
- `sortheap`: Amount of memory allocated to serve the sort operations. Self-tuning of the `sortheap` parameter is not supported when a database is created with the registry setting `DB2_WORKLOAD=ANALYTICS` (BLU accelerated column-organized tables).

If you want to activate STMM for the database `SAMPLE`, you can do so by executing the command:

```
CONNECT TO sample;
UPDATE DB CFG FOR sample USING SELF_TUNING_MEM ON;
```

To activate all of the memory areas managed by STMM, you can execute the command:

```
UPDATE DB CFG FOR sample USING PCKCACHESZ AUTOMATIC LOCKLIST AUTOMATIC
MAXLOCKS AUTOMATIC SORTHEAP AUTOMATIC SHEAPTHRES_SHR AUTOMATIC
DATABASE_MEMORY AUTOMATIC;
ALTER BUFFERPOOL <BufferpoolName> SIZE AUTOMATIC;
```

Starting from Db2 10.5 FP 5, the following listed cluster CF memory-related parameters can also be tuned automatically in a pureScale environment:

- `cf_db_mem_sz`: The total CF memory limit for the current database. The sum of the cluster caching facility structure memory limits for the `cf_gbp_sz`, `cf_lock_sz`, and `cf_sca_sz` parameters must be less than the CF structure memory limit for the `cf_db_mem_sz` parameter. If this is set to AUTOMATIC, the assigned value is based on the `cf_mem_sz` and the number of active databases.
- `cf_gbp_sz`: The amount of memory allocated by the CF for the group buffer pool for the current database.
- `cf_lock_sz`: The amount of memory allocated by the CF for the lock structure for the current database.
- `cf_sca_sz`: The amount of memory allocated by the CF for the shared communication area for the current database.

The CF self-tuning memory is set at the instance level, and you can enable it by setting the registry variable as follows:

```
db2set DB2_DATABASE_CF_MEMORY=AUTO
```

Automatic storage

The automatic storage feature makes storage management easier. In this mode, the database manager manages the space requirement at the storage group level, instead of DBAs managing the space at the table space container level. By default, all of the databases created in Db2 10.1 and above use the automatic storage feature. However, if the database was created with an explicitly stated AUTOMATIC STORAGE NO clause, it cannot use the automatic storage table spaces.

You can convert a non-automatic storage database, SAMPLE, to an automatic storage database via the following steps:

1. Create a storage group using the CREATE STOGROUP statement:

```
CONNECT TO sample;
```

```
CREATE STOGROUP SG_DATA ON '/data/fs1/' OVERHEAD 0.8 DEVICE READ RATE 512
DATA TAG 1;
CREATE STOGROUP SG_INDX ON '/indx/fs1/' OVERHEAD 0.8 DEVICE READ RATE 512
DATA TAG 2;
```

2. It is important to remember that the very first storage group you create will become the default storage group for the entire database. In the preceding example, the storage group SG_DATA will become the default storage group for the database SAMPLE.

3. Identify the DMS table spaces that you want to convert to automatic storage by using the table function SYSPROC.MON_GET_TABLESPACE():

```
SELECT SUBSTR (TBSP_NAME, 1, 12) AS TBSP_NAME, TBSP_ID, TBSP_TYPE,
TBSP_CONTENT_TYPE, TBSP_USING_AUTO_STORAGE
  FROM TABLE (SYSPROC.MON_GET_TABLESPACE ('',-2)) AS T
  WHERE TBSP_USING_AUTO_STORAGE=0;
```

4. Convert DMS table spaces to automatic storage table space using the ALTER TABLESPACE statement:

```
ALTER TABLESPACE <TableSpaceName> MANAGED BY AUTOMATIC STORAGE USING
STOGROUP SG_DATA;
```

In the preceding command, the following applies:

- TableSpaceName: Identifies the DMS table space name that needs conversion

5. Move the contents from the old DMS container to the automatic storage container by executing the ALTER TABLESPACE statement:

```
ALTER TABLESPACE <TableSpaceName> REBALANCE;
```

In the preceding command, the following applies:

- TableSpaceName: Identifies the table space name that needs a data rebalance

Let's dive deeper into storage groups. A storage group is a named set of storage paths where data can be stored. The storage groups can only be used by automatic storage table spaces, and one storage group can be associated with multiple table spaces; however, one table space cannot be created on two different storage groups.

Creating storage groups

You can create a storage group by using the CREATE STOGROUP statement. The basic syntax is:

```
CREATE STOGROUP [StogrpName] ON ['StoragePath']
OVERHEAD [DeviceOverHead]
DEVICE READ RATE [DeviceReadRate]
DATA TAG [DataTag] SET AS DEFAULT
```

In the preceding code, the following applies:

- StoGrpName: Identifies a unique name to assign to the storage group once it is created.
- StoragePath: Identifies storage paths to add for the named storage group.
- DeviceOverHead: Identifies the I/O controller time and the disk seek and latency time, in milliseconds. The default value is 6.725 milliseconds.
- DeviceReadRate: Identifies the device specification for the read transfer date in MB/second; the default value is 100 MB/second.
- DataTag: Identifies the tag name for the Db2 Workload Manager (WLM) to use to determine the processing priority of the database activities; the default setting is NONE.

If you want to create a storage group, SG_MKTG, to store the marketing department objects, you can do so by executing the CREATE STOGROUP statement via a user that has SYSCTRL or SYSADM authority:

```
CREATE STOGROUP SG_MKTG ON '/data/fs1/' OVERHEAD 0.8 DEVICE READ RATE 512
DATA TAG 1;
```

To create a table space, TBSP_MKTG_DATA, to store marketing department data by using the storage group SG_MKTG, you can execute the following command:

```
CREATE TABLESPACE TBSP_MKTG_DATA MANAGED BY AUTOMATIC STORAGE USING
STOGROUP SG_MKTG INITIALSIZE 1 G INCREASESIZE 1 G OVERHEAD INHERIT
TRANSFERRATE INHERIT;
```

The table space TBSP_MKTG_DATA inherits the transfer rate attribute from the storage group's device read rate using the following formula:

```
TRANSFERRATE = (1 /DEVICE READ RATE) * 1000 / 1024000 * PAGESIZE
```

Altering storage groups

You can use the `ALTER STOGROUP` statement to change the following storage group settings:

- `OVERHEAD` and `DEVICE READ RATE`
- `DATA TAG`
- Default storage group
- Add/remove storage paths

To add a new storage path to an existing storage group, you can execute the following `ALTER STOGROUP` statement:

```
ALTER STOGROUP SG_MKTG ADD '/data/fs2/';
```

To strip the table spaces which were created as part of the `SG_MKTG` storage group, you must use the `ALTER TABLESPACE` statement with the `REBALANCE` clause; for example:

```
ALTER TABLESPACE TBSP_MKTG_DATA REBALANCE;
```

To drop a storage path from an existing storage group, you can execute the following `ALTER STOGROUP` statement:

```
ALTER STOGROUP SG_MKTG DROP '/data/fs2/';
```

You can run the `ALTER TABLESPACE` statement with the `REBALANCE` clause to move all of the contents from the storage path `/data/fs2/` to the storage path `/data/fs1/`:

```
ALTER TABLESPACE TBSP_MKTG_DATA REBALANCE;
```

You can monitor the rebalance operation through the `SYSPROC.MON_GET_REBALANCE_STATUS ()` table function using the SQL statement shown here:

```
SELECT
    VARCHAR (TBSP_NAME, 15) AS TBSP_NAME,
    REBALANCER_MODE,
    REBALANCER_STATUS,
    REBALANCER_EXTENTS_REMAINING,
FROM TABLE (MON_GET_REBALANCE_STATUS (NULL,-2)) AS T;
```

Dropping storage groups

You can use the DROP STOGROUP statement to drop an existing storage group from the database using the following command:

```
DROP STOGROUP TBSP_MKTG;
```

A few things to remember before dropping a storage group are as follows:

- You cannot drop a DEFAULT storage group. For example, you may have two storage groups, such as:

```
CREATE STOGROUP SG_MKTG_DATA1 ON '/data/fs1/' OVERHEAD 0.8 DEVICE READ
RATE 512 DATA TAG 1 SET AS DEFAULT;
    CREATE STOGROUP SG_MKTG_DATA2 ON '/data/fs2/' OVERHEAD 0.8 DEVICE READ
RATE 512 DATA TAG 2;
```

- If you want to drop SG_MKTG_DATA1, you have to change the DEFAULT storage group from SG_MKTG_DATA1 to SG_MKTG_DATA2 using the statements shown here:

```
ALTER STOGROUP SG_MKTG_DATA2 SET AS DEFAULT;
DROP STOGROUP SG_MKTG_DATA1;
```

- In addition, if you have any table spaces created within the storage group that you want to drop, you must reassign them to a different storage group using the ALTER TABLESPACE statement, as shown here:

```
ALTER TABLESPACE TBSP_MKTG_DATA1 USING STOGROUP SG_MKTG_DATA2;
```

 Note: The remaining DB2 autonomic computing features will be discussed in detail in later chapters.

A word about Db2 workload manager (WLM)

The Db2 WLM is a feature that can help identify, manage, monitor, and control the database workload, to better reflect the organization and priorities of your business.

The WLM environment can be designed using the following four stages:

1. **Definition of the business goals**: It is necessary to understand the overall business goal you are trying to achieve for this system. For example, you may want to limit certain business processes to no more than 10% of system resources, while allowing a few critical business processes to utilize up to 80% of the resources.

2. **Identification of the work entering the database server**: Identification of the activities, in detail, for each of the business goals identified in step 1. For example, for critical business processes, identify the application user name or authorization ID that submits the query.

3. **Management of work when it is running in the database server**: Management of the activities identified in the earlier steps. This stage includes mechanisms for making steady progress towards the business goal, and necessary actions to take if a goal is not being met. For example, a greater percentage of CPU and I/O resources can be made available for business-critical applications, queries, and so on.

4. **Monitoring the database server to ensure it is being used efficiently**: Monitoring the state of activities on the database server to determine whether you are achieving the business goal. This is also a key element to determine necessary modifications to the earlier stages, if the business goals were not met.

The WLM objects

The Db2 WLM architecture consists of the following objects:

- Service class: A service class defines a unique execution environment in which units of work can run. This execution environment assigns system resources such as CPU and pre-fetch I/O priority, and controls work via thresholds. The service class will have subclasses defined, where all of the database work is executed within the service subclass. The following table shows the default Db2 WLM superclasses and subclasses:

Superclass	Subclass	Description
SYSDEFAULTUSERCLASS	SYSDEFAULTSUBCLASS SYSDEFAULTMANAGEDSUBCLASS	All user activities run in this class. The heavy weighted queries run in SYSDEFAULTMANAGEDSUBCLASS.

SYSDEFAULTMAINTENANCECLASS	SYSDEFAULTSUBCLASS	All of the maintenance activities run in this class, which includes asynchronous index cleanup (AIC). Health monitor initiated backup, `runstats`, and `reorg`.
SYSDEFAULTSYSTEMCLASS	SYSDEFAULTSUBCLASS	All of the Db2 internal system level tasks run in this class. The Db2 threads and connections that are tracked by this class are: `db2taskd`, `db2stmm`, `db2pfchr`, `db2pclnr`, `db2loggr`, `db2loggw`, `db2lfr`, `db2dlock`, `db2fw`, `db2evm`, `db2lused`, and `db2pcsd`.

The Db2 WLM default superclasses and subclasses

If you want to create a customized service class and subclasses, you can do so by executing the CREATE SERVICE CLASS statement, as seen in the following:

```
-- Create service super class
CREATE SERVICE CLASS sales;
-- Create service sub classes
CREATE SERVICE CLASS directsales UNDER sales;
CREATE SERVICE CLASS retailsales UNDER sales;
```

Workloads

A workload is an object that is used to identify submitted database work, based on the application user-name or authorization ID, so that it can be managed. At any given point in time, a unique application connection attribute can be assigned to one and only one workload; however, one workload can host multiple application connection attributes.

The connection attributes tracked by a Db2 workload are:

- Application name
- System authorization name
- Session authorization name
- Role session authorization name
- Group session authorization name
- Client user ID
- Client application name
- Client workstation name
- Client accounting string

The following table shows the default Db2 WLM workloads:

Workload	Description
SYSDEFAULTUSERWORKLOAD	This is a default user workload, created at database creation time, and it cannot be dropped.
SYSDEFAULTADMWORKLOAD	This is a default administration workload, created at database creation time, and it cannot be dropped. This workload permits ACCESSCTRL, DATAACCESS, DBADM, SECADM, or WLMADM users to query the database and perform administrative or monitoring tasks at any time.

The Db2 WLM default workloads

If you want to create customized workloads, you can do so by executing a CREATE WORKLOAD statement, like the one shown here:

```
CREATE WORKLOAD campaign APPLNAME ('dircamp') SESSION_USER GROUP ('SALES')
SERVICE CLASS directsales UNDER sales;
```

Thresholds

A threshold is an object that sets a predefined limit based on specific criteria, such as consumption of a specific system resource or duration of execution time. This is essential to maintaining the system stability by identifying work that behaves abnormally.

There are four types of Db2 WLM thresholds:

- **Connection thresholds:** This defines a limit as to how long a connection can sit idle, and can be defined using CONNECTIONIDLETIME.
- **Unit of work thresholds:** This defines a limit as to how long a unit of work can execute, and the clause is UOWTOTALTIME. This can only be applied to a unit of work, and not to a specific activity.
- **Activity thresholds:** This defines a limit as to how much of a system resource can be used or how long an individual activity can execute. The various activity thresholds are:
    - **ACTIVITYTOTALTIME**: Controls the amount of time that any given activity can take, from submission to completion.
    - **ACTIVITYTOTALRUNTIME**: Controls the amount of time that an activity can take while executing.

- **ACTIVITYTOTALRUNTIMEINALLSC**: Controls the maximum amount of runtime that an activity can take, running in a particular service subclass.
- **CPUTIME**: Controls the maximum amount of combined user and system processor time that an activity may consume on a particular member during the execution of the activity.
- **CPUTIMEINSC**: Controls the maximum amount of combined user and system processor time that an activity may consume on a particular member while executing in a specific service subclass.
- **DATATAGINSC**: Controls the data that can be touched (or not touched) by an activity while running a particular service subclass.
- **ESTIMATEDSQLCOST**: Controls DML activities that the query optimizer determines to have a large estimated cost.
- **SQLROWSREAD**: Controls the maximum number of rows which can be read on any member by an activity.
- **SQLROWSREADINSC**: Controls the maximum number of rows which can be read by an activity on a particular member while executing in a specific service subclass.
- **SQLROWSRETURNED**: Controls the number of rows returned when executing SQL.
- **SQLTEMPSPACE**: Controls the amount of temporary table space a given activity can consume on a member.

- **Aggregate thresholds:** This defines a limit across a set of multiple activities, and operates as a running total, to which any work tracked by the threshold contributes. The various aggregate thresholds are:
  - **AGGSQLTEMPSPACE**: Controls the maximum amount of system temporary table space that can be consumed, in total, across all activities in the service subclass.
  - **CONCURRENTWORKLOADOCCURRENCES**: Controls the number of active occurrences of a workload that can run on a coordinator member at the same time.
  - **CONCURRENTWORKLOADACTIVITIES**: Controls the number of individual activities that can run within a workload occurrence.
  - **CONCURRENTDBCOORDACTIVITIES**: Controls the number of concurrent activities in the domain that the threshold is associated with (database, work action, service superclass, or service subclass).

- **TOTALMEMBERCONNECTIONS**: Controls the number of database connections to a given member that can be established at the same time.
- **TOTALSCMEMBERCONNECTIONS**: Controls the number of database connections to a given member, for work executing within a given service class at the same time.

Actions that can be taken when a threshold is violated are:

- Stop execution (STOP EXECUTION): This action is to stop the execution of an activity when a threshold is violated.
- Continue execution (CONTINUE): This action allows the execution, or an activity, to continue when a threshold is violated. However, relevant data can be collected for an administrator to perform future analysis to determine how to prevent this condition from happening again.
- Force the application (FORCE APPLICATION): This action is to force off the users or application when the UOWTOTALTIME threshold is violated.
- Remap the activity (REMAP ACTIVITY TO): This action is to reassign different resource control to an activity when it violates a certain limit.
- Collect data (COLLECT ACTIVITY DATA): This action is to collect detailed information about the activity that violated the threshold.

If you want to create a threshold, you can do so by executing the CREATE THRESHOLD statement, as shown here:

```
CREATE THRESHOLD SALES_LONG_RUNNING
FOR SERVICE CLASS sales ACTIVITIES
ENFORCEMENT DATABASE
WHEN ACTIVITYTOTALTIME > 2 HOURS
COLLECT ACTIVITY DATA WITH DETAILS AND VALUES
CONTINUE;
```

Work action and work class sets

A work class set defines the characteristics of the work of interest, and a work action set dictates what happens when the work of interest is detected.

If you want to create a work class set and work action set to stop execution when Db2 detects a very high estimated cost, you can do so by using the CREATE WORK CLASS SET and CREATE WORK ACTION SET statements:

```
-- Creating work class set
CREATE WORK CLASS SET DIRECTSALES_QRY (WORK CLASS LONG_QRY WORK TYPE
READ FOR
TIMERONCOST FROM 100000 TO UNBOUNDED);
-- Creating work action set
CREATE WORK ACTION SET DBACTIONS FOR DATABASE USING WORK CLASS SET
DIRECTSALES_QRY
(WORK ACTION STOP_LONG_QRY ON WORK CLASS LONG_QRY
WHEN ESTIMATEDSQLCOST > 100000 COLLECT ACTIVITY DATA STOP EXECUTION);
```

Histogram templates

A histogram template is a graphical representation of tabulated frequencies. Histogram templates are used by service subclasses and work actions to define the bin values for the statistics that are maintained using histograms.

If you want to create a lifetime histogram for a direct sales high bin value of 50,000, you can do so by executing the CREATE HISTOGRAM statement, as shown in the following:

```
-- Creating a histogram
CREATE HISTOGRAM TEMPLATE HIST_DIRECTSALES HIGH BIN VALUE 50000;
-- Creating a subclass
CREATE SERVICE CLASS DIRECTSALES UNDER SALES ACTIVITY LIFETIME
HISTOGRAM TEMPLATE HIST_DIRECTSALES;
```

A word about IBM Data Server Manager (DSM)

The IBM Data Server Manager is an integrated database management tool platform for Db2 on Linux, UNIX, and Windows, and is built based on four key features:

- **Identify**:
  - Receive early notifications of problems before they impact the service
  - Quickly isolate problems across the database, network, and application layers
  - Get visibility into problems by workload, to prioritize response

- **Diagnose**:
    - Follow the well-proven guided workflows to diagnose
    - Provide a complete view of data, from real time to any specific time in the past
    - Dive deeply into root causes, with detailed drill-down capabilities
    - Use built-in integration to leverage data from other IBM solutions

- **Solve**:
    - Receive easy-to-understand, actionable recommendations for problem resolution
    - Tune entire workloads to balance costs across `query` and `insert` actions

- **Prevent**:
    - Capture all of the data necessary for root cause analysis
    - Real-time and historical data for capacity planning and growth
    - Proactively optimize performance of query workloads, databases, and applications
    - Minimize slowdowns that impact user productivity, revenue, and end user experience

The IBM Data Server Manager is available in two editions:

- **IBM Data Server Manager Base Edition offerings**:
    - Basic database administration
    - Basic real-time performance monitoring capabilities
    - No-charge edition

- **IBM Data Server Manager Enterprise Edition offerings**:
    - Advanced monitoring capabilities, including enhanced monitoring and access to real-time (or near real-time) and historical performance reports
    - Alerting and notification via customized email, SMTP, SNMP, alert history, and alert details
    - Captures database SQL performance statistics and creates a baseline to proactively send alerts about performance issues
    - Identifies potential data access bottlenecks for distributed applications
    - Provides advanced performance monitoring, including end-to-end transaction response time for any workload

- Advanced query tuning capabilities for both row-organized and column-organized databases
- Centralized configuration management, including change tracking at the server and client levels
- Identifies reclaimable space, compression, and multi-temperature data store opportunities

Data Server Manager Enterprise Edition is packaged with Db2 advanced editions or the Db2 Performance Management offering for non-advanced Db2 editions.

You can download the base edition at `https://www.ibm.com/developerworks/downloads/im/dsm/index.html` and install the product using the setup command `setup.bat` (Windows) or `setup.sh` (UNIX).

Summary

The objective of this chapter was to acquaint you with the following:

- The Db2 instance-specific commands, such as create, list, update, and drop
- The Db2 registry and operating system environment variables
- The Db2 instance and database configuration parameters and commands
- The Db2 autonomic computing features, and associated application or business benefits with STMM and automatic storage
- An introduction to the WLM feature and associated objects
- An introduction to IBM Data Server Manager and its capabilities

Practice questions

- **Question 1**: Which command can be used to display only the instance level registry settings for an instance `db2inst1`?
  1. `db2set -all db2inst1`
  2. `db2set -i db2inst1`
  3. `db2set -lr`
  4. `db2val`

- **Question 2**: Which of the following commands can be used to retrieve CURRENT and PENDING values of database manager configuration parameters for the instance db2inst1? (Choose two.)
    1. db2look -dbmcfg
    2. db2 "ATTACH TO db2inst1"; db2 "GET DBM CFG SHOW DETAIL"
    3. db2 "GET DBM CFG SHOW DETAIL"
    4. db2pd -dbmcfg
    5. db2greg

- **Question 3**: Which of the following table functions displays the registry setting?
    1. MON_GET_DATABASE ()
    2. MON_GET_INSTANCE ()
    3. ENV_GET_REG_VARIABLES ()
    4. MON_GET_UTILITY()

- **Question 4**: Which of the following parameters contributes to DATABASE_MEMORY usage? (Choose two.)
    1. dbheap
    2. stmtheap
    3. applheapsz
    4. appl_memory
    5. util_heap_sz

- **Question 5**: What is the order in which Db2 resolves the registry settings and the environment variables when configuring the system?
    1. Environment Variables, User Level, Instance Node Level, Instance Level, Global Level
    2. User Level, Instance Node Level, Instance Level, Global Level, Environment Variables
    3. Environment Variables, User Level, Instance Level, Instance Node Level, Global Level
    4. User Level, Instance Node Level, Instance Level, Environment Variables, Global Level

- **Question 6**: Which of the following commands or statements can be used to retrieve CURRENT and PENDING values of database configuration parameters for the database SAMPLE?

    1. db2look -dbcfg

    2. db2pd -dbcfg

    3. db2 "CONNECT TO SAMPLE"; db2 "SELECT NAME,SUBSTR (VALUE, 1, 20) AS VALUE, SUBSTR (DEFERRED_VALUE, 1, 20) AS DEFERRED_VALUE FROM TABLE (SYSPROC.DB_GET_CFG ())"

    4. db2 "CONNECT TO SAMPLE"; db2 "GET DB CFG FOR sample"

- **Question 7**: Which of the following commands can be used to enable STMM for the database SAMPLE?

    1. db2 "UPDATE DB CFG FOR sample USING SELF_TUNING_MEM ON"

    2. db2 "UPDATE DBM CFG USING SELF_TUNING_MEM ON"

    3. db2set DB2_DATABASE_CF_MEMORY=AUTO

    4. db2 "UPDATE DB CFG FOR sample USING DATABASE_MEMORY ON"

- **Question 8**: Which of the following statements can be used to strip the tablespace TBSP1 data across all of the storage paths when a new storage path is added to an existing storage group?

    1. db2 "ALTER TABLESPACE TBSP1 STRIP DATA ALL"

    2. db2 "ALTER TABLESPACE TBSP1 REBALANCE"

    3. db2 "ALTER TABLESPACE TBSP1 STRIP DATA"

    4. db2 "ALTER TABLESPACE TBSP1 BALANCE"

- **Question 9**: When a database SAMPLE is initially created with an AUTOMATIC STORAGE NO clause, which of the following commands will convert the database to an AUTOMATIC STORAGE enabled database?

    1. db2 "ALTER DATABASE sample ENABLE AUTOMATIC STORAGE"

    2. db2 "ALTER DATABASE sample AUTOMATIC STORAGE YES"

    3. db2 "CONNECT TO sample"; db2 "CREATE STOGROUP SG_DATA ON '/data/fs1/'"

    4. db2 "CONNECT TO sample"; db2 "CREATE TABLESPACE TBSP_DATA MANAGED BY AUTOMATIC STORAGE"

- **Question 10**: What actions are permitted when a threshold is violated? (Choose two.)
    1. Stop execution
    2. Drop the object
    3. Quiesce the database
    4. Remap the activity
    5. Quiesce the instance

Solutions

- **Question 1**:
  The correct answer is (2). Option (3) displays all of the supported registry variables. Option (4) is a Db2 copy validation command, and option (1) is invalid.
- **Question 2**:
  The correct answers are (2) and (4). Option (3) needs an instance attachment before running the SHOW DETAIL clause of the GET DBM CFG command. Option (5) is a global registry display command. Option (1) is invalid.
- **Question 3**:
  The correct answer is (3). Options (1), (2), and (4) are monitoring table functions, and will be discussed in the monitoring chapter.
- **Question 4**:
  The correct answers are (1) and (5). The parameter database_memory specifies the amount of shared memory that is reserved for the database shared memory region. When you set this parameter to AUTOMATIC, the initial memory requirement is calculated based on the underlying configuration settings:
    - **Buffer pools**: This specifies the amount of memory allocated to cache a table's index and data pages as they are read from the disk to be selected or modified
    - dbheap: This parameter specifies the amount of memory used to fulfill the global database memory requirements
    - locklist: This parameter specifies the amount of memory allocated to store the lock attributes
    - util_heap_sz: This parameter specifies the amount of memory allocated to the database utilities

- `pckcachesz`: This parameter specifies the amount of memory allocated to cache sections of static SQL, dynamic SQL, and XQuery statements
- `catalogcache_sz`: This parameter specifies the amount of memory of the `dbheap` allocated to cache the catalog information
- `sheapthres_shr`: This parameter specifies memory allocations to serve shared sorts
- **Overflow area**: The percentage of memory that can be controlled via the `DB2_MEM_TUNING_RANGE` registry variable, to manage the volatile memory requirement

- **Question 5**:
  The correct answer is (1). The second figure shows the order in which Db2 resolves the registry settings and the environment variables when configuring the system.
- **Question 6**:
  The correct answer is (3). Option (2) needs the database option and the database name for the `db2pd` command. Option (4) doesn't have the `SHOW DETAIL` clause in the `GET DB CFG` command. Option (1) has an invalid clause.
- **Question 7**:
  The correct answer is (1). Option (3) is to enable the self-tuning memory manager for CF, and options (2) and (4) are invalid.
- **Question 8**:
  The correct answer is (2). All other options are invalid.
- **Question 9**:
  The correct answer is (3). All other options are invalid.
- **Question 10**:
  The correct answers are (1) and (4). Actions that can be taken when a threshold is violated are:
    - **Stop execution** (`STOP EXECUTION`): This action is to stop the execution of an activity when a threshold is violated
    - **Continue execution** (`CONTINUE`): This action is to continue the execution of an activity when a threshold is violated; however, it can collect the relevant data for an administrator to perform future analysis to determine how to prevent this condition from happening again

- **Force the application (**FORCE APPLICATION**):** This action is to force off the users or application when the UOWTOTALTIME threshold is violated
- **Remap the activity (**REMAP ACTIVITY TO**):** This action is to reassign different resource control to an activity when it violates a certain limit
- **Collect data (**COLLECT ACTIVITY DATA**):** This action is to collect detailed information about the activity that violated the threshold

3
Physical Design

This chapter will prepare you to create, manage, and alter physical database objects. You will learn the proper use of compression, along with partitioning capabilities. We will discuss the implementation of Db2 BLU, along with the pureScale enhancements in the v11.1 release. We will also review the SQL enhancements in the Db2 v11.1 release. After the completion of this chapter, you will be able to demonstrate the ability to perform the following tasks:

- Creating, altering, and managing Db2 objects
- Implementing BLU acceleration
- Describing Db2 pureScale enhancements
- Properly use compression
- Describing SQL compatibility
- Describing partitioning capabilities

Certification test:

- Number of questions: 13
- Percentage of the exam: 22%

Database planning

Before creating a database, you should consider the rules for building a flexible Agile architecture. A flexible architecture is one that grows with the organization without impacting availability, reliability, or performance. It should be easy to maintain and upgrade as new releases of Db2 are made available. **Runtime Application Self-Protection (RASP)** and **Agile Database Implementation (ADI)** follows Agile constructs in the definition and use of database objects.

You can read about both **Optimal Flexible Architecture (OFA)** and ADI at www.enterprisedb2.com.

The following list shows the different areas of physical database design that should be considered before transforming a physical data model into a physical database, based on application requirements:

- Database partition groups
- Block-based buffer pools
- Tablespace volumetrics
- Very large tables
- Indexes
- Aliases, proper or base views, and multi-versioning for Agile flexibility
- Range-partitioned tables
- **Multidimensional Clustering (MDC)** tables
- **Materialized Query tables (MQT)**
- Multi-temperature management using storage groups
- **High Availability Disaster Recovery (HADR)** databases and registry settings
- Maintenance versus availability schedules
- Security and availability
- Active log space
- Sort overflow space

Creating a Db2 database

You can create a Db2 database by using the CREATE DATABASE command in all topologies (**Database Partitioning Feature (DPF)**, pureScale, or regular ESE), but there are differences to consider. In its simplest form, the syntax for the CREATE DATABASE command is as follows:

```
CREATE [DATABASE | DB] [DatabaseName]
```

In the preceding code, the following applies:

- `DatabaseName` identifies a unique name that is assigned to the database once it is created. Using the basic syntax, the database location is identified by the DBM parameter `DFTDBPATH`.
- The database that is created is unrestricted, and the default storage group, `IBMSTOGROUP`, is used. Storage groups are required for automatic storage, managed tablespaces. The Db2 instance must be started for this command to work. The only value that you must provide when executing this command is a name to assign to the new database. The rules for naming a database are as follows:
  - It can only consist of the characters a through z, A through Z, 0 through 9, @, #, $, and _ (underscore)
  - It cannot begin with a number
  - It must be eight characters or fewer in length
  - Mixed case is not supported
  - It cannot begin with the letter sequences `SYS`, `DBM`, or `IBM`
  - It cannot be the same as a name already assigned to another database within the same instance

We can see the database creation rules in the following table:

Object	Rules	Restriction	Application
Storage groups	Absolute path names	<= 175 characters	All
Storage paths	Must have >= 1 path	Unless database partition expressions	Partition DB
Database path	Drive letter	Unless `DB2_CREATE_DB_ON_PATH` is set	Windows
	No expressions	Cannot use database partition expressions	All

Database creation rules

Automatic storage management is required for most of the major new features in Db2, such as BLU and pureScale. Although you can still create a database using `AUTOMATIC STORAGE NO`, the functionality has been deprecated, and may soon be removed. In addition, Unicode is becoming the standard; so, we believe you should start moving in that direction.

Creating a custom defined database requires overriding the defaults, as follows:

```
CREATE [DATABASE | DB] [DatabaseName] <AT DBPARTITIONNUM>
```

You can also use the following command:

```
CREATE [DATABASE | DB] [DatabaseName]
<AUTOMATIC STORAGE [YES | NO]>
<ON [StoragePath ,...] <DBPATH [DBPath]>>
<ALIAS [Alias]>
<USING CODESET [CodeSet] TERRITORY [Territory]>
<COLLATE USING [CollateType]>
<PAGESIZE [4096 | Pagesize <K>]>
<NUMSEGS [NumSegments]>
<DFT_EXTENT_SZ [DefaultExtSize]>
<RESTRICTIVE>
<CATALOG TABLESPACE [TS_Definition]>
<USER TABLESPACE [TS_Definition]>
<TEMPORARY TABLESPACE [TS_Definition]>
<WITH "[Description]">
<AUTOCONFIGURE <USING [Keyword] [Value] ,...>
<APPLY [DB ONLY | DB AND DBM | NONE>>
```

In the preceding code, the following applies:

- DatabaseName: The unique name that is assigned to the database to be created.
- StoragePath: Identifies where tablespace containers will be placed.
- DBPath: Identifies where the directory hierarchy and metadata files associated with the database to be created should be physically stored. (If this parameter is not specified, and automatic storage is used, the metadata files will be stored in the first storage path specified in the StoragePath parameter.)
- Alias: Identifies the alias assigned to the database.
- CodeSet: Identifies the code set to be used for storing data in the database.
- Territory: Identifies the territory to be used for storing data in the database.
- CollateType: Specifies the collating sequence (that is, the sequence in which characters are ordered for the purpose of sorting, merging, and making comparisons) that is to be used by the database.
- NumSegments: Specifies the number of directories that are to be created and used to store files for the default SMS tablespace used by the database (TEMPSPACE1).
- DefaultExtSize: Specifies the default extent size to be used.

- `TS_Definition`: Specifies the definition used to create the tablespace that will be used to hold the system catalog tables (`SYSCATSPACE`), user-defined objects (`USERSPACE1`), and/or temporary objects (`TEMPSPACE1`).
- `Description`: A comment used to describe the database entry that will be made in the database directory for the database.
- `Keyword`: One or more keywords recognized by the `AUTOCONFIGURE` command.
- `Value`: Identifies the value that is to be associated with the keyword specified.
- `RESTRICTIVE`: If this clause is specified, the `RESTRICT ACCESS` database configuration parameter for the database being created will be set to `YES`, and no privileges will be granted to the group `PUBLIC`.

Here is an example of a custom-created database that provides settings for just about every database option, except encryption:

```
CREATE DATABASE AUTODB
AUTOMATIC STORAGE YES ON '/home' ALIAS TESTDB
USING CODESET UTF-8 TERRITORY en_US
PAGESIZE 32768
NUMSEGS 1
DFT_EXTENT_SZ 4 RESTRICTIVE
CATALOG TABLESPACE MANAGED BY AUTOMATIC STORAGE
EXTENTSIZE 32 PREFETCHSIZE -1 OVERHEAD -1 TRANSFERRATE -1
NO FILE SYSTEM CACHING AUTORESIZE YES INITIALSIZE 32 M INCREASESIZE 256 M
MAXSIZE 24576 M
USER TABLESPACE MANAGED BY AUTOMATIC STORAGE
EXTENTSIZE 32 PREFETCHSIZE -1 OVERHEAD -1 TRANSFERRATE -1
NO FILE SYSTEM CACHING AUTORESIZE YES INITIALSIZE 32 M INCREASESIZE 256 M
MAXSIZE 24576 M
TEMPORARY TABLESPACE MANAGED BY AUTOMATIC STORAGE
EXTENTSIZE 64 PREFETCHSIZE 512 OVERHEAD -1 TRANSFERRATE -1
WITH "Sample Auto DB"
AUTOCONFIGURE using mem_percent 35 workload_type mixed admin_priority
performance isolation ur bp_resizeable no
APPLY DB AND DBM;
```

Enabling automatic storage

While Db2 v11.1 does support non-automatic storage upgrades for DMS tablespaces, there is no upgrade support for SMS. We recommend that you convert all existing databases to automatic storage before you upgrade them.

You can convert an existing non-automatic storage database to automatic storage by using the CREATE STOGROUP command, as shown in the following command:

```
CREATE STOGROUP SG_HOT ON '/db/ts01';
```

Because there was no storage group defined, SG_HOT will be set to default, as follows:

```
db2pd -db sample -storagepaths

Address              SGID  Default  DataTag    Name
0x00007FFF01ECA500 0      Yes      0          SG_HOT
```

If IBMSTOGROUP (or some other storage group) is set as default, you can change SG_HOT to the default by running the ALTER command, as follows:

```
ALTER STOGROUP SG_HOT SET AS DEFAULT;
```

Now you can alter the tablespaces to automatic storage, as follows:

```
ALTER TABLESPACE TS_SMALL_DATA MANAGED BY AUTOMATIC STORAGE;
```

 Db2 pureScale and BLU only support databases that are defined with AUTOMATIC STORAGE.

Buffer pools

A buffer pool is an area within DATABASE_MEMORY that is allocated by the database manager during database activation to cache table and index pages that are read from the disk during the execution of a transaction. Buffer pools are allocated in the memory on the local server where the database is active, and they are referred to as **Local Buffer Pools (LBP)**.

Db2 reads and writes blocks of pages between disk storage devices and buffer pools. All data, except for **Large Binary Objects (LOB)**, is moved from the disk to the buffer pools before work is performed against the data. If compression is active, the page is compressed for storage in the buffer pools. In many cases, data is not decompressed until it is returned to the client.

Db2 can perform many types of I/O reads and writes, and tries to determine the best I/O for all work performed. Any I/O performed while the transaction waits is called synchronous. Any I/O performed without a transaction wait is called asynchronous. Prefetching is the process of reading data from the disk into the buffer pools asynchronously, before the transaction needs it; this is performed by I/O servers. With the exception of rare situations, all write I/O is performed asynchronously, using processes called cleaners.

I/O is important to any database solution, and minimizing its impact on workloads improves throughput and performance. All of the I/O operations are scheduled. Many devices will queue up to five I/Os on a device by default, while the remaining I/O is buffered in memory. Write I/O has a higher scheduling priority than read I/O. An I/O operation that is on the queue waiting for some time can be given an "execute immediate" priority, to prevent I/O stall.

Read and write I/O measurements can be found in the tables
`SYSIBMADM.BP_READ_IO` and `SYSIBMADM.BP_WRITE_IO`.

A buffer pool hit occurs when the necessary page is found in the buffer pool, and a miss occurs when the necessary page is not found in the buffer pool. The pages in the buffer pool can be in one of these three states:

- **In use:** Pages are currently being read or updated
- **Dirty:** Pages contain data that has been changed, but has not been written to the disk yet
- **Clean:** Pages contain data that has been changed and written to the disk

Buffer pool planning

Have you ever wondered which is better, one large buffer pool or many small ones? The answer depends on the data design and the transactional workloads that have been defined. As a general rule, one large buffer pool will perform better than several small ones. Db2 supports 4K, 8K, 16K, and 32K buffer pool page sizes. As a rule, a row cannot span a page, since page chaining can significantly degrade performance. To prevent this, a new DB CFG parameter was added in v10.5, named `EXTENDED_ROW_SZ`. When enabled, this setting will allow a row to span a page, creating chained pages. For example, it will allow a row larger than 4,005 to be stored in a 4,096 page size.

We recommend disabling DB CFG EXTENDED_ROW_SZ, unless it is really necessary for the application.

A key to retaining database performance is to optimize the buffer pool hit ratio. We recommend that you set a baseline for each buffer pool, and that you review it on a regular basis as data volume and workloads change.

This information can be found in SYSIBMADM.BP_HITRATIO and SYSIBMADM.MON_BP_UTILIZATION.

Creating a buffer pool

If you want to create a buffer pool of a page size 4K, with a total number of pages of 50,000, you can do so by executing the CREATE BUFFERPOOL command, as follows:

```
CREATE BUFFERPOOL bpool_04k SIZE 50000 PAGESIZE 4K;
```

If you want to specify the number of pages that should exist in the block-based area to improve the sequential prefetching, execute the following command:

```
CREATE BUFFERPOOL bpool_16k SIZE 10000 PAGESIZE 16K
NUMBLOCKPAGES 5000 BLOCKSIZE 128;
```

Finally, if you want to create a buffer pool that is automatic in nature, you can do so by executing the following command:

```
CREATE BUFFERPOOL auto_bpool_32k PAGESIZE 32K;
```

Altering a buffer pool

You can modify the following listed attributes of a buffer pool by using the ALTER BUFFERPOOL statement:

- SIZE: The number of pages allocated for the specific buffer pool
- NUMBLOCKPAGES: The block based total area
- BLOCKSIZE: The block size, within the block based total area

- `ESTORE`: Enabling or disabling the extended storage
- `DBPGNAME`: The database partition group

If you want to change the block based total area and the block size, you can do so by executing the following statement:

```
ALTER BUFFERPOOL bpool_08k NUMBLOCKPAGES 8000 BLOCKSIZE 256;
```

Storage groups

A storage group assigns tablespace containers to storage paths. These can be used to define the class of service for I/O. Storage groups help in segregating the different classes of storage available to the database system, such as **Solid State Drives (SSD)** (very fast disks), **Serial Attached SCSI (SAS)** (medium fast disks), and **Serial ATA (SATA)** (slow disks). Only automatic storage tablespaces can be assigned to storage groups. A storage group can have multiple tablespaces, but a tablespace can only be assigned to one storage group.

You can create a storage group by using the CREATE STOGROUP statement, as follows:

```
CREATE STOGROUP [StogrpName] ON ['StoragePath']
OVERHEAD [DeviceOverHead]
DEVICE READ RATE [DeviceReadRate]
DATA TAG [DataTag]
SET AS DEFAULT
```

In the preceding code, the following applies:

- `StoGrpName`: Identifies a unique name assigned to the storage group, once it is created.
- `StoragePath`: Identifies the storage paths to be added for the named storage group.
- `DeviceOverHead`: Identifies the I/O controller time and the disk seek and latency time, in milliseconds. Usually, this information comes from the storage manufacturer. The default value is 6.725 milliseconds.
- `DeviceReadRate`: Identifies the device specification for the read transfer date, in MBps. The default value is 100 Megabits per Second.
- `DataTag`: Identifies a tar name to be used by the Db2 workload manager to determine the processing priority of the database activities. The default setting is NONE.

If you want to create a storage group, SG_HOT, with an overhead rate of 0.8 and a device read date of 512 Megabits per Second, the statement is as follows:

```
CREATE STOGROUP SG_HOT ON '/data/hot_fs1' OVERHEAD 0.8
DEVICE READ RATE 512 DATA TAG 1;
```

If you want to create a tablespace, Q4_2014, to store recent data using the storage group SG_HOT, execute the following command:

```
CREATE TABLESPACE Q4_2014 MANAGED BY AUTOMATIC STORAGE
USING STOGROUP SG_HOT
INITIALSIZE 5M INCREASESIZE 5M
OVERHEAD INHERIT TRANSFERRATE INHERIT;
```

As you can see from the preceding statement, the automatic storage tablespace inherits the overhead and transfer rate attributes from the storage group. The Db2 database manager converts the device read rate into a transfer rate using the formula listed here:

$$TRANSFERRATE = (1 \div DEVICE\_READ\_RATE) * \frac{1000}{1024000} * PAGESIZE$$

Storage group planning

A storage group contains storage paths of similar characteristics; some
critical storage attributes that you need to consider while building the storage groups are as follows:

- Storage capacity
- Latency
- Data transfer rate
- RAID level

Altering storage groups

You can use the ALTER STOGROUP command to change the following listed storage group settings:

- OVERHEAD
- DEVICE READ RATE
- DATA TAG

You can also add or remove storage paths; if you want to add a new storage path to an existing storage group, execute the following command:

```
ALTER STOGROUP SG_HOT ADD '/data/hot_fs2';
ALTER TABLESPACE Q4_2014 REBALANCE;
```

If you want to drop a storage path, execute the following command:

```
ALTER STOGROUP SG_HOT DROP '/data/hot_fs2';
ALTER TABLESPACE Q4_2014 REBALANCE;
```

Renaming a storage group

You can use the RENAME STOGROUP command to rename an available storage group as follows:

```
RENAME STOGROUP SG_HOT TO SG_SSD;
```

Dropping a storage group

You can use the DROP STOGROUP command to drop an available storage group as follows:

```
DROP STOGROUP SG_HOT;
```

Before you drop an available storage group, any associated tablespaces will need to be moved to another storage group; you can do this by executing the following command:

```
ALTER TABLESPACE Q4_2014 USING STOGROUP IBMSTOGROUP;
```

Tablespaces

Tablespaces are database objects that provide a mapping between objects containing data to be retained and the operating system storage subsystem. Data can be retained in a transactional state or in a persisted state. For example, a sort overflow requires data to be retained until the sort process is completed, while base tables and indexes persist data until removed by a process.

Containers

Containers are the actual physical files that store data. Containers have the following three categories of management:

- **Database Managed Space (DMS)**
- **System Managed Space (SMS)**
- **Automatic Storage (AS)**

A disk storage device can be used by Db2 in its raw state; we call this a raw device. In the past, raw devices were used for Db2 active logs because of the RAID 5 write penalty. However, due to improved storage devices, this is no longer needed. When the device is assigned a mount point and is mounted, it becomes a filesystem. A container is a fully qualified file or raw device.

A typical Db2 container is as follows:

```
/ts1/data/db2inst1/NODE0000/DB1/T0000057/C0000001.LRG
```

In the preceding code, the following applies:

- `/ts1`: Filesystem
- `db2inst1`: Instance name
- `DB1`: Database name
- `T0000057`: Tablespace
- `C00000001.LRG`: Container

A tablespace can contain a mix of one or more tables and indexes. Each tablespace can span one or more containers, but a container can only be assigned to one tablespace. The disk space allocated in tablespace containers is formatted into pages and grouped into extents.

The following diagram shows the relationship between pages, extents, and tablespace containers:

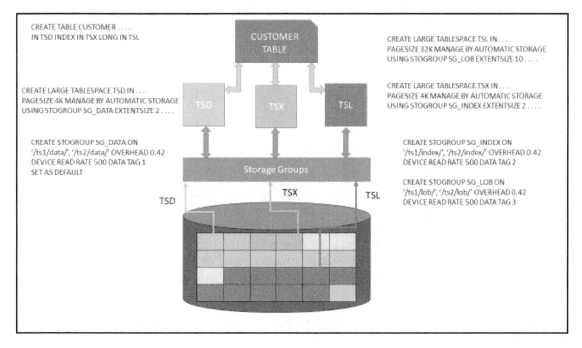

CREATE TABLE CUSTOMER . . . .
IN TSD INDEX IN TSX LONG IN TSL

CUSTOMER TABLE

CREATE LARGE TABLESPACE TSL IN . . .
PAGESIZE 32K MANAGE BY AUTOMATIC STORAGE
USING STOGROUP SG_LOB EXTENTSIZE 10 . . . .

CREATE LARGE TABLESPACE TSD IN . . .
PAGESIZE 4K MANAGE BY AUTOMATIC STORAGE
USING STOGROUP SG_DATA EXTENTSIZE 2 . . . .

CREATE LARGE TABLESPACE TSX IN . . .
PAGESIZE 4K MANAGE BY AUTOMATIC STORAGE
USING STOGROUP SG_INDEX EXTENTSIZE 2 . . . .

TSD TSX TSL

CREATE STOGROUP SG_DATA ON
'/ts1/data/', '/ts2/data/' OVERHEAD 0.42
DEVICE READ RATE 500 DATA TAG 1
SET AS DEFAULT

CREATE STOGROUP SG_INDEX ON
'/ts1/index/', '/ts2/index/' OVERHEAD 0.42
DEVICE READ RATE 500 DATA TAG 2

Storage Groups

CREATE STOGROUP SG_LOB ON
'/ts1/lob/', '/ts2/lob/' OVERHEAD 0.42
DEVICE READ RATE 500 DATA TAG 3

TSD TSX TSL

How data is written to tablespace containers

In Db2, an extent contains a number of contiguous pages in the storage device. An extent is configured using the DFT_EXTENT_SZ clause when creating the database, or using the EXTENTSIZE clause when creating the tablespace. Once specified, the extent size cannot be altered for the life of the database or the tablespace. The Db2 I/O works with extents; in this way, contiguous pages are read from the disk to the buffer pool in a single I/O. A good rule of thumb is to have an extent size of 256 Kilo byte (in other words, 8 Kilo byte per page x 32 pages) for OLTP, and 512 Kilo byte (16 Kilo byte per page x 32 pages) for data warehouse applications.

You can monitor the number of pages that the prefetcher read into the buffer pool that were never used before, by using one of the following table functions:

- `mon_get_bufferpool()`
- `mon_get_database()`
- `mon_get_database_details()`
- `mon_get_tablespace()`

Tablespace planning

Tablespaces are very important structures in Db2, containing tables, indexes, and large and long objects. In earlier versions of Db2, tablespaces were made up of a number of containers that mapped to the physical disk. Starting with Db2 10.1, storage groups were added to provide a layer of abstraction between tablespaces and the physical disk, allowing tablespaces to be moved between the storage groups based on business needs (fast SSD drives for the recent data, medium SAS drives for the previous month's data, and slow SATA drives for archived data).

Not all data is the same. Some data is written once and read often, while other data is changed often and seldom read. Some data arrives at the database in large bunches to be inserted or updated, while other data arrives in thousands of concurrent, single-row transactions. Understanding data behavior and size is important, in order to properly plan for its disk storage configuration and retention. When someone tells you that you should no longer be concerned about these data behaviors because solid state/flash and modern SAN systems will take care of it, be very skeptical, and make them prove it.

A poor tablespace design can lead to a significant negative impact on database server performance. The design principles around tablespaces are listed as follows:

- **Extent size**: This is the amount of data that is to be written to a single tablespace container, before another container will be used. Ideally, the size should be a multiple of the segment size of the disks and the page size. For example, a segment size of 32 Kilo byte and a page size of 4 Kilo byte will deliver an extent size of 128 Kilo byte. A good rule of thumb is to have an extent size of 256 Kilo byte; however, extent sizes of 128 Kilo byte or 512 Kilo byte are also good choices, based on the application type.

- **Page size**: This is the size of each page used by the tablespace being created. Selecting the proper page size is important, as a lot of wasted disk space can occur with the wrong page size. Page chaining is generally a bad idea, so a row must fit within a page. Choosing the wrong page size for a row length can leave unusable space within the page. Depending on the workloads executed against the table, smaller page sizes can also lead to higher I/O rates.

- **Filesystem caching**: `NO FILE SYSTEM CACHING` enables direct or concurrent I/O, and it is the default attribute for DMS and automatic storage tablespaces. The Db2 database manager caches regular data in respective buffer pools before sending the data back to the client. It is advisable to not cache the data in the operating system filesystem cache.

- **Prefetch size**: This is the amount of data that is to be read whenever a prefetch is triggered. Setting a prefetch size to a multiple of the extent size can cause multiple extents to be read in parallel. The recommendation is to set this parameter to `AUTOMATIC`.

- **Parallel IO**: The Db2 registry variable `DB2_PARALLEL_IO` can be used to explicitly specify a prefetch request for each container. For example, if a tablespace container exists on a `RAID 5 4+1` array filesystem, then set `DB2_PARALLEL_IO=*:5` to activate prefetch for each physical disk.

- **Use** `AUTOMATIC`: It is recommended to set the number of prefetchers and the number of page cleaners to `AUTOMATIC` as follows:

    - `TRUNCATE ... LOAD`: It is recommended to create `TRUNCATE` and `LOAD` tables in a separate tablespace, to eliminate the conflict between `BACKUP` and `TRUNCATE`

    - `NOT LOGGED INITIALLY`: It is recommended to create `NOT LOGGED INITIALLY` tables in a separate tablespace

- **Mixed organization**: It is recommended to keep row and column organized tables in separate tablespaces.

- **Highly volatile tables**: It is recommended to keep static and volatile tables in separate tablespaces.

Creating tablespaces

Tablespaces can be created by executing the `CREATE TABLESPACE` statement. The basic syntax for this statement is as follows:

```
CREATE
<REGULAR | LARGE | SYSTEM TEMPORARY | USER TEMPORARY>
```

```
TABLESPACE [TablespaceName]
<PAGESIZE [PageSize] <K>>
MANAGED BY AUTOMATIC STORAGE
<AUTORESIZE [YES | NO]>
<INITIALSIZE [InitSize <K | M | G>]>
<INCREASESIZE [IncSize <PERCENT | K | M | G>]>
<MAXSIZE [NONE | MaxSize <K | M | G>]>
<EXTENTSIZE [ExtentPages | ExtentSize <K | M | G>]> <PREFETCHSIZE
[AUTOMATIC | PrefetchPages |
PrefetchSize <K | M | G>]>
<BUFFERPOOL [BufferPoolName]>
<<NO> FILE SYSTEM CACHING>
<DROPPED TABLE RECOVERY <ON | OFF>>
```

In the preceding code, the following applies:

- `TablespaceName`: Identifies the name assigned to the tablespace to be created.
- `PageSize`: Specifies the size of each page used by the tablespace being created. The following values are valid for this parameter: 4,096; 8,192; 16,384; or 32,768 bytes. Unless otherwise specified, pages used by tablespaces are 4,096 bytes in size.
- `Container`: Identifies, by name, one or more containers that are to be used to store the data associated with the tablespace.
- `ContainerPages`: Identifies the amount of storage, by number of pages, which is to be pre-allocated for the container(s) identified in the `Container` parameter.
- `ContainerSize`: Identifies the amount of storage that is to be pre-allocated for the container(s) identified in the `Container` parameter. The value specified for this parameter is treated as the total number of bytes, unless the letter `K` (for kilobytes), `M` (for megabytes), or `G` (for gigabytes) is also specified. (If a `ContainerSize` value is specified, it is converted to a `ContainerPages` value by using the `PageSize` value provided.)
- `InitSize`: Identifies the amount of storage that is to be pre-allocated for an auto-resize DMS or automatic storage tablespace.
- `IncSize` : Identifies the amount by which a tablespace enabled for automatic resizing will be automatically increased when the tablespace is full and a request for more space is made.
- `MaxSize` : Identifies the maximum size to which a tablespace enabled for automatic resizing can be automatically increased.
- `ExtentPages` : Identifies the number of pages of data that are to be written to a single tablespace container before another container will be used.

- ExtentSize : Identifies the amount of data that is to be written to a single tablespace container before another container will be used. The value specified for this parameter is treated as the total number of bytes, unless the letter K (for kilobytes), M (for megabytes), or G (for gigabytes) is also specified. (If an ExtentSize value is specified, it is converted to an ExtentPages value by using the PageSize value provided.)
- PrefetchPages : Identifies the number of pages of data that are to be read from the tablespace when data prefetching is performed (prefetching allows the data needed by a query to be read before it is referenced, so that the query spends less time waiting for I/O).
- PrefetchSize : Identifies the amount of data that is to be read from the tablespace when data prefetching is performed. The value specified for this parameter is treated as the total number of bytes, unless the letter K (for kilobytes), M (for megabytes), or G (for gigabytes) is also specified. (If a PrefetchSize value is specified, it is converted to a PrefetchPages value by using the PageSize value provided.)
- BufferPoolName : Identifies the name of the buffer pool to be used by the tablespace. (The page size of the buffer pool specified must match the page size of the tablespace to be created, or the CREATE TABLESPACE statement will fail.)

If you want to create an automatic storage tablespace that has the name TS_LARGE_DATA and uses the buffer pool IBMDEFAULTBP, you can do so by executing a CREATE TABLESPACE statement as follows:

```
CREATE LARGE TABLESPACE TS_LARGE_DATA MANAGED BY AUTOMATIC STORAGE;
```

The maximum size of a regular 32K page size tablespace is 512 GB, and a large 32K page size tablespace is 64 Tera byte.

If you want to rename a tablespace, use the RENAME TABLESPACE command, as shown in the following code. Remember that SYSCATSPACE can't be renamed:

```
RENAME TABLESPACE TS_SMALL_DATA TO TS_NEW_DATA;
```

Other than the size of the containers, you can change the PREFETCHSIZE, OVERHEAD, and TRANSFERRATE of a tablespace by using the following command:

```
ALTER TABLESPACE TS_SMALL_DATA PREFETCHSIZE 64 OVERHEAD 1 TRANSFERRATE 128;
```

Adding containers to automatic storage tablespaces

You can use the ALTER STOGROUP statement to add a new storage path to an automatic storage tablespace. This can only be done after the database has been created. The basic syntax for this statement is as follows:

```
ALTER STOGROUP [StoGrpName]
ADD '[StoragePath]' ,...)
```

In the preceding code, the following applies:

- StoGrpName: Identifies the storage group name that is to have a new storage path added to its pool of storage paths that are used for automatic storage
- StoragePath: Identifies one or more new storage paths (absolute paths) that are to be added to the collection of storage paths that are used for automatic storage tablespaces

If you want to add the storage locations /database/path1 and /database/path2 to a database named SAMPLE, which is configured for automatic storage and resides on a UNIX system, you can do so by executing an ALTER STOGROUP statement as follows:

```
ALTER STOGROUP IBMSTOGROUP ADD '/database/path1', '/database/path2';
```

Tablespace rebalance operation

When you add a new storage path to an existing storage group, or when you remove an available storage path from an existing storage group using the ALTER STOGROUP statement, the Db2 database manager performs a rebalance operation. A forward rebalance happens when you add a storage path, and a reverse rebalance happens when you remove a storage path. Optionally, you can use the ALTER TABLESPACE statement with the REBALANCE clause to initiate an immediate rebalance operation.

The tablespace rebalance is not supported in pureScale. Use the ADMIN_MOVE_TABLE () procedure to manage disk storage allocations for tables in pureScale.

If you want to monitor the rebalance operation, you can do so by using the MON_GET_REBALANCE_STATUS () table function, as follows:

```
select
varchar (tbsp_name, 15) as tbsp_name,
rebalancer_mode,
rebalancer_status,
rebalancer_extents_remaining,
rebalancer_extents_processed,
rebalancer_start_time
from table (mon_get_rebalance_status (NULL,-2)) as t;
```

Reclaimable storage

For automatic storage tablespaces, you can use the ALTER TABLESPACE statement with the REDUCE MAX clause to release all of the unused space and reduce the high-water mark. This eliminates the process of running db2dart, dropping and recreating objects, and exporting and importing the data. The SQL statement is as follows:

```
ALTER TABLESPACE USERSPACE1 REDUCE MAX;
```

The REDUCE MAX clause is not supported in pureScale. For the Db2 pureScale environment, use ADMIN_MOVE_TABLE (), which is covered in detail later in this chapter.

Converting DMS tablespaces to use automatic storage

To simplify storage management, you can convert to an existing DMS tablespace to use automatic storage by using these steps:

1. Identify the tablespace that you want to convert from DMS non-automatic storage to DMS automatic storage. Then, identify the storage group that you want the tablespace to use.

2. You can use the MON_GET_TABLESPACE () table function to find the candidate for the conversion. A sample SQL statement is as follows:

```
SELECT SUBSTR (TBSP_NAME, 1, 12) AS TBSP_NAME,
TBSP_ID, TBSP_TYPE, TBSP_CONTENT_TYPE,
TBSP_USING_AUTO_STORAGE FROM TABLE (MON_GET_TABLESPACE ('', -2)) AS
T WHERE TBSP_USING_AUTO_STORAGE=0;
```

3. You can use the `ADMIN_GET_STORAGE_PATHS` () table function to find the most suitable storage group to place the tablespace:

```
SELECT SUBSTR(STORAGE_GROUP_NAME,1,15)  AS STOGROUP,
SUBSTR(DB_STORAGE_PATH,1,20)  AS STORAGE_PATH,
SUBSTR(DB_STORAGE_PATH_STATE,1,10)  AS DB_STORAGE_PATH_STATE
FROM TABLE (ADMIN_GET_STORAGE_PATHS ('',-1)) AS T;
```

4. Once you have the data ready, you can convert the tablespace to use automatic storage by executing the statement listed here:

```
ALTER TABLESPACE TS_DMS_DATA MANAGED BY AUTOMATIC STORAGE USING
STOGROUP SG_HOT;
```

5. Move the content from the old container to the new automatic storage path by executing the `REBALANCE` statement:

```
ALTER TABLESPACE TS_DMS_DATA REBALANCE;
```

6. Monitor the progress of the rebalance operation by using the statement shown here:

```
SELECT
    VARCHAR (TBSP_NAME, 15) AS TBSP_NAME,
    rebalancer_mode,
    rebalancer_status,
    rebalancer_extents_remaining,
    rebalancer_extents_processed,
    rebalancer_start_time
from table (mon_get_rebalance_status (NULL,-2)) as t;
```

Smart disk storage management

Not all tables (entities) have the same level of importance when it comes to product performance. Some tables are critical, while others are less important to the overall transactional throughput. Likewise, disk storage solutions deliver varying levels of velocity and volume. You can save money and deliver better levels of performance by placing data where it is needed most.

The way to do this is to define storage groups for each I/O **class of service** (**COS**). The following table shows an example:

Class of service	Service level	Storage group	Storage paths
Critical	.003 to .035 ms	sg_critical	/db/ts01, /db/ts02
Normal	1 to 35 ms	sg_normal	/db/ts30, /db/ts31
Low	No service level	sg_low	/db/ts50, /db/ts51

I/O class of service

Placing tables into storage groups according to their importance can reduce disk storage costs, while maintaining a high level of performance. A database is comprised of one or more tablespaces. The size of the database is the sum of the tablespaces it contains. The built-in procedure GET_DBSIZE_INFO can be used to find the database size and capacity. The syntax for this procedure is shown here:

```
CALL GET_DBSIZE_INFO (?,?,?,0);
```

The output from the procedure contains the parameter DATABASESIZE, which shows the actual database size in bytes.

Creating a table

At the heart of any database solution, you will find a table. Tables are logical structures used to manage data. The type of table is defined by the type of data it contains. Data can be identified as summary, temporary, persistent, results, partitioned, or dimensional. See the following table for a complete list:

Table group	Table type	Description
Base	Regular	General purpose.
	Multidimensional clustering (MDC)	Physical clusters on more than one key or dimension. Not supported in pureScale.
	Insert time (ITC)	Clustered on time of insert.
	Range-Clustered (RCT)	Tightly clustered (RID) access. Not supported in PS.
	Range Partitioned (RPT)	Data is divided across data partitions or ranges.
	Temporal	Time-based state information.

		Stores temporary data for different database operations and doesn't add to system catalog. It can be either a declared or created (DGTT, CGTT) temporary table.
Temporary	Temporary data storage	Stores temporary data for different database operations and doesn't add to system catalog. It can be either a declared or created (DGTT, CGTT) temporary table.
Query	**Materialized Query (MQT)**	Query content maintained by SYSTEM, USER, or FEDERATED_TOOL.
	Shadow	Column-organized copy of a row-organized table that includes all columns (or a subset of columns) and is implemented as a replicated MQT.

Types of tables

The create table DML statement is the most complex DML statement in database solutions. In its simplest form, the create table statement looks as follows:

```
CREATE TABLE [TableName]
( [Column | Unique Constraint | Referential Constraint | Check Constraint]
, ... )
<LIKE [Source] <CopyOptions>>
<IN [TS_Name]>
<INDEX IN [TS_Name]>
<LONG IN [TS_Name]>
<ORGANIZE BY [ROW | COLUMN]>
<PARTITION BY [PartitionClause]>
<COMPRESS [YES | NO]>
```

The following is an example of an MQT which is updated by a user:

```
CREATE SUMMARY TABLE INVENTORY_SUMMARY AS
(SELECT SKU, TYPE, COLOR, SIZE, COST, COUNT (*) AS ONHAND FROM IN_STORE S,
IN_ROUTE R, DEPLETION D WHERE S.SKU = R.SKU AND S.SKU = D.SKU GROUP BY
GROUPING SETS ((SKU), (TYPE, COLOR, SIZE))) DATA INITIALLY DEFERRED REFRESH
DEFERRED;

REFRESH TABLE INVENTORY_SUMMARY;
```

Alter table

The `alter table` statement is used to make modifications to tables, such as adding, dropping, or renaming columns, or changing column attributes. The `alter table` statement can also be used to:

- Add or drop a column
- Change the append mode
- Change PCTFREE
- Change the compress status
- Change the log index build status
- Set not logged operations

Other changes include adding, attaching, or detaching data partitions, adding or dropping versioning, and adding or dropping security. While the CREATE TABLE statement is the most complex statement in most relational database solutions, the alter statement is not far behind. Take a loot at the ALTER TABLE statement in the following command:

```
ALTER TABLE [TableName]
ALTER COLUMN [ColumnName] <Modification definition>
```

Examples of ALTER TABLE statements are as follows:

```
ALTER TABLE ... ALTER COLUMN ... SET DEFAULT ALTER TABLE ... ALTER COLUMN
... SET INLINE LENGTH 1024 ALTER TABLE ... ALTER COLUMN ... SET NOT NULL
ALTER TABLE ... ALTER COLUMN ... DROP NOT NULL|GENERATED|DEFAULT ALTER
TABLE ... ALTER COLUMN ... DROP COLUMN SECURITY ALTER TABLE ... ADD COLUMN
ALTER TABLE ... DROP COLUMN ALTER TABLE ... ALTER FOREIGN KEY|CHECK ...
ENFORCED|NOT ENFORCED
```

Many of the alter statements are dynamic in nature, and cause little to no disruption when executed. A few of the statement options, when executed, cause a version change, and place the table into a REORG pending state. The following table has a list of the following options:

DML statement	Utility
DROP COLUMN	Reorg to gain full access
ALTER COLUMN SET NOT NULL	Reorg to gain full access
ALTER COLUMN DROP NOT NULL	Reorg to gain full access
ALTER COLUMN SET DATA TYPE	Reorg to gain full access
ALTER COLUMN SET INLINE LENGTH integer	Reorg to take advantage

| ALTER COLUMN SET EXPRESSION AS | Integrity immediate checked with forced generated to take advantage |

Alter table DML statements

There are exceptions to the reorg requirement, including increasing the VARCHAR, VARBINARY, or VARGRAPHIC column lengths, or decreasing them and keeping the trailing blanks in the existing data. The column cannot be defined in any indexes. Three alter statements with reorg recommendations are allowed before a mandatory re-organization is required.

Expression-based indexes

Expression-based indexes are indexes whose keys are derived by applying a supported column expression. These indexes, like all others, are created using the CREATE INDEX statement. A typical opportunity when it comes to data, are mixed case searches, they are as follows:

```
-- Table Definition
CREATE TABLE CUSTOMER (LASTNAME VARCHAR (30), FIRSTNAME VARCHAR (30),
ADDRESS VARCHAR (2000));

-- SELECT Statement

SELECT ADDRESS, LASTNAME|| ', ' ||FIRSTNAME FROM CUSTOMER
    WHERE UPPER (LASTNAME) LIKE 'SMI%';
```

This SQL results in a table scan (TBSCAN), which can have poor results when run against a large table. Here, expression based indexes can help. We create an index on the LASTNAME, column with an UPPER function applied as follows:

```
CREATE INDEX XD1_CUSTOMER ON CUSTOMER                        (UPPER
(LASTNAME) ASC) ALLOW REVERSE SCANS;
```

The following table illustrates the performance differences before and after the expression based index creation:

OPERATION	TOTAL_COST	IO_COST	CPU_COST	FIRST_ROW_COST	
TBSCAN	7.577435	1	57523.66	7.5776912	BEFORE
IXSCAN	3.375112	0.444	49859.78	3.374467	AFTER

Expression-based indexes

Some data types are not supported in expression-based indexes, such as XML, LONG VARCHAR, LONG VARGRAPHICS, ARRAY, CURSOR, ROW, and User defined. In MPP (DPF) environments, this is supported only when a table is created in the catalog data partition.

Invalidation of database objects

Db2 supports two types of invalidation: soft and hard. During soft invalidation, active objects can be dropped, even if active transactions are using them. Currently, active transactions use a cached copy of the object, so these transactions are not impacted by the invalidation. However, any new transactions are prevented access to the invalidated object. Cached statements and packages with direct or indirect references to the objects are invalidated. Soft invalidation prevents lock timeouts when executing DDL against active objects.

If hard invalidation is in effect, exclusive locking is used when referencing an object, preventing access to the object. This method guarantees that all transactions use the same version of objects and are prevented from using any dropped object.

Soft invalidation is enabled by the registry variable DB2_DDL_SOFT_INVAL. By default, this variable is ON. The list of DDL statements supporting soft invalidation is as follows:

- ALTER TABLE...DETACH PARTITION
- CREATE OR REPLACE ALIAS
- CREATE OR REPLACE FUNCTION
- CREATE OR REPLACE TRIGGER
- CREATE OR REPLACE VIEW
- DROP ALIAS

- DROP FUNCTION
- DROP TRIGGER
- DROP VIEW

Revalidation of database objects

Many Db2 objects are dependent on other Db2 objects. A very common dependency between two base objects is the parent-child relationship, as defined by **referential integrity (RI)** constraints. Other dependent objects, such as triggers, views, and aliases, depend completely on base objects for their existence. When the status of base objects changes significantly, dependent objects can be invalidated. For example, if a base object is dropped (or in some cases, altered), then any dependent objects, such as triggers or indexes, become invalid.

Invalid database objects must be revalidated before they can be used. Revalidation is achieved by reprocessing the DDL to recreate the dependent object. Automatic revalidation takes invalid objects and revalidates them at runtime. An invalid package, for example, is rebound. A trigger is regenerated. A view is redefined. Automatic revalidation is enabled by setting the database configuration variable auto_reval. By default, this variable is set to DEFERRED.

AUTO_REVAL is set to DISABLED if upgraded from v9.5 or earlier.

The statements identified as follows support the automatic revalidation of dependent objects:

- ALTER MODULE DROP FUNCTION
- ALTER MODULE DROP PROCEDURE
- ALTER MODULE DROP TYPE
- ALTER MODULE DROP VARIABLE
- ALTER NICKNAME (altering the local name or the local type)
- ALTER TABLE ALTER COLUMN
- ALTER TABLE DROP COLUMN
- ALTER TABLE RENAME COLUMN

- CREATE OR REPLACE ALIAS
- CREATE OR REPLACE FUNCTION
- CREATE OR REPLACE NICKNAME
- CREATE OR REPLACE PROCEDURE
- CREATE OR REPLACE SEQUENCE
- CREATE OR REPLACE TRIGGER
- CREATE OR REPLACE VARIABLE
- CREATE OR REPLACE VIEW
- DROP FUNCTION
- DROP NICKNAME
- DROP PROCEDURE
- DROP SEQUENCE
- DROP TABLE
- DROP TRIGGER
- DROP TYPE
- DROP VARIABLE
- DROP VIEW
- RENAME TABLE

A list of invalid objects can be shown by executing the following query:

```
SELECT OBJECTNAME, ROUTINENAME, SQLCODE, SQLSTATE, ERRORMESSAGE,
INVALIDATE_TIME FROM SYSCAT.INVALIDOBJECTS WITH UR;
```

The ADMIN_REVALIDATE_DB_OBJECTS () procedure can be used to revalidate all (or a selected group of) objects. For example, the following statement can be used to revalidate all invalid objects in the database:

```
CALL "SYSPROC"."ADMIN_REVALIDATE_DB_OBJECTS" (NULL, NULL, NULL);
```

It is also possible to use the same SELECT statement to monitor the progress of revalidation. As each object is revalidated, it is removed from this table.

Online table move

Online Table Move (OTM) is the process of moving a table without a service disruption. Have you ever had the need to change something such as tablespace extent size? How about the need to reclaim tablespace filesystem storage when you're unable to use REDUCE MAX? If you can take the source table(s) out of service for some varying length of time, there are several possible solutions. But, what if the table(s) cannot be offline for any amount of time?

The stored procedure ADMIN_MOVE_TABLE can be used to move data in an active table to a new object with the same name, keeping the data online and available. A typical ADMIN_MOVE_TABLE statement looks like the following:

```
CALL SYSPROC.ADMIN_MOVE_TABLE
  (
    [TableSchema], [SourceTable], [TargetDataTS],
    [TargetIndexTS], [TargetLongTS], [MDC_Columns],
    [PartitionKeys], [DataPartitions], [ColumnDefs],
    [Options,...], [Operations]
);

CALL SYSPROC.ADMIN_MOVE_TABLE
('ERP',
'EMPLOYEE',
'TS_SMALL_DATA',
'TS_SMALL_INDEX',
'TS_LOB_DATA',
'',
'',
'',
'',
'',
'MOVE');
```

This procedure uses three tables: Source, Target, and Stage. **Source** is the original table, or the table being moved. **Target** is the new table, which can be created by the stored procedure. After the data is moved, the target table is renamed to match the source table. **Stage** contains recorded insert, update, and delete changes to the source, during the actual move. This table is dropped when the process has completed.

The target table can be created by the stored procedure during execution, or it can be created before execution by using the CREATE TABLE statement. Some changes require you to create the target table before running the stored procedure. Changing the data partitioning scheme, for example, would require the creation of the target table before running the stored procedure, while recovering data storage space used by the source table can be done without specifying a target table.

ADMIN_MOVE_TABLE can be used to:

- Change the MDC (ORGANIZE BY DIMENSION) specification for a table
- Change the ITC (ORGANIZE BY INSERT TIME) specification for a table
- Modify a table's partitioning keys (DISTRIBUTE BY HASH)
- Change the range partitioning (PARTITION BY RANGE) specification for a table
- Add or remove columns from a table, or alter a column's data type
- Create a new compression dictionary for a table that has static compression enabled
- Change tablespace attributes by moving the table(s) to newly created tablespaces (for example, extent size)

ADMIN_MOVE_TABLE is particularly important in pureScale deployments, because REDUCE MAX and REORG TABLE ... INPLACE are not supported.

Tracking the execution of online table move

The following diagram shows the six stages of execution for the ADMIN_MOVE_TABLE() procedure:

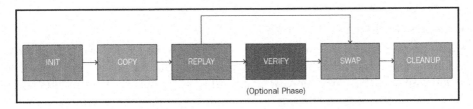

Stages of the ADMIN_MOVE_TABLE procedure

Let us see what each stage stands for:

- INIT: Initializes all of the objects required for the operation, including the staging table that is necessary for capturing all of the data changes during the move.
- COPY: Creates a copy of the source table per the current definition and copies the data into the target table.
- REPLAY: Replays all of the changes captured in the staging table into the target table, just before swapping the source and target tables.
- VERIFY: An optional phase that checks the table contents between source and target, to make sure they are identical before the swap.
- SWAP: Performs a swapping of source and target tables. The source table will be taken offline briefly, to complete the REPLAY.
- CLEANUP: Drops all of the intermediate tables created during the online move, such as the staging table, any non-unique indexes, and triggers.

Online table move planning

There are a lot of operational considerations that need to be taken into account when using the ADMIN_MOVE_TABLE() procedure. For example, moving a table during low activity is preferred. Other considerations are as follows:

- Avoid concurrent moves into the same tablespace.
- Run during low activity on the source table, if possible.
- Run using multi-step operations. Execute the REPLY phase several times, to keep the STAGE table small, and then run SWAP when activity is low. Run INIT and COPY any time.
- Always consider an offline move first.
- The staging table is populated using triggers on the source. Keep in mind that some DDL and utilities can occur without firing a trigger. A new table-level state flag prevents these between INIT and CLEANUP phases. These events include:
    - TRUNCATE TABLE
    - IMPORT...REPLACE INTO
    - LOAD TABLE
    - ALTER TABLE
    - REORG

Online table move-running changes

The procedure ADMIN_MOVE_TABLE_UTIL can be used to adjust a running ADMIN_MOVE_TABLE procedure attribute. The ADMIN_MOVE_TABLE procedure must be running under the authority of the user executing ADMIN_MOVE_TABLE_UTIL. The procedure modifies values in the ADMIN_MOVE_TABLE protocol table. The syntax of the call is as follows:

```
SYSPROC.ADMIN_MOVE_TABLE_UTIL
([TableSchema], [TableName], [Action], [Key], [Value])
```

Let's review a use case. Move the table ERP.EMPLOYEE, keeping the table in the same tablespace(s). Before the COPY phase, set the commit frequency to 20 to keep log usage low:

```
CALL SYSPROC.ADMIN_MOVE_TABLE         -- Starts the Move
('ERP','EMPLOYEE','','','','','','','','INIT');
CALL SYSPROC.ADMIN_MOVE_TABLE_UTIL  -- Set commit frequency
('ERP','EMPLOYEE','UPSERT','COMMIT_AFTER_N_ROWS','20');
CALL SYSPROC.ADMIN_MOVE_TABLE_UTIL  -- Run Copy Phase
('ERP','EMPLOYEE','','','','','','','','COPY');
CALL SYSPROC.ADMIN_MOVE_TABLE_UTIL  -- Run Replay Phase
('ERP','EMPLOYEE','','','','','','','','REPLAY');
CALL SYSPROC.ADMIN_MOVE_TABLE_UTIL  -- Run Swap Phase
('ERP','EMPLOYEE','','','','','','','','SWAP');
```

Copy schema procedure

The procedure ADMIN_COPY_SCHEMA can be used to copy a schema and its contents. The same object names will be used and placed into the target schema specification. The new tables can be created with or without data from the source. The syntax for the copy schema procedure is:

```
SYSPROC.ADMIN_COPY_SCHEMA
([SourceSchema], [TargetSchema], [CopyMode], [ObjectOwner],
[SourceTBSP], [TargetTBSP], [ErrorTableSchema], [ErrorTable])
CALL SYSPROC.ADMIN_COPY_SCHEMA ('ERP', 'TEST', 'COPY', NULL, '', '
','ERROR', 'ERP_ERROR_INFO');
```

 If ADMIN_COPY_SCHEMA copies a schema, guess what ADMIN_DROP_SCHEMA does? It drops a specific schema, and all of the objects contained it.

Range clustering and range partitioning tables

Rows of data can be grouped into ranges and assigned to tablespaces. This is done when the table is created by using the CREATE TABLE statement. This determines how data is physically stored on the disk. Data ranges are created using range-clustered tables, or by taking advantage of range partitioning tables.

Range clustered tables

A **range clustered table (RCT)** is a table whose data is organized by a unique, not null integer record key, with a predetermined set of ranges based on each column of the key. These tables are useful when data is tightly clustered across one or more columns in a table. Each possible key value in the defined range has a predetermined location in the physical table, preassigned by an internal **record ID (RID)**. The storage required for an RCT must be pre-allocated and available when the table is created, and it must be sufficient to store the number of rows found in the specified range, multiplied by the row size. RCTs have no need for free space, because space is reserved for use by the table even when rows do not yet exist.

RCTs can result in significant performance advantages during query processing, because fewer input/output (I/O) operations are required, and no free space controls are needed. RCTs require less buffer pool memory, maintenance, and logging, because there are no secondary objects to maintain.

RCTs are created by specifying the ORGANIZE BY KEY SEQUENCE clause of the CREATE TABLE statement when a table is created. The syntax for this optional clause is:

```
ORGANIZE BY KEY SEQUENCE
([ColumnName]
  <STARTING <FROM> [Start]>
  ENDING <AT> [End] ,...)
<ALLOW OVERFLOW | DISALLOW OVERFLOW>
<PCTFREE [PercentFree]>
```

In the preceding code, the following applies:

- ColumnName: Identifies, by name, one or more columns whose values are to be used to determine the sequence of the RCT.
- Start: Specifies the low end of the range of values allowed. (Values less than the starting value specified are allowed only if the ALLOW OVERFLOW option is specified.)
- End: Specifies the high end of the range of values allowed. (Values greater than the ending value specified are allowed only if the ALLOW OVERFLOW option is specified.)
- PercentFree: Specifies the percentage of each page that is to be left as free space. (The first row of each page is added without restriction; when additional rows are added to a page, a check is performed to ensure the specified percentage of the page is left free.)

If the DISALLOW OVERFLOW clause is specified, key values will not be allowed to exceed the defined range; otherwise, overflow data will be assigned to a dynamically allocated area with poor performance.

CUSTOMERS is an RCT that has two columns, named CUSTOMER_ID and CUSTOMER_NAME, where the CUSTOMER_ID column will become the unique key that determines how records are physically stored, and where only unique values between 1 and 100 can be assigned to the CUSTOMER_ID column. Rows outside of that range will be rejected:

```
CREATE TABLE CUSTOMERS
(CUSTOMER_id    INTEGER NOT NULL,
 CUSTOMER_name VARCHAR(80))
 ORGANIZE BY KEY SEQUENCE
(CUSTOMER_id STARTING FROM 1 ENDING AT 100) DISALLOW OVERFLOW;
```

When reading from the CUSTOMERS table, Db2 will look for the requested row by using a predetermined offset from the logical start of the table. Row order is maintained and guaranteed meaning, like index RIDs. When a row that changes the key column value is updated, the updated row is copied to the new location, and the old copy of the row is deleted.

RCTs are not supported in Db2 pureScale.

Range clustered table planning

There are cases where RCTs cannot be used, and there are certain utilities that cannot operate on an RCT. The restrictions are as follows:

- RCT cannot be used in pureScale environment
- A partitioned table cannot be an RCT
- Declared and created temporary tables cannot be RCTs
- Automatic summary tables cannot be RCTs
- The LOAD command is not supported
- The REORG command is not supported
- Multidimensional clustering and clustering indexes are not compatible with RCTs
- Compression is not supported
- Reverse scans are not supported on RCTs
- The IMPORT command's REPLACE parameter is not supported
- The WITH EMPTY TABLE clause is not supported on the ALTER TABLE ... ACTIVATE NOT LOGGED INITIALLY

Range partitioned tables

A **range partitioned table (RPT)**, whose verb form is *Range partitioning*, is a table with a data organization scheme in which data is divided across multiple storage objects called data partitions. Each data partition is uniquely named and assigned to data, index, and LOB tablespaces. Data partitions can share tablespaces or be assigned to private tablespaces. Table partitioning improves performance and eliminates the need to create a partitioned database using the Data Partitioning feature. Other advantages of using table partitioning include:

- It is easy to roll-in and roll-out data. Rolling in a partitioned table data allows a new range to be easily incorporated into a partitioned table as an additional data partition. Rolling out a partitioned table data allows you to easily separate ranges of data from a partitioned table for subsequent purging or archiving. Data can be rolled in and out quickly by using the ATTACH PARTITION and DETACH PARTITION clauses of the ALTER TABLE statement.

- Easier administration of large tables. Table-level administration becomes more flexible, because administrative tasks can be performed on individual data partitions. Such tasks include the detaching and reattaching of a data partition, backing up and restoring individual data partitions, and reorganizing individual indexes. In addition, time-consuming maintenance operations can be shortened by breaking them down into a series of smaller operations. For example, backup operations can be performed at the data-partition level when each data partition is placed in a separate tablespace. Thus, it is possible to back up one data partition of a partitioned table at a time.
- Flexible index placement. With table partitioning, indexes can be placed in different tablespaces, allowing for more granular control of index placement.
- Better query processing. In the process of resolving queries, one or more data partitions may be automatically eliminated, based on the query predicates used. This functionality, known as Data Partition Elimination, improves the performance of many decision support queries, because less data has to be analyzed before a result data set can be returned.

Data from a given table is partitioned into multiple storage objects based on the specifications provided in the PARTITION BY clause of the CREATE TABLE statement. The syntax for this optional clause is:

```
PARTITION BY <RANGE>
([ColumnName] <NULLS LAST | NULLS FIRST> ,...)
(STARTING <FROM>
<(> [Start | MINVALUE | MAXVALUE] < ,...)>
<INCLUSIVE | EXCLUSIVE>
ENDING <AT>
<(> [End | MINVALUE | MAXVALUE] < ,...)>
<INCLUSIVE | EXCLUSIVE>
EVERY <(>[Constant] <DurationLabel><)> )
```

The syntax can also be:

```
PARTITION BY <RANGE>
( [ColumnName] <NULLS LAST | NULLS FIRST> ,... )
( <PARTITION [PartitionName]>
STARTING <FROM>
<(> [Start | MINVALUE | MAXVALUE] < ,...)>
<INCLUSIVE | EXCLUSIVE>
ENDING <AT>
<(> [End | MINVALUE | MAXVALUE] < ,...)>
<INCLUSIVE | EXCLUSIVE>
<IN [TableSpaceName] INDEX IN (IndexSpaceName) LONG IN (LObSPaceName) > )
```

In the preceding code, the following applies:

- `ColumnName`: Identifies, by name, one or more columns whose values are to be used to determine which data partition a row is to be stored in. (The group of columns specified makes up the partitioning key for the table.)
- `PartitionName`: Identifies the unique name that is to be assigned to the data partition.
- `Start`: Specifies the low end of the range for each data partition.
- `End` : Specifies the high end of the range for each data partition.
- `Constant` : Specifies the width of each data-partition range when the automatically generated form of the syntax is used. Data partitions will be created starting at the STARTING FROM value, and will contain this number of values in the range. This form of the syntax is supported only if the partitioning key is made up of a single column that has been assigned a numeric, date, time, or timestamp data type.
- `DurationLabel`: Identifies the duration that is associated with the *Constant* value specified if the partitioning key column has been assigned a date, time, or timestamp data type. The following values are valid for this parameter: YEAR, YEARS, MONTH, MONTHS, DAY, DAYS, HOUR, HOURS, MINUTE, MINUTES, SECOND, SECONDS, MICROSECOND, and MICROSECONDS.
- `TableSpaceName` : Identifies the tablespace in which each data partition is to be stored.
- `IndexSpaceName` : Identifies the tablespace in which each index partition is to be stored.
- `LobSpaceName` : Identifies the tablespace in which each LOB partition is to be stored.

To create an RPT named SALES that is partitioned by column sales_date into three consecutive month intervals, with each partition in a different tablespace, execute a CREATE TABLE statement that looks something like this:

```
CREATE TABLE sales
  (sales_date      DATE,
   sales_amt       NUMERIC(5,2))
  IN tbsp0, tbsp1, tbsp2, tbsp3
  PARTITION BY RANGE (sales_date NULLS FIRST)
    (STARTING '1/1/2014' ENDING '12/31/2014' EVERY 3 MONTHS);
```

To create an RPT named DEPARTMENTS that is partitioned by dept_no into four partitions stored in separate tablespaces, with the ranges 0-9, 10-19, 20-29, and 30-39, execute a CREATE TABLE statement that looks something like this:

```
CREATE TABLE departments
    (dept_no   INT
     desc      CHAR(3))
    PARTITION BY (dept_no NULLS FIRST)
        (STARTING 0 ENDING 9 IN tbsp0,
         STARTING 10 ENDING 19 IN tbsp1,
         STARTING 20 ENDING 29 IN tbsp2,
         STARTING 30 ENDING 39 IN tbsp3);
```

An index created on an RPT can be either partitioned or non-partitioned (global). Any unique index created on an RPT that does not include all of the partition key columns is global. Any non-unique index created on an RPT is partitioned, unless specifically created with NOT PARTITIONED. Partitioned indexes can only be created on an RPT.

There are three create DDL statements for the index dept_idx, shown as follows. The first two statements place the index partitions with the data partitions. The IN TBSP3 clause is ignored in the second DDL statement. The third statement creates a global index, which is placed in the tablespace TBSP3:

```
CREATE INDEX dept_idx ON departments (dept_no);
CREATE INDEX dept_idx ON departments (dept_no) IN tbsp3;
CREATE INDEX dept_idx ON departments (dept_no)
    NOT PARTITIONED IN tbsp3;
```

We can create a compressed RPT named STAGING.SALES_ORDER_INCR_STG, with private tablespaces assigned to each data, index, and lob partition, by using the following DML statement:

```
CREATE TABLE STAGING.SALES_ORDER_INCR_STG
(
  INSTANCE_ID INTEGER
  , COMPANY_ORDER VARCHAR(10)
  , DOCUMENT_NO INTEGER
  , ORDER_TYPE VARCHAR(5)
  , LINE_NO INTEGER
  , RECORD_LOAD_TIMESTAMP TIMESTAMP
  , ORDER_CONTENT CLOB(1M)
)
COMPRESS YES STATIC
PARTITION BY RANGE (INSTANCE_ID)
(
  PART0 STARTING(0) ENDING(0) IN TBSP0 INDEX IN
```

```
TBSP_IX0,LONG IN TBSP_LOB0
 ,PART101 STARTING(101) ENDING(101) IN TBSP1 INDEX IN
TBSP_IX1,LONG IN TBSP_LOB1,
 ,PART102 STARTING(102) ENDING(102) IN TBSP2 INDEX IN
TBSP_IX2,LONG IN TBSP_LOB2,
 ,PART112 STARTING(112) ENDING(112) IN TBSP3 INDEX IN
TBSP_IX3,LONG IN TBSP_LOB3,
 ,PART183 STARTING(183) ENDING(183) IN TBSP4 INDEX IN
TBSP_IX4,LONG IN TBSP_LOB4,
 ,PART191 STARTING(191) ENDING(191) IN TBSP5 INDEX IN
TBSP_IX5,LONG IN TBSP_LOB5,
 ,PART192 STARTING(192) ENDING(192) IN TBSP6 INDEX IN
TBSP_IX6,LONG IN TBSP_LOB6,
 ,PART400 STARTING(400) ENDING(400) IN TBSP7 INDEX IN
TBSP_IX7,LONG IN TBSP_LOB7
);
```

Listing the data partitions

If you want to list the data partition attributes, such as the partition ID, partition name, tablespace ID, access mode, and range, you can use the DESCRIBE DATA PARTITIONS statement:

```
DESCRIBE DATA PARTITIONS FOR TABLE STAGING.SALES_ORDER_INCR_STG SHOW
DETAIL;
```

Detaching a data partition

Detaching a data partition from the base table consists of two phases: the logical partitions detach, and converting the detached partition into a standalone base table through an asynchronous index clean-up process.

You can use the ALTER TABLE ... DETACH PARTITION statement to detach a data partition from the base table:

```
ALTER TABLE STAGING.SALES_ORDER_INCR_STG
DETACH PARTITION PART102 INTO STAGING.SALES_ORDER_INCR_STG_102;
```

You can view the asynchronous partition detach operation by executing the LIST UTILITIES command:

```
LIST UTILITIES SHOW DETAIL;
```

Attaching a data partition

Attaching a data partition to a base table consists of two steps: attaching the partition to the base table, and then performing the data integrity checks, such as range validation and constraint checking.

You can use the ALTER TABLE ... ATTACH PART statement to attach a data partition to the base table:

```
alter table STAGING.SALES_ORDER_INCR_STG attach part PART102
starting (102) ending (102) from STAGING.SALES_ORDER_INCR_STG_102;
```

You can query the system catalog table to identify the tables that are in a SET INTEGRITY pending state, as shown here:

```
SELECT substr (rtrim (TABSCHEMA) ||'.'||rtrim (TABNAME), 1, 50) FROM
SYSCAT.TABLES WHERE STATUS = 'C';
```

To resolve the SET INTEGRITY pending state on a table, the following command can be used:

```
set integrity for STAGING.SALES_ORDER_INCR_STG immediate checked;
```

MDC

Multidimensional clustering (MDC) provides a method for clustering data in tables along multiple dimensions in a flexible, continuous, and automatic way. MDC allows a table to be physically clustered on more than one key or dimension, simultaneously. Like any other table, an MDC table can have views, MQTs, referential integrity, triggers, RID indexes, and replication defined for the table. Range queries involving any combination of the specified dimensions of the clustered table will perform better, because they will only need to access those pages that have records with the specified dimension values.

When an MDC table is created, the dimensional key (or keys) along which to cluster the table's data are specified. Each of the specified dimensions can be defined with one or more columns, like an index key. A dimension block index will automatically be created for each of the dimensions specified, and will be used to quickly and efficiently access data along each of the specified dimensions. The dimension block indexes point to extents instead of individual rows, and are smaller than regular indexes. These dimension block indexes can be used to quickly access only those extents of the table that contain dimension values. In addition, a block index containing all dimension key columns will be automatically created. The block index will be used to maintain the clustering of the data during insert and update activity, as well as to provide quick and efficient access to the data. A composite block index containing all of the dimension key columns is also created automatically. The composite block index is used to maintain the clustering of data during insert and update activity. The composite block index is also used in query processing, to access data in the table that has specific dimension values.

Multidimensional clustering tables are created by specifying the ORGANIZE BY DIMENSIONS clause of the CREATE TABLE statement when a table is created. The syntax for this optional clause is:

```
ORGANIZE BY DIMENSIONS
( <(>[ColumnName] ,...<)> ,...)
```

In the preceding code, the following applies:

- ColumnName: Identifies, by name, one or more columns whose values are to be used to cluster the table's data. The use of parentheses within the column list specifies that a group of columns is to be treated as a single dimension.

Thus, if you wanted to create an MDC table named SALES, in such a way that its data is organized into extents based on unique combinations of values found in the REGION and SALES_YEAR columns, you can do so by executing a CREATE TABLE statement that looks something like this:

```
CREATE TABLE SALES
    (CUSTOMER      VARCHAR (80),
    REGION        CHAR (5),
    SALES_YEAR    INTEGER,
    Volume        INTEGER,
    PERIOD        INTEGER,
    REC_LOAD_DT   TIMESTAMP   )
ORGANIZE BY DIMENSIONS (REGION, SALES_YEAR);
```

Along with the table, three indexes are created, shown as follows. Two dimension block indexes and one composite index are created:

```
SELECT SUBSTR (INDSCHEMA, 1, 10) AS INDSCHEMA,
SUBSTR (INDNAME, 1, 25) AS INDNAME, INDEXTYPE,
SUBSTR (COLNAMES, 1, 30) AS COLNAMES
FROM SYSCAT.INDEXES WHERE TABNAME='SALES';

INDSCHEMA INDNAME INDEXTYPE COLNAMES
---------- ------------------------- ---------------
SYSIBM SQL141229141543060 BLOK +REGION+SALES_YEAR
SYSIBM SQL141229141543170 DIM +SALES_YEAR
SYSIBM SQL141229141543200 DIM +REGION
```

The following diagram shows how the SALES MDC is organized across REGION and SALES_YEAR dimensions, and the block indexes that are created:

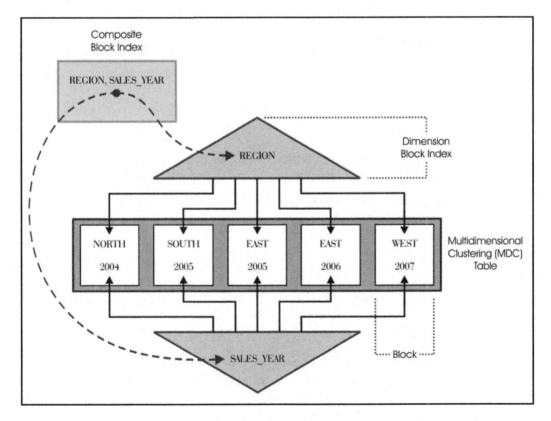

MDC sales table

MQT

A **Materialized Query Table (MQT)** is a table that is defined on the result of a SQL statement. It is generally used to avoid repetitive calculations by storing pre-computed aggregated results in the table. If the Db2 database manager determines that a portion of an SQL statement can be resolved using an MQT, the database manager will rewrite the access plan to use the appropriate MQT on behalf of a regular base table. This process is very transparent to the application or the end user.

It is a two-step process to create and maintain an MQT. First, create an MQT based on the needs of the business logic, and then refresh the data in the MQT table. If you want to build an MQT to record the SUM of SALES_AMOUNT for each SALES_DATE, you can do so by executing the following statements:

```
CREATE TABLE SALES_MQT AS
(SELECT SUM (SALES_AMOUNT) AS TOTAL_SUM, SALES_DATE
   FROM SALES
   GROUP BY SALES_DATE)
   DATA INITIALLY DEFERRED REFRESH DEFERRED;

REFRESH TABLE SALES_MQT;
```

When you have REFRESH DEFERRED MQTs available, try setting the DFT_REFRESH_AGE database configuration parameter to ANY.

If you execute the SQL statement shown on the database SAMPLE, the database manager will try to use any available MQT to quickly return the data to the client:

```
select sum (sales_amOUNT), sales_date
from sales group by sales_date;
```

ITC

Insert Time Clustering (ITC) tables provide an effective way of maintaining data clustering based on the insert time, along with easier space management. The characteristics of ITC tables are as follows:

- ITC table records are clustered based on their insert times.
- ITC tables have characteristics similar to MDC tables—they use block-based data allocation and a dimension block index. However, the data organization scheme is based on an implicitly created virtual dimension (record insert time) instead of explicitly stated dimension columns.

- ITC tables are created using the CREATE TABLE ... ORGANIZE BY INSERT TIME clause.
- ITC tables' space reclamation can be done by executing the REORG TABLE ... RECLAIM EXTENTS command.

If you want to create an ITC table, SALES_ITC, you can do so by executing the following statement:

```
CREATE TABLE SALES_ITC
    (CUSTOMER            VARCHAR (80),
     REGION              CHAR (5),
     YEAR                INTEGER,
     Volume              INTEGER,
     PERIOD              INTEGER,
     REC_LOAD_DT         TIMESTAMP)
ORGANIZE BY INSERT TIME;

CREATE INDEX IX1_SALES_ITC ON SALES_ITC (REGION, YEAR, PERIOD);
```

This creates one dimension block index and one regular index, as shown here:

```
SELECT SUBSTR (INDSCHEMA, 1, 10) AS INDSCHEMA,
SUBSTR (INDNAME, 1, 25) AS INDNAME, INDEXTYPE,
SUBSTR (COLNAMES, 1, 30) AS COLNAMES
FROM SYSCAT.INDEXES WHERE TABNAME='SALES_ITC'

INDSCHEMA INDNAME INDEXTYPE COLNAMES
----- --------------------- --- ------------------------
SYSIBM SQL150109091701660 DIM +SQL000000000000000
SALES  IX1_SALES_ITC        REG +REGION+YEAR+PERIOD
```

Db2 BLU Acceleration

This was introduced in Db2 v10.5, and significantly improved in Db2 v11.1. Db2 with BLU acceleration integrating innovative new technology, delivering exceptional performance and compression directed specifically at predictive analytical workloads. Db2 BLU speeds up reporting by a factor of 10x to 50x, with a compression factor of up to 10x, compared to traditional row-organized tables.

The following elements make BLU different from other columnar technologies:

- **Compression duration**: Data and indexes are compressed, and remain compressed, even through most predicate evaluations.

- **Radix parallel sort**: A faster sort method from Watson Labs, executed in column form.
- **MPP (DPF) Technology with BLU**: Hybrid Transactional and Analytical Processing (HTAP) just got a lot closer to reality. One single database that supports all workload types; for example, DW, DSS, OLTP, Document, Graphic, and Analytics.
- **SIMD Advances**: New feature that takes advantage of SIMD hardware.
- **IBM wrapped BLU into Basic Db2**: Other vendors make you learn new commands and new ways of setting up and managing columnar. BLU is wrapped into basic Db2. There is very little to learn, outside of normal Db2, to get BLU to work.

Configuring a Db2 instance for BLU workloads is easy. Set the instance-aggregated registry variable DB2_WORKLOAD=ANALYTICS. All databases created with this setting in place will have the following parameters:

- Degree of parallelism: (DFT_DEGREE) = ANY
- Default tablespace extent size (pages): (DFT_EXTENT_SZ) = 4
- Default table organization: (DFT_TABLE_ORG) = COLUMN
- Database page size: 32768

Other notable DBM and DB configuration settings for BLU workloads are:

Parameter Type	Parameter	Value
DBM CFG	INTRA_PARALLEL	YES
DB CFG	SHEAPTHRES_SHR	Calculated and set based on workload AUTOMATIC is not allowed. A good value is 50% DATABASE_MEMORY.
DB CFG	SORTHEAP	Calculated and set based on workload AUTOMATIC is not allowed. Good ROT is 10-20% of SHEAPTHRES_SHR.
DB CFG	UTIL_HEAP_SZ	Start with a minimum size of 6M pages; the best option is to set to AUTOMATIC.

Db2 DBM and DB configuration settings for BLU

Make sure that you have plenty of operating system paging space available on the BLU server:

RAM 64G-128G 32G Paging Space

RAM 128G-256G 64G Paging Space
RAM >= 256G 128G Paging Space

UTIL_HEAP_SZ is not limited by INSTANCE_MEMORY

Implementing BLU

The steps to implementing Db2 with BLU acceleration are shown here:

1. Create a Db2 instance (db2icrt command).
2. Configure the Db2 instance for a BLU workload.
   Set the Db2 registry variables as follows:

   ```
   db2set DB2COMM=TCPIP
   db2set DB2_WORKLOAD=ANALYTICS
   ```

3. Restart the Db2 instance:

   ```
   db2stop
   db2start
   ```

4. Create a Db2 database, as described earlier in this chapter.
5. Set the following DBM and DB parameters:
   - INSTANCE_MEMORY: If this is the only instance on this server, set to 95 percent of RAM; otherwise, take 95 percent of RAM and divide it among the instances, per workloads and importance. (If Production does not use AUTOMATIC.)
   - DATABASE_MEMORY: If this is the only database in the instance, then use 80 percent of INSTANCE_MEMORY; otherwise, take 80 percent of INSTANCE_MEMORY and divide it out among the databases according to workloads and importance. (If Production do not use AUTOMATIC.)
   - The other parameters: Set SHEAPTHRES_SHR, SORTHEAP, and UTIL_HEAP_SZ, as discussed earlier in this chapter.

BLU compression and statistics

Compression efficiency is at the heart of BLU performance. Each columnar table has a column compression dictionary made up of small symbols representing repeated bytes of data. The dictionaries are of fixed size, so there is a limited number of slots. Populating these slots with a valid representation of the data in the table is important. Text data generally compresses better than numeric and random values; those from encryption would result in poor compression results. Compression and statistics collection are automatic.

 If implementing data at rest encryption, it is best to perform compression before encryption. You should expect lower disk storage savings resulting from compression because of encryption.

The load utility has an analyze phase, which only executes when the dictionary must be built. This happens any time there is no dictionary, or if the dictionary is being replaced. Populating a columnar table using inserts does not enforce the creation of a column compression dictionary until a threshold number of values is reached. Until then, the data is stored uncompressed.

Once the column compression dictionary is full, new data not represented in the dictionary will result in a decreased compression ratio that may reduce performance. This can be fixed by unloading and reloading the data with LOAD REPLACE, to get a new dictionary; when table sizes get up into the billions, that can take a long time.

Another option is to build a second copy of the table; then, using an alias, you can direct traffic to the corrected table. After the data is copied, you will need a way to apply changes made to the source table to the target table so that they are identical.

Real-time statistics collection (RTS) output is stored in the statistics cache and can be used by database agents for subsequent statements. The cached statistics are later written to the database catalog by a daemon process in servicing a WRITE_STATS request. A COLLECT_STATS request can be issued by a db2agent process during a statement compilation, and the status can be queried using the following:

```
SELECT    QUEUE_POSITION,
          REQUEST_STATUS, REQUEST_TYPE,
          OBJECT_TYPE, VARCHAR (OBJECT_SCHEMA, 10) AS SCHEMA,
          VARCHAR (OBJECT_NAME, 10) AS NAME
    FROM TABLE (MON_GET_RTS_RQST ()) AS T
    ORDER BY QUEUE_POSITION, SCHEMA, NAME;
```

There are three possible statuses for REQUEST_STATUS: EXECUTING, QUEUED, or PENDING. At most, you can have one table with an EXECUTING status. RTS checks for PENDING requests every five minutes, and places the requests on the run queue.

You can check the column compression values with the following statement:

```
SELECT TRIM (SYSCAT.COLUMNS.TABNAME) AS TABLE,
       TRIM (COLNAME) AS COLUMN, PCTENCODED,
       TYPENAME, LENGTH, CARD AS ROWS
  FROM SYSCAT.COLUMNS, SYSCAT.TABLES
 WHERE SYSCAT.COLUMNS.TABNAME = SYSCAT.TABLES.TABNAME
       AND SYSCAT.COLUMNS.TABSCHEMA = SYSCAT.TABLES.TABSCHEMA
       AND NOT SYSCAT.TABLES.TABSCHEMA LIKE 'SYS%'
       AND TYPE = 'T'
       AND TABLEORG = 'C'
       AND SYSCAT.TABLES.TABNAME = 'CUSTOMER'
 ORDER BY COLUMN, PCTENCODED DESC, TABLE
 WITH UR;
```

A sample output from this statement is shown as follows. The CUSTOMER_ID is a GENERATE_UNIQUE randomized value, as a pseudo key:

TABLE	COLUMN	PCTENCODED	TYPENAME	LENGTH	CARD
CUSTOMER	CUSTOMER_ID	4	VARCHAR	32	6378719906
CUSTOMER	ZIPCODE	100	INTEGER	4	6378719906
CUSTOMER	LAST_NAME	100	VARCHAR	100	6378719906
CUSTOMER	ADDRESS	100	VARCHAR	1000	6378719906

BLU disk space management

Db2 performs what is called logical deletion of rows. This is different from pseudo deletion, because in logical deletion, the space occupied by the deleted row on the data page can be overwritten with an inserted row. Pseudo deleted rows are not available until additional cleanup operations are performed.

For column-organized tables, data is pseudo deleted; for row organized tables, it is logically deleted. Thus, for column-organized tables, space reclaims are performed at the extent level, and the extent space is returned to the table space for use with any defined table.

To reclaim extents, execute a `REORG` command:

```
REORG TABLE CUSTOMER RECLAIM EXTENTS;
```

 The storage extents whose pages held data that was completely deleted are the only candidates for space reclamation. The records in a columnar table are never updated; however, they are deleted, then inserted.

Let's take a look at an example. The following table shows the CUSTOMER table before space was reclaimed:

TABSCHEMA	TABNAME	COL_OBJECT_L_SIZE	COL_OBJECT_P_SIZE
DEMO	CUSTOMER	24977408	24977408

CUSTOMER table before space was reclaimed

The following table shows the CUSTOMER table after the space is reclaimed. A saving of 10,715,136 pages, or 334,848 MB, is seen for this example:

TABSCHEMA	TABNAME	COL_OBJECT_L_SIZE	COL_OBJECT_P_SIZE
DEMO	CUSTOMER	24977408	14262272

CUSTOMER table after space was reclaimed

To get the table size, use the following statement:

```
SELECT TABSCHEMA, TABNAME, COL_OBJECT_L_SIZE, COL_OBJECT_P_SIZE
FROM SYSIBMADM.ADMINTABINFO
where tabschema = 'DEMO'
WITH UR;
```

BLU platform management

While you can run OLTP and analytical workloads on the same server, it is best to isolate analytical workloads, even from each other. While it is also possible to run BLU on a virtual image, it is not recommended for production environments. There are several different options for configuring BLU:

- Option 1: BLU and OLTP workloads on separate servers:
    - Best option
    - Minimizes risk to workloads

- Fewer controls to manage, configure, and set up
- Best security
- Ease of resource and capacity management
- Option 2: One server with separate Db2 instances:
  - Good option
  - Set Db2 instance resources to guarantee each instance gets specific levels of server resources
  - Allow registry/instance controls to manage, configure, and set up
  - Good security
  - Local ETL if OLTP is source for BLU analytical data
- Option 3: One server, one instance, one or more databases:
  - Can be done, but not recommended
  - Requires setting resource limits at the DB level
  - Instance level changes requiring a cycle to take both down
  - Instance upgrades impact both
  - Can join between OLTP (row) and BLU (column) tables
  - One SQL can access both table types without federation (within a single DB)
  - ETL, if OLTP is source for BLU analytical data, is contained within one DB

Row- and column-organized tables can coexist in the same database, in the same schema or tablespace, and can be accessed by a single SQL statement. However, this configuration is not recommended from a manageability and performance perspective. The following table shows the same table created for row and column organization.

To build a mix of row and column configured databases in a single instance, start with the database instance configured for row-based tables. Build the databases you need, then set the DB2_WORKLOAD=ANALYTICS registry setting and restart the instance. Finally, create the database configured for column-based tables.

When running a Db2 instance with row and column organized databases, configure the database manager and database configuration settings for column workloads. Row workloads (OLTP) will run fine in a column-configured Db2 instance, but not vice versa.

Anatomy of a columnar table

Db2 organizes data as rows or as columns. A single data page will contain data from one column, and data is deleted or inserted, but never updated. Isolation level Currently Committed (CC) is supported in column organized pages, by keeping track of both current and previous copies of the slot.

The DDL differences between a row- and column-organized table are minimal, and can be seen in the following table:

Column-Organized Table	Row-Organized Table
CREATE TABLE "DEMO"."T3" ("ID" INTEGER NOT NULL, "NAME" VARCHAR(20 OCTETS) , "ADDRESS" VARCHAR(50 OCTETS) , "SALARY" INT) DISTRIBUTE BY HASH("ID") IN "USERSPACE1" ORGANIZE BY COLUMN;	CREATE TABLE "DEMO"."T4" ("ID" INTEGER NOT NULL, "NAME" VARCHAR(20 OCTETS) , "ADDRESS" VARCHAR(50 OCTETS) , "SALARY" INT)COMPRESS YES STATIC DISTRIBUTE BY HASH("ID") IN "USERSPACE1" ORGANIZE BY ROW;
Records Loaded: 62,914,560	Records Loaded: 62,914,560

Column and row table structure comparison

Each columnar table, when created, will result in the creation of a system maintained columnar synopsis table. In the synopsis table, there is one entry for every 1,024 records inserted in the user table, or every commit, whichever is fewer. Db2 uses this table to implement data skipping. The description of a columnar table T3 synopsis table is shown below:

```
DESCRIBE TABLE SYSIBM.SYN170323092546645613_T3

Column
name          schema      Data type    Column
                          name         Length  Scale  Nulls

----------    ----------  ---------    ------  -----  ----
IDMIN         SYSIBM      INTEGER      4       0      NO
IDMAX         SYSIBM      INTEGER      4       0      NO
NAMEMIN       SYSIBM      VARCHAR      20      0      Yes
NAMEMAX       SYSIBM      VARCHAR      20      0      Yes
ADDRESSMIN    SYSIBM      VARCHAR      50      0      Yes
ADDRESSMAX    SYSIBM      VARCHAR      50      0      Yes
SALARYMIN     SYSIBM      INT         8       0      Yes
SALARYMAX     SYSIBM      INT         8       0      Yes
TSNMIN        SYSIBM      BIGINT      8       0      No
TSNMAX        SYSIBM      BIGINT      8       0      No
```

User-defined indexes cannot be created on columnar tables. This does not mean that there are no indexes; it just means that you cannot run the `CREATE INDEX` statement. Adding a unique or primary key constraint on a columnar table will result in the creation of an index. When a user-defined, column-organized table is created using the `CREATE TABLE` statement, two tables (both column-organized) and one index are created. The synopsis table and a CPMA index are created along with the user table.

To manage the uniqueness for a columnar table, a `UNIQUE` or `PRIMARY KEY` constraint can be added using the following statements:

```
ALTER TABLE DEMO.T3 ADD CONSTRAINT UNIQ UNIQUE (ID) ENFORCED
ALTER TABLE DEMO.T3 ADD CONSTRAINT PK_T3 PRIMARY KEY (ID) ENFORCED
```

 Guess what happens if you run both?
The second DDL statement is ignored. It runs with no errors, but does nothing.

To see the indexes created for the `T3` columnar table, a DML statement such as the one shown here can be executed:

```
SELECT TRIM (TABNAME) AS TABNAME, TRIM(INDNAME) AS INDNAME, INDEXTYPE,
COMPRESSION
from syscat.indexes where tabname like '%T3%'
```

The following table shows two CPMA indexes (one for each columnar table) and one unique index, created to support the unique constraint:

TABNAME	INDNAME	INDEXTYPE	COMPRESSION
T3	SQL171021221512775194	CPMA	Y
SYN171021221512557055_T3	SQL171021221512788992	CPMA	Y
T3	UNIQ	REG	Y

Column-organized table indexes

 What is CPMA?
A column page map index (CPMA) is an internal index, created for each column-organized table, to maintain the mapping between a TSN (Tuple Sequence Number) and the page that it belongs to.

Db2 V11.1 BLU advances

Db2 Massively Parallel Processing (MPP) now supports column-organized tables. The following diagram shows a simple BLU MPP (DPF) topology:

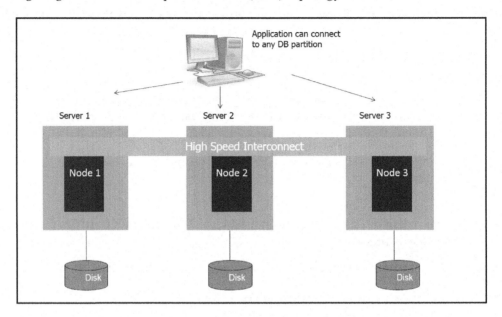

Db2 Massively Parallel Processing (MPP) topology

With Db2 MPP, it is possible to deliver a true massively parallel columnar store. Data exchanges during distributed joins and aggregations are performed entirely in a native columnar format.

Core technologies added to Db2 BLU for MPP processing are as follows:

- Column Vector Processing Engine is MPP aware
- Partition communication uses optimized vector format
- Common table dictionary keeps data compressed across network
- Multi-core optimized infrastructure for communications

Other BLU technologies added in this release are:

- Nest loop join support
- Faster SQL merge operation
- Advanced de-correlation technique

- Better memory management
- Advances in SIMD
- Radix sort
- SQL parallelism
- Identity support
- Expression generated columns
- Not logged initially support

Data is distributed across data partitions, based on distribution keys. Each table has its own distribution key, which can be one or more columns. The performance of queries that join tables will typically be increased if the join is collocated. Db2 automation makes data loading simple, because it detects and adapts to available memory and cores. The same happens for FCM buffers and parallelism.

A RANDOM distribution should be used when the following are true:

- Collocated joins are not possible
- Collocated joins are not necessary, due to smaller table sizes
- Distribution by hash results in a significant data skew across the data partitions

Columnar tables perform well for reading, but are slower than row tables when it comes to changing data. v11.1.2.2 has parallel inserts for columnar tables. In v11.1.1.1, improvements were made to the synopsis table regarding small sized transactions performing data changes. Transactions that insert or update fewer than 100 rows will see a significant improvement.

db2convert

There are several ways to convert data from row- to column-organized. Db2convert is an executable program wrapper for ADMIN_MOVE_TABLE, with a few nice features included.

It is possible to convert all of the tables in a database with one command. The tables, such as range clustered, typed, MQT, declared global temporary, and created global temporary, cannot be converted to column-organized tables, and are skipped automatically. Using the -force parameter will convert all other tables, including range partition, MDC and ITC tables:

```
db2convert -d mydb
```

During the conversion process, it is possible to stop execution in specific phases. For example, the -stopbeforeswap option will halt the move operation at swap, preventing INIT, COPY, and REPLAY phases until the requester responds to the prompt. This will allow the requester to take an online backup before continuing.

Another nice option is -check, which allows the user to run the db2convert program for validation, without making any changes. This allows the user to ensure that all conditions are met before running the final conversion.

Some row-organized table dependent objects that are not supported for columnar tables will not be converted, including:

- Triggers
- User-defined indexes
- Foreign keys (no referential integrity constraints)
- Check constraints

 Since column-organized tables don't support triggers being created, they can't be used as source tables in an ADMIN_MOVE_TABLE () procedure; however, they can be target tables.

Db2 pureScale

The IBM Db2 cluster technology, called pureScale, was introduced in 2010, in v9.8. Leveraging the architecture and design principles of Db2 data sharing on Z, pureScale has rapidly become a technological force in delivering shared data performance and unparalleled scalability. Db2 pureScale is comprised of four major components, which are shown in the following diagram:

- Members (Db2 data sharing LPARS on Z)
- Cluster caching facility (coupling facility on Z)
- Shared disk storage
- Cluster services and interconnect

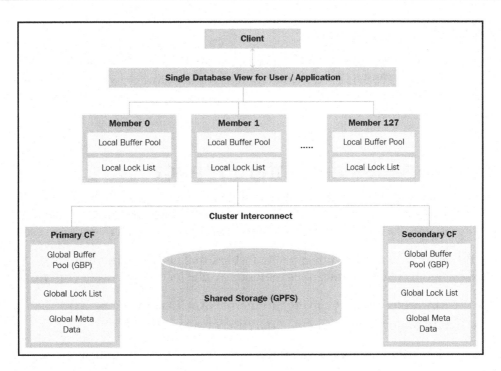

Db2 pureScale architecture

Members

Db2 pureScale is made up of one or more Db2 LUW instances. Each Db2 instance is completely independent and runs workloads assigned to it. These are called members. They can be started, stopped, installed, dropped, or upgraded, independently. Members have their own `db2sysc` process, threads, local buffer pools, memory regions, and active logs.

Cluster-caching facility (CF)

The CF is the communication switchboard. It is a software application managed by Db2 Cluster Services, which maintains a centralized global locking registry and a data page caching registry. Global Lock Manager (GLM) controls locking events, and Global Buffer Pool Manager (GBP) controls data page events. A global event occurs any time two or more members want the same data at the same time.

Shared disk storage

The tablespace containers used to store data must be available to all members. A **General Parallel File System** (**GPFS**) is used to manage shared disk storage, which is then mounted on each member server defined to the cluster. This includes SYSCATSPACE, SYSTEM TEMP, and USER TABLESPACES.

Cluster services and interconnect

Db2 pureScale has a sophisticated monitoring system, which manages all of the services required to operate the cluster. IBM's **Reliable Services Cluster Technology** (**RSCT**) detects failures, and **Tivoli System Automation** (**TSA**) automates recovery processes.

To make this work, you need a high-capacity fast internal network. There are two supported interconnect communications methods available, listed in order of performance:

- RDMA protocol over Converged Ethernet (RoCE) network
- TCP/IP protocol over Ethernet (TCP/IP) network

The **Remote Direct Memory Access** (**RDMA**) is a set of instructions that allows servers to access each other's memory.

  InfiniBand is no longer supported.

Db2 v11.1 pureScale advances

IBM continues to enhance the Db2 pureScale platform. With v11.1, IBM delivers on several key, customer-focused enhancements. They are listed in the following sections.

Availability

Db2 HADR support was introduced in v10.5, allowing for asynchronous modes. The SYNC and NEARSYNC HADR synchronization modes were added in v11.1. With SYNC and NEARSYNC, near zero data loss is possible, with the scalability and cost improvements of cluster technology.

Geographically Dispersed pureScale Cluster (**GDPC**) now supports 10GE RoCE and a TCP/IP network within all pureScale supported operating systems. This feature includes multi-adapter ports for each member of the cluster. In addition, the CF allows for high bandwidth, and eliminates a **single point of failure** (**SPOF**) in the event of a loss of a single member or CF. For production clusters, dual switch configurations should always be used, giving dual cabling to each switch.

Installation and upgrades

The Db2 pureScale installation requires tools to share data in a UNIX environment. RSCT, TSA, and GPFS are products included with Db2 to make pureScale installations easier. In V11.1, IBM has added smarts and checks to the pre-check, installation, and verification processes. Getting GPFS set up and replicated across servers is also easier. Db2/HADR support was introduced with V10.5, allowing for asynchronous modes.

The installation process itself includes problem identification during a step-by-step deployment, along with restart logic.

V11.1 now includes a direct V9.7 upgrade. A streamlined HADR upgrade is available for those upgrading from V10.5 Fix Packs (or later). This eliminates the need to reinitialize the standby database after upgrading the primary database.

With V11.1, database version upgrades no longer require an offline backup if upgrading from V10.5 FP7 (or later).

pureScale V11 now runs on Power Linux **Little Endian** (**LE**), as well as with RDMA support for Linux Virtual. RHEL 7.2 is now supported for pureScale.

Management and performance

The management is the ability to perform online table reorgs at the data partition level in a range partition table. With v11.1.2.2, pureScale member crash recovery is faster, thanks to a better hashing algorithm and increased parallelism in GLM recovery, benefiting larger clusters the most. pureScale now supports database rebuild functionality.

Work around **group buffer pool** (**GBP**) locking and storage management was done in v11.1, with significant improvements, especially for large tables involving
TRUNCATE|DROP|LOAD|INGEST WITH REPLACE commands.

Member subsets were introduced in v10.5. These are database objects that define a relationship between a database alias and a server list. The server list is made up of members in a Db2 pureScale cluster. Member subsets allow you to centrally manage how an application views the cluster topology of the database environment. Remote applications connect to a specific database alias that is assigned to a member subset. Member subsets can be adjusted dynamically.

V11.1 includes improved monitoring of pureScale resources. The `db2cluster -verify` command has been improved to include validations for:

- Configuration settings in peer domains and GPFS clusters
- Communications between members and CFs
- GFPS replication settings for each filesystem
- Status of each disk in the filesystem
- Remote access with db2sshid, among all nodes through db2locssh and db2scp

Features

V11.1 pureScale supports text search. Additional functionality was added for JSON/SQL. The member sets and subsets were added in V10.5, and were improved in V11.1 with additional options.

Self-tuning database memory manager (STMM) in pureScale

Db2 pureScale has one STMM per member. STMM actively tunes memory configurations, based on local resources, dynamic workloads, and what configuration settings are set to `AUTOMATIC`.

The Db2 STMM can be activated by setting the DB CFG variable `SELF_TUNING_MEM` to `ON`. For pureScale, STMM is activated if any member in the cluster has it on.

You can turn off STMM for any database on any member by setting `SELF_TUNING_MEM` to `OFF`. If you want STMM on, but you do not want it changing a DB configuration variable like `DATABASE_MEMORY`, then just remove `AUTOMATIC` from that variable.

Just like DB configuration variables can be tuned by STMM when set to AUTOMATIC, so can buffer pools. A buffer pool with AUTOMATIC will be tuned by STMM if it is on for that member. Remember that these are local buffer pools (LBP).

The buffer pool exceptions can prevent a buffer pool from being STMM tuned. You can check for exceptions using the statement:

```
SELECT * FROM SYSCAT.BUFFERPOOLEXCEPTIONS;
```

To remove an exception, you can perform one of the following:

- Alter the buffer pool to set the size to a fixed value
- Alter the buffer pool to set the size on a member to the default
- Alter the buffer pool to set the size on a member to be AUTOMATIC

Self-tuning CF memory in pureScale

In Db2 V11.1, CF self-tuning memory is enabled by default. CF self-tuning memory is set at the instance level by setting the registry variable Db2_DATABASE_CF_MEMORY to AUTO:

```
db2set DB2_DATABASE_CF_MEMORY = AUTO
```

Setting DB2_DATABASE_CF_MEMORY to AUTO turns on CF self-tuning memory for all active databases that have CF the memory variables CF_GBP_SZ (group buffer pool), CF_LOCK_SZ (global lock list), and CF_SCA_SZ (shared communication area) set to AUTOMATIC.

Let's take a closer look at how to set these, and what Db2 STMM will do.

Db2_DATABASE_CF_MEMORY (DB2 registry variable)

It can be set to -1, a percentage, or AUTO. -1 will cause the CF resources to be allocated equally, by percentage, to each database created. For example, if there are two databases, then each will get 50% of the resources. Using a percentage will cause all of the databases to receive the percentage of resources specified. For example, the value 33 would cause all created databases to get 33% of the CF resources.

CF_DB_MEM_SZ (DB CFG in 4K pages)

It can be set to a fixed size amount, or a fixed size amount and AUTOMATIC, as seen below:

```
UPDATE DB CFG FOR sample USING CF_DB_MEM_SZ 6492672 AUTOMATIC;
```

If set to automatic, STMM will tune this amount based on dynamic workload demands. Other CF settings, such as CF_GBP_SZ, CF_LOCK_SZ, and CF_SCA_SZ, will adjust dynamically, also, because their percentage of CF is based on CF_DB_MEM_SZ.

$CF\_DB\_MEM\_SZ = (CF\_GBP\_SZ + CF\_LOCK\_SZ + CF + SCA\_SZ)$

CF_GBP_SZ, CF_LOCK_SZ, CF_SCA_SZ (DB CFG in 4K pages)

All three of these must be set to AUTOMATIC for CF self-tuning to work. If CF_DB_MEM_SZ is fixed, then these three can adjust in the percentages of CF_DB_MEM_SZ, but the amount of CF resources assigned to the database will not grow. If set to AUTOMATIC, then self-tuning CF can increase CF resources assigned to this database. This may mean taking CF resources away from another active database.

Data compression

In Db2, compression has been evolutionary, going back to the column compression days of Db2 for MVS, and later, the row compression algorithm Lempel-Ziv. Popular compression algorithms are lossless-based, meaning they remove repeating values when you deflate, or zip when data is stored and inflate or unzip when read. In this section, we are going to focus on V11.1 data compression, and specifically, table and index compression.

There are four types of compression in Db2. The following table lists the types of compression, with some details about each:

Object	Dictionary	Type	Controlled
Table	Row	Static	ALTER/CREATE TABLE ... COMPRESS YES STATIC
Table	Column	Adaptive	Controlled by Db2. Cannot be changed by user.
Table	Value	Value	ALTER/CREATE TABLE VALUE COMPRESSION

Page	Page and row	Adaptive	Compression of the page. ALTER/CREATE TABLE ... COMPRESS YES ADAPTIVE

Db2 table compression types

In Db2, just about everything can be compressed, and remains compressed longer than in other technologies. All indexes, data, and temp tables can be compressed. Many SQL operations are performed on compressed data. This is important, because savings related to compression are seen in buffer pool storage, disk IO, utilities, large queries, and sort performance. Temp table compression is enabled automatically if the Storage Optimization Feature is available.

Static row compression

Table row compression, sometimes referred to as static or classic compression, involves identifying repeating values and replacing them with a 12-bit symbol key. These keys are stored in a table-level dictionary, specific for that table. The dictionary is stored with the table data rows in the data object portions of the table. All data and log records, except for long data objects, are eligible for compression. To use data row compression with a table, two prerequisites must be satisfied:

- Compression must be enabled at the table level.
- A compression dictionary must be built for the table. Automatic Dictionary Creation (ADC) rules apply, in some cases.

A new table can be created with static row compression using the CREATE TABLE statement, as follows:

```
CREATE TABLE DEPARTMENTS
    (DEPT_NO    INT
    DESC       CHAR (3))
    PARTITION BY (DEPT_NO NULLS FIRST)
        (STARTING  0 ENDING  9 IN tbsp0,
         STARTING 10 ENDING 19 IN tbsp1,
         STARTING 20 ENDING 29 IN tbsp2,
         STARTING 30 ENDING 39 IN tbsp3)
COMPRESS YES STATIC;
```

Indexes corresponding to this table can be compressed (or not). To compress new indexes on this table, use the CREATE INDEX statement, as follows:

```
CREATE UNIQUE INDEX UX_DEPARTMENTS ON DEPARTMENTS
            (DEPT_NO ASC)
             PARTITIONED
             ALLOW REVERSE SCANS
             COMPRESS YES;

CREATE INDEX UD1_DEPARTMENTS ON DEPARTMENTS
            (DESC ASC)
             PARTITIONED
             ALLOW REVERSE SCANS
             COMPRESS NO;
```

For all new indexes that support compression, the default is COMPRESS YES if the table is compressed.

To compress an existing table, use the ALTER TABLE statement, as follows:

```
ALTER TABLE DEPARTMENTS COMPRESS YES STATIC;
```

Any new rows added to the table will be compressed. This means that INSERT or LOAD INSERT, INGEST INSERT, or IMPORT INSERT utilities will add compressed rows to the table. To compress rows which existed in the table before the ALTER TABLE was executed, existing data will need be reloaded. This means that EXPORT/LOAD REPLACE, REORG TABLE, EXPORT/IMPORT REPLACE, or ADMIN_MOVE_TABLE can be used.

Should the table be compressed?

If the table is small, it should probably not be compressed. There are thresholds required for a dictionary to be built. If there are not enough rows, or if the compression value is low, a dictionary might not be created, and therefore, no rows can be compressed.

It is possible to estimate the potential impact of compression on a table. The old method was to run the INSPECT command, and then format the results using db2inspf. The INSPECT command produces a file stored in the same location as the current db2diag.log file for that Db2 instance (a DIAGPATH database manager configuration parameter).

A better way is to make sure that valid statistics have been collected on the table by running the RUNSTATS utility. Run a DML statement, as follows:

```
SELECT TRIM(TABSCHEMA) as SCHEMA, TRIM(TABNAME) AS TAB,  OBJECT_TYPE AS
OTYP, AVGROWSIZE_CURRENT AS AROWC, AVGROWSIZE_STATIC AS AROWS,
PCTPAGESSAVED_STATIC AS PPSS, AVGROWSIZE_ADAPTIVE as AROWA,
PCTPAGESSAVED_ADAPTIVE AS PPSA    FROM
TABLE("SYSPROC"."ADMIN_GET_TAB_COMPRESS_INFO"(CAST ('DEMO' AS VARCHAR
(128)), CAST ('DEPARTMENTS' AS VARCHAR (128)))) AS UDF FOR FETCH ONLY;
```

The object type, as we already know, is DATA. The average row size of the table is 676. The static row compression average row size is estimated to be 144, and the page savings is at 78%. Using adaptive compression, the average row size would drop to 68, and the estimated page savings using adaptive compression would be 87%. This table is currently using 195,753, and the page size is 8K. Using static row compression, this data would take 1,193 MB less disk space:

SCHEMA	TAB	OTYP	AROWC	AROWS	PPSS	AROWA	PPSA
DEMO	DEPARTMENTS	DATA	676	144	78	68	87

Wondering the two methods give the same results? The INSPECT formatted output for the preceding table is shown as followings, with the same results:

```
Table phase start (ID Signed: 140, Unsigned: 140; Tablespace ID: 678):
XX.DEPARTMENTS
Data phase start. Object: 140 Tablespace: 678
Row compression estimate results:
Percentage of pages saved from compression: 78
Percentage of bytes saved from compression: 78
Compression dictionary size: 46720 bytes.
Expansion dictionary size: 32768 bytes.
Data phase end.
Table phase end.
```

Getting information about the compression dictionary

It is a good idea to monitor compression effectiveness for tables with high insert, update, and delete rates. Tables that have little to no data change or completely reloaded data do not to be checked.

The following DML can be used to evaluate the compression dictionary for a table:

```
SELECT TRIM(TABSCHEMA) AS SCHEMA, TRIM(TABNAME) AS TAB, DATAPARTITIONID AS
PART, OBJECT_TYPE AS OTYP, ROWCOMPMODE AS COMPM, BUILDER, BUILD_TIMESTAMP
AS BDT, SIZE, ROWS_SAMPLED AS SAMPSIZE, PCTPAGESSAVED AS PPS,
AVGCOMPRESSEDROWSIZE AS ACRS
FROM TABLE (
   "SYSPROC"."ADMIN_GET_TAB_DICTIONARY_INFO" (
   CAST ('DEMO' AS VARCHAR (128)),
   CAST ('CUSTOMER' AS VARCHAR (128)))) AS UDF
FOR FETCH ONLY;
```

The CUSTOMER table, as we can see, has five partitions. The dictionaries were built on different days, using regular insert processing. This means that the table partitions were built with insert processing in mind, because the dictionaries were not all built on the same day. We can also see that the dictionary sizes are not the same, and neither is the sampling size that was used to define the dictionary. In addition, the percentage of pages saved and the average compressed row size have gotten worse:

SCHEMA	TAB	PART	OTYP	COMPM	BUILDER	BDT	SIZE	SAMPSIZE	PPS	ACRS
DEMO	CUSTOMER	0	DATA	A	TABLE GROWTH	2015-02-23 19:35:43.000000	46720	15758	72	39
DEMO	CUSTOMER	1	DATA	A	TABLE GROWTH	2015-02-23 21:38:07.000000	47360	15736	70	41
DEMO	CUSTOMER	2	DATA	A	TABLE GROWTH	2015-02-23 19:31:23.000000	46848	15740	71	41
DEMO	CUSTOMER	3	DATA	A	TABLE GROWTH	2016-09-14 10:56:55.000000	40576	14420	65	53
DEMP	CUSTOMER	4	DATA	A	TABLE GROWTH	2016-09-14 13:02:29.000000	41344	14446	65	53

Building a row compression dictionary

Data compression will never take place without a compression dictionary. From time to time, it might be necessary to rebuild an existing compression dictionary, so that the symbols accurately reflect the contents of the table. To truly understand compression and manage it effectively, one must understand how the contents of the dictionary are identified.

With an empty compressed table, data can be inserted over time. Initially, no compression dictionary will exist; but once the required number of rows has been inserted, the dictionary will start being populated. The population of the dictionary will coincide with the growth of the table, so we call this method of building the compression dictionary TABLE GROWTH. The INSERT, IMPORT, and INGEST utilities are also table growth methods.

A second method of building the compression dictionary is called LOAD. It is called that because the LOAD REPLACE utility is used to populate the dictionary. If no dictionary exists at the time that LOAD is run, it will automatically build the dictionary. With LOAD REPLACE, it is possible to use KEEPDICTIONARY, RESETDICTIONARY, or RESETDICTIONARYONLY. For LOAD REPLACE, KEEPDICTIONARY is the default for row-organized tables, while RESETDICTIONARY is the default for column-organized tables.

We have already explained how to build the initial compression dictionary for a table. If a table with uncompressed data exists, first, perform the compression estimate check (as we explained previously) to determine whether the table data should be compressed. To compress the data, execute the ALTER TABLE statement, with either static or adaptive compression. Once that is done, any new rows added to the table will be compressed (once the ACD rules are met). To compress all of the data rows in the table, execute an offline REORG, ADMIN_MOVE_TABLE, or LOAD REPLACE RESETDICTIONARY utility.

If the REORG command is executed with either option specified, and a compression dictionary does not exist, a new dictionary will be built; if the REORG command is executed with either option specified, and a dictionary already exists, the data in the table will be reorganized/compressed, and the existing dictionary will either be recreated (RESETDICTIONARY) or left as it is (KEEPDICTIONARY). Thus, if you want to create a new compression dictionary (and compress the existing data) for a table named CUSTOMER that has been enabled for data row compression, you can do so by executing a REORG command:

```
ALTER TABLE CUSTOMER COMPRESS YES STATIC;
REORG TABLE CUSTOMER RESETDICTIONARY;
```

When this command is executed, data stored in the CUSTOMER table will be analyzed, and a compression dictionary will be constructed and stored in pages within the data object area. The same results will occur when using the LOAD REPLACE utility command:

```
ALTER TABLE CUSTOMER COMPRESS YES ADAPTIVE;
EXPORT TO CUSTOMER.del of DEL SELECT * FROM CUSTOMER;
LOAD FROM CUSTOMER.del of del REPLACE RESETDICTIONARY INTO CUSTOMER;
```

Index data is not affected by data row compression. Indexes created on a compressed table are automatically compressed.

Index compression

Many databases supporting OLTP and DSS workloads have large numbers of indexes per table. These indexes take server resources, including memory and disk storage. All indexes, including those on declared or created temporary tables, can be compressed. You can enable compression on existing indexes by using the ALTER INDEX ...COMPRESS YES command. The only indexes that cannot be compressed are MDC block indexes and XML path indexes.

You can use the ADMIN_GET_INDEX_COMPRESS_INFO table function to determine the potential index compression storage savings as follows:

```
SELECT TRIM (INDSCHEMA) || '.' ||TRIM (INDNAME) AS INDNAME,
COMPRESS_ATTR AS ATTR, INDEX_COMPRESSED AS ISCOMP, PCT_PAGES_SAVED AS PPS,
NUM_LEAF_PAGES_SAVED AS NLPS
FROM TABLE (SYSPROC.ADMIN_GET_INDEX_COMPRESS_INFO ('T', 'DEMO', 'CUSTOMER',
NULL, NULL)) AS t;

INDNAME              ATTR ISCOMP PPS NLPS

---------------- ----- ----- --- -------

DEMO.IX1_CUSTOMER N N 69 816
```

If you wanted to enable compression on the IX1_CUSTOMER index, execute the following command:

```
ALTER INDEX DEMO.IX1_CUSTOMER COMPRESS YES;
REORG INDEXES ALL FOR TABLE DEMO.CUSTOMER;
```

LOBs and XML compression

Large objects (LOBs) and XML documents are generally stored in a location separate from the table row that references them. However, you can choose to store a LOB or XML document (up to 32 KB in size) inline, in a base table row, to simplify access to it. LOBs and XML documents that are stored inline can be compressed along with other relational data. Additionally, XML data in the XML storage object of a table is eligible for compression if the XML columns are created using Db2 9.7, and if you enable the table for data row compression. (XML columns created prior to Db2 9.7 are not eligible for compression.)

Temporary tables and replication support

With the Db2 storage optimization feature, temporary table compression is enabled by default. The Db2 optimizer considers the storage savings and the SQL statement performance before compressing the temporary data for aggregated or ORDER BY clause queries. You can use the access plan or the db2pd command to see whether the optimizer used compression for temporary tables:

```
db2pd -db DB1 -temptable
System Temp Table Stats:
        Number of System Temp Tables    : 43614764
        Comp Eligible Sys Temps         : 52
        Compressed Sys Temps            : 52
        Total Sys Temp Bytes Stored     : 5489976234667
        Total Sys Temp Bytes Saved      : 459808462230
        Total Sys Temp Compressed Rows  : 10930175985
    Total Sys Temp Table Rows:          : 91368293421

User Temp Table Stats:
        Number of User Temp Tables      : 235
        Comp Eligible User Temps        : 0
        Compressed User Temps           : 0
        Total User Temp Bytes Stored    : 2826
        Total User Temp Bytes Saved     : 0
        Total User Temp Compressed Rows : 0
        Total User Temp Table Rows:     : 226
```

Starting with Db2 9.7, the SQL replication, Q replication, and event publishing is supported from compressed and partitioned source tables to any target table. This is done mainly through enhancing the log read interface to read compressed log records, and un-compressing it before passing this to the replication capture program at the source.

Adaptive compression

Adaptive row compression adds a second level of compression, with a dictionary built at the page level, and compresses patterns within the page that are not part of the static dictionary. This way, adaptive compression not only yields a better performance ratio, but also adapts to changing data characteristics.

The following table shows the differences between static row compression (also called classic compression) and adaptive compression:

Static Row Compression	Adaptive Compression
This creates a global compression dictionary at the table level.	This creates a local compression dictionary at the page level.
This is the base level compression required to enable adaptive compression.	This needs static row compression to be enabled before activating the adaptive compression.
This needs frequent REORG on the table to eliminate stale patterns.	This is dynamic in nature, and it always complements classic/static row compression by making use of global dictionary patterns inside the local dictionary patterns.
Compression ratio is anywhere between 30% and 50%.	Compression ratio is anywhere between 50% and 80%.
This needs a little more maintenance, such as REORG and RUNSTATS at regular intervals.	No maintenance is necessary.
Base data objects, such as CHAR, VARCHAR, INTEGER, FLOAT, inline LOB, and inline XML data, can be compressed.	Base data objects, such as CHAR, VARCHAR, INTEGER, FLOAT, inline LOB, and inline XML data, can be compressed.
Syntax to enable static compression is as follows: CREATE TABLE ... COMPRESS YES STATIC It can also be: ALTER TABLE ... COMPRESS YES STATIC	Syntax to enable adaptive compression is as follows: CREATE TABLE ... COMPRESS YES ADAPTIVE It can also be: ALTER TABLE ... COMPRESS YES ADAPTIVE

The `ADMIN_GET_TAB_COMPRESS_INFO` table function provides compression estimates.	The `ADMIN_GET_TAB_COMPRESS_INFO` table function provides compression estimates.
This is an add-on feature, available as part of the Advanced Enterprise Server Edition and the Advanced Workgroup Server Edition.	This is an add-on feature, available as part of the Advanced Enterprise Server Edition and the Advanced Workgroup Server Edition.
The system catalog view statement `SELECT SUBSTR (TABSCHEMA, 1, 10) AS TABSCHEMA,` `SUBSTR (TABNAME, 1, 12) AS TABNAME, COMPRESSION, ROWCOMPMODE FROM SYSCAT.TABLES WHERE TABNAME='<tabname>'` can be used to validate the mode of compression. `ROWCOMPMODE S` indicates static row compression.	The system catalog view statement `SELECT SUBSTR (TABSCHEMA, 1, 10) AS TABSCHEMA,` `SUBSTR (TABNAME, 1, 12) AS TABNAME, COMPRESSION, ROWCOMPMODE FROM SYSCAT.TABLES WHERE TABNAME='<tabname>'` can be used to validate the mode of compression. `ROWCOMPMODE A` indicates adaptive compression.

Db2 static and adaptive compression comparison

Finally, you can compress the transaction archive log files in Db2 10.1 by updating the database configuration parameter, as shown here:

```
UPDATE DB CFG FOR DB1 USING LOGARCHCOMPR1 ON LOGARCHCOMPR2 ON;
```

If the database is not enabled for archive logging, or if the database configuration parameters `LOGARCHMETH1` and `LOGARCHMETH2` are not set, you will get the following error:

```
UPDATE DB CFG FOR DB1 USING LOGARCHCOMPR1 ON LOGARCHCOMPR2 ON;
```

SQL compatibilities

Unlike other database technologies, Db2 can run applications developed in other database technologies with minimal changes.

The Db2 registry variable `DB2_COMPAT_VECTOR` is used to active this compatibility. Compatibility can be set at different levels. For example, to set compatibility for Oracle, use the `db2set` command as follows:

```
db2set DB2_COMPAT_VECTOR=ORA
db2stop
db2start
```

The following is the list of other databases that are supported under `DB2_COMPAT_VECTOR`:

- **Oracle (ORA)**
- **Sybase (SYB)**
- **MySQL (MYS)**

Some compatibility features are always active. For example, `DISTINCT` can be replaced with `UNIQUE`, and `MINUS` can replace `EXCEPT`. Most of the features that are automatically active provide an application portability bridge between Db2 and PostgreSQL or Netezza.

 When `DB2_COMPAT_VECTOR=ORA` is set, the `NUMBER`, `VARCHAR2`, and `DATE` Oracle data types will be compatible with Db2.

Compatibility features for Netezza

Db2 11.1 provides features that enable applications that were written for a **Netezza Platform Software (NPS)** database to use a Db2 database, without having to be rewritten. To activate fully fledged NPS compatibility features, including the optional features, set the `SQL_COMPAT` global variable to `NPS`:

```
SET SQL_COMPAT='NPS'
```

The following table shows optional compatibility features for Netezza:

Feature	Format	NPS Interpretation
Double-dot notation	<NPS_DB>..<NPS_Object>	<Schema>.<Object>
Translate Scalar Function Syntax	translate('12345', '143', 'ax')	a2x5
Operators	^ and **	Exponential Operators

Grouping by SELECT clause columns	SELECT c1 AS a, c2+c3 AS b, COUNT(*) AS c FROM t1 GROUP BY 1, 2;	Can specify the ordinal position or exposed name of a SELECT clause column when grouping the results of a query
Expressions refer to column aliases	SELECT c1 AS a, a+3 AS b FROM t1;	An expression can refer to either a column name or a column alias that is set in the select list
Routines written in NZPLSQL		The NZPLSQL language can be used in addition to the SQL PL language

Optional compatibility features for Netezza

There are following few limitations for routines within Netezza:

- The routine must define exactly one alias for each of its parameters
- The routine must return an integer, Boolean, or null value. If the routine returns a non-integer or non-Boolean value, it must use a return; (or return NULL;) statement
- The routine cannot contain argument lists or variable arguments
- The use of the following syntax keywords is restricted:
    - ARRAY
    - AUTOCOMMIT
    - FOR
    - IN EXECUTE
    - INTERVAL
    - LAST_OID
    - RAISE
    - REFTABLE
    - RUN AS
    - SELECT
    - TIMETZ
    - TRANSACTION_ABORTED

Summary

The objective of this chapter was to acquaint you with the following:

- Creating, altering, and managing Db2 objects
- The implementation of Db2 BLU acceleration
- A description of pureScale enhancements
- The proper use of compression techniques
- The new Db2 v11.1 SQL compatibilities
- New partitioning capabilities, such as massively parallel processing (MPP) and range partitioning

You should now be equipped with sufficient knowledge to answer the server management questions in the Db2 v11.1 DBA certification exam.

Practice questions

- **Question 1:** When a new database, SAMPLE, is created after setting the DB2_WORKLOAD to ANALYTICS, which of the following statements are true? (Choose two.)
    1. The degree of parallelism (DFT_DEGREE) will be set to NO
    2. The default tablespace extent size (DFT_EXTENT_SZ) will be set to 4
    3. The default table organization (DFT_TABLE_ORG) will be set to COLUMN
    4. The database page size will be set to 64
    5. The automatic table reorganization (AUTO_REORG) will be set to NO

- **Question 2:** Which of the following db2cluster command options can be used to retrieve current state and cluster domain information? (Choose two.)
    1. -verify
    2. -extract
    3. -list
    4. -get
    5. -show

- **Question 3:** When you run the `db2convert -d SAMPLE -force` command, what will happen to the existing MDC table, `SALES`?
    1. The `SALES` table will be converted to a column-organized MDC table
    2. The `SALES` table will not be converted to a column-organized table, but would remain
    3. The `SALES` table will be converted to a column-organized regular non-MDC table
    4. The `SALES` table will be dropped from the database `SAMPLE`, due to the `-force` option

- **Question 4:** Which of the following statements will cause a version change and place the table in a `REORG` pending state? (Choose two.)
    1. `ALTER TABLE employee RENAME COLUMN id TO empid;`
    2. `ALTER TABLE employee ALTER COLUMN id DROP NOT NULL;`
    3. `ALTER TABLE employee ADD COLUMN cell VARCHAR(10);`
    4. `ALTER TABLE employee ALTER COLUMN id SET NOT NULL;`
    5. `ALTER TABLE employee ADD CONSTRAINT con_empdept FOREIGN KEY      (deptid) REFERENCES department (deptid);`

- **Question 5:** Which command can be used to copy the data from an existing DMS tablespace to a newly created automatic storage tablespace, without impacting the application?
    1. The `EXPORT` and `LOAD` commands
    2. The `ADMIN_MOVE_TABLE_UTIL` procedure
    3. The `ADMIN_COPY_SCHEMA` procedure
    4. The `ADMIN_MOVE_TABLE` procedure

- **Question 6:** Which of the following system commands can be used to get database design recommendations?
    1. `db2exfmt`
    2. `db2bfd`
    3. `db2expl`
    4. `db2advis`

- **Question 7:** Which data type is NOT supported to create expression-based indexes?
    1. INTEGER
    2. XML
    3. VARCHAR
    4. TIMESTAMP

- **Question 8:** Which command will enable hardware accelerated backup and log file compression for the database SAMPLE on AIX Power 7 and 8 servers?
    1. ```
db2set DB2_BCKP_COMPRESSION=NX842
db2 "UPDATE DB CFG FOR sample USING LOGARCHCOMPR1
NX842"
```
    2. ```
db2set DB2_PMAP_COMPATIBILITY=NX842
db2 "UPDATE DB CFG FOR sample USING LOGARCHCOMPR1
NX842"
```
    3. ```
db2set DB2_BCKP_COMPRESSION=YES
db2 "UPDATE DB CFG FOR sample USING LOGARCHCOMPR1 ON"
```
    4. ```
db2set DB2_BCKP_COMPRESSION=NX842
db2 "UPDATE DB CFG FOR sample USING LOGARCHCOMPR1 ON"
db2 "UPDATE DB CFG FOR sample USING LOGARCHCOMPR2 ON"
```

- **Question 9:** What of the following statements is true about the database partitioning feature (also called Massively Parallel Processing (MPP)?
    1. It is a shared-everything architecture
    2. It doesn't allow database maintenance, such as backup, restore, and load, at the database partition level
    3. It enables the parallel execution of database operations or utilities
    4. It always uses the RANDOM data placement method to distribute the data across database partitions

- **Question 10:** Which of the following settings are valid for the DB2_COMPATIBILITY_VECTOR registry variable?
    1. SYB
    2. SYBASE
    3. ORACLE
    4. MYS
    5. MYSQL

Solutions

- **Question 1:**
  The correct answers are **2** and **3**. When you set the instance aggregated registry variable DB2_WORKLOAD=ANALYTICS, all databases created with this setting in place will have the following parameters:
  - Degree of parallelism (DFT_DEGREE) = ANY
  - Default tablespace extent size (pages) (DFT_EXTENT_SZ) = 4
  - Default table organization (DFT_TABLE_ORG) = COLUMN
  - Database page size = 32768

- **Question 2:**
  The correct answers are **1** and **3**.
  The database cluster health check is made easier with one single command, db2cluster -verify, checking:
  - Configuration settings in the peer domain and GPFS cluster
  - Communication between members and CFs
  - The replication setting for each filesystem
  - The status of each disk in the filesystem
  - Remote access with db2sshid among all nodes through db2locssh and db2scp

  The cluster command db2cluster -list returns details about the following:

  - -tiebreaker
  - -alert
  - -HostFailureDetectionTime
  - -LocalHostVersion
  - -DomainCommittedVersin
  - -pprimary
  - -autofailback

- **Question 3:**
  The correct answer is **3**. The `-force` option specifies that all table types are to be converted, including range partitioned tables, multidimensional clustering (MDC) tables, and insert time clustering (ITC) tables, to a regular column-organized table.

- **Question 4:**
  The correct answers are **2** and **4**. A few of the `ALTER TABLE` statement options will cause a version change and place the table into a `REORG` pending state. The following is the full list of `REORG` recommended `ALTER` statements:

  - `DROP COLUMN`
  - `ALTER COLUMN SET NOT NULL`
  - `ALTER COLUMN DROP NOT NULL`
  - `ALTER COLUMN SET DATA TYPE`

An exception is increasing the length of a VARCHAR or VARGRAPHIC column and decreasing the length of a VARCHAR or VARGRAPHIC column without truncating trailing blanks from existing data, when no indexes exist on the column.

- **Question 5:**
  The correct answer is **4**. You can use the `SYSPROC.ADMIN_MOVE_TABLE ()` procedure to move the table online without impacting the application; an example statement is as follows:

- **CALL SYSPROC.ADMIN_MOVE_TABLE**

```
('DB2INST1',
'EMP_PHOTO',
'TS_SMALL_DATA',
'TS_SMALL_INDEX',
'TS_LOB_DATA',
' ',
' ',
' ',
' ',
' ',
'MOVE')
```

- **Question 6:**

  The correct answer is **4**. The Design Advisor is a tool that identifies indexes, MQTs, MDCs, and the repartitioning opportunities for tables, to improve query performance in the database environment. You can invoke the Design Advisor by executing the `db2advis` command. A basic command example is as follows:

  - `db2advis -d sample -i db2advis.sql -t 5`

- **Question 7:**

  The correct answer is **2**. The following data types are not supported as input to the expression-based index key:
    - LONG VARCHAR and LONG VARGRAPHIC (deprecated data types)
    - XML
    - User-defined distinct types on any of the types listed previously
    - User-defined weakly typed distinct types that include a data type constraint
    - User-defined structured types and reference types
    - Array, cursor, and row types

- **Question 8:**

  The correct answer is **2**. To enable hardware backup compression by default, set the registry variable `DB2_BCKP_COMPRESSION` to `NX842`; otherwise, you will have to specify the compression library `libdb2nx842.a` in the `BACKUP` command. To enable log archive compression, change the `LOGARCHCOMPR1` or `LOGARCHCOMPR2` database configuration to `NX842`.

- **Question 9:**

  The correct answer is **3**. Database partitioning is built based on the following characteristics:
    - Shared-nothing architecture
    - Enables parallel execution of database operations or utilities
    - SQL optimizer limit processing to selected database partitions
    - If a table is defined on a subset of the database partitions, only that subset will perform SQL processing
    - Some SQL predicates allow the optimizer to direct SQL processing to a single database partition, where data records will be stored
    - Enables maintenance management at the partition level (backup, restore, and load)

- **Question 10:**

  The correct answers are **1** and **4**. The following values can be set for the DB2_COMPATIBILITY_VECTOR registry variable:

    - NULL: This value specifies that no compatibility features are activated. This is the default setting.
    - ORA: This value specifies that Oracle compatibility features are activated.
    - SYB: This value specifies that Sybase compatibility features are activated.
    - MYS: This value specifies that MySQL compatibility features are activated.

Implementing Business Rules

4

This chapter will prepare you for creating and using constraints to enforce business rules at the database layer. You will also learn how to use triggers and constraints to enforce data integrity rules. This chapter will introduce you to the key system catalog tables, which describe the physical and logical structure of the data stored in the database.

After the completion of this chapter, you will be able to demonstrate the ability to:

- Understand various constraints, such as NOT NULL, DEFAULT, CHECK, UNIQUE, referential integrity, and NOT ENFORCED informational constraints and to determine when and how to use them
- Create views with CHECK OPTION
- Use the SET INTEGRITY command
- Create and use triggers
- Understand constraint behavior in a column-organized database
- Examine the content of the system catalog tables

Certification test:
Number of questions: 6
Percentage in the exam: 10%

Business rules

A business rule is a statement that defines some characteristics of the business. In most businesses, the data must adhere to a specific set of rules and restrictions such as an employee having a valid employee ID. These restrictions can be effectively implemented at the database layer using constraints.

The types of constraints available within Db2 are:

- NOT NULL
- DEFAULT
- CHECK
- UNIQUE
- NOT ENFORCED informational
- Referential integrity

The constraints are usually defined during table creation, however they can also be added to existing tables by using the ALTER TABLE statement.

NOT NULL constraints

In Db2, you can use the NULL value to represent an unknown state or missing information for a column. By default, every column in a table will accept a NULL value. However, some business rules might dictate that a value must always be provided for a column. In those situations, the NOT NULL constraint can be used to ensure that a given column of a table is never assigned the NULL value. Once a NOT NULL constraint has been defined on a column or set of columns, any INSERT or UPDATE operation that attempts to insert a NULL value into that column will fail. The following diagram shows how to use the NOT NULL constraint to avoid NULL values:

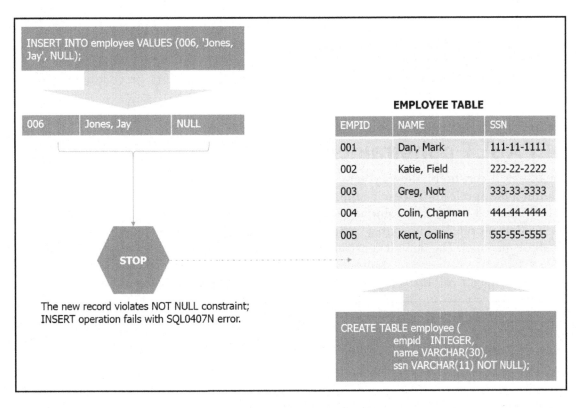

INSERT INTO employee VALUES (006, 'Jones, Jay', NULL);

| 006 | Jones, Jay | NULL |

EMPLOYEE TABLE

EMPID	NAME	SSN
001	Dan, Mark	111-11-1111
002	Katie, Field	222-22-2222
003	Greg, Nott	333-33-3333
004	Colin, Chapman	444-44-4444
005	Kent, Collins	555-55-5555

STOP

The new record violates NOT NULL constraint; INSERT operation fails with SQL0407N error.

CREATE TABLE employee (
        empid   INTEGER,
        name VARCHAR(30),
        ssn VARCHAR(11) NOT NULL);

How the NOT NULL constraint prevents NULL value

The NOT NULL constraints are associated with a single column or a set of specific columns in the table, which are usually defined during the table creation process using the CREATE TABLE statement. They can also be changed to an existing table using the ALTER TABLE statement as follows:

```
-- Table Creation Process

CREATE TABLE DEMO.EMPLOYEE (
            EMPID INTEGER NOT NULL,
            NAME VARCHAR (30),
            SSN VARCHAR (11) NOT NULL)
            IN USERSPACE1;
-- Table Attribute Modification Process

ALTER TABLE DEMO.EMPLOYEE ALTER COLUMN SSN SET NOT NULL;
```

The ALTER TABLE... SET NOT NULL constraint is not supported (SQL1667N) on an existing column-organized table. In these situations, the only option is to create a new table with the NOT NULL constraint and copy the data. Remember, you cannot use the ADMIN_MOVE_TABLE () procedure to copy from a column-organized table to another table.

DEFAULT constraints

The DEFAULT constraint allows you to specify a predefined value that is written to a column if the application doesn't supply a value. The predefined value provided can be NULL (if the NOT NULL constraint has not been defined for the column), a user, or an application-supplied value with a compatible data type or a value provided by the Db2 database manager. The default constraints are only applied to new rows inserted into the table via INSERT, IMPORT, LOAD or INGEST commands. For existing records, the Db2 database manager will furnish a default value as shown in the following table:

Column data type	Default value provided
SMALLINT, INTEGER, DECIMAL, NUMERIC, NUM, REAL, FLOAT, DOUBLE, DOUBLE RECISION	0
CHARACTER, GRAPHIC	A string of blank characters
CHARACTER VARYING, CHAR VARYING, or VARCHAR, LONG VARCHAR, VARGRAPHIC, LONG VARGRAPHIC, BLOB, CLOB, DBCLOB	A zero-length string
DATE	The system date obtained from the CURRENT_DATE special register at the time the row is added to the table (when a date column is added to an existing table, existing rows are assigned the date January 01, 0001)
TIME	The system time obtained from the CURRENT_TIME special register at the time the row is added to the table (when a time column is added to an existing table, existing rows are assigned the time 00:00:00)

Column data type	Default value provided
TIMESTAMP	The system date and time obtained from CURRENT_TIMESTAMP special register (including microseconds) at the time the row is added to the table (when a timestamp column is added to an existing table, existing rows are assigned a timestamp that corresponds to January 01, 0001 - 00:00:00.000000)
XML	Not applicable
Any distinct user-defined data type	The default value provided for the built-in data type that the distinct user-defined data type is based on (typecast to the distinct user-defined data type)

The following diagram shows how to use the DEFAULT constraint to insert a default value when no data is provided for the default column:

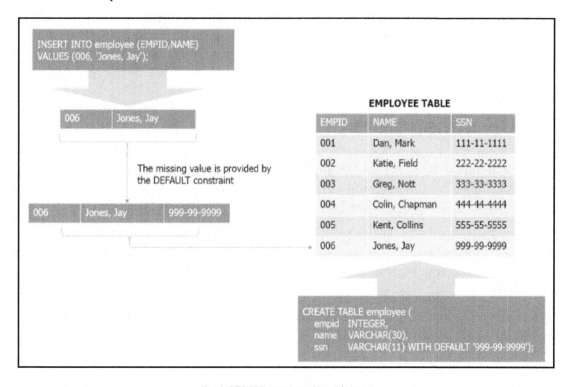

How the DEFAULT constraint provides a default value

The DEFAULT constraints are associated with a single column or a set of specific columns in the table. They are usually defined during the table creation process using the CREATE TABLE statement and can be applied to an existing table using the ALTER TABLE statement as follows:

```
-- Table Creation Process

CREATE TABLE DEMO.EMPLOYEE (
            EMPID INTEGER NOT NULL,
            NAME VARCHAR (30),
            SSN VARCHAR (11) WITH DEFAULT '999-99-9999')
            IN USERSPACE1;
-- Table Attribute Modification Process

ALTER TABLE DEMO.EMPLOYEE ALTER COLUMN SSN SET DEFAULT '999-99-9999';
```

The ALTER TABLE... SET DEFAULT constraint is not supported (SQL1667N) on an existing column organized table. In those situations, the only option is to create a new table with the DEFAULT constraint and copy the data.

CHECK constraints

The CHECK constraint accepts a range of values allowed for a specific column. A simple CHECK constraint can be built using multiple comparison operators such as >, <, >=, <=, =, and <>. A complex CHECK constraint can also be built using AND, OR, NOT (Boolean operators), and LIKE (using wildcard characters such as % and _) or IN predicates.

The CHECK constraints are evaluated to return a value of TRUE or FALSE. The value that passes the CHECK constraint is inserted or updated into the table. The value that does not pass the CHECK constraint is rejected and SQL error SQL0545N is returned to the application.

The following diagram shows how to use the CHECK constraint to control what data values are allowed by a column or set of columns:

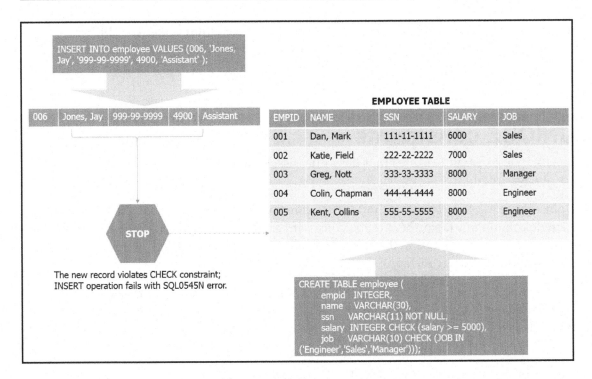

How the CHECK constraint controls what data values are acceptable

The CHECK constraints are associated with a single column or a set of specific columns in the table, which are usually defined during the table creation process using the CREATE TABLE statement. They can also be added to an existing table using the ALTER TABLE statement as follows:

```
-- Table Creation Process

CREATE TABLE demo.employee (
        empid    INTEGER,
        name     VARCHAR(30),
        ssn      VARCHAR(11) NOT NULL,
        salary   INTEGER CHECK (salary >= 5000),
        job      VARCHAR(10) CHECK (JOB IN ('Engineer','Sales','Manager')));
-- Table Attribute Modification Process

ALTER TABLE demo.employee ADD CONSTRAINT check_salary CHECK (salary >=5000)
ADD CONSTRAINT check_job CHECK (JOB in ('Engineer','Sales','Manager'));
```

The CHECK constraint is not supported in a column-organized (BLU acceleration database) table and will receive SQL error SQL1666N if you attempt to create a CHECK constraint.

UNIQUE constraints

The UNIQUE constraint ensures that the values assigned to one or more columns in a table are always unique.

Unlike the NOT NULL, DEFAULT, and CHECK constraints, which can be associated with only a single column in a table, the UNIQUE constraint can be associated with either a single column or a set of columns in the table. The columns specified in a UNIQUE constraint must also have a NOT NULL constraint.

When a UNIQUE constraint is created, the Db2 database manager checks this to determine whether an index for the columns that the UNIQUE constraint refers to already exists. If so, that index will be marked as unique and system required. If not, an appropriate index is created with a SYSIBM schema and marked as unique and system required.

Any record which violates the UNIQUE constraint during an INSERT or an UPDATE operation will be rejected, and SQL error SQL0803N will be returned to the application. The following diagram illustrates how to use the UNIQUE constraint:

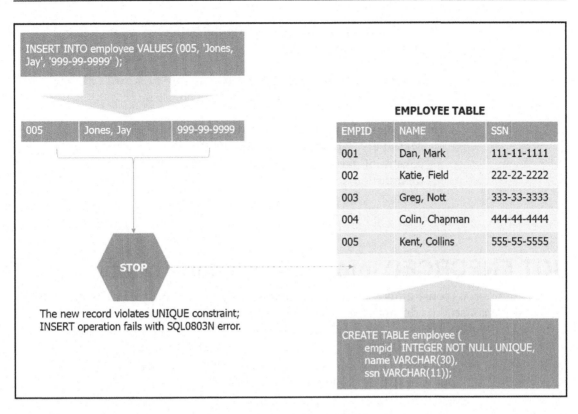

How the UNIQUE constraint controls the duplication of data values

The UNIQUE constraints can be defined during the table creation process using the CREATE TABLE statement, or can be added to an existing table using the ALTER TABLE statement as follows:

```
-- Table Creation Process

CREATE TABLE demo.employee (
        empid    INTEGER NOT NULL UNIQUE,
        name     VARCHAR(30),
        ssn      VARCHAR(11));
-- Table Attribute Modification Process

ALTER TABLE demo.employee
        ADD CONSTRAINT u1_employee UNIQUE (empid);
```

- UNIQUE constraints are supported in both row-organized and column-organized tables

- Columns with an XML data type, structure type, or LOB data type cannot participate in the UNIQUE constraint

- In a **database partitioning feature (DPF)**, also called a **Massively Parallel Processing** (MPP) environment, the UNIQUE constraint participating column key must be a superset of the distribution key specified in the DISTRIBUTE BY clause of the CREATE TABLE statement

NOT ENFORCED informational constraints

Defining numerous constraints can require a considerable amount of system resources to enforce those constraints during INSERT and UPDATE operations. If an application is coded with data validation, it may be more efficient to create NOT ENFORCED informational constraints rather than creating other constraints. The NOT ENFORCED informational constraint will not enforce the constraint during data INSERT or UPDATE operations, however the Db2 optimizer will evaluate the information which is provided by the NOT ENFORCED informational constraint when considering the best access path to resolve a query.

The following diagram illustrates how to use the NOT ENFORCED informational constraint:

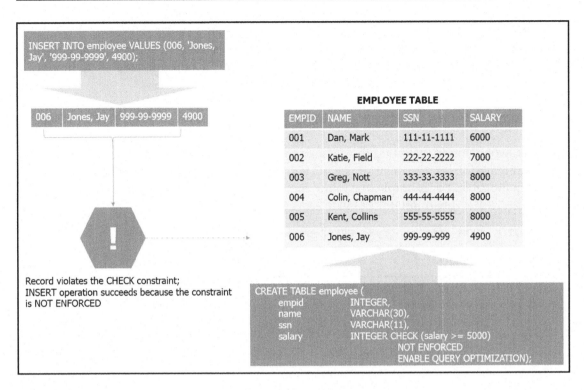

INSERT INTO employee VALUES (006, 'Jones, Jay', '999-99-9999', 4900);

| 006 | Jones, Jay | 999-99-9999 | 4900 |

EMPLOYEE TABLE

EMPID	NAME	SSN	SALARY
001	Dan, Mark	111-11-1111	6000
002	Katie, Field	222-22-2222	7000
003	Greg, Nott	333-33-3333	8000
004	Colin, Chapman	444-44-4444	8000
005	Kent, Collins	555-55-5555	8000
006	Jones, Jay	999-99-999	4900

Record violates the CHECK constraint;
INSERT operation succeeds because the constraint is NOT ENFORCED

```
CREATE TABLE employee (
    empid         INTEGER,
    name          VARCHAR(30),
    ssn           VARCHAR(11),
    salary        INTEGER CHECK (salary >= 5000)
                      NOT ENFORCED
                      ENABLE QUERY OPTIMIZATION);
```

How to use the NOT ENFORCED informational constraint

A NOT ENFORCED informational constraint can be defined during the table creation process using the CREATE TABLE statement, and it can also be added to an existing table using the ALTER TABLE statement as follows:

```
-- Table Creation Process

CREATE TABLE employee (
      empid   INTEGER,
      name        VARCHAR(30),
      ssn             VARCHAR(11),
      salary      INTEGER CHECK (salary >= 5000)
    NOT ENFORCED
    ENABLE QUERY OPTIMIZATION);
-- Table Attribute Modification Process

ALTER TABLE demo.employee ADD CONSTRAINT check_Sal_employee
        CHECK (SALARY >= 5000)
        NOT ENFORCED
        ENABLE QUERY OPTIMIZATION;
```

It is important to understand how the Db2 optimizer evaluates NOT ENFORCED informational constraints when performing a SELECT operation, since some queries may not return records that have been inserted into a table. The Db2 optimizer lets you insert a value which violates the CHECK constraint as follows:

```
INSERT INTO demo.employee  VALUES (006, 'Jones, Jay', '999-99-9999', 4900);
DB20000I  The SQL command completed successfully.
```

However, when you try selecting the data using an equality predicate with a CHECK constraint that violates the constraints, Db2 will not return the result even when it is present in the table. For example, the following will not be returned because of the NOT ENFORCED CHECK constraint CHECK_SAL_EMPLOYEE:

```
SELECT * FROM demo.employee WHERE salary=4900;

EMPID        NAME                                   SSN            SALARY
-----------  ------------------------------------   -----------    -------

    0 record(s) selected.
```

 The CHECK constraint, by itself, is not supported in a column-organized table, however it is supported when the CHECK constraint is defined with the NOT ENFORCED clause.

The NOT ENFORCED constraint can also be used in conjunction with a primary key constraint and is supported in both row-organized and column-organized tables. The following listed example shows the behavior of PRIMARY KEY NOT ENFORCED:

```
CREATE TABLE demo.employee (
                id INTEGER NOT NULL,
                name VARCHAR(20),
                location VARCHAR(10),
                create_date TIMESTAMP );

ALTER TABLE demo.employee ADD PRIMARY KEY (id) NOT ENFORCED;

INSERT into demo.employee values (1,'Tom', 'Dallas', CURRENT_TIMESTAMP);
INSERT into demo.employee values (2,'Trey', 'Fort Worth',
CURRENT_TIMESTAMP);
INSERT into demo.employee values (3,'Greg', 'Plano', CURRENT_TIMESTAMP);
INSERT into demo.employee values (1,'Charles', 'Houston',
CURRENT_TIMESTAMP);

SELECT * FROM demo.employee;
ID              NAME           LOCATION   CREATE_DATE
```

```
----------  ----------  ----------  ----------------------------
         1 Tom         Dallas      2017-11-11-01.26.39.612916
         2 Trey        Fort Worth  2017-11-11-01.26.49.789062
         3 Greg        Plano       2017-11-11-01.26.57.690662
         1 Charles     Houston     2017-11-11-01.27.07.215106

  4 record(s) selected.
```

When you define a column with `PRIMARY KEY NOT ENFORCED`, it will allow duplicate values to be inserted into a column. When you perform a `SELECT` via the primary key column predicate in a column-organized table, it will return the row which was inserted first. On the other hand, `SELECT` will return all the matching records in a row-organized table:

```
-- Column Organized Table Behavior

SELECT * FROM demo.employee WHERE id=1;

ID           NAME                LOCATION    CREATE_DATE
----------  --------------------  ----------  --------------------
         1 Tom                  Dallas      2017-11-11-01.29.22.201775

  1 record(s) selected.

 -- Row Organized Table Behavior

ID           NAME                LOCATION    CREATE_DATE
----------  --------------------  ----------  --------------------
         1 Tom                  Dallas      2017-11-11-01.26.39.612916
         1 Charles              Houston     2017-11-11-01.27.07.215106

  2 record(s) selected.
```

Referential integrity constraints

Referential integrity constraints (also known as *foreign key constraints* or *referential constraints*) enable you to define required relationships between and within different tables. Referential integrity is the state of a database in which all values of all foreign keys are valid. A foreign key is a column or a set of columns in a table whose values are required to match at least one primary key or unique key value of a row in its parent table.

To understand how referential constraints work, let's establish a relationship between the EMPLOYEE and DEPARTMENT tables, as shown in the following diagram. In this example, a single column DEPTID defines the parent key and the foreign key of the referential constraint. However, as with UNIQUE constraints, you can use multiple columns to define both the parent and the foreign keys of a referential constraint:

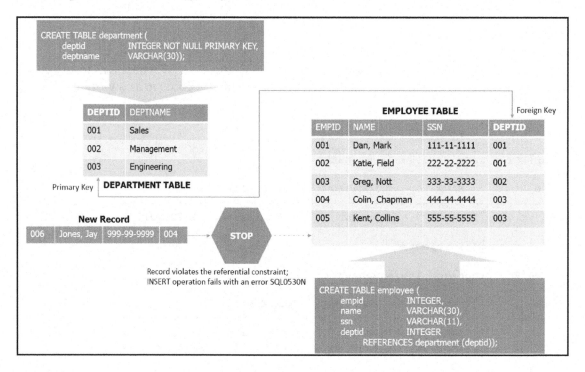

How to use a referential constraint to define a relationship between two tables

You can only insert rows into the EMPLOYEE table when you have a matching row available in the DEPARTMENT table:

```
INSERT INTO demo.employee VALUES (006, 'Jones, Jay', '999-99-9999', 001);
DB20000I  The SQL command completed successfully.
```

However, if you try inserting a record into the EMPLOYEE table when you have no matching record in the DEPARTMENT table, it will fail with an error of SQL0530N:

```
INSERT INTO demo.employee VALUES (007, 'Jones, Jay', '999-99-9999', 004);

SQL0530N The INSERT or UPDATE value of the FOREIGN KEY
"DEMO.EMPLOYEE.SQL171105040442910" is not equal to any value of the parent
key of the parent table. SQLSTATE=23503
```

- The names of the columns used to create the foreign key of a referential constraint do not have to be the same as the names of the columns used to create the primary key of the constraint. However, the data types used for the column or columns that make up the primary key and the foreign key of a referential constraint must be identical.

- Referential integrity constraints are not supported in column-organized tables.

The referential constraint is much more complex than NOT NULL, DEFAULT, CHECK, and UNIQUE constraints. It is important to understand the different terminology that makes up the referential integrity constraints. The following table shows the complete list:

Terminology	Description
Unique key	A column or set of columns in which every row of values is different from the values of all other rows.
Primary key	A special unique key that does not accept NULL values. Each table can contain only one primary key, and every column that defines the primary key must have a NOT NULL constraint defined.
Foreign key	A column or set of columns in a child table whose values must match those of a parent key in a parent table.
Parent key	A primary key or unique key in a parent table that is referenced by a foreign key in a referential constraint.
Parent table	A table that contains a parent key of a referential constraint (a table can be both a parent table and a dependent table of any number of referential constraints).
Parent row	A row in a parent table that has at least one matching row in a dependent table.

Dependent or child table	A table that contains at least one foreign key that references a parent key in a referential constraint (a table can be both a dependent table and a parent table of any number of referential constraints).
Dependent or child row	A row in a dependent table that has at least one matching row in a parent table.
Descendent table	A dependent table or a descendent of a dependent table.
Descendent row	A dependent row or a descendent of a dependent row.
Referential cycle	A set of referential constraints defined in such a way that each table in the set is a descendent of itself.
Self-referencing table	A table that is both a parent table and a dependent table in the same referential constraint (the constraint is known as a self-referencing constraint).
Self-referencing row	A row that is a parent of itself.

The primary reason for creating a referential constraint is to guarantee that table relationships are maintained and that data entry rules are followed. As long as the referential constraint is in effect, the database manager guarantees that for each row in a child table that has a non-null value in its foreign key columns, a row exists in a corresponding parent table that has a matching value in its parent key.

What happens when a user attempts to change data in such a way that referential integrity will be violated? Let's take a look at a few scenarios that can compromise data integrity if the referential integrity checks are not provided:

- **INSERT operation**: When a user tries to add a record to a child table that does not have a matching value in the corresponding parent table. For example, a user tries to insert a record into the EMPLOYEE table with a value that does not exist in the DEPARMENT table.
- **UPDATE operation (child)**: When a user tries to update an existing record in a child table so that it no longer has a matching value in the corresponding parent table. For example, if a user tries to update a record in the EMPLOYEE table with a value which does not exist in the DEPARTMENT table.

- **UPDATE operation (parent)**: When a user tries to update an existing record in the parent table, thus leaving rows in a child table with values that no longer match those in the parent table. For example, if a user tries to update an existing record in the DEPARTMENT table so that records in the EMPLOYEE table no longer have a corresponding value in the DEPATMENT table.
- **DELETE operation**: When a user tries to delete an existing record from a parent table, leaving records in a child table with values that no longer match those in the parent table. For example, if a user tries to delete an existing record from the DEPARTMENT table without deleting the child rows in the EMPLOYEE table.

The Db2 database manager controls these types of situations by enforcing a set of rules that are associated with each referential constraint. The rules are as follows:

- An INSERT rule
- An UPDATE rule
- A DELETE rule

Now that you know the referential integrity rules, let's dive deep into each rule to understand how Db2 implements each of these rules.

The INSERT rule for referential constraints

The INSERT rule is applicable to the child table and it guarantees that a value can never be inserted into the foreign key of a child table unless a matching value exists in the corresponding primary key of the associated parent table. Any attempt to insert a record into a child table that violates the INSERT rule will result in an SQL0530N error and the INSERT operation will fail.

Remember, this rule is not applicable to the parent table and no data validation occurs when records are added to the parent key of the parent table.

The following diagram shows how a record that conforms to the INSERT rule for a referential constraint is successfully added to the child table:

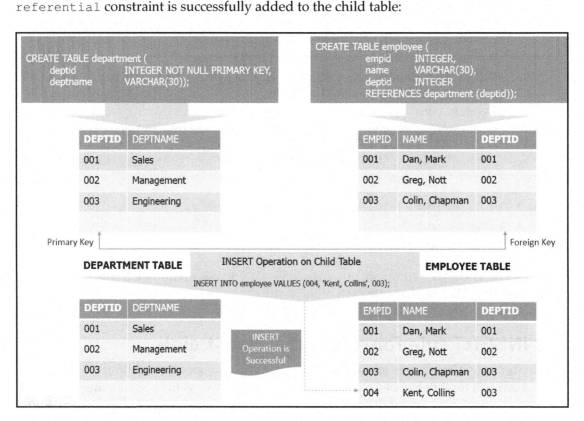

How an INSERT operation is performed that conforms to the INSERT rule of the referential integrity constraint

A successful INSERT statement snippet is shown as follows:

```
INSERT INTO demo.employee VALUES (004, 'Kent, Collins', 003);
DB20000I The SQL command completed successfully.
```

The following diagram shows how a record that violates the INSERT rule for a referential constraint is rejected from being added to the child table:

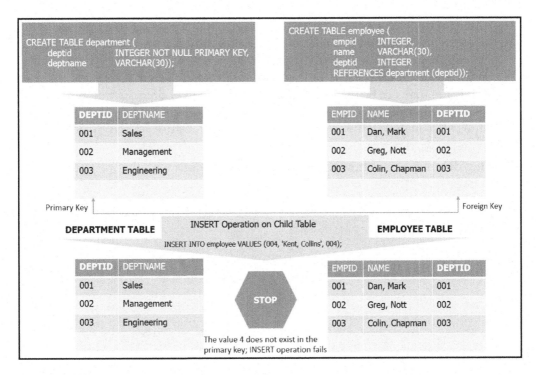

How an INSERT operation is rejected if it violates the INSERT rule of the referential integrity constraint

An unsuccessful `INSERT` statement snippet is shown as follows:

```
INSERT INTO demo.employee VALUES (004, 'Kent, Collins', 004);
SQL0530N The INSERT or UPDATE value of the FOREIGN KEY
"DEMO.EMPLOYEE.SQL171105210910870" is not equal to any value of the parent
key of the parent table.  SQLSTATE=23503
```

The update rule for referential constraints

The update rule controls how the update operations are performed against parent and child tables participating in a referential integrity constraint. There are two possible behaviors that occur with an update rule and they are as follows:

- **ON UPDATE RESTRICT**: This ensures that whenever an update operation is performed on a parent table of a referential integrity constraint, the value for the foreign key of each record in the child table will have the exact same matching value in the primary key of the parent table that it had before the update operation was performed.

- **ON UPDATE NO ACTION**: This ensures that whenever an update operation is performed on either table in a referential integrity constraint, the value of the foreign key of each record in the child table will have a matching value in the primary key of the corresponding parent table. Unlike in ON UPDATE RESTRICT, the value may not be the same as it was before the update operation was performed. If no update rule clause is specified while building the referential integrity constraint, the ON UPDATE NO ACTION clause is used by default.

The following diagram shows how the update rule is imposed with the ON UPDATE RESTRICT clause:

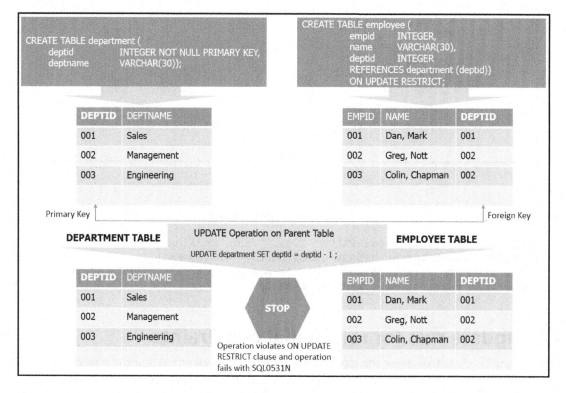

How an update operation is rejected due to the ON UPDATE RESTRICT definition

A failed update operation when the ON UPDATE RESTRICT clause is defined in shown as follows:

```
UPDATE demo.department SET deptid = deptid - 1;
SQL0531N The parent key in a parent row of relationship
"DEMO.EMPLOYEE.SQL171105212154870" cannot be updated.  SQLSTATE=23001
```

The following diagram shows how the update rule is imposed when you use the ON UPDATE NO ACTION clause:

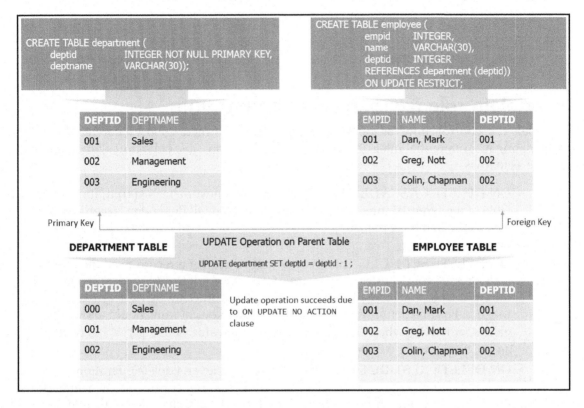

How an update operation succeeds due to the ON UPDATE NO ACTION definition

A successful update operation when the ON UPDATE NO ACTION clause is defined is shown as follows:

```
UPDATE demo.department SET deptid = deptid - 1;
DB20000I  The SQL command completed successfully.

SELECT * FROM demo.department;

DEPTID       DEPTNAME
-----------  -------------------------------
          0  Sales
          1  Management
          2  Engineering
```

```
SELECT * FROM demo.employee;

EMPID        NAME                                      DEPTID
-----------  --------------------------------  ------------
          1 Dan, Mark                                     1
          2 Greg, Nott                                    2
          3 Colin, Chapman                                2
```

The delete rule for referential constraints

The delete rule controls how the delete operations are performed against a parent table participating in a referential integrity constraint. The four possible behaviors with a delete rule are as follows:

- **ON DELETE CASCADE**: This ensures that whenever a record from the parent table of a referential integrity constraint is deleted, all dependent records in the child table that have matching primary key values in their foreign key are deleted as well.
- **ON DELETE SET NULL**: This ensures that whenever a record from the parent table of a referential integrity constraint is deleted, all the dependent records in the child table that have matching primary key values in their foreign key are set to NULL. For this definition to work, the foreign key column should allow NULL values, otherwise when Db2 attempts to set the value of the NOT NULL column, an SQL0629N error will be received.
- **ON DELETE RESTRICT**: This ensures that whenever a delete operation is performed on the parent table of a referential integrity constraint, the value for the foreign key of each row in the child table will have the exact same matching value in the primary key of the parent table that it had before the delete operation was performed.
- **ON DELETE NO ACTION**: This ensures that whenever a record from the parent table of a referential integrity constraint is deleted, the value of the foreign key of each record in the child table will have a matching value in the primary key of the corresponding parent table. Unlike the ON DELETE RESTRICT clause, the value may not be the same as it was before the delete operation was performed. If no delete rule clause is specified while building the referential integrity constraint, the ON DELETE NO ACTION clause is used by default.

The following diagram shows how the delete rule is imposed when you use the ON DELETE CASCADE clause:

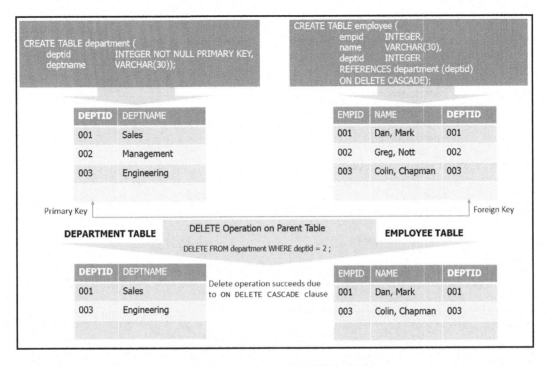

How a delete operation succeeds due to an ON DELETE CASCADE definition

A successful delete operation when the `ON DELETE CASCADE` clause is defined is shown as follows:

```
SELECT * FROM demo.department;

DEPTID        DEPTNAME
-----------   -------------------------------
          1   Sales
          2   Management
          3   Engineering


SELECT * FROM demo.employee;

EMPID         NAME                               DEPTID
-----------   -------------------------------    -----------
          1   Dan, Mark                                    1
          2   Greg, Nott                                   2
          3   Colin, Chapman                               3
```

```
DELETE FROM demo.department WHERE deptid = 2;
DB20000I  The SQL command completed successfully.

SELECT * FROM demo.department;

DEPTID      DEPTNAME
----------- ---------------------------------
          1 Sales
          3 Engineering

SELECT * FROM demo.employee;

EMPID       NAME                              DEPTID
----------- --------------------------------- -----------
          1 Dan, Mark                                   1
          3 Colin, Chapman                              3
```

The following diagram shows how the delete rule is imposed when you use the ON DELETE SET NULL clause:

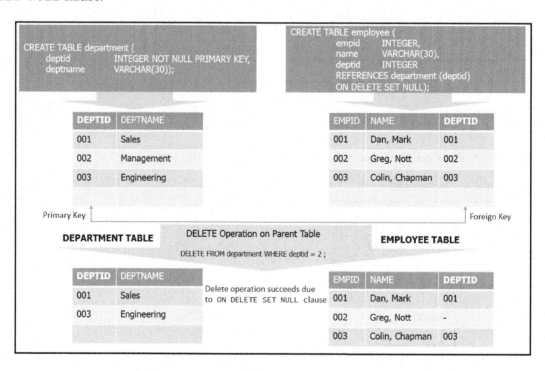

How a delete operation succeeds due to an ON DELETE SET NULL definition

A successful delete operation when the ON DELETE SET NULL clause is defined is shown as follows:

```
SELECT * FROM demo.department;

DEPTID      DEPTNAME
----------- ------------------------------
          1 Sales
          2 Management
          3 Engineering

SELECT * FROM demo.employee;

EMPID       NAME                            DEPTID
----------- ------------------------------- ------------
          1 Dan, Mark                                 1
          2 Greg, Nott                                2
          3 Colin, Chapman                            3

DELETE FROM demo.department WHERE deptid = 2;
DB20000I  The SQL command completed successfully.

SELECT * FROM demo.department;

DEPTID      DEPTNAME
----------- ------------------------------
          1 Sales
          3 Engineering

SELECT * FROM demo.employee;

EMPID       NAME                            DEPTID
----------- ------------------------------- ------------
          1 Dan, Mark                                 1
          2 Greg, Nott                                -
          3 Colin, Chapman                            3
```

The following diagram shows how the delete rule is imposed when the ON DELETE SET RESTRICT clause is defined:

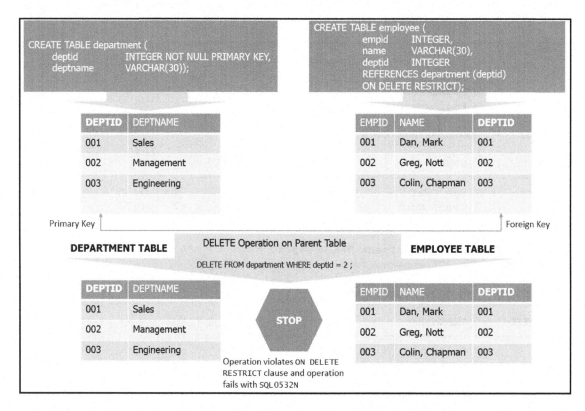

How a delete operation fails due to the ON DELETE RESTRICT definition

An unsuccessful delete operation when the ON DELETE RESTRICT clause is defined is shown as follows:

```
SELECT * FROM demo.department;

DEPTID       DEPTNAME
------------ -------------------------------
           1 Sales
           2 Management
           3 Engineering

SELECT * FROM demo.employee;

EMPID        NAME                            DEPTID
```

```
----------- ------------------------------ -----------
          1 Dan, Mark                                 1
          2 Greg, Nott                                2
          3 Colin, Chapman                            3
```

```
DELETE FROM department WHERE deptid = 2;
SQL0532N A parent row cannot be deleted because the relationship
"DEMO.EMPLOYEE.SQL171111120757110" restricts the deletion.  SQLSTATE=23001
```

The following diagram shows how the delete rule is imposed when the ON DELETE NO ACTION clause is defined:

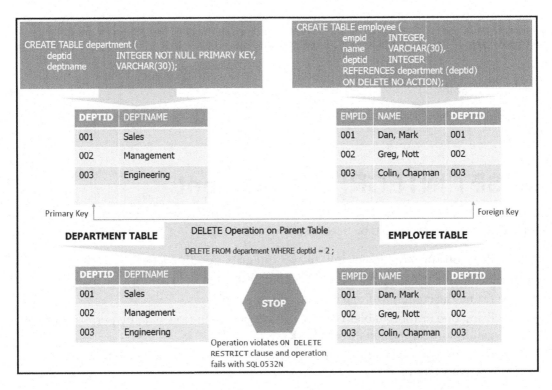

How a delete operation fails due to the ON DELETE NO ACTION definition

An unsuccessful delete operation when the ON DELETE NO ACTION clause is defined is shown as follows:

```
SELECT * FROM demo.department;

DEPTID      DEPTNAME
----------- ------------------------------
```

```
                   1 Sales
                   2 Management
                   3 Engineering

SELECT * FROM demo.employee;

EMPID          NAME                                DEPTID
-----------    --------------------------------    -----------
           1 Dan, Mark                                       1
           2 Greg, Nott                                      2
           3 Colin, Chapman                                  3

DELETE FROM department WHERE deptid = 2;
SQL0532N A parent row cannot be deleted because the relationship
"DEMO.EMPLOYEE.SQL171111121724840" restricts the deletion.  SQLSTATE=23504
```

 Referential integrity constraints are not supported on column-organized tables.

The SET INTEGRITY statement

The SET INTEGRITY statement can be used to temporarily suspend constraint checking on a table. This statement can also be used to perform the following operations:

- Place one or more tables into the set integrity pending state
- Place one or more tables into the full access state
- Prune the contents of one of more staging tables
- Bring one or more tables out of a set integrity pending state by performing data validation via the constraint check
- Bring one or more tables out of a set integrity pending state without performing data validation

The basic syntax for the SET INTEGRITY statement is:

```
SET INTEGRITY FOR [TableName] [OFF | FULL ACCESS | PRUNE] | [IMMEDIATE
CHECKED | IMMEDIATE UNCHECKED] <AccessMode>
```

In the preceding statement, the following applies:

- **TableName**: Identifies the name of one table on which to perform an integrity check or suspend the integrity check.
- **AccessMode**: Identifies whether the specified table can be accessed in read-only mode while checking the data's integrity. The valid options are READ ACCESS and NO ACCESS.

If you want to suspend the data integrity check on the EMPLOYEE table, you can do so by executing the following statement:

```
SET INTEGRITY FOR demo.employee OFF;
```

The preceding statement places the EMPLOYEE table into CHECK PENDING state. In this state, any SELECT, INSERT, UPDATE, and DELETE operations on the table will not be allowed. The only operation allowed at this point is the ALTER TABLE statement.

Once the data integrity check has been turned off, you can use the IMMEDIATE CHECK or UNCHECK option to turn on the constraint checking on a table using the following code:

```
SET INTEGRITY FOR demo.employee IMMEDIATE CHECKED;
SET INTEGRITY FOR demo.employee IMMEDIATE UNCHECKED;
```

The IMMEDIATE CHECK option enables the data integrity check and performs data validation in a single step. If there is a constraint violation, the integrity check will be cancelled and the table will be placed in the CHECK PENDING state once more. The IMMEDIATE UNCHECKED option enables the data integrity check, but it doesn't perform data validation.

If there are data integrity violations, you may want to place the violating records into a separate table. You can do so by specifying an exception table in the SET INTEGRITY command, which is shown in the following code snippet. This statement also brings the table out of the CHECK PENDING state:

```
CREATE TABLE demo.employee_exception LIKE demo.Employee;
DB20000I  The SQL command completed successfully.

SET INTEGRITY FOR demo.employee IMMEDIATE CHECKED
FOR EXCEPTION IN demo.employee USE demo.employee_exception;
SQL3602W  Check data processing found constraint violations and moved them
to exception tables.  SQLSTATE=01603
```

In the case of a range partition table, the SET INTEGRITY statement must be run before any new partition is brought online after the ALTER TABLE... ATTACH operation. The operations that are performed by the SET INTEGRITY statement on a range partitioned table are as follows:

- To validate the data in the newly added partition to make sure that all the data matches the range defined for the new partition
- To update any generated columns and to check for any constraints that may be on the table
- To update any **materialized query tables** (**MQTs**) that may be defined on the base table
- To update the index keys for the new records

The following example illustrates the use of the SET INTEGRITY statement during the ALTER TABLE... ATTACH operation:

```
-- Create partition table

CREATE TABLE demo.sales
   (sale_date   DATE CHECK (sale_date >= '01/01/2016'),
    sale_amount    NUMERIC (8,2))
PARTITION BY RANGE (sale_date)
   (STARTING '01/01/2016' ENDING '10/31/2017' EVERY 1 MONTH);
DB20000I  The SQL command completed successfully.


--  Create a partition for November 2017

CREATE TABLE demo.sales_112017 (
sale_date    DATE,
   sale_amount    NUMERIC (8,2));
DB20000I  The SQL command completed successfully.

-- Populate a few sample records into new November 2017 table

INSERT INTO demo.sales_112017 VALUES ('11/01/2017', 100000);
DB20000I  The SQL command completed successfully.

INSERT INTO demo.sales_112017 VALUES ('11/02/2017', 60000);
DB20000I  The SQL command completed successfully

-- Attach the table as a new partition

ALTER TABLE demo.sales ATTACH PART "PART37" STARTING ('11/01/2017') ENDING
('11/30/2017') FROM demo.sales_112017;
SQL3601W  The statement caused one or more tables to automatically be
```

```
        placed in the Set Integrity Pending state.   SQLSTATE=01586

        -- Verify the check pending status

        SELECT SUBSTR(RTRIM(TABSCHEMA)||'.'||RTRIM(TABNAME),1,30) AS
        CHECK_PENDING_TABLE FROM syscat.tables WHERE STATUS='C';

        CHECK_PENDING_TABLE
        ------------------------------
        DEMO.SALES

          1 record(s) selected.

        -- Perform the data integrity check

        SET INTEGRITY FOR demo.sales IMMEDIATE CHECKED;
        DB20000I  The SQL command completed successfully.

        -- Verify the check pending status again

        db2 "SELECT SUBSTR(RTRIM(TABSCHEMA)||'.'||RTRIM(TABNAME),1,30) AS
        CHECK_PENDING_TABLE FROM syscat.tables WHERE STATUS='C';

        CHECK_PENDING_TABLE
        ------------------------------

          0 record(s) selected.
```

Views with CHECK OPTION

A view is a way of representing data without the need to store and maintain it. A view is not an actual table and requires no storage. It also provides a different way of looking at the data in one or more base tables.

For example, if you want to restrict users from accessing SSN and SALARY information, you can easily do so by creating a view without these columns and limit the user's access to only the view. An example of this is shown as follows:

```
CREATE TABLE demo.employee (
             empid INTEGER,
             name VARCHAR(30),
              ssn  VARCHAR(11),
             salary INTEGER );

SELECT * FROM demo.employee;
```

EMPID	NAME	SSN	SALARY
1	Robert, Colin	999-99-9999	90000
2	Milan, Mohan	111-11-1111	80000
3	Colin, Chapman	222-22-2222	90000

```
CREATE OR REPLACE VIEW demo.v_employee AS SELECT empid, name FROM
demo.employee;

SELECT * FROM demo.v_employee;
```

EMPID	NAME
1	Robert, Colin
2	Milan, Mohan
3	Colin, Chapman

You can create or replace a view by executing the CREATE or REPLACE VIEW statement, and the basic syntax for this statement is:

```
CREATE OR REPLACE VIEW [ViewName]
<([ColumnName],[ColumnName],..>
AS [SELECTStatement]
<WITH <LOCAL | CASCADE> CHECK OPTION
```

Where,

- **ViewName**: Identifies the name to be assign to the view which is going to be created
- **ColumnName**: Identifies the names of one or more columns which are going to be in the view that is being created; if a list of column names is specified, the number of column names provided must match the number of columns that will be returned by the SELECT statement used to create the view
- **SELECTStatement**: Identifies a SELECT SQL statement that, when executed, will produce data that will populate the view

If you want to create a view that references only a SALARY over 6,000 in the EMPLOYEE table, you can do so by creating a view, which is shown as follows:

```
CREATE VIEW demo.v_employee AS SELECT * FROM demo.employee WHERE SALARY >
6000;
```

If you specify `WITH LOCAL CHECK OPTION` in the view definition, the `INSERT` and `UPDATE` operations performed against the view are validated to ensure that all the records being inserted into or updated in the base table the view refers to conforms to the view's definition. The following diagram shows how the `INSERT` operation works when 2 `LOCAL CHECK OPTION` is defined on a view:

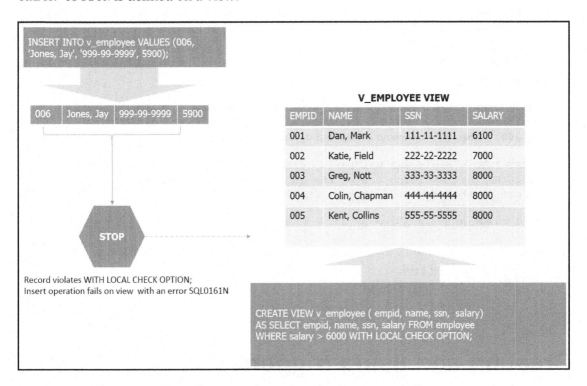

How an INSERT operation fails due to the LOCAL CHECK OPTION definition

However, since the check option is only applied to the view, you can insert the same record into the base table `EMPLOYEE` without errors. The example is shown as follows:

```
CREATE VIEW demo.v_employee ( empid, name, ssn,  salary)
AS SELECT empid, name, ssn, salary FROM demo.employee
WHERE salary > 6000 WITH LOCAL CHECK OPTION;
DB20000I  The SQL command completed successfully.

INSERT INTO demo.v_employee VALUES
(006, 'Jones, Jay', '999-99-9999', 5900);
SQL0161N  The resulting row of the INSERT or UPDATE operation does not
conform to the view definition.  SQLSTATE=44000
```

```
-- Record insertion into the base table EMPLOYEE

INSERT INTO demo.employee VALUES
(006, 'Jones, Jay', '999-99-9999', 5900);
DB20000I  The SQL command completed successfully.
```

A second option that can be used to create a view is the WITH CASCADED CHECK OPTION. If you specify this option, the newly created view will inherit the check condition of the parent view. For example, if you create a view v_employee2 on v_employee using the WITH CASCADED CHECK OPTION, it will inherit the CHECK condition SALARY > 6000 from the view v_employee:

```
CREATE VIEW v_employee2 ( empid, name, ssn,  salary)  AS SELECT empid,
name, ssn,  salary  FROM v_employee WITH CASCADED CHECK OPTION;
DB20000I  The SQL command completed successfully.

INSERT INTO v_employee2 VALUES (7,'Jones, Jay', '999-99-9999', 5500);
SQL0161N  The resulting row of the INSERT or UPDATE operation does not
conform to the view definition.  SQLSTATE=44000
```

The SELECT operation will also exhibit the exact same behavior as the INSERT operation.

> The views with the CHECK OPTION are not supported on column-organized tables.

Creating and using triggers

A trigger is a database object that can perform a set of actions in response to events such as an INSERT, UPDATE, or DELETE operation on a specified table or view. You can use triggers, along with referential constraints and CHECK constraints, to enforce data integrity rules.

Five major components are associated with any trigger:

- The subject on which the trigger is defined–tables or views
- The event which initiates the trigger–an INSERT, UPDATE, or DELETE operation
- The activation time of the trigger–a BEFORE or AFTER the event
- The granularity which specifies whether the trigger's actions are performed once for the statement or once for each of the affected rows–a FOR EACH STATEMENT or FOR EACH ROW action

- The action, which the trigger performs–one or more of the following elements:
    1. CALL statement
    2. DECLARE and/or SET variable statement
    3. WHILE and/or FOR loop
    4. IF, SIGNAL, ITERATE, LEAVE, and GET DIAGNOSTIC statements
    5. SELECT SQL statement
    6. INSERT, UPDATE, DELETE, and MERGE SQL statements (only for AFTER and INSTEAD OF triggers)

In Db2, triggers are classified as BEFORE, AFTER, or INSTEAD OF:

- **BEFORE** triggers are activated before an update or INSERT operation, and the values that are being updated or inserted can be changed before the database data is modified in the table. Generally, this trigger is used for data cleansing and modification.
- **AFTER** triggers are activated after an INSERT, UPDATE, or DELETE operation and are used to maintain relationships between data or to keep audit trail information.
- **INSTEAD OF** triggers define how to perform an INSERT, UPDATE, or DELETE operation on a view where these operations are otherwise not allowed.

Triggers can be created or replaced (if already present) by executing the CREATE or REPLACE TRIGGER SQL statement. The basic syntax for this statement is:

```
CREATE OR REPLACE TRIGGER [TriggerName]
<NO CASCADE>|<AFTER | BEFORE | INSTEAD OF> [TriggerEvent]
ON [TableName |ViewName]
REFERENCING <OLD AS | NEW AS | OLD TABLE AS | NEW TABLE AS>
[CorrelationName |Identifier]
<FOR EACH ROW | FOR EACH STATEMENT>
<Action>
```

Where,

- TriggerName: Identifies the name to assign to the trigger to be created
- TriggerEvent: Specifies that the triggered action associated with the trigger is to be executed whenever one of the events is applied to the subject table or subject view
- TableName: Identifies the name of the table (subject) on which the trigger is defined

- `ViewName`: Identifies the name of the view (subject) on which the trigger is defined
- `CorrelationName`: Specifies a correlation name that identifies the row state before triggering the SQL operation
- `Identifier`: Specifies a temporary table name that identifies the set of affected rows before triggering the SQL operation
- `Action`: Specifies the action to perform when a trigger is activated; a triggered action is composed of an SQL procedure statement and an optional condition for the execution of the SQL procedure statement

The following example illustrates a `BEFORE` trigger that is activated when an `INSERT` statement is executed on the `EMPLOYEE` table. The trigger `EMPLOYEEJOINDATE` assigns a value of the next day when it detects a `NULL` being inserted into the `EMPSTARTDATE` column of the `EMPLOYEE` table:

```
CREATE OR REPLACE TRIGGER employeeJoinDate
NO CASCADE BEFORE INSERT ON employee
REFERENCING NEW AS N
FOR EACH ROW
MODE DB2SQL
WHEN (N.EMPSTARTDATE IS NULL)
SET N.EMPSTARTDATE = CURRENT DATE + 1 DAY
```

In the following example, an `AFTER` trigger is activated when an `INSERT` statement is executed on the `EMPLOYEE` table. If the row being inserted into the `EMPLOYEE` table is due to a new hire, the trigger statement will update the employee head count in the company statistics table `COMPANY_STATS`:

```
CREATE OR REPLACE TRIGGER employeeNewHire
    NO CASCADE AFTER INSERT ON employee
    FOR EACH ROW
    MODE DB2SQL
    UPDATE COMPANY_STATS SET EMP_TCOUNT = EMP_TCOUNT + 1;
```

Consider an example where the HR department wants to check for an employee pay rise before the salary change is made in the `EMPLOYEE` table. For any employee, if the pay rise is double the current salary, it must be recorded in the `SALARY_AUDIT` table for analysis purposes. An `AFTER` trigger can be created to insert the appropriate data into the `SALARY_AUDIT` table:

```
CREATE OR REPLACE TRIGGER employeeSalaryUpdate
AFTER UPDATE OF salary ON employee
REFERENCING NEW AS N OLD AS O
```

```
FOR EACH ROW
MODE DB2SQL
WHEN (N.SALARY > O.SALARY * 2)
  INSERT INTO SALARY_AUDIT
         (EMPNO, OLD_SALARY, NEW_SALARY, RATING) VALUES
            (N.EMPID, O.SALARY, N.SALARY, N.RATING);
```

Triggers can also be used to raise errors through the SIGNAL statement and to prevent specific operations on the tables. For example, if there is an HR department rule that no pay rise can exceed 300 percent, you can create a trigger that will check for this condition. It would look something like this:

```
CREATE TRIGGER salaryRaiseLimit
AFTER UPDATE OF SALARY ON EMPLOYEE
REFERENCING NEW AS N OLD AS O
FOR EACH ROW
WHEN (N.SALARY > O.SALARY * 3)
SIGNAL SQLSTATE '75000' SET MESSAGE_TEXT='Salary increase>300%'
DB20000I  The SQL command completed successfully.

UPDATE employee SET SALARY=400000 WHERE EMPID=2;
SQL0438N  Application raised error or warning with diagnostic text: "Salary
increase>300%". SQLSTATE=75000
```

When you use an INSTEAD OF trigger, the requested modified operation against the view is replaced by the trigger logic, which performs the operation on behalf of the view. From the application's perspective, this happens transparently, since all operations are performed against the view. Only one INSTEAD OF trigger is allowed for each kind of operation on a given subject view.

The following listed example illustrates the INSTEAD OF trigger behaviour:

```
CREATE TABLE demo.employee (
                empid INTEGER,
                name VARCHAR(30),
                 ssn  VARCHAR(11),
                salary INTEGER );
DB20000I  The SQL command completed successfully.
ALTER TABLE demo.employee ADD CONSTRAINT check_salary CHECK
                (SALARY >= 5000)
        ENFORCED
        ENABLE QUERY OPTIMIZATION;
DB20000I  The SQL command completed successfully.

CREATE VIEW demo.v_emp AS SELECT empid, name, ssn, salary FROM
demo.employee;
```

```
DB20000I   The SQL command completed successfully.

CREATE TRIGGER InsteadOfTriger
INSTEAD OF INSERT ON demo.v_emp
      REFERENCING NEW AS N
   FOR EACH ROW
INSERT INTO demo.employee ( empid, name, ssn, salary) VALUES ( empid, name,
ssn, salary);
DB20000I   The SQL command completed successfully.

INSERT INTO demo.v_emp VALUES (1,'Robert, Colin', '999-99-9999', 90000);
DB20000I   The SQL command completed successfully.

SELECT * FROM demo.employee;

EMPID        NAME                                SSN           SALARY
------------ ----------------------------- ------------ ------------
          1 Robert, Colin                 999-99-9999        90000

   1 record(s) selected.

INSERT INTO demo.v_emp VALUES (2,'Milan, Mohan', '111-11-1111', 4000);
SQL0723N   An error occurred in a triggered SQL statement in trigger
"DEMO.INSTEADOFTRIGER".   Information returned for the error includes
SQLCODE "-545", SQLSTATE "23513" and message tokens
"DEMO.EMPLOYEE.CHECK_SALARY".   SQLSTATE=09000
```

A trigger definition cannot be directly modified when there is a need to change the trigger code. The CREATE or REPLACE statement can be used to update the trigger. This statement will internally drop and then recreate the trigger. In addition, you can explicitly drop the trigger by using the DROP TRIGGER command and create it by using the CREATE TRIGGER statement.

Triggers are not supported on column-organized tables.

The system catalog views

The system catalog consists of a set of special SYSIBM schema tables and special SYSCAT views (these are built on SYSIBM base special tables) which include information about all the objects within a database. These tables contain information about the logical and physical structure of the database objects and security information including the type of access that users have to access these objects.

Understanding the system catalog tables and views is essential to effectively administer and maintain the database. The following table shows the available system catalog views and the information each provides:

System Catalog View	Description
SYSCAT.ATTRIBUTE	Provides information about user-defined structured data types.
SYSCAT.AUDITPOLICIES	Provides information about an audit policy.
SYSCAT.AUDITUSE	Provides information about an audit policy that is associated with an object.
SYSCAT.BUFFERPOOLDBPARTITIONS	Provides information about buffer pools and members, in which the size of the buffer pool on that database partition member is different from its default size for other database partition members in the same database partition group.
SYSCAT.BUFFERPOOLS	Provides information about all the buffer pools.
SYSCAT.CASTFUNCTIONS	Provides information about cast functions.
SYSCAT.CHECKS	Provides information about check constraints.
SYSCAT.COLAUTH	Provides information about a user, group, or role that has been granted one or more privileges on a column.
SYSCAT.COLCHECKS	Provides information about a column that is referenced by a check constraint or by the definition of a materialized query table.

SYSCAT.COLDIST	Provides information about the nth most frequent value of some column, or the nth quantile (cumulative distribution) value of the column.
SYSCAT.COLGROUPCOLS	Provides information about a column that makes up a column group.
SYSCAT.COLGROUPDIST	Provides information about the value of the column in a column group that makes up the nth most frequent value of the column group or the nth quantile value of the column group.
SYSCAT.COLGROUPDISTCOUNTS	Provides information about the distribution statistics that apply to the nth most frequent value of a column group or the nth quantile of a column group.
SYSCAT.COLGROUPS	Provides information about a column group and statistics that apply to the entire column group.
SYSCAT.COLIDENTATTRIBUTES	Provides information about an identity column that is defined for a table.
SYSCAT.COLOPTIONS	Provides information about column-specific option values.
SYSCAT.COLUMNS	Provides information about a column defined for a table, view, or nickname.
SYSCAT.COLUSE	Provides information about a column that is referenced in the DIMENSIONS clause of a CREATE TABLE statement.
SYSCAT.CONDITIONS	Provides information about a condition defined in a module.
SYSCAT.CONSTDEP	Provides information about a dependency of a constraint on some other object.
SYSCAT.CONTEXTATTRIBUTES	Provides information about a trusted context attribute.
SYSCAT.CONTEXTS	Provides information about a trusted context.

SYSCAT.CONTROLDEP	Provides information about a dependency of a row permission or column mask on some other object.
SYSCAT.CONTROLS	Provides information about a row permission or column mask.
SYSCAT.DATAPARTITIONEXPRESSION	Provides information about an expression for that part of the table partitioning key.
SYSCAT.DATAPARTITIONS	Provides information about a data partition. Note that the data partition statistics represent one database partition if the table is created on multiple database partitions.
SYSCAT.DATATYPEDEP	Provides information about a dependency of a user-defined data type on some other object.
SYSCAT.DATATYPES	Provides information about a built-in or user-defined data type.
SYSCAT.DBAUTH	Provides information about a user, group, or role that has been granted one or more database-level authorities.
SYSCAT.DBPARTITIONGROUPDEF	Provides information about a database partition that is contained in a database partition group.
SYSCAT.DBPARTITIONGROUPS	Provides information about a database partition group.
SYSCAT.EVENTMONITORS	Provides information about an event monitor.
SYSCAT.EVENTS	Provides information about an event that is being monitored.
SYSCAT.EVENTTABLES	Provides information about the target table of an event monitor that writes to SQL tables.
SYSCAT.FULLHIERARCHIES	Provides information about the relationship between a subtable and a supertable, a subtype and a supertype, or a subview and a superview. All hierarchical relationships, including immediate ones, are included in this view.

SYSCAT.FUNCMAPOPTIONS	Provides information about a function mapping option value.
SYSCAT.FUNCMAPPARMOPTIONS	Provides information about a function mapping parameter option value.
SYSCAT.FUNCMAPPINGS	Provides information about function mapping
SYSCAT.HIERARCHIES	Provides information about the relationship between a subtable and its immediate supertable, a subtype and its immediate supertype, or a subview and its immediate superview. Only immediate hierarchical relationships are included in this view.
SYSCAT.HISTOGRAMTEMPLATEBINS	Provides information about a histogram template bin.
SYSCAT.HISTOGRAMTEMPLATES	Provides information about a histogram template.
SYSCAT.HISTOGRAMTEMPLATEUSE	Provides information about a relationship between a workload management object that can use histogram templates and a histogram temp.
SYSCAT.INDEXAUTH	Provides information about a user, group, or role that has been granted CONTROL privilege on an index.
SYSCAT.INDEXCOLUSE	Provides information about a column that participates in an index.
SYSCAT.INDEXDEP	Provides information about a dependency of an index on some other object.
SYSCAT.INDEXES	Provides information about an index.
SYSCAT.INDEXEXPLOITRULES	Provides information about an index exploitation rule.
SYSCAT.INDEXEXTENSIONDEP	Provides information about a dependency of an index extension on some other object.
SYSCAT.INDEXEXTENSIONMETHODS	Provides information about a search method.

SYSCAT.INDEXEXTENSIONPARMS	Provides information about an index extension instance parameter or source key column.
SYSCAT.INDEXEXTENSIONS	Provides information about an index extension.
SYSCAT.INDEXOPTIONS	Provides information about an index-specific option value.
SYSCAT.INDEXPARTITIONS	Provides information about a partitioned index piece located on one data partition.
SYSCAT.INDEXXMLPATTERNS	Provides information about a pattern clause in an index over an XML column.
SYSCAT.INVALIDOBJECTS	Provides information about an invalid object.
SYSCAT.KEYCOLUSE	Provides information about a column that participates in a key defined by a unique key, primary key, or foreign key constraint.
SYSCAT.MEMBERSUBSETATTRS	Provides information about a member subset attribute.
SYSCAT.MEMBERSUBSETMEMBERS	Provides information about a member that is associated with a member subset.
SYSCAT.MEMBERSUBSETS	Provides information about a member subset.
SYSCAT.MODULEAUTH	Provides information about a user, group, or role that has been granted a privilege on a module.
SYSCAT.MODULEOBJECTS	Provides information about a function, procedure, global variable, condition, or user-defined type that belongs to a module.
SYSCAT.MODULES	Provides information about a module.
SYSCAT.NAMEMAPPINGS	Provides information about the mapping between a logical object and the corresponding implementation object that implements the logical object.
SYSCAT.NICKNAMES	Provides information about a nickname.

`SYSCAT.PACKAGEAUTH`	Provides information about a user, group, or role that has been granted one or more privileges on a package.
`SYSCAT.PACKAGEDEP`	Provides information about a dependency of a package on some other object.
`SYSCAT.PACKAGES`	Provides information about a package that has been created by binding an application program.
`SYSCAT.PARTITIONMAPS`	Provides information about a distribution map that is used to distribute the rows of a table among the database partitions in a database partition group, based on hashing the table's distribution.
`SYSCAT.PASSTHRUAUTH`	Provides information about a user, group, or role that has been granted pass-through authorization to query a data source.
`SYSCAT.PERIODS`	Provides information about the definition of a period for use with a temporal table.
`SYSCAT.PREDICATESPECS`	Provides information about a predicate specification.
`SYSCAT.REFERENCES`	Provides information about a referential integrity (foreign key) constraint.
`SYSCAT.ROLEAUTH`	Provides information about a role granted to a user, group, role, or public.
`SYSCAT.ROLES`	Provides information about a role.
`SYSCAT.ROUTINEAUTH`	Provides information about a user, group, or role that has been granted an `EXECUTE` privilege on either a routine in the database that is not defined in a module or all routines in a schema in the database that are not defined in a module.
`SYSCAT.ROUTINEDEP`	Provides information about a dependency of a routine on some other object.
`SYSCAT.ROUTINEOPTIONS`	Provides information about a routine-specific option value.
`SYSCAT.ROUTINEPARMOPTIONS`	Provides information about a routine parameter-specific option value.

`SYSCAT.ROUTINEPARMS`	Provides information about a parameter, an aggregation state variable, or the result of a routine defined in `SYSCAT.ROUTINES`.
`SYSCAT.ROUTINES`	Provides information about a user-defined routine (scalar function, table function, sourced function, aggregate interface function, method, or procedure).
`SYSCAT.ROUTINESFEDERATED`	Provides information about a federated procedure.
`SYSCAT.ROWFIELDS`	Provides information about a field that is defined for a user-defined row data type.
`SYSCAT.SCHEMAAUTH`	Provides information about a user, group, or role that has been granted one or more privileges on a schema.
`SYSCAT.SCHEMATA`	Provides information about a schema.
`SYSCAT.SCPREFTBSPACES`	Provides information about preferred system temporary table space for the service class.
`SYSCAT.SECURITYLABELACCESS`	Provides information about a security label that was granted to the database authorization ID.
`SYSCAT.SECURITYLABELCOMPONENTELEMENTS`	Provides information about an element value for a security label component.
`SYSCAT.SECURITYLABELCOMPONENTS`	Provides information about a security label component.
`SYSCAT.SECURITYLABELS`	Provides information about a security label.
`SYSCAT.SECURITYPOLICIES`	Provides information about a security policy.
`SYSCAT.SECURITYPOLICYCOMPONENTRULES`	Provides information about the read and write access rules for a security label component of the security policy.
`SYSCAT.SECURITYPOLICYEXEMPTIONS`	Provides information about a security policy exemption that was granted to a database authorization ID.

`SYSCAT.SEQUENCEAUTH`	Provides information about a user, group, or role that has been granted one or more privileges on a sequence.
`SYSCAT.SEQUENCES`	Provides information about a sequence or alias.
`SYSCAT.SERVEROPTIONS`	Provides information about a server-specific option value.
`SYSCAT.SERVERS`	Provides information about a data source.
`SYSCAT.SERVICECLASSES`	Provides information about a service class.
`SYSCAT.STATEMENTS`	Provides information about an SQL statement in a package.
`SYSCAT.STOGROUPS`	Provides information about a storage group object.
`SYSCAT.STATEMENTTEXTS`	Provides information about a user-provided SQL statement for statement thresholds.
`SYSCAT.SURROGATEAUTHIDS`	Provides information about a user or a group that has been granted a `SETSESSIONUSER` privilege on a user or public.
`SYSCAT.TABAUTH`	Provides information about a user, group, or role that has been granted one or more privileges on a table or view.
`SYSCAT.TABCONST`	Provides information about a table constraint of type `CHECK`, `UNIQUE`, `PRIMARY KEY`, or `FOREIGN KEY`.
`SYSCAT.TABDETACHEDDEP`	Provides information about a detached dependency between a detached dependent table and a detached table.
`SYSCAT.TABLES`	Provides information about a table, view, alias, or nickname.
`SYSCAT.TABLESPACES`	Provides information about a table space.
`SYSCAT.TABOPTIONS`	Provides information about an option that is associated with a remote table.
`SYSCAT.TBSPACEAUTH`	Provides information about a user, group, or role that has been granted the `USE` privilege on a table space in the database.

SYSCAT.THRESHOLDS	Provides information about a threshold.
SYSCAT.TRANSFORMS	Provides information about the functions that handle transformations between a user-defined type and a base SQL type, or the reverse.
SYSCAT.TRIGDEP	Provides information about the dependency of a trigger on some other object.
SYSCAT.TRIGGERS	Provides information about a trigger.
SYSCAT.TYPEMAPPINGS	Provides information about the data type mapping between a locally-defined data type and a data source data type.
SYSCAT.USAGELISTS	Provides information about a usage list for a table or index object.
SYSCAT.USEROPTIONS	Provides information about a server-specific user option value.
SYSCAT.VARIABLEAUTH	Provides information about a user, group, or role that has been granted one or more privileges by a specific granter on a global variable in the database that is not defined in a module.
SYSCAT.VARIABLEDEP	Provides information about a dependency of a global variable on some other object.
SYSCAT.VARIABLES	Provides information about a global variable.
SYSCAT.VIEWS	Provides information about a view or materialized query table.
SYSCAT.WORKACTIONS	Provides information about a work action that is defined for a work action set.
SYSCAT.WORKACTIONSETS	Provides information about a work action set.
SYSCAT.WORKCLASSATTRIBUTES	Provides information about an attribute in the definition of a work class.
SYSCAT.WORKCLASSES	Provides information about a work class defined for a work class set.
SYSCAT.WORKCLASSSETS	Provides information about a work class set.

SYSCAT.WORKLOADAUTH	Provides information about a user, group, or role that has been granted the USAGE privilege on a workload.
SYSCAT.WORKLOADCONNATTR	Provides information about a connection attribute in the definition of a workload.
SYSCAT.WORKLOADS	Provides information about a workload.
SYSCAT.WRAPOPTIONS	Provides information about a wrapper-specific option.
SYSCAT.WRAPPERS	Provides information about a registered wrapper.
SYSCAT.XDBMAPGRAPHS	Provides information about a schema graph for an XDB map.
SYSCAT.XDBMAPSHREDTREES	Provides information about a shred tree for a given schema graph identifier.
SYSCAT.XMLSTRINGS	Provides information about a single string and its unique string ID, used to condense structural XML data.
SYSCAT.XSROBJECTAUTH	Provides information about a user, group, or role that has been granted the USAGE privilege on an XSR object.
SYSCAT.XSROBJECTCOMPONENTS	Provides information about an XSR object component.
SYSCAT.XSROBJECTDEP	Provides information about a dependency of an XSR object on some other object.
SYSCAT.XSROBJECTDETAILS	Provides information about an XML schema repository object.
SYSCAT.XSROBJECTHIERARCHIES	Provides information about a hierarchical relationship between an XSR object and its components.
SYSCAT.XSROBJECTS	Provides information about an XML schema repository object.
SYSIBM.SYSDUMMY1	This is a special in-memory table containing only one record.

These tables can be used either to extract the information about an object or to extract the data definition for an object. For example, if you want to extract CHECK constraint information, you can do so by querying the SYSIBM.CHECK_CONSTRAINTS system catalog base table as follows:

```
SELECT
VARCHAR (CONSTRAINT_CATALOG, 10) CONSTRAINT_CATALOG,
VARCHAR (CONSTRAINT_NAME, 30) CONSTRAINT_NAME,
VARCHAR (CHECK_CLAUSE, 40) CHECK_CLAUSE
FROM SYSIBM.CHECK_CONSTRAINTS;
```

If you want to find referential constraint information for a specific table, you can do so by querying the SYSCAT.REFERENCES and SYSCAT.TABCONST system catalog table views as follows:

```
SELECT
VARCHAR (CONSTNAME, 20) CONSTNAME,
VARCHAR (TABNAME, 10) TABNAME,
VARCHAR (REFKEYNAME, 20) REFKEYNAME,
VARCHAR (REFTABNAME, 10) REFTABNAME,
COLCOUNT,
UPDATERULE,
DELETERULE,
VARCHAR (FK_COLNAMES, 7) FK_COLNAMES,
VARCHAR (PK_COLNAMES, 7) PK_COLNAMES
FROM SYSCAT.REFERENCES;

SELECT
VARCHAR (CONSTNAME, 25) CONSTNAME,
VARCHAR (TABNAME, 10) TABNAME,
TYPE,
ENFORCED,
ENABLEQUERYOPT
FROM SYSCAT.TABCONST
WHERE TABNAME IN ('EMPLOYEE', 'DEPARTMENT');
```

If you want to find the trigger definition, you can do so by querying the SYSCAT.TRIGGERS system catalog table view as follows:

```
SELECT
VARCHAR (TRIGNAME, 20) TRIGNAME,
VARCHAR (TEXT, 400) TEXT
FROM SYSCAT.TRIGGERS WHERE TRIGNAME='EMPLOYEEJOINDATE';
```

Summary

The objective of this chapter was to provide sufficient knowledge to answer the server management questions on the following topics:

- The different constraints available within Db2 and their implementation aspects
- The SET INTEGRITY statement and the exception table to copy the constraint violated data
- The types of triggers and the implementation aspects of each one
- The different check options available within Db2 and their implementation aspects
- System catalog tables and how to find the information you might need in them

Practice questions

Question 1

Which statement regarding the CHECK constraint is TRUE?

1. The CHECK constraint is supported in both row-organized and column-organized tables.
2. A table can have only one CHECK constraint defined.
3. When there are some rows that do not meet the CHECK constraint, the CHECK constraint can still be created.
4. The ALTER TABLE statement can be used to define a CHECK constraint on an existing table.

Question 2

What are NOT ENFORCED informational constraints used for?

1. To influence the Db2 optimizer data access plan during referential integrity constraint enforcement.
2. To influence the Db2 optimizer data access plan for the SELECT operation without impacting the INSERT and UPDATE operations.
3. To influence the Db2 optimizer to use the primary key index during the SELECT operation.
4. To influence the Db2 optimizer to always cache the data in the buffer pool for faster access.

Question 3

Consider the following SQL statements:

```
CREATE TABLE department (
    deptid     INT NOT NULL PRIMARY KEY,
    deptname VARCHAR (10));

CREATE TABLE employee (
    empid      INT,
    name       VARCHAR(20),
    deptid     INT);

ALTER TABLE employee ADD CONSTRAINT fk_emp_dept
    FOREIGN KEY (deptid) REFERENCES department (deptid)
    ON UPDATE RESTRICT;

INSERT INTO department VALUES (1, 'Research'), (2, 'Finance'),(3, 'Sales');

INSERT INTO employee VALUES (1, 'Milan, Mohan', 3);

UPDATE department SET deptid = deptid + 1;
```

What will be the result of using an UPDATE statement?

1. The UPDATE operation will fail.
2. The UPDATE operation will succeed.
3. The UPDATE operation will place both the DEPARTMENT and EMPLOYEE tables into the CHECK PENDING state.
4. The UPDATE operation will place the DEPARTMENT table into the CHECK PENDING state.

Question 4

Consider the following SQL statements:

```
CREATE TABLE employee (
    empid      INT NOT NULL PRIMARY KEY,
    empname    VARCHAR(20) NOT NULL,
    deptid     INT NOT NULL,
    salary     INT NOT NULL CHECK (salary >=5000),
    job        VARCHAR(10) CHECK (JOB in ('Engineer','Sales','Manager')));
```

How many constraints are defined in the EMPLOYEE table?

    1. 5
    2. 6
    3. 7
    4. 8

Question 5

Which statement about the primary key is TRUE?

1. A table can have more than one primary key defined.
2. A primary key accepts one, and only one, NULL value.
3. A unique index, with matching columns of the primary key, must be created before a primary key can be created.
4. A unique bidirectional index is automatically created for the columns of the primary key, if an appropriate unique index does not already exist.

Question 6

Which statements about SET INTEGRITY are TRUE? (Choose two)

1. It prunes the contents of one of more staging tables.
2. It places the table in the LOAD PENDING state.
3. It places one or more tables in the SET INTEGRITY pending state.
4. It places the table in the REORG pending state.
5. It places the table space in the BACKUP pending state.

Question 7

Consider the following SQL statements:

```
CREATE TABLE employee (
    empid       INT NOT NULL,
    empname     VARCHAR(20) NOT NULL,
    salary      INT NOT NULL);

CREATE VIEW v1_employee AS SELECT * FROM employee WHERE salary > 5000;

CREATE VIEW v2_employee AS SELECT * FROM v1_employee WHERE salary < 8000
WITH CHECK OPTION;

CREATE VIEW v3_employee AS SELECY * FROM v2_employee WHERE salary < 10000;
```

```
INSERT INTO v3_employee VALUES (1, 'Milan, Mohan', 11000);
```

What will be the result of using an INSERT statement?

    1. The INSERT operation will fail due to the v3_employee definition.

    2. The INSERT operation will fail due to the v2_employee definition.

    3. The INSERT operation will succeed.

    4. The INSERT operation will place the EMPLOYEE tables into CHECK PENDING state.

Question 8

What are the valid types of CHECK OPTIONS in Db2? (Choose two)

    1. WITH LOCAL CHECK OPTION.

    2. WITH REMOTE CHECK OPTION.

    3. WITH CASCADED CHECK OPTION.

    4. WITH SERVER CHECK OPTION.

    5. WITH CLIENT CHECK OPTION.

Question 9

Which trigger activation times are invalid?

    1. The AFTER trigger.

    2. The BEFORE trigger.

    3. The INSTEAD OF trigger.

    4. The RUNTIME trigger.

Question 10

What are the components of trigger definition? (Choose two)

    1. Event.

    2. Time zone.

    3. Locale.

    4. Action.

    5. Duration.

Answers

Question 1

The correct answer is **4**:

- The CHECK constraint is not support in a column-organized table. However, a NOT ENFORCED CHECK constraint is supported to enable query optimization.
- A table can have multiple CHECK constraints defined.
- When there are some rows that do not meet the CHECK constraint, the CHECK constraint will fail with an SQL0544N error.
- The ALTER TABLE statement can be used to define a CHECK constraint on an existing table. A sample ALTER TABLE statement is shown as follows:

```
ALTER TABLE demo.employee ADD CONSTRAINT check_salary CHECK (salary >=5000)
ADD CONSTRAINT check_job CHECK (JOB in ('Engineer','Sales','Manager'));
```

Question 2

The correct answer is **2**.

Unlike other constraints, information constraints are not enforced during the INSERT, UPDATE operation. However, the Db2 optimizer will evaluate the information provided by the information constraint so that it can use a best access plan to resolve a query.

Question 3

The correct answer is **1**:

```
CREATE TABLE ABC.department ( deptid              INT NOT NULL PRIMARY KEY,
deptname        VARCHAR (10))
DB20000I   The SQL command completed successfully.

CREATE TABLE ABC.employee ( empid              INT, name
VARCHAR(20), deptid              INT)
DB20000I   The SQL command completed successfully.

ALTER TABLE ABC.employee ADD CONSTRAINT fk_emp_dept FOREIGN KEY (deptid)
REFERENCES ABC.department (deptid) ON UPDATE RESTRICT
DB20000I   The SQL command completed successfully.

INSERT INTO ABC.department VALUES (1, 'Research'), (2, 'Finance'),(3,
'Sales')
DB20000I   The SQL command completed successfully.
```

```
INSERT INTO employee VALUES (1, 'Milan, Mohan', 3)
DB20000I  The SQL command completed successfully.

UPDATE department SET deptid = deptid +1;
SQL0531N  The parent key in a parent row of relationship
"EMPLOYEE.FK_EMP_DEPT" cannot be updated.  SQLSTATE=23001
```

Question 4

The correct answer is **3**:

```
CREATE TABLE employee (
    empid       INT NOT NULL PRIMARY KEY,
    empname   VARCHAR(20) NOT NULL,
    deptid      INT NOT NULL,
    salary      INT NOT NULL CHECK (salary >=5000),
    job         VARCHAR(10) CHECK (JOB in ('Engineer','Sales','Manager')));
```

The following table lists all the constraints and the count:

Column Name	Constraints	Count
empid	NOT NULL and PRIMARY KEY	2
empname	NOT NULL	1
DEPTID	NOT NULL	1
SALARY	NOT NULL and CHECK	2
JOB	CHECK	1
TOTAL		7 Constraints

Question 5

The correct answer is **4**. When you create a primary key, the Db2 database manager automatically creates a unique bidirectional index. If an appropriate unique index is present, then Db2 uses the existing index and marks it as system required. You can create one, and only one, primary key in a table; however, the primary key can have multiple columns defined. A primary key does not accept NULL values, but a unique index does accept one NULL value.

Question 6

The correct answers are **1** and **3**. The SET INTEGRITY statement can be used to temporarily suspend constraint checking on a table. This statement can also be used to perform the following listed operations:

- Placing one or more tables in the SET INTEGRITY pending state
- Placing one or more tables into the FULL ACCESS state
- Pruning the contents of one of more staging tables
- Bringing one or more tables out of the SET INTEGRITY PENDING state by performing data validation via the constraint check
- Bringing one or more tables out of the SET INTEGRITY PENDING state without performing data validation

Question 7

The correct answer is **3**:

```
CREATE TABLE employee ( empid           INT NOT NULL, empname
VARCHAR(20) NOT NULL, salary            INT NOT NULL);
DB20000I  The SQL command completed successfully.

CREATE VIEW v1_employee AS SELECT * FROM employee WHERE salary > 5000 WITH
CASCADED CHECK OPTION;
DB20000I  The SQL command completed successfully.

CREATE VIEW v2_employee AS SELECT * FROM v1_employee WHERE salary < 8000;
DB20000I  The SQL command completed successfully.

CREATE VIEW v3_employee AS SELECT * FROM v2_employee WHERE salary < 10000;
DB20000I  The SQL command completed successfully.

INSERT INTO v3_employee VALUES (1, 'Milan, Mohan', 11000);
DB20000I  The SQL command completed successfully.
```

Question 8

The correct answers are **1** and **3**. We have two types of CHECK OPTIONS in Db2 and they are WITH LOCAL CHECK OPTION and WITH CASCADED CHECK OPTION:

- The WITH LOCAL CHECK OPTION can also be specified when creating a view. If a view is defined with the LOCAL CHECK OPTION, the definition of the view is used when checking for any INSERT or UPDATE operations. However, the view does not inherit the search conditions from any updatable views on which the view depends on.
- If a view is defined with the WITH CASCADED CHECK OPTION or just the WITH CHECK OPTION (CASCADED is the default value of the WITH CHECK OPTION), the definition of the view is used when checking for any INSERT or UPDATE operations. In addition, the view inherits the search conditions from any updatable views on which the view depends.

Question 9

The correct answer is **4**. In Db2, triggers are classified as BEFORE, AFTER, or INSTEAD OF:

- BEFORE triggers are activated before an update or INSERT operation, and the values that are being updated or inserted can be changed before the database data is modified in the table. Generally, this trigger is used during data cleansing and modification.
- AFTER triggers are activated after an INSERT, UPDATE, or DELETE operation and are used to maintain the relationship between data or to keep audit trail information.
- INSTEAD OF triggers define how to perform an INSERT, UPDATE, or DELETE operation on a view where these operations are otherwise not allowed.

Question 10

The correct answers are **1** and **4**.

Five major components are associated with any trigger:

- The subject, on which the trigger is defined - basically, tables or views
- The event, which initiates the trigger - basically, an INSERT, UPDATE, or DELETE operation
- The activation time of the trigger - basically, a BEFORE or AFTER the event

- The granularity, which specifies whether the trigger's actions are performed once for the statement or once for each of the affected rows - basically, a FOR EACH STATEMENT or FOR EACH ROW action
- The action, which the trigger performs - basically, one or more of the following elements:
    - CALL statement
    - DECLARE and/or SET variable statement
    - WHILE and/or FOR loop
    - IF, SIGNAL, ITERATE, LEAVE, and GET DIAGNOSTIC statements
    - SELECT SQL statement
    - INSERT, UPDATE, DELETE, and MERGE SQL statements (only for AFTER and INSTEAD OF triggers)

Monitoring Db2 Activity 5

This chapter will teach you how to monitor Db2 instances, databases, objects, and workloads using monitor table functions and administrative views. You will be able to troubleshoot instance, database, and application-related issues using the Db2 problem determination (db2pd) and Db2 text-based monitoring (dsmtop) tool commands. You will also learn how to utilize the event monitors and explain facilities within Db2.

After the completion of this chapter, you will be able to demonstrate the ability to:

- Use the monitoring table functions and administrative views to collect the activity data and analyze it in an ESE, BLU Acceleration, and pureScale database environment
- Create and activate event monitors and analyze event monitor information
- Use the explain facility to capture and analyze comprehensive explaination information
- Use the MONREPORT module to generate various text reports of monitoring data
- Use the problem determination and validation tools available within Db2, such as db2pd and dsmtop

Certification Test:
Number of Questions: 7
Percentage in the Exam: 12%

Monitoring infrastructure

The new in-memory metrics monitoring infrastructure introduced in Db2 9.7 accesses the monitoring information through new table functions and event monitors. This is an improvement from expensive snapshot-based statistics used in the earlier Db2 releases.

The monitoring table functions and administrative views allow you to capture the state of a database or application connections at a specific point in time, whereas event monitors capture and record information as specific database events occur. The monitoring information collected in both tools is stored in entities called monitor elements. The monitor elements are data structures used to store information about a specific aspect of the database system's status. For example, the monitor element *deadlocks* reflects the total number of deadlocks that have occurred in the database system since its last activation. Each monitor element specifically reflects one of the following types of data:

- **Counter**: This records a precise count of the number of times an activity or event has occurred in the database system. For example, the `pool_col_l_reads` monitor element records the number of column-organized page requests from the buffer pool for regular and large table spaces. The other examples of the counters include `direct_reads`, `direct_writes`, `pool_data_l_reads`, `pool_data_p_reads`, and `pool_col_p_reads`.
- **Gauge**: This reflects the current value for a monitoring element based on how much of something is happening or is used. For example, the `num_locks_held` monitoring element shows how many locks are being currently held in the database. The other examples include `db_status`, `lock_waiting`, `lock_list_in_use`, `num_coord_agents`, and `active_sorts`.
- **Watermark**: This signifies the highest value for a given monitoring element. For example, the `connections_top` monitoring element shows the highest number of simultaneous connections to the database since the database's activation. The other examples are `agents_top`, `coord_agents_top`, `sort_shrheap_top`, `sort_heap_top`, and `tbsp_max_page_top`.
- **Text**: This is the text value that monitoring elements report. For example, the `bp_name` monitoring element states the name of the buffer pool. The other examples are `db_name`, `host_name`, `stmt_text`, `appl_name`, and `tbsp_name`.

- **Timestamp**: This monitor element reports the time that an event happened. For example, the `last_backup` monitoring element lists the date and time that the latest database backup was completed. The other examples include `last_overflow_time`, `db2start_time`, `db_conn_time`, `lock_wait_start_time`, and `uow_stop_time`.

The monitor elements are broadly categorized into the following groups based on the type of in-memory metrics they contain:

- **Request monitor elements (request metrics)**: These measure the volume of work or effort spent by the database server to process different types of requests, including opening a connection from a client to the server and executing a set of SQL statements.
- **Activity monitor elements (activity metrics)**: These measure the data server processing related to executing activities, such as processing undertaken to execute SQL statement sections, locking, sorting, and row processing. These are a subset of request monitor elements.
- **Monitor element collection levels:** These provide a control to activate or deactivate the data collection for the activity, request, and data monitor elements. You can activate specific monitor elements by setting the following database configuration parameters:
  - `mon_obj_metrics`: This parameter activates the object metric's data collection for the entire database. The values it can take are NONE, BASE, and EXTENDED.
  - `mon_act_metrics`: This parameter activates the activity metrics data collection for the entire database. The values it can take are NONE, BASE, and EXTENDED.
  - `mon_req_metrics`: This parameter activates the request metrics data collection for the entire database. The values it can take are NONE, BASE, and EXTENDED.

If you want to update all of the previously listed metrics, you can do so by executing the following command:

```
UPDATE DB CFG FOR <dbname> USING MON_OBJ_METRICS BASE MON_ACT_METRICS BASE
MON_REQ_METRICS BASE;
```

Monitoring table functions

The monitoring table functions are designed to collect and view data for systems, activities, and data objects at a specific point in time. The monitoring table functions are logically categorized based on the monitoring elements and are as follows:

- Table functions for monitoring system information
- Table functions for monitoring activities
- Table functions for monitoring data objects
- Table functions for monitoring locks
- Table functions for monitoring system memory
- Table functions for monitoring the pureScale environment
- Table functions for monitoring routines

The basic syntax to construct a SQL statement that references table functions for monitoring the system information is as follows:

```
SELECT * FROM TABLE ([FunctionName] ([FunctionSpecifics],[Member] )) AS
[CorrelationName]
```

Where,

- **FunctionName**: Identifies the name of the monitoring table function
- **FunctionSpecifics**: Identifies the monitor table function's specific parameters
- **Member**: Identifies the member for which to collect the monitor information; the value of -1 is for the current member, and -2 for all the members in the pureScale cluster, or in massively parallel processing systems
- **CorrelationName**: Specifies a correlation name that identifies the row state before triggering the SQL operation

The SYSPROC schema holds the built-in monitoring table functions and it requires EXECUTE, DATAACCESS, DBADM, or SQLADM authorizations to run these table functions.

Monitoring system information

The system's monitoring information includes the complete volume of work and effort spent by the data server manager to process the application requests. This information provides an overview of how the database server is performing. The following table shows the table functions available in Db2 v11.1 for accessing current system monitoring information:

Table Function	Information Returned
MON_GET_DATABASE	Returns database-level metrics
MON_GET_DATABASE_DETAILS	Returns detailed database-level metrics in an XML document
MON_GET_SERVICE_SUBCLASS	Returns metrics for one or more service subclass(es)
MON_GET_SERVICE_SUBCLASS_DETAILS	Returns detailed metrics for one or more service subclasses in an XML document
MON_GET_WORKLOAD	Returns metrics for one or more workloads

Table Function	Information Returned
MON_GET_WORKLOAD_DETAILS	Returns detailed metrics for one or more workloads in an XML document
MON_GET_CONNECTIONS	Returns metrics for one or more connections
MON_GET_CONNECTIONS_DETAILS	Returns detailed metrics for one or more connections
MON_GET_UNIT_OF_WORK	Returns metrics for one or more unit(s) of work
MON_GET_UNIT_OF_WORK_DETAILS	Returns detailed metrics for one or more unit(s) of work in an XML document

If you want to collect database-level information such as the shared sort reservation levels, execute the following SQL statement:

```
WITH DBCFG AS

(SELECT INTEGER (VALUE) AS SHEAPTHRES_SHR FROM SYSIBMADM.DBCFG WHERE NAME =
'sheapthres_shr')

SELECT MEMBER,

SHEAPTHRES_SHR AS "SHARED_SORT_HEAP",
```

```
SORT_SHRHEAP_ALLOCATED AS "SHARED_SORT_ALLOCATED",

DEC ((100 * SORT_SHRHEAP_ALLOCATED)/SHEAPTHRES_SHR, 5, 2) AS
"PERCENT_SORT_HEAP_USED",

DEC ((100* SORT_SHRHEAP_TOP)/SHEAPTHRES_SHR, 5, 2) AS "PERCENT_MAX
SORT_HEAP_USED",

SORT_OVERFLOWS AS "SORT_OVERFLOWS",

TOTAL_SORTS AS "TOTAL_SORTS"

FROM DBCFG, TABLE (MON_GET_DATABASE (-2)) AS MONGETDB

ORDER BY MEMBER DESC;
```

Similarly, if you want to collect information about the lock list usage, execute the SQL statement as follows:

```
WITH LockListdbcfg AS

(SELECT FLOAT (INTEGER (VALUE) * 4096) AS LOCKLIST, ((VALUE * 4)/1024) AS
LOCKLIST_MB FROM SYSIBMADM.DBCFG WHERE NAME = 'locklist'),

MaxLocksdbcfg AS

(SELECT FLOAT (INT (VALUE)) AS MAXLOCKS, (VALUE) AS MAXLOCKS_PERCENTAGE
FROM SYSIBMADM.DBCFG WHERE NAME = 'maxlocks')

SELECT

LOCKLIST_MB,

MAXLOCKS_PERCENTAGE,

DEC ((MONGETDB.LOCK_LIST_IN_USE/LOCKLIST)*100, 4, 1) AS "PERCENT_LOCKLIST",

DEC ((MONGETDB.LOCK_LIST_IN_USE/ (LOCKLIST*(MAXLOCKS/100))*100), 4, 1) AS
"PERCENT_MAXLOCK",

MONGETDB.APPLS_CUR_CONS AS "NO_APPLICATIONS_CONNECTED",

MONGETDB.LOCK_LIST_IN_USE/MONGETDB.APPLS_CUR_CONS AS
"AVG_LOCK_MEMORY_PER_CONNECTION_BYTES"

FROM LockListdbcfg, MaxLocksdbcfg, TABLE (MON_GET_DATABASE (-2)) AS
mongetdb;
```

We will get the following output:

MEMBER	SHARED_SORT_HEAP	SHARED_SORT_ALLOCATED	PERCENT_SORT_HEAP_USED	PERCENT_MAX SORT_HEAP_USED	SORT_OVERFLOWS	TOTAL_SORTS
0	4410409	6	0.00	9.00	5872	194814

Detailed database-level statistics, such as the number of lock waits, the number of rows read, and total CPU time, can be extracted in an XML document format using the `SYSPROC.MON_GET_DATABASE_DETAILS()` table function.

If you want to collect the total CPU time spent in milliseconds and the number of application requests completed for all the superclasses and subclasses in the system, execute the following SQL statement:

```
SELECT VARCHAR (SERVICE_SUPERCLASS_NAME, 30) AS SERVICE_SUPERCLASS,

VARCHAR (SERVICE_SUBCLASS_NAME, 30) AS SERVICE_SUBCLASS,

(SUM (TOTAL_CPU_TIME))/1000 AS TOTAL_CPU_MS,

SUM (APP_RQSTS_COMPLETED_TOTAL) AS TOTAL_REQUESTS

FROM TABLE (MON_GET_SERVICE_SUBCLASS ('','',-2)) AS T

GROUP BY SERVICE_SUPERCLASS_NAME, SERVICE_SUBCLASS_NAME

ORDER BY TOTAL_CPU_MS DESC;
```

We will get the following output: (Another image)

LOCKLIST_MB	MAXLOCKS_PERCENTAGE	% LOCKLIST	% MAXLOCK	# APPLICATIONS_CONNECTED	AVG_LOCKLIST_MEMORY_PER_CONNECTION (BYTES)
570.5	98	0.0	0.0	6	19264

If you want to capture the locking and log buffer information, such as the number of deadlocks, lock timeouts, lock escalations, and log buffer wait time in milliseconds, use the `SYSPROC.MON_GET_WORKLOAD()` table function as follows:

```
SELECT VARCHAR (WORKLOAD_NAME, 30) AS WORKLOAD_NAME,

SUM (DEADLOCKS) AS NUM_OF_DLOCKS,

SUM (LOCK_WAIT_TIME) AS TOTAL_LOCK_WAIT_TIME_MS,

SUM (LOCK_WAITS) AS TOTAL_LOCK_WAITS,

SUM (LOCK_TIMEOUTS) AS TOTAL_LOCK_TIMEOUTS,
```

```
SUM (LOCK_ESCALS) AS TOTAL_LOCK_ESCALS,

SUM (LOG_BUFFER_WAIT_TIME) AS LOG_BUF_WAIT_MS

FROM TABLE (MON_GET_WORKLOAD ('',-2)) AS t

GROUP BY WORKLOAD_NAME;
```

We will get the following output:

SERVICE_SUPERCLASS	SERVICE_SUBCLASS	TOTAL_CPU_MS	TOTAL_REQUESTS
SYSDEFAULTUSERCLASS	SYSDEFAULTMANAGEDSUBCLASS	126512876	0
SYSDEFAULTUSERCLASS	SYSDEFAULTSUBCLASS	37871193	868135
SYSDEFAULTMAINTENANCECLASS	SYSDEFAULTSUBCLASS	169645	17209
SYSDEFAULTSYSTEMCLASS	SYSDEFAULTSUBCLASS	0	0

If you want to capture the wait times for active connections to a database, you can use the `SYSPROC.MON_GET_CONNECTION ()` table function as follows:

```
SELECT

APPLICATION_HANDLE AS APPL_ID,

TOTAL_WAIT_TIME,

POOL_READ_TIME,

POOL_WRITE_TIME,

LOG_DISK_WAIT_TIME,

LOCK_WAIT_TIME

FROM TABLE (MON_GET_CONNECTION (NULL,-2))

ORDER BY TOTAL_WAIT_TIME DESC;
```

We will get the following output:

WORKLOAD_NAME	NUM_OF_DLOCKS	TOTAL_LOCK_WAIT_TIME_MS	TOTAL_LOCK_WAITS	TOTAL_LOCK_TIMEOUTS	TOTAL_LOCK_ESCALS	LOG_BUF_WAIT_MS
SYSDEFAULTADMWORKLOAD	0	0	0	0	0	0
SYSDEFAULTUSERWORKLOAD	4	73967924	286762	1203	0	0

If you want to capture the pre-fetch efficiency (number of pre-fetch requests and the average number of pages read per pre-fetch) of applications, you can use the `SYSPROC.MON_GET_CONNECTION ()` table function as follows:

```
SELECT

APPLICATION_HANDLE,

POOL_QUEUED_ASYNC_DATA_REQS AS PREFETCH_REQS,

POOL_QUEUED_ASYNC_DATA_PAGES AS PREFETCH_PAGES,

CASE

WHEN POOL_QUEUED_ASYNC_DATA_REQS > 0 THEN

DECIMAL (FLOAT (POOL_QUEUED_ASYNC_DATA_PAGES)/FLOAT
(POOL_QUEUED_ASYNC_DATA_REQS), 10, 2)

ELSE -1

END AS PAGES_PER_PREFETCH,

POOL_FAILED_ASYNC_DATA_REQS AS FAILED_PREFETCH,

PREFETCH_WAIT_TIME,

PREFETCH_WAITS

FROM TABLE (MON_GET_CONNECTION (NULL,-2)) AS MONGETCONNECTION;
```

We will get the following output:

APPL_ID	TOTAL_WAIT_TIME	POOL_READ_TIME	POOL_WRITE_TIME	LOG_DISK_WAIT_TIME	LOCK_WAIT_TIME
24405	333009	16034	0	0	0
24256	2169	0	0	50	0
27578	1995	37	0	0	0
27674	1252	0	0	979	0
24353	985	0	0	2	0
25637	70	0	0	0	0

If your database monitoring indicates that a large amount of active transaction log space has been allocated, you can capture information about the oldest transaction holding the transaction log space by using the SYSPROC.MON_GET_UNIT_OF_WORK () and SYSPROC.MON_GET_TRANSACTION_LOG () table functions. The SQL statement is as follows:

```
SELECT

MONGETUOW.MEMBER,

SUBSTR (MONGETUOW.WORKLOAD_OCCURRENCE_STATE, 1, 20) AS "STATUS",

SUBSTR (MONGETUOW.SESSION_AUTH_ID, 1, 10) AS "AUTHID",

MONGETUOW.APPLICATION_HANDLE AS "APPL_HANDLE",

INTEGER (MONGETUOW.UOW_LOG_SPACE_USED/1024/1024) AS "LOG_USED_MB",

(MONGETUOW.TOTAL_ACT_TIME/1000) AS "TOTAL_ACTIVITY_TIME_SEC",

(MONGETUOW.TOTAL_ACT_WAIT_TIME/1000) AS "TOTAL_ACTIVITY_WAIT_TIME_SEC",

MONGETUOW.UOW_START_TIME AS "UOW_START_TIME"

FROM

TABLE (MON_GET_TRANSACTION_LOG (-2)) AS MONGETTLOG,

TABLE (MON_GET_UNIT_OF_WORK (NULL,-2)) AS MONGETUOW

WHERE MONGETUOW.APPLICATION_HANDLE = MONGETTLOG.APPLID_HOLDING_OLDEST_XACT;
```

We will get the following output:

APPLICATION_HANDLE	PREFETCH_REQS	PREFETCH_PAGES	PAGES_PER_PREFETCH	FAILED_PREFETCH	PREFETCH_WAIT_TIME	PREFETCH_WAITS
24256	1221	137551	112.65	0	0	0
27578	3	3	1.00	0	0	0
25637	0	0	-1.00	0	0	0
24353	0	0	-1.00	0	0	0
24405	0	0	-1.00	0	4572	478
27674	0	0	-1.00	0	0	0

MEMBER	STATUS	AUTHID	APPL_HANDLE	LOG_USED_MB	TOTAL_ACTIVITY_TIME_SEC	TOTAL_ACTIVITY_WAIT_TIME_SEC	UOW_START_TIME
0	UOWWAIT	DB2ANL01	25637	43	2	0	5/12/2018 2:08:26 AM

To collect the request metrics information, update the database configuration parameter `MON_REQ_METRICS` to `BASE` or `EXTENDED`.

Monitoring activities

The activity monitoring elements are a subset of the request monitor elements. The elements focus on the activities related to the execution of SQL statements. For activities that are in progress, the metrics are accumulated in memory and for activities that are SQL statements, the metrics are accumulated in the package cache. In the package cache, the activity metrics are aggregated over all the executions of each SQL statement section.

The following table shows the table functions available in Db2 v11.1 for accessing current activity information:

Table Function	Information Returned
MON_GET_ACTIVITY_DETAILS	Returns information about an activity, including the SQL statement text and set of activities
MON_GET_PKG_CACHE_STMT	Returns a point-in-view of both static and dynamic SQL statements in the database package cache
MON_GET_PKG_CACHE_STMT_DETAILS	Returns detailed metrics for one or more package caches

To find details about all the activities currently running in the system, use the `SYSPROC.MON_GET_ACTIVITY_DETAILS ()` table function as follows:

```
WITH METRIC AS

(SELECT *

FROM TABLE (WLM_GET_WORKLOAD_OCCURRENCE_ACTIVITIES (NULL, -2))

WHERE ACTIVITY_ID > 0)

SELECT METRIC.APPLICATION_HANDLE, METRIC.ACTIVITY_ID, METRIC.UOW_ID,

METRIC.TOTAL_ACT_TIME, METRIC.TOTAL_ACT_WAIT_TIME, SUBSTR
(ACTMETRICS.STMT_TEXT, 1,
```

```
250) AS STMT_TEXT

FROM METRIC, TABLE (MON_GET_ACTIVITY_DETAILS (METRIC.APPLICATION_HANDLE,

METRIC.UOW_ID, METRIC.ACTIVITY_ID, -1)) AS ACTDETAILS, XMLTABLE

(XMLNAMESPACES (DEFAULT 'http://www.ibm.com/xmlns/prod/db2/mon'),

'$ACTMETRICS/db2_activity_details' PASSING XMLPARSE (DOCUMENT

ACTDETAILS.DETAILS) AS "ACTMETRICS"

COLUMNS "STMT_TEXT" VARCHAR (1024) PATH 'stmt_text',

"TOTAL_ACT_TIME" INTEGER PATH 'activity_metrics/total_act_time',
"TOTAL_ACT_WAIT_TIME" INTEGER PATH 'activity_metrics/total_act_wait_time')

AS ACTMETRICS;
```

We will get the following output:

APPLICATION_HANDLE	ACTIVITY_ID	UOW_ID	TOTAL_ACT_TIME	TOTAL_ACT_WAIT_TIME	STMT_TEXT
36783	1	27729	0	0	DECLARE ACK_WTRX_CUR CURSOR FOR SELECT VARCHAR_FORMAT(T2.TRAN_TL_DT,'YYYY-MM-DD'), T2.TRAN_TL_FILE, T2.TRAN_TL_OFST, T2.ST...
39657	2	33	433570	422268	SELECT TRAN.TRAN_TL_DT, TRAN.TRAN_TL_FILE, TRAN.TRAN_TL_OFST, TRAN.ST_OFST, TRAN.TRAN_TYP, HEAD.INTERFACE_TYP, RETEN.RETEN_H...
39657	1	32	36117	202	call EDIUTIL.SP_COLLECT_TRANS_BOUNDED(?, ?, ?, ?, ?,?,?)
40531	1	59	0	0	WITH METRIC AS (SELECT * FROM TABLE (WLM_GET_WORKLOAD_OCCURRENCE_ACTIVITIES (NULL, -2)) WHERE ACTIVITY_ID > 0) SELECT ...
40701	2	1	11232	9082	DECLARE UNMATCHED_AKS_CUR CURSOR WITH HOLD FOR select distinct VARCHAR_FORMAT(t.tran_tl_dt,'YYYY-MM-DD'), t.tran_tl_file, t.tran_tl_ofst ...

The `SYSPROC.MON_ACTIVITY_DETAILS ()` table function can be used to display a hierarchical breakdown of all the wait times in the entire database.

If you want to monitor the performance of static (S) and dynamic (D) SQL statements, use the `SYSPROC.MON_GET_PKG_CACHE_STMT ()` table function to analyze the number of executions, time spent in execution, average execution time, and the number of sorts per SQL statement, as follows:

```
SELECT

NUM_EXECUTIONS AS "NUM_EXECS",

TOTAL_ACT_TIME AS TOTAL_TIME, (TOTAL_ACT_TIME / NUM_EXECUTIONS) AS
"AVG_TIME_MS",

TOTAL_SORTS AS "NUM SORTS",

(TOTAL_SORTS / NUM_EXECUTIONS) AS "SORTS_PER_STMT",
```

```
TOTAL_SECTION_SORT_TIME,

VARCHAR (STMT_TEXT, 100) AS "SQL_STMT"

FROM TABLE (MON_GET_PKG_CACHE_STMT ('D', NULL, NULL,-1)) AS MONGETPKG

WHERE NUM_EXECUTIONS > 0 AND TOTAL_ROUTINE_TIME = 0 ORDER BY 2 DESC FETCH
FIRST 10 ROWS ONLY;
```

If you want to monitor and analyze the SQL statement preparation time, use the following SQL. If the time the Db2 optimizer takes to compile and optimize a query is almost as long as it takes for the query to execute, you might want to look at the optimization class that you are using:

```
SELECT

NUM_EXECUTIONS,

STMT_EXEC_TIME AS TOTAL_EXEC_TIME,

CASE

WHEN NUM_EXECUTIONS > 0 THEN

(STMT_EXEC_TIME / NUM_EXECUTIONS)

ELSE -1

END AS AVG_EXEC_TIME,

PREP_TIME,

CASE

WHEN (STMT_EXEC_TIME/NUM_EXECUTIONS) > 0 THEN

((100 * PREP_TIME) / (STMT_EXEC_TIME/NUM_EXECUTIONS))

ELSE -1

END AS PCT_PREP,

VARCHAR (STMT_TEXT, 100) AS "SQL_TEXT"

FROM TABLE (MON_GET_PKG_CACHE_STMT ('D', NULL, NULL,-1)) AS MONGETPKG

WHERE STMT_EXEC_TIME > 1000 ORDER BY PREP_TIME DESC;
```

We will get the following output:

NUM_EXECS	TOTAL_TIME	AVG_TIME_MS	NUM SORTS	SORTS_PER_STMT	TOTAL_SECTION_SORT_TIME	SQL_STMT
303	1127380316	3720727	0	0	0	select b.LINE_SGMT_NBR,b.SRC_FILE_ROW_NBR, b.SRC_FILE_NME, b.MP_OFSET_FT, b.MP_NBR, b...
118	165690629	1404157	0	0	0	select b.LINE_SGMT_NBR,b.SRC_FILE_ROW_NBR, b.SRC_FILE_NME, b.MP_OFSET_FT, b.MP_NBR, b...
243	51316677	211179	0	0	0	select b.LINE_SGMT_NBR,b.SRC_FILE_ROW_NBR, b.SRC_FILE_NME, b.MP_OFSET_FT, b.MP_NBR, b...
181	49843934	275380	0	0	0	select SRC_FILE_ROW_NBR, SRC_FILE_NME, MP_OFSET_FT, MP_NBR, GMTRY_CAR_TEST_DT, LINE_...
244	36865684	151088	488	2	0	select GMTRY_CAR_TEST_DT,TRAK_TYP_CD,TRAK_SDTRAK_NBR,CALCD_MP_NBR,GAGE_IN,ALGNMT...
181	30349168	167674	0	0	0	select SRC_FILE_ROW_NBR ,SRC_FILE_NME ,MP_OFSET_FT ,MP_NBR ,GMTRY_CAR_TEST_DT ,LINE_...

If you are interested in capturing expensive dynamic and static SQL statements that make heavy data reads over a period of time, use the following SQL statement:

```
WITH SUM_REC_TAB (SUM_REC_READ) AS (

SELECT SUM (ROWS_READ)

FROM TABLE (MON_GET_PKG_CACHE_STMT (NULL, NULL, NULL, -2)) AS T)

SELECT

ROWS_READ, DECIMAL (100*(FLOAT (ROWS_READ)/ NULLIF
(SUM_REC_TAB.SUM_REC_READ, 0)), 5, 2) AS PCT_TOTAL_RECORDS_READ,

ROWS_RETURNED,

CASE

WHEN ROWS_RETURNED > 0 THEN

DECIMAL (FLOAT (ROWS_READ)/FLOAT (ROWS_RETURNED), 10, 2)

ELSE -1

END AS READ_EFFICIENCY,

NUM_EXECUTIONS,

VARCHAR (STMT_TEXT, 200) AS STATEMENT

FROM TABLE (MON_GET_PKG_CACHE_STMT (NULL, NULL, NULL, -2)) AS MONGETPKG,
SUM_REC_TAB

ORDER BY ROWS_READ DESC FETCH FIRST 5 ROWS ONLY WITH UR;
```

We will get the following output:

NUM_EXECUTIONS	TOTAL_EXEC_TIME	AVG_EXEC_TIME	PREP_TIME	PCT_PREP	SQL_TEXT
1	11476	11476	2457	21	with LOCOS (LOCO_INIT, LOCO_NUMB, START_TS, STOP_TS) as (values (?, ?, to_timestamp(?,
36	2537	70	1076	1537	DELETE FROM EQ.TB_BNSF_ONLY WHERE TRNSP_EQP_ID = ? AND BNSF_ONLY_EFF_TS = ? AND CAR_KND_ABBR = ?
2	3830	1915	825	43	SELECT SM.SHPMT_MSTR_ID, SM.SHPMT_MSTR_VRSN_NBR AS SHPMT_MSTR_VRSN_NBR, SM.SPM_CHNG_RQST_ID,
9	19329	2147	703	32	SELECT A1."LOCO_CLASS" C0, COUNT(*) C1, SYSIBM.MONTH(A1."BLD_D") C2 FROM "OY", "TLOCO_INV" A0, "EQ"."
39	1994891	51151	659	1	SELECT OFCR.OFCR_USER_ID AS OFCR_USER_ID, (TRIM(OFCR.OFCR_FNME)||' '||TRIM(OFCR.OFCR_LNME)) AS OF
1	1406	1406	637	45	SELECT SUM(D.ERWRN_WGT), EQP_INIT, EQP_NUMB FROM ME.THSCOR_ACT_ALRM_EQP B LEFT JOIN ME.THSCOR_ERWRN

If you want to establish the efficiency of dynamic SQL statements such as pre-fetch wait time, total activity time, total CPU time, and number of lock-waits, execute the following query:

```
SELECT CURRENT_TIMESTAMP,

SUM (NUM_EXECUTIONS) AS EXEC,

SUM (ROWS_READ) AS ROWS_READ,

SUM (ROWS_RETURNED) AS ROWS_RETURNED,

(SUM (ROWS_READ)/SUM (NUM_EXECUTIONS)) AS AVG_ROWS_READ,

(SUM (ROWS_RETURNED)/SUM (NUM_EXECUTIONS)) AS AVG_ROWS_RETURNED,

MAX (ROWS_READ) AS MAX_ROWS_READ,

MAX (ROWS_RETURNED) AS MAX_ROWS_RETURNED,

SUM (TOTAL_CPU_TIME)/SUM (NUM_EXEC_WITH_METRICS) as AVG_CPU_TIME_US,

CAST (STMT_TEXT AS VARCHAR (32000)) as SQL_STMT,

SUM (PREFETCH_WAIT_TIME) AS PREFETCH_WAIT_TIME_MS,

SUM (PREFETCH_WAITS) AS PREFETCH_WAITS,

SUM (TOTAL_ACT_TIME) AS ACT_TIME_MS,

SUM (TOTAL_ACT_WAIT_TIME) AS TOTAL_ACT_WAIT_TIME_MS,

SUM (TOTAL_CPU_TIME) AS TOTAL_CPU_TIME_US,

SUM (LOCK_WAIT_TIME) AS LOCK_WAIT_MS,

SUM (LOCK_WAITS) AS LOCK_WAITS
```

```
FROM TABLE (MON_GET_PKG_CACHE_STMT ('D', NULL, NULL, -2)) as T

WHERE T.NUM_EXEC_WITH_METRICS <> 0

GROUP BY CURRENT_TIMESTAMP, CAST (STMT_TEXT AS VARCHAR (32000))

ORDER BY SUM (NUM_EXECUTIONS) DESC

FETCH FIRST 10000 ROWS ONLY;
```

ROWS_READ	PCT_TOTAL_RECORDS_READ	ROWS_RETURNED	READ_EFFICIENCY	NUM_EXECUTIONS	STATEMENT
119469802343	19.71	281774	423991.57	27956	select emplcertst0_.empl_cert_msg_id as empl_ce13_9_0_, emplcertst0_.empl_cert_stat_id as empl_cer1_...
99825466736	16.47	231818	430619.99	23489	select emplcertst0_.empl_cert_msg_id as empl_ce13_9_0_, emplcertst0_.empl_cert_stat_id as empl_cer1_...
84359236321	13.92	198131	425775.04	19829	select emplcertst0_.empl_cert_msg_id as empl_ce13_9_0_, emplcertst0_.empl_cert_stat_id as empl_cer1_...
77471783640	12.78	178544	433908.63	18132	select msgprocess0_.empl_cert_msg_id as empl_cer1_8_1_, msgprocess0_.cret_ts as cret_ts2_8_1_, msg...
65878512835	10.87	148434	443823.60	15503	select msgprocess0_.empl_cert_msg_id as empl_cer1_8_1_, msgprocess0_.cret_ts as cret_ts2_8_1_, msg...

1 *	EXEC	ROWS_READ	ROWS_RETURNED	AVG_ROWS_READ	AVG_ROWS_RETURNED	MAX_ROWS_READ	MAX_ROWS_RETURNED	AVG_CPU_TIME_US	SQL_STMT
5/12/2018 9:09:50 PM	3927282	0	3927282	0	1	0	945965	17	select :L0 from sysibm.sysdu
5/12/2018 9:09:50 PM	3845168	36102886	3475	9	0	17994552	2251	77	SELECT * FROM WN
5/12/2018 9:09:50 PM	3189250	0	0	0	0	0	0	537	SELECT CAST(NULL AS
5/12/2018 9:09:50 PM	2886805	1593351399	0	551	0	1092120437	0	73	UPDATE PM_RECOVERY SET
5/12/2018 9:09:50 PM	1725341	0	1725341	0	1	0	685676	16	SELECT :L0 FROM SYSIBM.
5/12/2018 9:09:50 PM	1537980	1537980	0	1	0	1537980	0	77	UPDATE NP_CRM1.BILL_

To collect the activity metrics information, update the database configuration parameter MON_ACT_METRICS to BASE or EXTENDED.

Monitoring data objects

Data object monitoring focuses on providing information about operations performed on the data objects such as tables, indexes, buffer pools, table spaces, and containers. The following table shows the table functions available in Db2 v11.1 for accessing data object information:

Table Function	Information Returned
MON_GET_BUFFERPOOL	Returns monitor metrics for one or more buffer pools
MON_GET_TABLESPACE	Returns monitor metrics for one or more table spaces
MON_GET_CONTAINERS	Returns monitor metrics for one or more table space containers
MON_GET_TABLE	Returns monitor metrics for one or more tables
MON_GET_INDEXES	Returns monitor metrics for one or more indexes

If you want to monitor the performance of database buffer pools, use the
SYSPROC.MON_GET_BUFFERPOOL () table function and the monitoring SQL statement as
follows:

```
SELECT

VARCHAR (BP_NAME, 20) AS BP_NAME,

POOL_DATA_L_READS,

POOL_DATA_P_READS,

CASE

WHEN POOL_DATA_L_READS > 0 THEN

(100 * (POOL_DATA_L_READS - POOL_DATA_P_READS)) / (POOL_DATA_L_READS)

ELSE -1

END AS DATA_HIT_PCT,

POOL_INDEX_L_READS,

POOL_INDEX_P_READS,

CASE

WHEN POOL_INDEX_L_READS > 0 THEN

(100 * (POOL_INDEX_L_READS - POOL_INDEX_P_READS)) / (POOL_INDEX_L_READS)

ELSE -1

END AS INDEX_HIT_PCT

FROM TABLE (MON_GET_BUFFERPOOL (NULL,-2)) AS MONGETBUF

WHERE BP_NAME NOT LIKE 'IBMSYSTEM%'

ORDER BY DATA_HIT_PCT DESC;
```

We will get the following output:

BP_NAME	POOL_DATA_L_READS	POOL_DATA_P_READS	DATA_HIT_PCT	POOL_INDEX_L_READS	POOL_INDEX_P_READS	INDEX_HIT_PCT
BP00_04K	133014287	9239	99	249684651	4137	99
BP01_16K	4213008	1841	99	132088	66	99
BP01_32K	166972824	906237	99	2145144	3557	99
BP00_04K	131320231	9423	99	243368698	4399	99
BP01_16K	3631275	1930	99	136451	73	99
BP01_32K	172247310	749099	99	1065002	3275	99
BP00_04K	36957603	9595	99	160826383	4341	99

To collect the number of column-organized pages, physical read, and logical read metrics, use the POOL_COL_L_READS and POOL_COL_P_READS monitor elements within the SYSPROC.MON_GET_BUFFERPOOL () table function. In general, the column-organized monitor elements will have _COL_ in their name, and the row-organized monitor elements will have _DATA_ in their name.

In Db2, table space is a fundamental logical storage structure of a database. If you want to find the table space attributes such as table space type, state, used pages, and allocated pages, use the SYSPROC.MON_GET_TABLESPACE () table function as follows:

```
SELECT

VARCHAR (TBSP_NAME, 20) AS TBSP_NAME,

VARCHAR (TBSP_STATE, 10) AS TBSP_STATE,

TBSP_TYPE,

TBSP_TOTAL_PAGES AS TOTAL_PAGES,

TBSP_USED_PAGES AS USED_PAGES,

(100 * TBSP_USED_PAGES / TBSP_TOTAL_PAGES) AS PCT_USED,

TBSP_PAGE_TOP AS HIGH_WATER_MARK,

(100 * TBSP_PAGE_TOP / TBSP_TOTAL_PAGES) AS PCT_HWM,

CASE (TBSP_USING_AUTO_STORAGE) WHEN 1 THEN 'YES' ELSE 'NO' END AS
AUTO_STORAGE

FROM TABLE (MON_GET_TABLESPACE (NULL,-2)) AS MONGETTBSP ORDER BY TBSP_NAME;
```

If you want to check the performance of table space containers, you can use the `SYSPROC.MON_GET_CONTAINER ()` table function:

```
SELECT VARCHAR (CONTAINER_NAME, 40) AS CONTAINER_NAME,

VARCHAR (TBSP_NAME, 20) AS TBSP_NAME,

POOL_READ_TIME AS POOL_READ_TIME_MS,

POOL_WRITE_TIME AS POOL_WRITE_TIME_MS,

FS_ID,

FS_USED_SIZE/1024/1024/1024 AS FS_USED_SIZE_GB,

FS_TOTAL_SIZE/1024/1024/1024 AS FS_TOTAL_SIZE_GB,

CASE WHEN FS_TOTAL_SIZE > 0

THEN DEC (100*(FLOAT (FS_USED_SIZE)/FLOAT (FS_TOTAL_SIZE)), 5, 2)

ELSE -1

END AS UTILIZATION

FROM TABLE (MON_GET_CONTAINER ('',-2)) AS MONGETCONT

ORDER BY UTILIZATION DESC;
```

We will get the following output:

TBSP_NAME	TBSP_STATE	TBSP_TYPE	TOTAL_PAGES	USED_PAGES	PCT_USED	HIGH_WATER_MARK	PCT_HWM	AUTO_STORAGE *
AEA01000	NORMAL	DMS	36960	8576	23	14208	38	YES
AEA01000	NORMAL	DMS	36960	8576	23	14208	38	YES
AEA01000	NORMAL	DMS	36960	8576	23	14208	38	YES
AEL01000	NORMAL	DMS	4160	160	3	160	3	YES
AEL01000	NORMAL	DMS	4160	160	3	160	3	YES
AEL01000	NORMAL	DMS	4160	160	3	160	3	YES
AEX01000	NORMAL	DMS	69760	13440	19	21888	31	YES

```
SELECT

VARCHAR (TBSP_NAME, 20) AS TBSPNAME,

SUM (POOL_READ_TIME) AS POOL_READ_TIME,
```

```
SUM (DIRECT_READS) AS DIRECT_READS,

SUM (DIRECT_WRITES) AS DIRECT_WRITES,

SUM (DIRECT_READ_TIME) AS DIRECT_READ_TIME,

SUM (DIRECT_WRITE_TIME) AS DIRECT_WRITE_TIME

FROM TABLE (MON_GET_CONTAINER ('',-2)) AS MONGETCONT

GROUP BY (TBSP_NAME);
```

We will get the following output:

CONTAINER_NAME	TBSP_NAME	POOL_READ_TIME_MS	POOL_WRITE_TIME_MS	FS_ID	FS_USED_SIZE_GB	FS_TOTAL_SIZE_GB	UTILIZATION
/db/ts01/db2anl01/NODE0000/TITO1000/T0000000/C0000000.CAT	SYSCATSPACE	2236	1	64783	336	709	47.46
/db/ts02/db2anl01/NODE0000/TITO1000/T0000000/C0000001.CAT	SYSCATSPACE	2559	3	64784	336	709	47.46
/db/ts03/db2anl01/NODE0000/TITO1000/T0000000/C0000002.CAT	SYSCATSPACE	1879	353	64785	336	709	47.46
/db/ts04/db2anl01/NODE0000/TITO1000/T0000000/C0000003.CAT	SYSCATSPACE	2218	50	64786	336	709	47.46
/db/ts04/db2anl01/NODE0000/TITO1000/T0000001/C0000000.LRG	EVICA400	1006	0	64786	336	709	47.46
/db/ts03/db2anl01/NODE0000/TITO1000/T0000001/C0000001.LRG	EVICA400	938	0	64785	336	709	47.46
/db/ts02/db2anl01/NODE0000/TITO1000/T0000001/C0000002.LRG	EVICA400	736	0	64784	336	709	47.46

You can use the SYSPROC.MON_GET_TABLE () table function to determine expensive table scans using the following SQL statement:

```
SELECT

VARCHAR (TABNAME, 30) AS TABNAME,

TABLE_SCANS,

ROWS_READ,

ROWS_INSERTED,

ROWS_DELETED

FROM

TABLE (MON_GET_TABLE ('', '', -1))

ORDER BY TABLE_SCANS DESC

FETCH FIRST 10 ROWS ONLY
```

We will get the following output:

TBSPNAME	POOL_READ_TIME	DIRECT_READS	DIRECT_WRITES	DIRECT_READ_TIME	DIRECT_WRITE_TIME
EVICA100	451203	1210400768	0	5401373	0
EVICA200	13094	573440	0	3130	0
EVICA300	82251196	9115598848	0	13962264	0
EVICA400	3384	1835008	0	18053	0
EVICA500	103	4608	0	220	0
EVICX100	1199178	774717440	0	2102259	0
EVICX200	5248	573440	0	2810	0

To list the aggregated activity on all tables that have been accessed since the database's activation, you can use the following query:

```
SELECT

VARCHAR (TABSCHEMA, 10) AS TABSCHEMA,

VARCHAR (TABNAME, 30) AS TABNAME,

SUM (ROWS_READ) AS TOTAL_ROWS_READ,

SUM (ROWS_INSERTED) AS TOTAL_ROWS_INSERTED,

SUM (ROWS_UPDATED) AS TOTAL_ROWS_UPDATED,

SUM (ROWS_DELETED) AS TOTAL_ROWS_DELETED

FROM TABLE (MON_GET_TABLE ('','',-2)) AS MONGETTAB GROUP BY TABSCHEMA,
TABNAME

ORDER BY TOTAL_ROWS_READ DESC;
```

We will get the following output:

TABNAME	TABLE_SCANS	ROWS_READ	ROWS_INSERTED	ROWS_DELETED
SYSDATATYPES	13026	53861	0	0
SYN1708261134504605265_TEVIC_GM	5780	14021173071	0	0
TEVIC_CSP_GIS_LOG	1120	92819671	163	0
TEVIC_GMTRY_FILE	816	64549662	4743	0
SYSBUFFERPOOLS	322	2576	0	0
SYSMODULES	213	768	0	0
SYSCOMMENTS	69	41	0	0

You can use the `SYSPROC.MON_GET_INDEX ()` table function to determine unused, inefficient indexes in the database. The SQL statement is listed as follows:

```
SELECT

VARCHAR (INDX.INDSCHEMA, 10) AS INDSCHEMA,

VARCHAR (INDX.INDNAME, 30) AS INDNAME,

MONGETINDEX.INDEX_SCANS,

MONGETINDEX.INDEX_ONLY_SCANS

FROM TABLE (MON_GET_INDEX ('','', -2)) AS MONGETINDEX, SYSCAT.INDEXES AS
INDX

WHERE

MONGETINDEX.TABSCHEMA = INDX.TABSCHEMA AND

MONGETINDEX.TABNAME = INDX.TABNAME AND

MONGETINDEX.IID = INDX.IID AND

MONGETINDEX.INDEX_SCANS = 0 AND

MONGETINDEX.INDEX_ONLY_SCANS = 0 AND

INDX.INDSCHEMA <> 'SYSIBM';
```

We will get the following output:

TABSCHEMA	TABNAME	TOTAL_ROWS_READ	TOTAL_ROWS_INSERTED	TOTAL_ROWS_UPDATED	TOTAL_ROWS_DELETED
ZDENGPUB	TEVIC_GMTRY_CAR_2	537809585476	29942904	0	0
SYSIBM	SYN170826113450465265_TEVIC_GM	14021173071	0	0	0
ZDENGPUB	TEVIC_GMTRY_CAR_STG	161194320	23724565	23181032	29942904
ZDENGPUB	TEVIC_CSP_GIS_LOG	92832757	163	3579	0
ZDENGPUB	TEVIC_GMTRY_FILE	64549662	4743	7183	0
DB2ANL01	T100	262143	262144	0	0
SYSIBM	SYSCOLUMNS	185754	2	0	0

If you want to find efficient indexes in a database, execute the following SQL statement:

```
SELECT

VARCHAR (S.INDSCHEMA, 10) AS INDSCHEMA,

VARCHAR (S.INDNAME, 30) AS INDNAME,

T.NLEAF,

T.NLEVELS,

T.INDEX_SCANS,

T.INDEX_ONLY_SCANS,

T.KEY_UPDATES,

T.BOUNDARY_LEAF_NODE_SPLITS + T.NONBOUNDARY_LEAF_NODE_SPLITS AS PAGE_SPLITS

FROM

TABLE (MON_GET_INDEX ('', '', -2)) AS T, SYSCAT.INDEXES AS S

ORDER BY

T.INDEX_ONLY_SCANS DESC

FETCH FIRST 5 ROWS ONLY;
```

INDSCHEMA *	INDNAME *	INDEX_SCANS	INDEX_ONLY_SCANS
ZDENGP	XD1_TEVIC_CSP_GIS_LOG	0	0
ZDENGP	XD3_TEVIC_GMTRY_CAR_STG	0	0
ZDENGP	XD2_TEVIC_GMTRY_CAR_STG	0	0
ZDENGP	XD1_TEVIC_GMTRY_CAR_STG	0	0
ZDENGP	UNIQ_TEVIC_GMTRY_CAR_2	0	0
ZDENGP	XPK_EVIC_GMTRY_CAR_ALGNMT_RPT	0	0

INDSCHEMA *	INDNAME *	NLEAF	NLEVELS	INDEX_SCANS	INDEX_ONLY_SCANS	KEY_UPDATES	PAGE_SPLITS
DB2ANL	ARG_I1	52	2	122952	110016	577	1
DB2ANL	EXP_DIAG_DAT_I1	52	2	122952	110016	577	1
DB2ANL	IDX_I1	52	2	122952	110016	577	1
DB2ANL	IDX_I2	52	2	122952	110016	577	1
DB2ANL	MQT_I1	52	2	122952	110016	577	1

 To collect the data object metrics information, update the database configuration parameter MON_OBJ_METRICS to BASE or EXTENDED.

Monitoring locks

Lock monitoring focuses on providing information about lock-wait and deadlock performance problems in a database. In Db2 v11.1, we can also monitor latching at the memory structure level. The following table shows the difference between Lock and Latches in Db2:

Lock	Latch
Protects transactional data consistency.	Lightweight synchronization object that protects the data consistency at an internal data structure in memory such as a buffer pool.

Locks are applied based on different isolation levels: • **Uncommitted Read (UR)** • **Cursor Stability (CS)** • **Read Stability (RS)** • **Repeatable Read (RR)** Lock statuses are: G (granted), W (waiting), and C (converting state).	Latches being applied at the EDU (Engine Dispatchable Unit) level, and the status would generally be: H- EDU holding a latch W- EDU waiting on a latch C- Latches are contested (just like lock-waits)
Locks can be monitored using the `SYSPROC.MON_GET_LOCKS ()` table function. The `SYSPROC.MON_GET_APPL_LOCKWAIT ()` table function can be used to find the information about locks for which an application is waiting.	Latches can be monitored using the `SYSPROC.MON_GET_LATCH ()` table function. The `SYSPROC.MON_GET_EXTENDED_LATCH_WAIT ()` table function can be used to find the latch waits between the members and the time it spends in waiting.

The following table shows the table functions available in Db2 v11.1 for accessing lock and latch information:

Table Function	Information Returned
`MON_GET_LOCKS`	Returns a list of all locks in the currently connected database.
`MON_GET_APPL_LOCKWAIT`	Returns information about all the locks that each application's agents connected to the current database are waiting to acquire.
`MON_GET_LATCH`	Returns a list of all latches in the current member.
`MON_GET_EXTENDED_LATCH_WAIT`	Returns information about latches that have been involved in extended latch waits. This information includes latch name, the number of extended waits, and the time spent in extended waits.

To capture and analyze a potential locking problem, use the `SYSPROC.MON_GET_LOCKS ()` table function as follows:

```
SELECT

APPLICATION_HANDLE,

VARCHAR (LOCK_OBJECT_TYPE, 10) AS OBJECT_TYPE,

LOCK_MODE,

LOCK_STATUS,

COUNT (*) AS LOCK_COUNT

FROM TABLE (MON_GET_LOCKS (NULL, -2)) AS MONLOCKS

WHERE LOCK_OBJECT_TYPE IN ('TABLE','ROW','CATALOG','TABLESPACE')

GROUP BY APPLICATION_HANDLE, LOCK_OBJECT_TYPE, LOCK_MODE, LOCK_STATUS

ORDER BY APPLICATION_HANDLE, LOCK_OBJECT_TYPE, LOCK_MODE, LOCK_STATUS;
```

If you want to find the lock holding application handle and the lock waiting application handle, execute the SQL statement as follows:

```
SELECT DISTINCT

B.APPLICATION_HANDLE,

A.HLD_APPLICATION_HANDLE,

A.LOCK_NAME,

A.HLD_MEMBER,

A.LOCK_STATUS FROM TABLE (MON_GET_APPL_LOCKWAIT (NULL, -2)) A JOIN

TABLE (MON_GET_LOCKS (CLOB
('<lock_name>'||A.LOCK_NAME||'</lock_name>'),-2)) B

ON A.LOCK_NAME=B.LOCK_NAME

WHERE A.HLD_APPLICATION_HANDLE IS NOT NULL;
```

APPLICATION_HANDLE	OBJECT_TYPE	LOCK_MODE	LOCK_STATUS	LOCK_COUNT *
454	TABLE	IX	G	5
455	TABLE	IX	G	5
456	TABLE	IX	G	5
457	TABLE	IX	G	5
458	TABLE	IX	G	5
459	TABLE	IX	G	5
460	TABLE	IX	G	5

If you want to capture the latching information, use the `SYSPROC.MON_GET_LATCH ()` table function as follows:

```
SELECT

VARCHAR (LATCH_NAME, 40) AS LATCH_NAME,

VARCHAR (MEMORY_ADDRESS, 20) AS MEMORY_ADDRESS,

EDU_ID,

VARCHAR (EDU_NAME, 20) EDU_NAME,

APPLICATION_HANDLE,

MEMBER,

LATCH_STATUS,

LATCH_WAIT_TIME

FROM TABLE (MON_GET_LATCH (NULL, -2)) ORDER BY LATCH_NAME, LATCH_STATUS;
```

APPLICATION_HANDLE	HLD_APPLICATION_HANDLE	LOCK_NAME	HLD_MEMBER	LOCK_STATUS
28701	28701	0F00040100000000000000000054	0	W
29782	28701	0F00040100000000000000000054	0	W

Monitoring system memory

System memory monitoring focuses on providing information about the system memory allocations from the operating system into memory sets. The following table shows the table functions available in Db2 v11.1 for accessing system memory information:

Table Function	Information Returned
MON_GET_MEMORY_SET	Returns a list of all locks in the currently connected database
MON_GET_MEMORY_POOL	Returns information about all of the locks that each application's agents connected to the current database are waiting to acquire

If you want to view the overall memory utilization by the database manager, database, applications, **fenced mode process** (FMP), and private memory agent, use the following SQL statement:

```
SELECT VARCHAR (MEMORY_SET_TYPE, 20) AS SET_TYPE,

VARCHAR (DB_NAME, 20) AS DBNAME,

(MEMORY_SET_SIZE/1024) AS "MEMORY_SET_SIZE_MB",

(MEMORY_SET_USED/1024) AS "MEMORY_SET_USED_MB",

(MEMORY_SET_USED_HWM/1024) AS "MEMORY_SET_USED_HWM_MB"

FROM TABLE (

MON_GET_MEMORY_SET (NULL, NULL, -2));
```

We will get the following output:

LATCH_NAME	MEMORY_ADDRESS	EDU_ID	EDU_NAME	APPLICATION_HANDLE	MEMBER	LATCH_STATUS	LATCH_WAIT_TIME
SQLO_LT_SQLE_KRCB__EDUChainLatch	0x000000020083F2D2	8765	db2agent (TITO1000)	30310	0	H	{null}
SQLO_LT_sqeWLDispatcher__m_tunerLatch	0x00000002OB110470	14	db2wlmt 0	{null}	0	H	{null}

To find a detailed level of memory utilization for each memory pool within the memory set, use the `SYSPROC.MON_GET_MEMORY_POOL ()` table function:

```
SELECT VARCHAR (MEMORY_SET_TYPE, 10) AS SET_TYPE,

VARCHAR (MEMORY_POOL_TYPE, 20) AS POOL_TYPE,

(MEMORY_POOL_USED/1024) AS "MEMORY_POOL_USED_MB",

(MEMORY_POOL_USED_HWM/1024) AS "MEMORY_POOL_USED_HWM_MB"

FROM TABLE (

MON_GET_MEMORY_POOL ('DBMS', CURRENT_SERVER, -2));
```

We will get the following output:

SET_TYPE	DBNAME	MEMORY_SET_SIZE_MB	MEMORY_SET_USED_MB	MEMORY_SET_USED_HWM_MB
DBMS	{null}	251	176	213
FMP	{null}	1	1	1
PRIVATE	{null}	131	76	222
DATABASE	TITO1000	119425	70734	73291
APPLICATION	TITO1000	36	26	6394

If you want to monitor database memory usage for a specific database, use the following SQL statement:

```
SELECT

VARCHAR (MEMORY_POOL_TYPE, 20) AS POOL_TYPE,

MEMORY_POOL_USED,

MEMORY_POOL_USED_HWM

FROM TABLE (MON_GET_MEMORY_POOL ('DATABASE', NULL, NULL)) AS MONGETMEM
ORDER BY 1 DESC;
```

We will get the following output:

SET_TYPE	POOL_TYPE	MEMORY_POOL_USED_MB	MEMORY_POOL_USED_HWM_MB
DBMS	FCM_LOCAL	0	0
DBMS	FCM_SESSION	8	8
DBMS	FCM_CHANNEL	4	4
DBMS	FCMBP	85	141
DBMS	FCM_CONTROL	2	2
DBMS	MONITOR	1	1
DBMS	RESYNC	0	0
DBMS	OSS_TRACKER	0	0
DBMS	APM	14	24
DBMS	KERNEL	33	50
DBMS	BSU	6	7
DBMS	SQL_COMPILER	6	6
DBMS	FEDERATED	0	0
DBMS	KERNEL_CONTROL	6	6
DBMS	EDU	7	7

Monitoring the pureScale environment

pureScale monitoring focuses on providing information about page reclaims, local and group buffer pool efficiency, and CF operations. The following table shows the table functions available in Db2 v11.1 for accessing pureScale-specific monitoring information:

Table Function	Information Returned
MON_GET_PAGE_ACCESS_INFO	Returns information about buffer pool pages that are being waited on for a specified table
MON_GET_CF_WAIT_TIME	Returns information on the total time of measurements for cluster **caching facility** (CF) commands
MON_GET_CF_CMD	Returns information about the processing times for cluster CF commands
MON_GET_GROUP_BUFFERPOOL	Returns information about the group buffer pool (GBP)

When an application on a member needs to make a change to a page that is currently held exclusively by another member, the CF can request that the p-lock is released early. This process of releasing a page early is called page reclaiming.

This helps to eliminate page lock waits across members, however these reclaims are expensive and so this should be monitored using the `SYSPROC.MON_GET_PAGE_ACCESS_INFO ()` table function as follows:

```
SELECT

VARCHAR (TABNAME, 30) AS NAME,

VARCHAR (OBJTYPE, 10) AS TYPE,

PAGE_RECLAIMS_X AS PGRCX,

PAGE_RECLAIMS_S AS PGRCS,

SPACEMAPPAGE_PAGE_RECLAIMS_X AS SMPPGRCX,

SPACEMAPPAGE_PAGE_RECLAIMS_S AS SMPPGRCS,

RECLAIM_WAIT_TIME

FROM TABLE (MON_GET_PAGE_ACCESS_INFO ('','', NULL)) AS RECLAIMMETRICS ORDER
BY RECLAIM_WAIT_TIME DESC;
```

We will get the following output:

POOL_TYPE	MEMORY_POOL_USED	MEMORY_POOL_USED_HWM
XMLCACHE	448	448
UTILITY	64	167808
SHARED_SORT	2560	2630976
PACKAGE_CACHE	45440	45440
LOCK_MGR	612800	612800
DATABASE	183808	183808
CAT_CACHE	3072	3072
BP	19828288	19828288
BP	9914688	9914688
BP	1748672	1748672
BP	218880	218880
BP	6609792	6609792
BP	33047808	33047808
BP	167104	167104

If you want to monitor the number of CF-specific operations, such as getting the LFS number and registering and deregistering a page, use the SYSPROC.MON_GET_CF_WAIT_TIME () table function as follows:

```
SELECT

VARCHAR (CF_CMD_NAME, 30) AS CF_CMD_NAME,

TOTAL_CF_WAIT_TIME_MICRO AS WAIT_TIME_MICRO,

TOTAL_CF_REQUESTS AS TOTAL_REQUESTS

FROM TABLE (MON_GET_CF_WAIT_TIME (-1))

WHERE ID = '128';
```

We will get the following output:

NAME	TYPE	PGRCX	PGRCS	SMPPGRCX	SMPPGRCS	RECLAIM_WAIT_TIME
QRTZ_SCHEDULER_STATE	TABLE	2224	0	1391	0	67149
T_CUST_ORDR_MGMT_BUSNS_EVT	INDEX	13032	88	0	0	61956
NODEINSTANCELOG	INDEX	6778	0	0	0	50711
NODEINSTANCELOG	TABLE	7055	737	2580	734	41425
VARIABLEINSTANCELOG	INDEX	3696	0	0	0	35079
T_SHPMT_COND_GRP_VRSN	TABLE	6492	31	1605	31	31071
WORKITEMINFO	TABLE	4063	19	357	19	20518
T_NTFCTN_HIST	TABLE	4607	0	13	0	18705
T_CMDTY_GRP_VRSN_ELE	TABLE	2180	2	917	2	16738
T_CMDTY_GRP_VRSN	INDEX	1599	418	1	0	16265

If you want to find the number of requests made from members to the CF, use the SYSPROC.MON_GET_CF_CMD () table function as follows:

```
SELECT

VARCHAR (CF_CMD_NAME, 40) AS CF_CMD_NAME,

TOTAL_CF_REQUESTS AS REQUESTS

FROM TABLE (MON_GET_CF_CMD (129)) AS CF_REQ_METRICS;
```

We will get the following output:

CF_CMD_NAME	WAIT_TIME_MICRO	TOTAL_REQUESTS
DeletePage	802426003	39898123
DeletePageList	0	0
DeleteSA	27708088	1712346
DeleteSAList	138163	192
DeregisterPage	2114328	112571
DeregisterPageList	235407	1452
GetAndIncLFS	306658264	6141760
GetLFS	1253	28
GetLSN	1893217029	112805967
GetNotification	0	0
GetStatus	0	2

Group buffer pool conditions are undesirable in pureScale. In order to check the number of times a group buffer pool has been full, use the SYSPROC.MON_GET_GROUP_BUFFERPOOL () table function as follows:

```
SELECT

SUM (MONGETGROUP.NUM_GBP_FULL) AS NUM_GBP_FULL

FROM TABLE (MON_GET_GROUP_BUFFERPOOL (-2)) AS MONGETGROUP;
```

We will get the following output:

CF_CMD_NAME	REQUESTS
ReadAndRegister	403379724
WriteAndRegister	248721789
WriteAndRegisterMultiple	11799705
ReadCastoutClass	2048
ReadCCInfo	2
ReadForCastout	0
ReadForCastoutMultipleList	0
ReadForCastoutMultiple	0
ReleaseCastoutLocks	0
ReadCacheInfo	72
AttachLocalCache	24
ReadSetLFS	27249799
TryInstant	0
SetLockStateCommands	0

Additional monitoring table functions

The following table shows a few additional table functions available in Db2 v11.1 for accessing information such as routines, transaction log usage, and HADR status information:

Table Function	Information Returned
MON_GET_ROUTINE	Returns the execution metrics for routines in a relational format
MON_GET_TRANSACTION_LOG	Returns information about the transaction logging subsystem for the currently connected database
MON_GET_HADR	Returns information about high availability disaster recovery (HADR) monitoring information

To analyze stored procedure performance, you can execute the following query, which will show the total CPU time consumption in microseconds:

```
SELECT

ROUTINE_TYPE,

ROUTINE_NAME,

TOTAL_CPU_TIME,

TOTAL_TIMES_ROUTINE_INVOKED

FROM

TABLE (MON_GET_ROUTINE (NULL, NULL, NULL, NULL, -2)) AS T

ORDER BY

TOTAL_CPU_TIME DESC;
```

If you want to capture transaction logging information such as the transaction log used, allocated, and log free, you can execute the following query:

```
SELECT

INTEGER TOTAL_LOG_USED/1024/1024) AS "LOG_USED_MB",

INTEGER (TOTAL_LOG_AVAILABLE/1024/1024) AS "LOG_SPACE_FREE_MB",

INTEGER ((FLOAT (TOTAL_LOG_USED) / FLOAT
(TOTAL_LOG_USED+TOTAL_LOG_AVAILABLE))*100) AS "PCT_USED",

INTEGER (TOT_LOG_USED_TOP/1024/1024) AS "MAX_LOG_USED_MB",

INTEGER (SEC_LOG_USED_TOP/1024/1024) AS "MAX_SEC_USED_MB",

INTEGER (SEC_LOGS_ALLOCATED) AS "#SECONDARY_LOGS"

FROM TABLE (MON_GET_TRANSACTION_LOG (-2)) AS MONGETTRAN;
```

If you want to analyze your database active transaction log performance by measuring the average log writes and reads per millisecond, you can execute the following query:

```
SELECT

MEMBER,

SEC_LOG_USED_TOP,

SEC_LOGS_ALLOCATED,

LOG_WRITES,

NUM_LOG_WRITE_IO,

LOG_WRITE_TIME,

CASE WHEN LOG_WRITE_TIME > 0 THEN

(NUM_LOG_WRITE_IO / CAST (LOG_WRITE_TIME AS DECIMAL (18, 6)))

ELSE 0

END AS LOG_WRITES_MS,

CASE WHEN NUM_LOG_WRITE_IO > 0 THEN

(CAST (LOG_WRITE_TIME AS DECIMAL (18, 6)) / NUM_LOG_WRITE_IO)

ELSE 0

END AS IO_COMPLETE_PER_MS,

CASE WHEN NUM_LOG_WRITE_IO > 0 THEN

(LOG_WRITES / NUM_LOG_WRITE_IO)

ELSE 0

END AS PAGES_PER_WRITE,

CASE WHEN LOG_READ_TIME > 0 THEN

(NUM_LOG_READ_IO / CAST (LOG_READ_TIME AS DECIMAL (18, 6)))

ELSE 0
```

```
END AS LOG_READS_MS,

CASE WHEN NUM_LOG_READ_IO > 0 THEN (LOG_READS / NUM_LOG_READ_IO)

ELSE 0

END AS PAGES_PER_READ

FROM TABLE ("SYSPROC"."MON_GET_TRANSACTION_LOG"(CAST (-2 AS INTEGER))) AS
MONGETTRAN FOR FETCH ONLY;
```

If you want to verify the HADR status for a specific HADR pair, you can use the
SYSPROC.MON_GET_HADR () table function as follows:

```
SELECT

HADR_ROLE,

STANDBY_ID,

HADR_STATE,

PRIMARY_MEMBER_HOST,

STANDBY_MEMBER_HOST

FROM TABLE (MON_GET_HADR (NULL));
```

Monitoring table functions: a quick reference

The following table provides a summary of table functions with corresponding monitoring levels and database configuration parameters that control monitoring data collection:

Table Function	Monitor Level	Database Configuration Parameter Control	WLM Service Class Setting
MON_GET_SERVICE_SUBCLASS	Database server	mon_req_metrics	COLLECT REQUEST METRICS
MON_GET_SERVICE_SUBCLASS_DETAILS			
MON_GET_WORKLOAD			
MON_GET_WORKLOAD_DETAILS			
MON_GET_CONNECTION			
MON_GET_CONNECTION_DETAILS			
MON_GET_UNIT_OF_WORK			
MON_GET_UNIT_OF_WORK_DETAILS			
MON_GET_ACTIVITY_DETAILS	Current executing activities	mon_act_metrics	COLLECT ACTIVITY METRICS
MON_GET_PKG_CACHE_STMT			
MON_GET_PKG_CACHE_STMT_DETAILS			
MON_GET_BUFFERPOOL	Data object	mon_obj_metrics	None
MON_GET_TABLESPACE			
MON_GET_CONTAINER			
MON_GET_TABLE		Always collected	
MON_GET_INDEX			

MON_GET_LOCKS	Locks	Always collected	None
MON_GET_APPL_LOCKWAIT			
MON_GET_MEMORY_SET	Database server	Always collected	None
MON_GET_MEMORY_POOL			
MON_GET_ROUTINE	Functions, Procedures, Triggers	mon_rtn_data and mon_rtn_execlist	COLLECT REQUEST METRICS
MON_GET_ROUTINE_DETAILS			
MON_GET_ROUTINE_EXEC_LIST			
MON_GET_SECTION_ROUTINE			
MON_GET_HADR	HADR	Always collected	None
MON_GET_TRANSACTION_LOG	Transaction Log	Always collected	None
MON_GET_FCM	FCM and Table space	Always collected	None
MON_GET_FCM_CONNECTION_LIST			
MON_GET_EXTENT_MOVEMENT_STATUS			

Monitoring table functions: a quick reference

Administrative views for monitoring

A new set of administrative views are available in the SYSIBMADM schema to extract database monitoring information in a relational table format. Unlike monitoring table functions, administrative views do not require input parameters.

The SYSIBMADM schema holds the built-in monitoring administrative views and it requires one of the following authorizations to run these views:

- SELECT privilege on a specific view
- CONTROL privilege on a specific view
- DATAACCESS authority
- DBADM authority
- SQLADM authority

The following table lists the monitoring administrative views constructed on the newer lightweight, high-speed monitoring solution:

Administrative View Name	Information Returned
MON_BP_UTILIZATION	Returns key monitoring metrics for buffer pools, including hit ratio and average read and write times across all the database partitions in the currently connected database
MON_CONNECTION_SUMMARY	Returns key metrics for all connections, including the application handle, total commits, average amount of CPU time spent, and lock waits per activity in the currently connected database
MON_CURRENT_SQL	Returns key metrics for all activities that were submitted across all members of the database and have not yet been completed, including a point-in-time view of both dynamic and static SQL statements presently being executed in the currently connected database
MON_CURRENT_UOW	Returns key metrics for all units of work submitted across all members of the database; it shows long-running units of work statements and helps prevent performance problems
MON_DB_SUMMARY	Returns key metrics aggregated over all service classes across all members in the currently connected database; it is designed to help monitor the system in a high-level manner by providing a concise summary of the database

MON_LOCKWAITS	Returns information about agents working on behalf of applications that are waiting to obtain locks in the currently connected database; it is very useful when it comes to resolving locking problems
MON_PKG_CACHE_SUMMARY	Returns key metrics for both dynamic and static SQL statements in the cache, providing a high-level summary of the database package cache; the metrics returned are aggregated over all executions of the statement across all members of the database
MON_SERVICE_SUBCLASS_SUMMARY	Returns key metrics for all service subclasses in the currently connected database; it is designed to help monitor the system in a high-level manner, showing work executed per service class.
MON_TBSP_UTILIZATION	Returns key monitoring metrics for table spaces in the currently connected database, including all table space attributes, utilization percentage, high watermark, and hit ratio
MON_TRANSACTION_LOG_UTILIZATION	Returns information about transaction log utilization for the currently connected database, including transaction log used as a percentage, in KB, and available log space
MON_WORKLOAD_SUMMARY	Returns key metrics for all workloads in the currently connected database; it is designed to help monitor the system in a high-level manner, showing incoming work per workload

If you want to capture performance metrics for buffer pools, such as data and index hit ratio and the average buffer pool response time in milliseconds, use the following SQL statement:

```
SELECT

VARCHAR (BP_NAME, 30) AS BPOOL_NAME,

DATA_HIT_RATIO_PERCENT,

INDEX_HIT_RATIO_PERCENT,
```

```
XDA_HIT_RATIO_PERCENT,

AVG_PHYSICAL_READ_TIME,

AVG_WRITE_TIME

FROM

SYSIBMADM.MON_BP_UTILIZATION;
```

We will get the following output:

If you want to capture expensive SQL statements that are currently running in your database, execute the following:

```
SELECT

APPLICATION_HANDLE,

ELAPSED_TIME_SEC,

VARCHAR (ACTIVITY_STATE, 10) AS ACTIVITY_STATE,

VARCHAR (ACTIVITY_TYPE, 10) AS ACTIVITY_TYPE,

TOTAL_CPU_TIME,

(ROWS_READ/NULLIF (ROWS_RETURNED, 0)) AS INDEX_EFFICIENCY,

QUERY_COST_ESTIMATE,

VARCHAR (STMT_TEXT, 200) AS STMT_TEXT

FROM SYSIBMADM.MON_CURRENT_SQL

ORDER BY ELAPSED_TIME_SEC DESC;
```

You can also use the SYSIBMADM.MON_PKG_CACHE_SUMMARY administrative view to capture expensive SQL statements:

```
SELECT

SECTION_TYPE,
```

```
    TOTAL_STMT_EXEC_TIME,

    AVG_STMT_EXEC_TIME,

    TOTAL_CPU_TIME,

    AVG_CPU_TIME,

    TOTAL_IO_WAIT_TIME,

    PREP_TIME,

    ROWS_READ_PER_ROWS_RETURNED,

    VARCHAR (STMT_TEXT, 200) AS STMT_TEXT

    FROM

    SYSIBMADM.MON_PKG_CACHE_SUMMARY

    ORDER BY

    TOTAL_CPU_TIME DESC;
```

We will get the following output:

BPOOL_NAME	DATA_HIT_RATIO_PERCENT	INDEX_HIT_RATIO_PERCENT	XDA_HIT_RATIO_PERCENT	AVG_PHYSICAL_READ_TIME	AVG_WRITE_TIME
BP00_32K	99.85	99.72	{null}	7	0
BP03_32K	99.96	{null}	{null}	1	0
BP01_32K	99.99	99.96	{null}	2	0
BP01_04K	99.99	50.00	{null}	13	0
BP02_32K	99.99	99.99	{null}	7	0
BPT01_32K	100.00	100.00	100.00	{null}	{null}

If you want to analyze locking problems in your database, you can use the SYSIBMADM.MON_LOCKWAITS administrative view as follows:

```
    SELECT

    VARCHAR (HLD_APPLICATION_NAME, 10) AS LOCK_HOLDING_APP,

    VARCHAR (HLD_USERID, 10) AS LOCK_HOLDING_USER,

    VARCHAR (REQ_APPLICATION_NAME, 10) AS LOCK_WAITING_APP,

    VARCHAR (REQ_USERID, 10) AS LOCK_WAITING_USER,
```

```
LOCK_MODE,

LOCK_OBJECT_TYPE,

VARCHAR (TABSCHEMA, 10) AS TABSCHEMA,

VARCHAR (TABNAME, 10) AS TABNAME,

VARCHAR (HLD_CURRENT_STMT_TEXT, 20) AS STMT_HOLDING_LOCK,

VARCHAR (REQ_STMT_TEXT, 20) AS STMT_WAITING_LOCK,

LOCK_WAIT_ELAPSED_TIME AS LOCK_WAIT_TIME

FROM

SYSIBMADM.MON_LOCKWAITS;
```

We will get the following output:

APPLICATION_HANDLE	ELAPSED_TIME_SEC	ACTIVITY_STATE	ACTIVITY_TYPE	TOTAL_CPU_TIME	INDEX_EFFICIENCY	QUERY_COST_ESTIMATE	STMT_TEXT
42715	150786	EXECUTING	CALL	584698	{null}	-1	CALL MEDAJAVA.SP_DA_COLLECTOR(?,?,?)
42715	150786	IDLE	READ_DML	1363798	1	6	SELECT DA_PURGE_CNTL_ID,SCHMA_NME,TBL_NME,DA_D..
9766	82255	EXECUTING	CALL	38735040	{null}	-1	CALL MEDAJAVA.SP_DA_PURGE_DATA(?,?,?)
9766	82255	IDLE	READ_DML	32136	5	7	SELECT DISTINCT C.DA_PURGE_CNTL_ID,C.SCHMA_NME,C.
42715	13991	IDLE	READ_DML	760818612	1	15134	SELECT 'MEDA1','TDA_MSG_EQP_CST','(DA_MSG_ID, DA_E..

If you want to list the non-automatic storage-enabled table spaces whose utilization is greater than 95% and may potentially be full, you can use the following SQL statement:

```
SELECT

TBSP_NAME,

TBSP_UTILIZATION_PERCENT

FROM SYSIBMADM.MON_TBSP_UTILIZATION

WHERE

TBSP_UTILIZATION_PERCENT > 95 AND

TBSP_AUTO_RESIZE_ENABLED=0 AND

TBSP_CONTENT_TYPE NOT IN ('SYSTEMP','USRTEMP');
```

It is important that you understand the entire database server workload and performance with respect to the number of commits, the number of rollbacks, and the number of application requests, overall I/O wait time, and overall lock wait time. You can use the `SYSIBMADM.MON_DB_SUMMARY` administrative view to define the overall health of a database:

```
SELECT

APP_RQSTS_COMPLETED_TOTAL,

AVG_RQST_CPU_TIME,

RQST_WAIT_TIME_PERCENT,

ACT_WAIT_TIME_PERCENT,

IO_WAIT_TIME_PERCENT,

AGENT_WAIT_TIME_PERCENT,

LOCK_WAIT_TIME_PERCENT,

NETWORK_WAIT_TIME_PERCENT,

TOTAL_BP_HIT_RATIO_PERCENT

FROM

SYSIBMADM.MON_DB_SUMMARY;
```

We will get the following output:

SECTION_TYPE	TOTAL_STMT_EXEC_TIME	AVG_STMT_EXEC_TIME	TOTAL_CPU_TIME	AVG_CPU_TIME	TOTAL_IO_WAIT_TIME	PREP_TIME	ROWS_READ_PER_ROWS_RETURNED	STMT_TEXT
D	333334713	1556	106411509256	510793	4336340	106	227	SELECT 'S' AS MEAS_CAT
D	286656468	1343	106421632679	498777	3888318	111	227	SELECT 'S' AS MEAS_CAT
D	296010169	1390	106272262463	499111	3856844	109	228	SELECT 'S' AS MEAS_CAT
D	281073204	1352	103708606822	499122	3902012	78	228	SELECT 'S' AS MEAS_CAT
D	267921437	1299	102442655188	497031	3712466	88	226	SELECT 'S' AS MEAS_CAT

The SYSIBMADM.MON_DB_SUMMARY administrative view can be used to display a hierarchical breakdown of all the wait times in the entire database.

If you want to find expensive table scans over the entire database, you can use the following SQL statement:

```
SELECT

APPLICATION_HANDLE,

VARCHAR (APPLICATION_NAME, 20) AS APPL_NAME,

IO_WAIT_TIME_PERCENT AS PERCENT_IO_WAIT,

ROWS_READ_PER_ROWS_RETURNED AS ROWS_READ_VS_RETURNED

FROM

SYSIBMADM.MON_CONNECTION_SUMMARY ORDER BY 4 DESC;
```

We will get the following output:

HLD_APPLICATION_HANDLE	LOCK_HOLDING_USER	REQ_APPLICATION_HANDLE	LOCK_WAITING_USER	LOCK_MODE	LOCK_OBJECT_TYPE	TABSCHEMA	TABNAME	STMT_HOLDING_LOCK	STMT_WAITING_LOCK	LOCK_WAIT_TIME
30657 DB2ANL01		30650 DB2ANL01		S	TABLE	DB2ANL01	T100	(null)	update T100 set id=;	22

A word about the MONREPORT module

The Db2 has a built-in monitoring reporting tool called the MONREPORT module to help DBAs effectively monitor the databases. The following table shows available programs within the MONREPORT module:

Report Name	Procedure Name	Related Table Functions	Description
Summary report	MONREPORT.DBSUMMARY	MON_GET_SERVICE_SUBCLASS, MON_GET_CONNECTION, MON_GET_WORKLOAD	Provides a summary of the system and application performance metrics
Connection report	MONREPORT.CONNECTION	MON_GET_CONNECTION	Provides monitor data for each connection
Current Application report	MONREPORT.CURRENTAPPS	MON_GET_CONNECTION, MON_GET_UNIT_OF_WORK, WLM_GET_SERVICE_CLASS_AGENTS	Provides the current state of processing of units of work, agents, and activities for each connection

Current SQL report	MONREPORT.CURRENTSQL	MON_GET_PKG_CACHE_STMT	Provides information about the top currently running activities
Package Cache report	MONREPORT.PKGCACHE	MON_GET_PKG_CACHE_STMT	Provides top statement metrics by CPU, wait time, and so on
Current Lock-Wait report	MONREPORT.LOCKWAIT	MON_GET_APPL_LOCKWAIT, MON_GET_CONNECTION, WLM_GET_SERVICE_CLASS_AGENTS	Provides information about current lock-wait processes

You can use these reports to troubleshoot SQL performance problems and to create baseline reports for daily monitoring. To invoke the procedure, use the CALL command as follows:

```
CALL MONREPORT.DBSUMMARY ();
```

We will get the following output:

APP_RQSTS_COMPLETED_TOTAL	AVG_RQST_CPU_TIME	RQST_WAIT_TIME_PERCENT	ACT_WAIT_TIME_PERCENT	IO_WAIT_TIME_PERCENT	AGENT_WAIT_TIME_PERCENT	LOCK_WAIT_TIME_PERCENT	NETWORK_WAIT_TIME_PERCENT
3718612633	233	34.92	90.71	91.42	0.00	0.01	0.81

The MONREPORT.DBSUMMARY () procedure can be used to display a hierarchical breakdown of all the wait times in the entire database.

Event monitors

The monitoring table functions and administrative views return the monitoring information for the specific point in time that the routine or the view was run. This is useful when you want to check the current state of your system. However, there are times when you need to capture information about the state of your system at the exact time a specific event occurs. Event monitors serve this purpose.

Event monitors can be created to capture point-in-time information related to different kinds of events that take place within your system. For example, you can create an event monitor to capture information whenever a deadlock cycle or a lock timeout event occurs.

To create an event monitor, use the CREATE EVENT MONITOR SQL statement as follows:

```
CREATE EVENT MONITOR [EventMonName]

FOR [DATABASE |

BUFFERPOOLS |

TABLESPACES |

TABLES |

LOCKING |

UNIT OF WORK |

ACTIVITIES |

PACKAGE CACHE |

STATISTICS |

THRESHOLD VIOLATIONS |

DEADLOCKS <WITH DETAILS> <HISTORY> <VALUES> |

CONNECTIONS <WHERE [EventCondition]> |

STATEMENTS <WHERE [EventCondition]> |

TRANSACTIONS <WHERE [EventCondition]>,] |

CHANGE HISTORY <WHERE EVENT IN [EventControl]>]

WRITE TO [PIPE [PipeName] |

TABLE (TABLE [TableName]) <BLOCKED | NONBLOCKED>|

FILE [DirectoryName] <BLOCKED | NONBLOCKED>]

[MANUALSTART | AUTOSTART]

[ON DBPARTITIONNUM [PartitionNumber]]

[LOCAL | GLOBAL]
```

Where,

- **EventMonName**: Identifies the name to assign to the event monitor that is to be created
- **EventCondition**: Identifies a condition that determines the CONNECTION, STATEMENT, or TRANSACTION events that the event monitor is to collect
- **TableName**: Identifies the name of the database table where all collected event monitor data is to be written
- **EventControl**: Identifies the event controls that specify which events the event monitor is to capture
- **PipeName**: Identifies the name assigned to the named pipe where all collected event monitor data is to be written
- **DirectoryName**: Identifies the name assigned to the directory where one or more files containing event monitor data are to be written
- **PartitionNumber**: Identifies the database partition number or member on which the event monitor needs to collect the data in a partitioned database or pureScale environment

There are several different types of event monitors that can be created in Db2:

- **ACTIVITIES**: Records activity events that occur as the database is used.
- **BUFFERPOOLS**: Records a buffer pool event when the last application disconnects from the database.
- **CONNECTIONS**: Records a connection event when an application disconnects from the database.
- **DATABASE**: Records a database event when the last application disconnects from the database.
- **DEADLOCKS**: Records a deadlock event whenever a deadlock occurs. However, this monitor is depreciated and the LOCKING event should be used instead.
    - DEADLOCKS WITH DETAILS
    - DEADLOCKS WITH DETAILS HISTORY
    - DEADLOCKS WITH DETAILS HISTORY VALUES
- **STATEMENTS**: Records a statement event whenever a SQL statement finishes running.
- **STATISTICS**: Record statistics events that occur when using the database.
- **TABLES**: Records a table event for each active table when the last application disconnects from the database.

- **TABLESPACES**: Records a table space event for each table space when the last application disconnects from the database.
- **THRESHOLD VIOLATIONS**: Records threshold violation events that occur when using the database.
- **TRANSACTIONS**: Records a transaction event whenever a transaction completes. This is deprecated and will be removed in future releases.
- **UNIT OF WORK**: Records events when a unit of work completes.
- **LOCKING**: Records a lock event whenever a lock-related event occurs, such as lock timeout, lock waits, and deadlocks.
- **PACKAGE CACHE**: Records events related to the package cache statement.
- **CHANGE HISTORY**: Records events related to changes to the DB CFG, DBM CFG, and Db2 registry settings. This will also track the execution of utilities such as LOAD, online backup, REORG, and RUNSTATS.

If you want to create an activity event monitor, use the following SQL statement:

```
CREATE EVENT MONITOR activity FOR ACTIVITIES WRITE TO TABLE

CONTROL (TABLE CONTROL_activity),

ACTIVITY (TABLE ACTIVITY_activity),

ACTIVITYSTMT (TABLE ACTIVITYSTMT_activity),

ACTIVITYVALS (TABLE ACTIVITYVALS_activity);
```

The preceding `create` statement will create four tables internally (`ACTIVITYSTMT_ACTIVITY`, `ACTIVITYVALS_ACTIVITY`, `ACTIVITY_ACTIVITY`, and `CONTROL_ACTIVITY`) to record all of the activities happening on the database server.

To initiate event monitor data collection, activate the event monitor using the `SET EVENT MONITOR` statement:

```
SET EVENT MONITOR activity STATE 1;
```

If you want to stop the data collection, you can deactivate the event monitor by using the `SET EVENT MONITOR` statement again:

```
SET EVENT MONITOR activity STATE 0;
```

To review the event monitor information, you can use the following SQL statement:

```
SELECT
ACTIVITY.QUERY_CARD_ESTIMATE,
ACTIVITY.ROWS_RETURNED,
ACTIVITY.POOL_DATA_L_READS + ACTIVITY.POOL_INDEX_L_READS AS LOGICAL_READS,
ACTIVITY.TOTAL_SORTS,
VARCHAR (STMT.STMT_TEXT, 100) AS SQL_TEXT
FROM
ACTIVITYSTMT_ACTIVITY AS STMT,
ACTIVITY_ACTIVITY AS ACTIVITY
WHERE
STMT.APPL_ID = ACTIVITY.APPL_ID AND
STMT.ACTIVITY_ID = ACTIVITY.ACTIVITY_ID AND
STMT.UOW_ID = ACTIVITY.UOW_ID;
```

 The event monitor data can be reviewed while the event monitor is active and collecting the information. It is not necessary to deactivate the event monitor just to review the information.

EXPLAIN facility tools

The EXPLAIN facility provides the capability to capture and view detailed information about the access plan chosen for a particular SQL statement. This information includes performance data that can be used to identify poorly written or executing queries.

The EXPLAIN facility uses a special set of tables to store the information about the queries. These tables can be created by running the EXPLAIN.DDL script found in the sqllib/misc directory or by executing the SYSINSTALLOBJECTS procedure:

```
CALL SYSPROC.SYSINSTALLOBJECTS

('EXPLAIN', 'C', CAST (NULL AS VARCHAR (128)), 'DBA');
```

The following table showcases the different tools available within the Db2 Explain facility. The visual explain tool is a graphical interface provided through the IBM **Data Server Manager (DSM)** to view the access plans for a set of SQL statements. The `db2exfmt` tool provides a more comprehensive set of explain information and is best suited for complex SQL statement analysis. The `db2expln` tool works directly with a package and does not use explain snapshot data:

Attribute	Visual Explain	db2expln	db2exfmt
Type of Output	GUI	Text	Text
Static SQL Statement	No	Yes	Yes
Dynamic SQL Statement	Yes	Yes	Yes
Requires Explain Tables	Yes	No	Yes
Detailed Optimizer Information	Yes	No	Yes

If you want to use the `db2expln` tool to generate an access plan, use the following command:

```
db2expln -d SAMPLE -t -g -statement "SELECT * FROM employee"
```

This will generate access plan information that looks something like the following:

```
Statement:

SELECT *

FROM employee

Intra-Partition Parallelism Degree = 4

Section Code Page = 1208

Estimated Cost = 21.522827

Estimated Cardinality = 1000.000000

Process Using 4 Subagents

| Access Table Name = DB2INST1.EMPLOYEE ID = 2,7

| | #Columns = 14

| | Parallel Scan
```

| | Skip Inserted Rows

| | Avoid Locking Committed Data

| | Currently Committed for Cursor Stability

| | May participate in Scan Sharing structures

| | Scan may start anywhere and wrap, for completion

| | Fast scan, for purposes of scan sharing management

| | Scan can be throttled in scan sharing management

| | Relation Scan

| | | Prefetch: Eligible

| | Lock Intents

| | | Table: Intent Share

| | | Row: Next Key Share

| | Sargable Predicate(s)

| | | Insert Into Asynchronous Local Table Queue ID () = q1

| Insert Into Asynchronous Local Table Queue Completion () ID = q1

Access Local Table Queue ID () = q1 #Columns = 14

Return Data to Application

| #Columns = 14

End of section

Optimizer Plan:

Rows

Operator

(ID)

Cost

```
1000

RETURN

( 1)

21.5228

|

1000

LTQ

( 2)

21.5228

|

1000

TBSCAN

( 3)

21.3901

|

1000

Table:

DB2INST1

EMPLOYEE
```

If you want to generate a detailed report containing all of the explain data, you can execute the db2exfmt command in a sequence shown as follows:

1. Enable the Explain facility by setting the current explain mode to EXPLAIN. This will configure the CURRENT EXPLAIN MODE special register so that the EXPLAIN facility can capture the explain information without executing the SQL statement:

   1. SET CURRENT EXPLAIN MODE EXPLAIN;

2. Run the actual SQL statement in the same session:

   1. `db2 -tvf employee.ddl > employee.log`

3. Disable the Explain facility by setting the current explain mode to NO:

   3. `SET CURRENT EXPLAIN MODE NO`

4. Run the db2exfmt tool:

   4. `db2exfmt -d SAMPLE -g TIC -w -1 -s % -n % -# 0 -o employee.db2exfmt.out`

The detailed explain report will look something like the following:

```
Original Statement:

-------------------

Select * from employee

Optimized Statement:

-------------------

SELECT

Q1.EMPNO AS "EMPNO",

Q1.FIRSTNME AS "FIRSTNME",

Q1.MIDINIT AS "MIDINIT",

Q1.LASTNAME AS "LASTNAME",

Q1.WORKDEPT AS "WORKDEPT",

Q1.PHONENO AS "PHONENO",

Q1.HIREDATE AS "HIREDATE",

Q1.JOB AS "JOB",
```

```
Q1.EDLEVEL AS "EDLEVEL",

Q1.SEX AS "SEX",

Q1.BIRTHDATE AS "BIRTHDATE",

Q1.SALARY AS "SALARY",

Q1.BONUS AS "BONUS",

Q1.COMM AS "COMM"

FROM

DB2INST1.EMPLOYEE AS Q1

Access Plan:

-----------

Total Cost: 21.5228

Query Degree: 4

Rows

RETURN

( 1)

Cost

I/O

 |

1000

LTQ

( 2)

21.5228

3

 |
```

1000

TBSCAN

(3)

21.3901

3

|

1000

TABLE: DB2INST1

EMPLOYEE

Q1

Operator Symbols :

Symbol Description

--------- ---

ATQ : Asynchrony

BTQ : Broadcast

CTQ : Column-organized data

DTQ : Directed

LTQ : Intra-partition parallelism

MTQ : Merging (sorted)

STQ : Scatter

RCTQ : Column-organized data with row as the source

XTQ : XML aggregation

TQ* : Listener

```
Plan Details:

--------------

1) RETURN: (Return Result)

Cumulative Total Cost: 21.5228

Cumulative CPU Cost: 2.73691e+06

Cumulative I/O Cost: 3

Cumulative Re-Total Cost: 0.244257

Cumulative Re-CPU Cost: 1.72372e+06

Cumulative Re-I/O Cost: 0

Cumulative First Row Cost: 7.07554

Estimated Bufferpool Buffers: 3

Arguments:

---------

BLDLEVEL: (Build level)

DB2 v11.1.3.3 : s1803021700

ENVVAR : (Environment Variable)

DB2_ANTIJOIN=EXTEND

HEAPUSE : (Maximum Statement Heap Usage)

96 Pages

PLANID : (Access plan identifier)

41f5e77e71817356

PREPTIME: (Statement prepare time)

15 milliseconds

SEMEVID : (Semantic environment identifier)
```

```
431f78d03d9bb07e

STMTHEAP: (Statement heap size)

16384

STMTID : (Normalized statement identifier)

20314d5950426a1f

Input Streams:

-------------

3) From Operator #2

Estimated number of rows: 1000

Number of columns: 14

Subquery predicate ID: Not Applicable

Column Names:

------------

+Q2.COMM+Q2.BONUS+Q2.SALARY+Q2.BIRTHDATE

+Q2.SEX+Q2.EDLEVEL+Q2.JOB+Q2.HIREDATE

+Q2.PHONENO+Q2.WORKDEPT+Q2.LASTNAME+Q2.MIDINIT

+Q2.FIRSTNME+Q2.EMPNO

....

....

Objects Used in Access Plan:

---------------------------

Schema: DB2INST1

Name: ADEFUSR

Type: Materialized View (reference only)
```

```
Schema: DB2INST1

Name: EMPLOYEE

Type: Table

Time of creation: 2018-05-13-20.43.49.871419

Last statistics update:

Number of columns: 14

Number of rows: 1000

Width of rows: 88

Number of buffer pool pages: 3

Number of data partitions: 1

Distinct row values: No

Tablespace name: USERSPACE1

Tablespace overhead: 6.725000

Tablespace transfer rate: 0.320000

Source for statistics: Single Node

Prefetch page count: 32

Container extent page count: 32

Table overflow record count: 0

Table Active Blocks: -1

Average Row Compression Ratio: -1

Percentage Rows Compressed: -1

Average Compressed Row Size: -1
```

A word about the EXPLAIN operators

An operator is either an action that must be performed on data, or the output from a table or an index, when the access plan for a SQL or XQuery statement is executed.

The operators that appear in an explain plan graph are as follows:

```
CMPEXP IXAND RETURN CTQ

DELETE IXSCAN RIDSCN UNIQUE

FILTER MSJOIN SHIP UPDATE

GENROW NLJOIN SORT UNION

GRPBY PIPE TBSCAN XANDOR

HSJOIN REBAL TEMP ZZJOIN
```

Db2 troubleshooting tools

This section explores two key monitoring and troubleshooting tools: db2pd and dsmtop.

The db2pd command

You can use the Db2 problem determination tool, db2pd, to obtain troubleshooting information from database system memory sets, without acquiring any lock or latch in the database. Since the db2pd tool works directly with memory, it is possible to retrieve information that is changing as it is being collected using minimal Db2 engine resources.

If the database is running in a **Massively Parallel Processing** (**MPP**) setup, a pureScale configuration, or an HADR setup, this command must be run on all the nodes or members of the cluster. However, if you have logical partitions within one physical server in an MPP setup, it collects information for all the logical nodes of the current host.

If you want to see the HADR database status, you can execute the db2pd command either on the primary or on the standby server.

Use the following command to execute the tool:

```
db2pd -db SAMPLE -hadr

Database Member 0 -- Database SAMPLE -- Active -- Up 170 days 08:17:44 --
Date 2018-05-13-20.23.52.606937

HADR_ROLE = PRIMARY

REPLAY_TYPE = PHYSICAL

HADR_SYNCMODE = NEARSYNC

STANDBY_ID = 1

LOG_STREAM_ID = 0

HADR_STATE = PEER

HADR_FLAGS =

PRIMARY_MEMBER_HOST = DB2AXNODE001

PRIMARY_INSTANCE = db2inst1

PRIMARY_MEMBER = 0

STANDBY_MEMBER_HOST = DB2AXNODE002

STANDBY_INSTANCE = db2inst1

STANDBY_MEMBER = 0

HADR_CONNECT_STATUS = CONNECTED

HADR_CONNECT_STATUS_TIME = 11/24/2017 11:08:30.948572 (1511543310)

HEARTBEAT_INTERVAL(seconds) = 30

HEARTBEAT_MISSED = 3

HEARTBEAT_EXPECTED = 21499

HADR_TIMEOUT(seconds) = 120

TIME_SINCE_LAST_RECV(seconds) = 0

PEER_WAIT_LIMIT(seconds) = 300
```

```
LOG_HADR_WAIT_CUR(seconds) = 0.000

LOG_HADR_WAIT_RECENT_AVG(seconds) = 0.000681

LOG_HADR_WAIT_ACCUMULATED(seconds) = 787983.115

LOG_HADR_WAIT_COUNT = 529872503

SOCK_SEND_BUF_REQUESTED,ACTUAL(bytes) = 0, 262088

SOCK_RECV_BUF_REQUESTED,ACTUAL(bytes) = 0, 262088

PRIMARY_LOG_FILE,PAGE,POS = S0135197.LOG, 33536, 21171039888078

STANDBY_LOG_FILE,PAGE,POS = S0135197.LOG, 33521, 21171039826535

HADR_LOG_GAP(bytes) = 2508

STANDBY_REPLAY_LOG_FILE,PAGE,POS = S0135197.LOG, 33520, 21171039822144

STANDBY_RECV_REPLAY_GAP(bytes) = 3728

PRIMARY_LOG_TIME = 05/13/2018 20:23:52.000000 (1526261032)

STANDBY_LOG_TIME = 05/13/2018 20:23:49.000000 (1526261029)

STANDBY_REPLAY_LOG_TIME = 05/13/2018 20:23:48.000000 (1526261028)

STANDBY_RECV_BUF_SIZE(pages) = 131072

STANDBY_RECV_BUF_PERCENT = 0

STANDBY_SPOOL_LIMIT(pages) = 33423360

STANDBY_SPOOL_PERCENT = 0

STANDBY_ERROR_TIME = NULL

PEER_WINDOW(seconds) = 300

PEER_WINDOW_END = 05/13/2018 20:28:50.000000 (1526261330)

READS_ON_STANDBY_ENABLED = N
```

If you want to extract all of the locking information on the SAMPLE database, you can run the db2pd command without actually locking or latching any resource in the database using the following command:

```
db2pd -db SAMPLE -locks

Database Member 0 -- Database SAMPLE -- Active -- Up 170 days 08:19:35 --
Date 2018-05-13-20.25.43.409995

Locks:

Address TranHdl Lockname Type Mode Sts Owner Dur HoldCount Att ReleaseFlg
rrIID

0x0A000300464B7B80 132 FFFA801500390006C0F6000252 RowLock ..X G 132 1 0
0x00200020 0x40000000 0

0x0A000300464CCA00 132 00CE00040000000143DD009952 RowLock ..X G 132 1 0
0x00200008 0x40000000 0

0x0A000300464E4800 132 00CE00040000000143DC00BA52 RowLock ..X G 132 1 0
0x00200008 0x40000000 0

0x0A000300464CDF80 132 00CE00040000000143DE002E52 RowLock ..X G 132 1 0
0x00200008 0x40000000 0

0x0A000300464D5A80 132 00CE00040000000143DD004F52 RowLock ..X G 132 1 0
0x00200008 0x40000000 0

0x0A000300464DAA80 132 00CE00040000000143DC007052 RowLock ..X G 132 1 0
0x00200008 0x40000000 0

0x0A000300464E5C00 132 FFFA80150039000644FF000052 RowLock ..X G 132 1 0
0x00200020 0x40000000 0

0x0A0003010EE78480 97 FFFA8015FFFF00000000000054 TableLock .IX G 97 1 0
0x00202000 0x40000000 0

0x0A0003003D5D6A00 132 FFFA8015FFFF00000000000054 TableLock .IX G 132 255 1
0x00203000 0x40000000 0

0x0A000300D59DC500 116 FFFA8015FFFF00000000000054 TableLock .IN G 116 1 1
0x00002000 0x40000000 0

0x0A000300D59C3880 116 FFFA800F004000000000000054 TableLock .IX G 116 11 1
0x00203000 0x40000000 0
```

```
0x0A0003010EE6B400 97 FFFA8015004000000000000054 TableLock .IX G 97 1 0
0x00203000 0x40000000 0

0x0A000300D59D2980 116 FFFA8015004000000000000054 TableLock .IN G 116 1 1
0x00002000 0x40000000 0
```

The dsmtop command

The `dsmtop` command is a text-based monitoring tool similar to the `db2top` command. The `dsmtop` command uses `MON_GET_*` table functions to gather monitoring information. `MON_GET` table functions are built on a low overhead, lightweight monitoring infrastructure, so it is highly recommended to use `dsmtop` instead of `db2top` on databases that are running on version Db2 10.1 and higher.

The dsmtop command can provide information about:

- **Sessions**: The connections that are active, blocked, or idle.
- **SQL statements**: Recently executed SQL statements. The tool also provides a drill down to see the full SQL text or to run an explain on a statement.
- **Top consumers**: Connections or activities are consuming the most CPU, IO, or another resource.
- **Time spent metrics**: The breakdown of overall time spent by the database.

You can invoke the `dsmtop` tool by running the following command:

```
dsmtop -d <DBNAME> -n <HOSTNAME> -r <PORT NUMBER> -u <USER NAME>
```

For example, to monitor the `SAMPLE` database that is running on the `DB2HOST001` server, you can execute the following command:

```
dsmtop -d SAMPLE -n DB2HOST001 -r 50000 -u db2inst1
```

APPLICATION_HANDLE	APPL_NAME	PERCENT_IO_WAIT	ROWS_READ_VS_RETURNED
39657	db2jcc_application	86.51	749
36783	tlog2DB	79.90	171
36992	toad.exe	80.89	58
36775	tlog2DB	72.27	29
18230	db2jcc_application	41.46	28
36771	tlog2DB	83.15	6

Summary

The objective of this chapter was to acquaint you with the following concepts:

- Monitoring table functions and administrative views to collect and analyze the health and performance of a database
- Event monitors to capture and analyze certain event information in a database
- The EXPLAIN facility tool to capture and analyze explain information for SQL queries
- A few database problem determination tools to monitor and troubleshoot database- or application-related problems

Practice questions

Question 1: How do you activate database objects monitoring elements such as `object_data_l_reads` **and** `object_data_p_reads`?

1. `UPDATE DBM CFG DFT_MON_TABLE to ON`
2. `UPDATE DB CFG USING MON_OBJ_METRICS BASE`
3. `UPDATE MONITOR SWITCHES USING TABLE ON`
4. `UPDATE DBM CFG USING HEALTH_MON ON`

Question 2: Which of the following are column-organized monitoring elements? (Choose two)

1. `POOL_COL_L_READS`
2. `POOL_DATA_L_READS`
3. `POOL_DATA_P_READS`
4. `POOL_COL_P_READS`
5. `POOL_DATA_WRITES`

Question 3: Which statement will modify the current explain mode special register so that explain can capture without actually running the SQL statement?

1. SET CURRENT EXPLAIN MODE YES
2. SET CURRENT EXPLAIN MODE NO
3. SET CURRENT EXPLAIN MODE EXPLAIN
4. SET CURRENT EXPLAIN REOPT

Question 4: Which statement is FALSE about the Db2 problem determination tool (db2pd)?

1. The db2pd tool can obtain quick and immediate information from the Db2 database system memory sets.
2. The db2pd tool does not require a connection to an active database to obtain information about it.
3. The db2pd tool can obtain information about an instance that has stopped prematurely.
4. Because db2pd works directly with memory, it is possible to retrieve information that will change as it is being collected.

Question 5: What information can you obtain by analyzing db2exfmt command output data?

1. Access plan, optimized statement, total execution time in timerons.
2. Access plan, optimized statement, total execution time in minutes.
3. Access plan, optimized statement, total execution time in milliseconds.
4. Access plan, optimized statement, total execution time in seconds.

Question 6: Which tool should you use to capture the lock-wait information?

1. db2pdcfg
2. db2pd
3. db2mtrk
4. db2top

Question 7: Which of the following is NOT a valid table queue explain operator?

1. DTQ
2. BTQ
3. CTQ
4. COLQ

Question 8: How does dsmtop capture monitoring information?

1. It captures information using administrative views.
2. It captures information using event monitors.
3. It captures information using monitoring table functions.
4. It captures information using the db2top tool command.

Question 9: Which tool should you use to analyze a database for architectural integrity without taking the applications down?

1. db2dart
2. db2fodc
3. inspect
4. db2support

Question 10: Which is the best way to retrieve buffer pool metrics information?

1. Ensure the MON_OBJ_METRICS configuration parameter is enabled, and query the BP_HITRATIO table function.
2. Ensure the MON_ACT_METRICS configuration parameter is enabled, and query the BP_HITRATIO administrative view.
3. Ensure the MON_OBJ_METRICS configuration parameter is enabled, and query the MON_GET_BUFFERPOOL table function.
4. Ensure the MON_ACT_METRICS configuration parameter is enabled, and query the MON_GET_BUFFERPOOL administrative view.

Solutions

- **Question 1**:

    The correct answer is B. The database configuration parameter MON_OBJ_METRICS controls the collection of data object metrics of an entire database.

- **Question 2**:

    The correct answers are A and D. The column-organized monitor elements will have _COL_ in their name and the row-organized monitor elements will have _DATA_ in their name.

- **Question 3**:

    The correct answer is C. If you want to generate a detailed report consisting of all the explain data, you can execute the db2exfmt command in a sequence like the following:

    Step 1: Enable the Explain facility by setting the current explain mode to EXPLAIN. This will change the CURRENT EXPLAIN MODE special register so that the EXPLAIN facility can capture the explain information without actually executing the SQL statement:

    ```
    SET CURRENT EXPLAIN MODE EXPLAIN;
    ```

    Step 2: Run the actual SQL statement in the same session.

    Step 3: Disable the EXPLAIN facility by setting the current explain mode to NO:

    ```
    SET CURRENT EXPLAIN MODE NO
    ```

    Step 4: Run the db2exfmt tool.

- **Question 4**:

    The correct answer is C. The db2pd command cannot obtain information about an instance that has stopped prematurely. However, the remaining statements are correct.

- **Question 5**:

    The correct answer is A. The `db2exfmt` command output will always display total execution time information in timerons. A timeron is an IBM invented relative unit of measurement and its values are determined by the optimizer, based on internal values such as statistics that change as the database is used and the available resources on the server.

- **Question 6**:

    The correct answer is B. The `db2pd` command can be used to capture lock-wait information. The `db2pdcfg` command can be used to set flags in the database memory sets to influence the system's behavior for troubleshooting purposes. The `db2mtrk` command can be used to determine the memory usage and `db2top` is a depreciated text-based tool command.

- **Question 7**:

    The correct answer is D. There is no `COLQ` operator in Db2. The other operators are valid Db2 table queue operators:

    DTQ – Directed Table Queue

    BTQ – Broadcast Table Queue

    CTQ – Column Table Queue – to transition the data being processed from column-organized to row-organized

- **Question 8**:

    The correct answer is C. The `dsmtop` command uses `MON_GET` table functions to gather monitoring information and, as you are aware, `MON_GET` table functions are built on a low overhead, lightweight monitoring infrastructure.

- **Question 9**:

  The correct answer is C. The `inspect` command verifies the database and database objects for architectural integrity, checking the pages of the database for page consistency. This can be run even when the database is actively serving the application connections. The `db2dart` command also examines databases for architectural correctness and reports any encountered errors, but it is recommended to deactivate the database before running the `db2dart` command. The `db2fodc` command captures symptom-based data about the Db2 instance to help in problem determination situations. It is intended to collect information about potential hangs, severe performance issues, and various types of errors, but does not verify the architectural integrity of the database. The `db2support` command collects diagnostic information for IBM Db2 product support analysis.

- **Question 10**:

  The correct answer is C. It is highly recommended that you use the `SYSPROC/MON_GET_BUFFERPOOL ()` table function (lightweight infrastructure) to retrieve buffer pool information.

6
Db2 Utilities

This chapter will introduce you to the data movement utilities, such as Import, Export, Load, and Ingest, that are available in Db2. You will be able to use online table movement procedures to copy a specific table and specific schema without impacting on applications. You will also be introduced to database maintenance utilities such as REORG, REORGCHK, REBIND, and RUNSTATS. In addition to this, you will learn how to use the db2look and db2move tool commands:

- Demonstrate the ability to use the Export utility to extract data from a database and store it in an external file
- Demonstrate the ability to use the Import and Load (bulk-load) utilities to load the data from an external file to a database table
- Demonstrate the ability to use the **Continuous Data Ingest** (**CDI**) utility to perform high-speed data transformation, and loading into a database table
- Demonstrate the ability to choose the appropriate data load utility based on business requirements
- Demonstrate the ability to use the `ADMIN_MOVE_TABLE ()` and `ADMIN_COPY_SCHEMA ()` built-in procedures to copy data without impacting application functionality
- Demonstrate the ability to use the `db2move` tool command to copy objects and data between databases
- Demonstrate the ability to use database maintenance utilities, such as `REORG`, `REORGCHK`, `REBIND`, `RUNSTATS` and `ADMIN_CMD ()`
- Demonstrate the ability to extract database and data definitions using the `db2look` tool command

 Certification test:
Number of Questions: 8
Percentage in the Exam: 13%

Data movement file formats

The Db2 data movement utilities recognize and support four different file formats; they are the following:

- **Delimited ASCII (DEL)**: This file format is used in several relational database management systems. In this format, each row is extracted to a single line. Within each line, data values are separated by a delimiter, a unique character other than data values themselves. By default, the column delimiter is a comma, the row delimiter is a new line character (0x0A), and the character delimiter is a double quotation mark (").

  For example, if you export a table data in DEL format using default delimiters, the content could look similar to the following:

  ```
  "000030","SALLY","C01","MANAGER "
  "000050","JOHN","E01","MANAGER "
  "000110","VINCENZO","A00","SALESREP"
  "000120","SEAN","A00","CLERK    "
  "000150","BRUCE","D11","DESIGNER"
  "000160","ELIZABETH","D11","DESIGNER"
  ```

  When you execute a SELECT statement on the EMPLOYEE table for the preceding set of records, it would look like the following:

  ```
  SELECT empno, firstnme, workdept, job FROM employee WHERE empno
  IN ('000030','000050','000110','000120','000150','000160');

  EMPNO  FIRSTNME      WORKDEPT  JOB
  ------ ------------- --------- --------
  000110 VINCENZO      A00       SALESREP
  000120 SEAN          A00       CLERK
  000150 BRUCE         D11       DESIGNER
  000160 ELIZABETH     D11       DESIGNER
  000030 SALLY         C01       MANAGER
  000050 JOHN          E01       MANAGER
  ```

- **Non-delimited or fixed-length ASCII (ASC)**: The non-delimited ASCII file format is also used by multiple software and database applications. In this format, each row is also extracted to a single line. Instead of using a delimiter, the data values have a fixed length and the position of each value in the file determines the column associated with the data. This file format is also known as the **fixed-length ASCII file format**.

For example, data could be extracted from a table called `EMPLOYEE` with the following definition:

```
Select * from EMPLOYEE;
```

This would produce a file that looks like the following:

```
000030SALLY         C01MANAGER
000050JOHN          E01MANAGER
000110VINCENZO      A00SALESREP
000120SEAN          A00CLERK
000150BRUCE         D11DESIGNER
000160ELIZABETH     D11DESIGNER
```

- **PC Integration Exchange Format (PC/IXF)**: The PC/IXF file format is a special file format used exclusively to move data between different Db2 databases. In this file format, table definitions and associated index definitions are stored in the export file, along with data. For example, if you export the data using PC/IXF format, the content might look similar to the following:

```
000051HIXF0002DB2      02.00201805192339190000060081901200
001604T012employee.ixf
000

CMPC   I00004                                  PK_EMPLOYEE

5EMPNO
NNYN000000000000000000000000000000000000000000000000000000000000
000000000000000000000000000000000000000000000000000000000000000000
00000000000000000000000000000000000000000000000
000000000000000000000000000000000000000000000000000000000000000000
000000000000000000000000000000000000000000000000000000000000000000
00000000000000000000000000000000000000000000000
000000000000000000000000000000000000000000000000000000000000000000
000000000000000000000000000000000000000000000000000000000000000000
00000000000000000000000000000000000000000000000
00000000000000000000000000000000000000872C008FIRSTNME
NNYN
000000000000000000000000000000000000000000000000000000000000000000
000000000000000000000000000000000000000000000000000000000000000000
0000000000000000000000
000000000000000000000000000000000000000000000000000000000000000000
000000000000000000000000000000000000000000000000000000000000000000
0000000000000000000000000000000000000000000000
000000000000000000000000000000000000000000000000000000000000000000
000000000000000000000000000000000000000000000000000000000000000000
00000000000000000000000000000000000000000000000
```

```
000000000000000000000000000000000000000000000000000000000000000
00000872C008WORKDEPT
```

Unlike DEL and ASC formats, PC/IXF is not stored in a native format readable by the user. This option is only for copying data between Db2 databases. It cannot be used to move data between Db2 and other vendor databases.

- **Cursor**: This is not exactly a file format type, but a way to move data between Db2 databases using the LOAD command.
  For example, if you want to load a table data from one database to another within the same instance or across the instances, you can execute the following statements:

```
DECLARE c1 CURSOR FOR SELECT * FROM employee;
LOAD FROM c1 OF CURSOR MESSAGES /ds/exp/load.msg INSERT INTO
employee;
```

Data movement utilities

Db2 provides various data movement utilities to transfer data between databases and external files and are as listed below:

- The Db2 Export utility
- The Db2 Import utility
- The Db2 Load utility
- The Db2 Ingest utility

The Db2 Export utility

The Export utility extracts data from a Db2 database table or view and externalizes it to a file, using the DEL format or the PC/IXF format. Such files can then be used to load data into other databases or can be used by other software applications such as spreadsheets and word processors to analyze the exported data.

The basic syntax for the EXPORT command is as shown:

```
EXPORT TO [FileName] OF [DEL | WSF | IXF]
<LOBS TO [LOBPath]>
<LOBFILE [LOBFileName]>
<XML TO [XMLPath]>
```

```
<XMLFILE [XMLFileName]>
<MODIFIED BY [Modifiers]>
<METHOD N ([ColumnNames])>
<MESSAGES [MsgFileName]>
[SELECTStatement]
```

Where,

- `FileName`: Identifies the name and location of the external file to which to export or copy data
- `LOBPath`: Identifies one or more locations to store LOB data
- `LOBFileName`: Identifies one or more base names to which LOB data values are to be written
- `XMLPath`: Identifies one or more locations to store XML documents
- `XMLFileName`: Identifies one or more base names to use to name the files to which XML documents are to be written
- `Modifiers`: Identifies one or more options to use to override the default behavior of the Export utility
- `ColumnNames`: Identifies one or more column names to write to the external file to which data is to be exported
- `MsgFileName`: Identifies the name and location of an external file to which messages produced by the Export utility are to be written as the export operation is performed
- `SELECTStatement`: Identifies a `SELECT` SQL statement that, when executed, will retrieve the data to copy to an external file

A simple `EXPORT` command is as shown here:

```
EXPORT TO employee.del OF DEL MESSAGES employee.msg SELECT *
FROM employee;
```

If you want to export data stored in a table named `EMP_PHOTO` to a PC/IXF format and all **large object values** (**LOB**) stored in the PICTURE column are written to individual files, you can do so by executing the `EXPORT` command:

```
EXPORT TO /ds/data/EMP_PHOTO.ixf OF IXF
LOBS TO /ds/lob
LOBFILE e_picture
MODIFIED BY lobsinfile
MESSAGES /ds/msg/emp_photo.msg
SELECT * FROM emp_photo;
-- Output would look something like below
```

```
         Number of rows exported: 8
         -- The message file will have information about the number of records
     exported and also record the errors if any during the execution
         ==> cat emp_photo.msg
         SQL3104N  The Export utility is beginning to export data to file
         "/db/home/db2inst1/data/EMP_PHOTO.ixf".
         SQL3105N  The Export utility has finished exporting "8" rows.
         -- The data export file would look like:
         ==> ls -ltr
         total 8
         -rw-rw---- 1 db2inst1 db2inst1 7845 May 20 08:04 EMP_PHOTO.ixf
         -- The LOB values were exported to individual files per record
         ==> ls -ltr
         total 392
         -rw-rw---- 1 db2inst1 db2inst1 43690 May 20 08:04 e_picture.001.lob
         -rw-rw---- 1 db2inst1 db2inst1 29540 May 20 08:04 e_picture.002.lob
         -rw-rw---- 1 db2inst1 db2inst1 71798 May 20 08:04 e_picture.003.lob
         -rw-rw---- 1 db2inst1 db2inst1 29143 May 20 08:04 e_picture.004.lob
         -rw-rw---- 1 db2inst1 db2inst1 73438 May 20 08:04 e_picture.005.lob
         -rw-rw---- 1 db2inst1 db2inst1 39795 May 20 08:04 e_picture.006.lob
         -rw-rw---- 1 db2inst1 db2inst1 63542 May 20 08:04 e_picture.007.lob
         -rw-rw---- 1 db2inst1 db2inst1 36088 May 20 08:04 e_picture.008.lob
```

- The authorizations required to invoke the EXPORT command is data access administration authority (DATAACCESS) or CONTROL privilege on each participating table or SELECT privilege on each participating table.
- The supported file formats are these: DEL, PC/IXF and Work Sheet File Format (WSF).

The Db2 Import utility

If you want to read data directly from an external file and insert it into a specific table or an updatable view, you can use the IMPORT utility. The external files can be in one of the file formats: DEL, ASC, PC/IXF, and WSF.

The basic syntax for IMPORT command is as shown here:

```
IMPORT FROM [FileName] OF [DEL | ASC | WSF | IXF]
<LOBS FROM [LOBPath]>
<XML FROM [XMLPath]>
<MODIFIED BY [Modifiers]>
<Method>
<XML PARSE [STRIP | PRESERVE] WHITESPACE>
<XMLVALIDATE USING [XDS | SCHEMA [SchemaID]]>
```

```
<ALLOW NO ACCESS | ALLOW WRITE ACCESS>
<COMMITCOUNT [CommitCount] | COMMITCOUNT AUTOMATIC>
<RESTARTCOUNT | SKIPCOUNT [RestartCount]>
<WARNINGCOUNT [WarningCount]>
<NOTIMEOUT>
<MESSAGES [MsgFileName]>
[CREATE | INSERT | INSERT_UPDATE | REPLACE | REPLACE_CREATE]
    INTO [TableName] <([ColumnNames])>
    <IN [TSName] <INDEX IN [TSName]> <LONG IN [TSName]>>
```

Where:

- FileName: Identifies the name and location of the external file from which to import data
- LOBPath: Identifies one or more LOB locations that are to be imported
- XMLPath: Identifies one or more XML locations that are to be imported
- Modifiers: Identifies one or more options to use to override the default behavior of the Import utility
- Method: Identifies the method to use to read data values from an external file
- SchemaID: Identifies the XML schema identifier against which to validate XML documents being imported
- CommitCount: Identifies the number of rows to copy to the table/updatable view specified before a commit operation is performed
- RestartCount: Identifies the number of rows of data to skip in the external file specified
- WarningCount: Identifies the number of warnings to allow before the import operation is terminated
- MsgFileName: Identifies the name and location of an external file to which to write messages produced by the Import utility as the import operation is performed
- TableName: Identifies the name of the table or updatable view to which data is to be copied
- ColumnNames: Identifies one or more specific columns to which to copy the data
- TSName: Identifies the table space to store the table and its regular data, indexes, and long data/large object data if the table specified is to be created

A simple `IMPORT` command and a sample output looks like the following:

```
IMPORT FROM /ds/data/EMP_PHOTO.ixf OF IXF
LOBS FROM /ds/lob
MODIFIED BY lobsinfile
MESSAGES /ds/log/import.msg
INSERT INTO emp_photo;
-- Output would look something like below
Number of rows read       = 8
Number of rows skipped    = 0
Number of rows inserted   = 8
Number of rows updated    = 0
Number of rows rejected   = 0
Number of rows committed  = 8
```

There are five data copy control options available with the `IMPORT` command and these control how the target table data to be copied. The options are as follows:

- `CREATE`: The target table is created along with all of its associated indexes, and data is then imported into the new table. This option can also control the table space for the new table. However, this option can only be used when importing data from PC/IXF formatted files. The PC/IXF file formats will store the table and associated index definitions along with actual data.

- `INSERT`: Data is inserted into the target table, and the table must be made available before the `INSERT` operation.

- `INSERT_UPDATE`: Data is either inserted into the target table if not already present or if the row exists the data is updated (applicable only if the row being imported has a primary key value that matches that of an existing record).

- `REPLACE`: Any existing data is deleted from the target table and then the new data is inserted. For this option to work, the table must be already exist in the database.

- `REPLACE_CREATE`: Any existing data is deleted from the target table if it already exists, and then the new data is inserted. However, if the target table does not exist, it will be created (only if the file format is PC/IXF) along with all the associated indexes. Data is then imported into the new table.

The authorizations required to invoke the `IMPORT` command based on the data copy control options are as stated below:

- **IMPORT with INSERT**: DATAACCESS authority or `CONTROL` privilege on each participating table, view, or nickname, or `INSERT` and `SELECT` privilege on each participating table or view

- **IMPORT with INSERT_UPDATE**: DATAACCESS authority or CONTROL privilege on each participating table, view, or nickname, or INSERT, SELECT, UPDATE, and DELETE privilege on each participating table or view
- **IMPORT with REPLACE_CREATE**: DATAACCESS authority or CONTROL privilege on each participating table, or view or INSERT, SELECT, and DELETE privilege on each participating table or view. If table does not exist, then DBADM and CREATETAB authority to create a new table, and copy data into it. The supported file formats are these: DEL, ASC, PC/IXF and WSF

The Db2 Load Utility

The Load utility also copies data from an external file of various file formats such as DEL, ASC, PC/IXF and CURSOR to a database. The following table lists the differences between the Import and the Load utilities.

Import Utility	Load Utility
The Import utility is slow when processing large amounts of data. This is because IMPORT command calls concurrent INSERT statements threads in the background, and it operates at row level.	The Load utility is significantly faster than the Import utility when processing large amounts of data. This is because LOAD command writes formatted pages directly into the database table space containers.
Tables and associated indexes can be created from IXF format files.	Tables and associated indexes must exist before data can be loaded into them.
The Import utility makes limited use of intra-partition parallelism.	The Load utility takes full advantage of intra-partition parallelism.
WSF formatted files are supported.	WSF formatted files are not supported.
Data can be imported into tables, views, or aliases that refer to tables or views.	Data can be loaded only into tables or aliases that refer to tables. With this method, data cannot be loaded into views or aliases that refer to views.
Table spaces in which the table and its indexes reside remain online during the import operation.	Table spaces in which the table and its indexes reside are marked load in progress (0x20000) during the load operation, and enforces a backup at the end of the operation if the LOAD is running RECOVERABLE.
Import utility transactions are recorded in the database's transaction log files.	Minimal logging is performed. Load utility transactions are not recorded in the database's transaction log files.

Triggers can be fired during processing.	Triggers are not fired during processing.
Import utility use space freed by the deleted rows.	Load utility builds new extents in sequential order.
If an import operation is interrupted, and a commit frequency was specified, the table will remain usable, and it will contain all rows that were inserted up to the moment the last commit operation was performed. The user has the option of restarting the import operation or leaving the table as it is.	If a load operation was interrupted, and a consistency point (commit frequency) value was specified, the table remains in the *Load pending* state and cannot be used until the following conditions are met: (1) The load process is restarted, and the load operation is completed, or (2) The table space in which the table resides is restored from a backup image that was created before the load operation was initiated, or (3) The load process is terminated, or (4) Run a REPLACE operation is run against the same table on which the load operation failed.
All constraint checking is performed during processing.	Only uniqueness checking is performed during processing. All other constraint checking such as check constraints, referential integrity constraints, etc. must be performed after the load operation has completed using the SET INTEGRITY SQL statement.
The index key values inserted for each row into an appropriate index during an import operation.	All index keys are sorted during a load operation, and the indexes are rebuilt when the load phase of the load operation has completed.
Statistics must be manually collected after an import operation is performed.	Statistics can be collected and updated during a load operation using STATISTICS USE PROFILE option.
A backup image is not created during an import operation.	A backup image (copy) of the LOAD operation can be created during the execution of Load utility by using the COPY YES option.
Hierarchical data is supported.	Hierarchical data is not supported.
Data conversion between code pages is not performed.	Character data (and numeric data expressed as characters) can be converted from one code page to another during processing.

Cannot override columns defined as GENERATED ALWAYS.	Can override columns defined as GENERATED ALWAYS by using the `GENERATEDIGNORE` and `IDENTITYIGNORE` file type modifiers.
Adapted from Db2 v11.1 Knowledge Center's *"Differences between the import and load utility"* section	

Differences between Import and Load utilities

- Import utility supports data copy into tables, views, and nicknames, whereas Load utility supports data copy only into tables.
- Triggers and constraints are activated when using Import utility, whereas it is not activated when using the Load utility.
- Both Import and Load utilities support XML and LOB data types.

The basic syntax for LOAD command is as shown:

```
LOAD <CLIENT> FROM [FileName OF [DEL | ASC | IXF] |
    PipeName | Device | CursorName OF CURSOR]
<LOBS FROM [LOBPath]>
<MODIFIED BY [Modifiers]>
<Method>
<SAVECOUNT [SaveCount]>
<ROWCOUNT [RowCount]>
<WARNINGCOUNT [WarningCount]>
<MESSAGES [MsgFileName]>
<TEMPFILES PATH [TempFilesPath]>
[INSERT | REPLACE | RESTART | TERMINATE]
INTO [TableName] < ([ColumnNames])>
<FOR EXCEPTION [ExTableName]>
<STATISTICS [NO | USE PROFILE]>
<NONRECOVERABLE | COPY YES TO [CopyLocation or TSM]>
<WITHOUT PROMPTING>
<DATA BUFFER [Size]>
<INDEXING MODE [AUTOSELECT | REBUILD | INCREMENTAL |
    DEFERRED]>
<ALLOW NO ACCESS | ALLOW READ ACCESS <USE [TmpTSName]>>
<SET INTEGRITY PENDING CASCADE [IMMEDIATE | DEFERRED]>
```

Let's explore some of the terms from the following code:

- `FileName`: Identifies the name and location of one or more external files from which to copy data
- `PipeName`: Identifies the name of one or more named pipes in Unix from which to copy data
- `Device`: Identifies the name of one or more devices from which to copy data
- `CursorName`: Identifies the name of one or more cursors from which to copy data
- `LOBPath`: Identifies one or more locations to store LOB data to be loaded
- `Modifiers`: Identifies one or more options to use to override the default behavior of the Load utility
- `Method`: Identifies the method to use to extract data values from an external files specified, and map them to one or more columns of the target table
- `SaveCount`: Identifies the number of rows to copy to the target table before the Load utility will establish a new consistency point
- `RowCount`: Identifies the number of rows to load from an external files into a table
- `WarningCount`: Identifies the number of warning conditions the Load utility should ignore before terminating the load operation
- `MsgFileName`: Identifies the name and location of an external file to which to write messages that the Load utility produces as the load operation is performed
- `TempFilesPath`: Identifies the location to store temporary files that the Load utility might need
- `TableName`: Identifies the name to assign to the table into which to load data (this cannot be the name of a system catalog table)
- `ColumnName`: Identifies one or more specific columns (by name) into which to load data
- `ExTableName`: Identifies the name to assign to the table to which to copy all rows that violate unique index or primary key constraints defined for the target table specified
- `CopyLocation`: Identifies the directory or device that is to store a backup copy of all data loaded into the target table
- `Size`: Identifies the number of 4 KB pages to use as buffered storage space for transferring data within the Load utility
- `TmpTSName`: Identifies the system temporary table space in which to build shadow copies of indexes before they are copied to the appropriate regular table space for final storage during the Index Copy phase of a load operation

A simple `LOAD` command and a sample output look like the following:

```
LOAD FROM /ds/data/EMP_PHOTO.ixf OF IXF
LOBS FROM /ds/lob
MODIFIED BY lobsinfile
MESSAGES /ds/log/load.msg
REPLACE INTO emp_photo
STATISTICS USE PROFILE;
-- Output would look something like below
SQL3501W  The table space(s) in which the table resides will not be
placed in backup pending state since forward recovery is disabled for the
database.
SQL3519W  Begin Load Consistency Point. Input record count = "0".
SQL3520W  Load Consistency Point was successful.
SQL3110N  The utility has completed processing.  "8" rows were read
from the input file.
SQL3519W  Begin Load Consistency Point. Input record count = "8".
SQL3520W  Load Consistency Point was successful.
SQL3515W  The utility has finished the "LOAD" phase at time "05/21/2018
08:36:54.443136".
SQL3107W  At least one warning message was encountered during LOAD
processing.
Number of rows read         = 8
Number of rows skipped      = 0
Number of rows loaded       = 8
Number of rows rejected     = 0
Number of rows deleted      = 0
Number of rows committed    = 8
```

The Load utility supports writing any row that violates a unique index or a primary key index into an exception table, however, this exception table must exist before running the Load utility. The required exception table can be created using the following `CREATE TABLE` statement:

```
CREATE TABLE emp_photo_exception LIKE emp_photo IN TS_DATA;
```

You can even add two optional columns to record the violated row, insert timestamp, and the reason for the violation using the `ALTER TABLE` statement.

```
ALTER TABLE emp_photo_exception
ADD COLUMN rec_ts TIMESTAMP
ADD COLUMN rec_log_msg CLOB (32K);
```

Basic syntax to use the exception table during the Load utility is as follows:

```
LOAD FROM /ds/data/EMP_PHOTO.ixf OF IXF
LOBS FROM /ds/lob
MODIFIED BY lobsinfile
MESSAGES /ds/log/load.msg
REPLACE INTO emp_photo
FOR EXCEPTION emp_photo_exception
STATISTICS USE PROFILE;
```

There are four data-copy control options available with the LOAD command, and these control how the target table data to be copied. The options are as follows:

- INSERT: Data is inserted into an existing target table. A LOAD INSERT operation into a column-organized table maintains table statistics by default.
- REPLACE: Any existing data is deleted from the target table, and then the new data is loaded. As in LOAD INSERT operation, a LOAD REPLACE operation into a column-organized table maintains table statistics by default.
- If you specify KEEPDICTIONARY, an existing compression dictionary is preserved across the LOAD REPLACE operation. Similarly, if you specify RESETDICTIONARY, the LOAD REPLACE operation rebuilds a new dictionary for the table data object.
- RESTART: Restarts an interrupted Load operation. The Load operation automatically continues from the last consistency point in the Load, Build, or Delete phase. This option is not supported for column-organized tables and any RANDOM distribution tables.
- TERMINATE: Terminates a previously interrupted load operation. And if the previous load operation was with INSERT, it rolls the operation back to the point in time at which it started. If the previous load operation was with REPLACE, data in the target table is truncated.

Phases of a load operation

A complete load operation consists of five distinct phases; they are as follows:

- Analyze phase
- Load phase
- Build phase
- Delete phase
- Index copy phase

Analyze phase: This phase of the Load process is only utilized when a column-organized table is being loaded and the column compression dictionaries need to be built. This happens during a LOAD REPLACE operation, a LOAD REPLACE RESETDICTIONARY operation, a LOAD REPLACE RESETDICTIONARYONLY operation, or a LOAD INSERT operation (if the column-organized table is empty). For column-organized tables, this phase is followed by the load, build, and delete phases. The following diagram showcases the steps involved in the analyze phase. The analyze phase is invoked if you are loading data for the first time into a column-organized BLU acceleration table using LOAD INSERT, or running a LOAD REPLACE with RESETDICTIONARY or RESETDICTIONARYONLY clause.

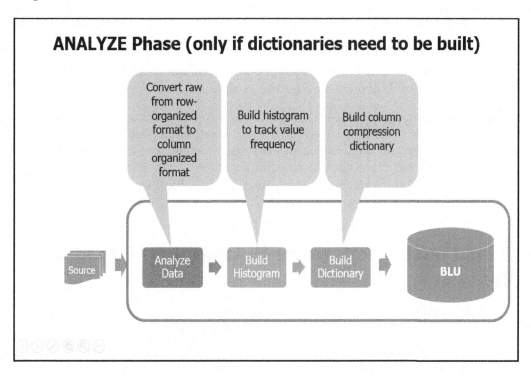

Analyze Phase (only if dictionaries need to be built)

Load phase: During this phase, data is loaded into the table, and index keys and table statistics are collected (if necessary). The save points, also called *points of consistency*, are established at intervals specified through the SAVECOUNT parameter in the LOAD command. The messages are generated, indicating how many input rows were successfully loaded at the time of the save point. You can use the LOAD QUERY TABLE command to monitor the progress of the load operation.

If you are loading data into a column-organized BLU Accelerated table, the load phase does the following:

- Compresses values
- Builds data pages
- Updates synopsis table
- Builds keys for page map indexes and any `UNIQUE` indexes

Build phase: During this phase, indexes are created based on the index keys collected during the load phase. The index keys are sorted during the load phase, and index statistics are collected if the `STATISTICS USE PROFILE` option was specified, and profile indicates collecting index statistics.

Delete phase: During this phase, the rows that caused a unique or primary key violation are removed from the table and inserted into an exception table if specified.

Index copy phase: During this phase, the index data is copied from a system temporary table space to the original table space where the index data associated with the table that was loaded is to reside. This will only occur if a system temporary table space was specified for index creation during a load operation with the `ALLOW READ ACCESS` and `USE [TablespaceName]` options specified. This phase is applicable only to row-organized tables.

Data load best practices for BLU Column-Organized Tables

- Batch up the data, at least 1,024 records per insert.
- Set `UTIL_HEAP_SZ` to `AUTOMATIC` and over 1M pages.
- Consider presorting data on column(s) that will frequently appear in query predicates to improve compression ratios and synopsis effectiveness.
- Reduce total time required for the first load of the table by reducing the duration of the ANALYZE phase. This can be achieved by `cdeanalyzefrequency` and/or `maxanalyzesize` file type modifier in the `LOAD` command.
  - `cdeanalyzefrequency`: Determines how frequently sample needs to be collected during Analyze phase.
  - `maxanalyzesize`: Determines how much data is sampled in the Analyze phase and the default is 128 GB and can be modified and the value `ZERO` means unlimited.

The Analyze phase is a unique phase within the Load utility for column-organized BLU accelerated tables.

Monitoring a Load operation

Like other DB2 database utilities, the Load utility can be monitored using two commands:

- `LIST UTILITIES SHOW DETAIL`
- `LOAD QUERY TABLE <TableName>`

The DB2 Ingest Utility

The Ingest utility (also known as Continuous Data Ingest, or CDI) is a high-speed, client-side, highly configurable, multithreaded DB2 utility that streams data from files and pipes into DB2 target tables by using SQL-like commands. Because the Ingest utility can move large amounts of real-time data without locking the target table, you do not need to choose between the data currency and availability.

The DB2 Ingest utility meets the current modern data warehouse expectations through several key capabilities:

- **Concurrent data access**: You can run concurrent SQL statements against the DB2 tables that are being loaded because the Ingest utility always uses row-level locking. You do not have to choose between tweaking data concurrency and data availability through isolation levels, as before.
- **Exception handling**: You can copy rejected records to a file or table, or discard them based on the business rule. If any data load failed operations, the data can easily be recovered by restarting the ingest operation from the last commit point.
- **Data transformations**: You can apply the data transformation techniques while continuously pumping data into DB2 tables.
- **Database partition awareness**: You can insert data directly into the appropriate partition in parallel instead of processing the whole data set through a coordinator partition. This is similar to the IBM Information Server Enterprise Stage.

- **Extensive DML support**: You can use `INSERT`, `UPDATE`, `DELETE`, `REPLACE`, and `MERGE` operations while streaming data into the data warehouse system. These DML operations can be used during the data transformation.
- **Configure anywhere**: The Ingest utility is part of the DB2 client feature (no additional licenses are necessary) and is very flexible and easily configurable. It is possible to install and configure the Ingest utility on an existing DB2 server, a dedicated ingest server, an existing shared **Extract, Transform, and Load** (ETL) server, or a coordinator node on the DPF system.
- **Data format support**: You can load data from delimited ASCII (DEL), non-delimited ASCII (ASC), columns in various orders and formats, positional text, and binary data file formats.
- **Various table support**: You can load data into regular tables, nicknames, MDC, and **insert time clustering** (ITC) tables, range-partitioned tables, **range-clustered tables** (RCT), MQT, temporal tables, and updatable views.

The following diagram shows the Ingest utility architecture. The data from source systems is exported into files or named pipes, which are then streamed into the Ingest utility as input sources. The data is then ingested into the target data warehouse system through a three-step process, which is as follows:

- **Transport**: The transporter thread reads data from the data source and puts records on the formatter queues. For insert and merge operations, there is one transporter thread for each input source (for example, one thread for each input file). For update and delete operations, there is only one transporter thread.
- **Format**: The formatter parses each record available in the formatter queue, converts the data into the format that DB2 database systems require, and places each formatted record on one of the flusher queues for that record's partition. The number of formatter threads is specified by the `NUM_FORMATTERS` ingest configuration parameter, and by default is set to (number of logical CPUs)/2.
- **Flush**: The flusher issues the SQL statements to perform the ingest operations on the data warehouse target tables. The number of flushers for each partition is specified by the `NUM_FLUSHERS_PER_PARTITION` ingest configuration parameter, and by default is set to max (1, ((number of logical CPUs)/2)/ (number of partitions)).

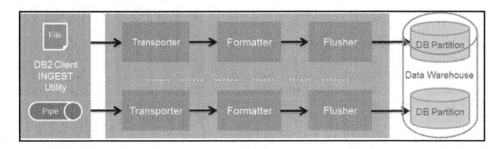

Ingest utility architecture

You invoke the Ingest utility by executing the INGEST command. The basic syntax for this command is as follows:

```
INGEST [DATA] FROM FILE [FileName] | PIPE [PipeName]
<FORMAT DELIMITED | POSITIONAL>
<DUMPFILE|BADFILE [ExFileName]>
<EXCEPTION TABLE [ExTableName]>
<WARNINGCOUNT n>
<MESSAGES MsgFileName>
[RESTART | CONTINUE | TERMINATE]
[INSERT | REPLACE | UPDATE | DELETE | MERGE]
INTO [TableName]
```

Where,

- FileName: Specifies the name and location of the external file from which to ingest data
- PipeName: Specifies the name of the pipe from which to ingest data
- ExFileName: Specifies the name of the file to which to write rows rejected by the formatters
- ExTableName: Specifies the table to which to write rows inserted by the Ingest utility and rejected by DB2 with certain SQLSTATE
- MsgFileName: Specifies the name of the file to record informational, warning, and error messages
- TableName: Specifies the target DB2 tables into which to write the Ingest utility flusher process

Before invoking the Ingest utility, it is mandatory to create the ingest control table, SYSTOOLS.INGESTRESTART. You can create this table through the SYSINSTALLOBJECTS () procedure, or by using the data definition of the object:

```
CALL SYSPROC.SYSINSTALLOBJECTS ('INGEST', 'C', 'SYSTOOLSPACE','SYSTOOLS');
```

Or, you can create the control table using the following table definition:

```
CREATE TABLE SYSTOOLS.INGESTRESTART (
    JOBID            VARCHAR (256)  NOT NULL,
    APPLICATIONID    VARCHAR (256)  NOT NULL,
    FLUSHERID        INT            NOT NULL,
    FLUSHERDISTID    INT            NOT NULL,
    TRANSPORTERID    INT            NOT NULL,
    BUFFERID         BIGINT         NOT NULL,
    BYTEPOS          BIGINT         NOT NULL,
    ROWSPROCESSED    INT            NOT NULL,
    PRIMARY KEY
    (JOBID,
    FLUSHERID,
    TRANSPORTERID,
    FLUSHERDISTID))
IN SYSTOOLSPACE;
```

If you want to ingest data stored in a DEL format external file, employee.del, into table EMPLOYEE, you can do so by executing the INGEST command:

```
INGEST FROM FILE employee.del FORMAT DELIMITED INSERT INTO EMPLOYEE
SQL2979I  The ingest utility is starting at "05/21/2018 20:53:30.791059".
SQL2914I  The ingest utility has started the following ingest job:
"DB21101:20180521.205330.791059:00003:00023".

Number of rows read        = 42
Number of rows inserted    = 42
Number of rows rejected    = 0

SQL2980I  The ingest utility completed successfully at timestamp
"05/21/2018 20:53:31.825854"
```

With the Ingest utility, you can use INSERT, UPDATE, DELETE, REPLACE, and merge DML operations to stream the source data into the target DB2 tables. The sample commands for each operation are as shown here:

```
-- Update Operation Example

INGEST FROM FILE myupdatefile.del
    FORMAT DELIMITED
        ($id         INTEGER EXTERNAL,
      $join_date   DATE 'yyyy/mm/dd',
      $name      CHAR (32))
    BADFILE exp_update.txt
    MESSAGES exp_update.msg
    UPDATE mytable
```

```
        SET (NAME, JOIN_DATE) = ($name, $join_date)
    WHERE ID=$id;

-- Delete Operation Example

INGEST FROM FILE mydeletefile.del
    FORMAT DELIMITED
        ($id         INTEGER EXTERNAL,
     $join_date  DATE 'yyyy/mm/dd',
         $name      CHAR (32))
    BADFILE exp_delete.txt
    MESSAGES exp_delete.msg
    DELETE FROM mytable WHERE ID=$id;

-- Merge Operation Example

INGEST FROM FILE mymergefile.del
    FORMAT DELIMITED
        ($id         INTEGER EXTERNAL,
     $join_date  DATE 'yyyy/mm/dd',
         $name      CHAR (32))
    BADFILE exp_merge.txt
    MESSAGES exp_merge.msg
    MERGE INTO mytable on (ID = $id)
    WHEN MATCHED THEN
        UPDATE SET (NAME, JOIN_DATE) = ($name, $join_date)
    WHEN NOT MATCHED THEN
        INSERT VALUES ($id, $name, $join_date);

-- Replace Operation Example

INGEST FROM FILE myreplacefile.txt
        FORMAT DELIMITED
            ($id             INTEGER EXTERNAL,
             $join_date      DATE 'yyyy/mm/dd',
             $name           CHAR (32))
        BADFILE exp_replace.txt
        MESSAGES exp_replace.msg
        REPLACE INTO mytable;
```

Monitoring an Ingest operation

Like other DB2 database utilities, the Ingest utility has two simple commands to monitor progress:

- INGEST LIST
- INGEST GET STATS FOR <id>

These commands must be run on the same machine running the Ingest utility. The command syntax and the following diagram showcase the output result:

```
INGEST LIST;
INGEST GET STATS FOR 1;
INGEST GET STATS FOR 1 EVERY 1 SECONDS;
```

```
INGEST LIST

Ingest job ID              = DB21101:20180521.211944.875017:00003:00023
Ingest temp job ID         = 1
Database Name              = SAMPLE
Target table               = DB2INST1.EMPLOYEE2
Input type                 = FILE
Start Time                 = 05/21/2018 21:19:45.321138
Running Time               = 00:00:01
Number of records processed = 0

DB20000I  The INGEST LIST command completed successfully.

INGEST GET STATS FOR 1

Ingest job ID              = DB21101:20180521.211944.875017:00003:00023
Database Name              = SAMPLE
Target table               = DB2INST1.EMPLOYEE2

Overall         Overall         Current         Current
ingest rate     write rate      ingest rate     write rate
(records/second) (writes/second) (records/second) (writes/second)  Total records
---------------- --------------- ---------------- ----------------- -------------
        86016              0            86016              0                0

DB20000I  The INGEST GET STATS command completed successfully.

INGEST GET STATS FOR 1 EVERY 1 SECONDS

Ingest job ID              = DB21101:20180521.211944.875017:00003:00023
Database Name              = SAMPLE
Target table               = DB2INST1.EMPLOYEE2

Overall         Overall         Current         Current
ingest rate     write rate      ingest rate     write rate
(records/second) (writes/second) (records/second) (writes/second)  Total records
---------------- --------------- ---------------- ----------------- -------------
        86016              0                0              0                0
        43008          43008                0          86016            86016

DB20000I  The INGEST GET STATS command completed successfully.
```

Monitoring ingest operation

DB2 utilities comparison – Import vs. Ingest vs. Load

The following table summarizes key differences between Ingest, Import, and Load utilities:

Attribute	Import	Ingest	Load
Speed	Slow: uses sequential insert statements	Fast: uses parallel insert threads	Very fast: writes formatted pages directly into table space containers
Concurrency	High: sometimes escalates to table-level lock	Very high: row-level locking	Low: allows read-only operations
Transaction logging	Every record change is logged	Every record change is logged	Very minimal logging
Behavior on failure	Rollback, and table is accessible	Rollback, and table is accessible	Table will remain in Load Pending state
LOBs and XML data	Supported data type	Unsupported data type	Supported data type
Utility type	Server-side	Client-side	Server-side
Triggers activation	Yes	Yes	No
Constraint validation	Yes	Yes	Only UNIQUE keys are validated
Is table space backup necessary?	No	No	Yes, but No if run using NONRECOVERABLE clause or with COPY YES
Utility throttling	Can use `UTIL_IMPACT_PRIORITY` or `util_impact_lim` to throttle the utility	No impact	Can use `UTIL_IMPACT_PRIORITY` or `util_impact_lim` to throttle the utility

DB2 utilities comparison

A word about the CATALOG STORAGE ACCESS command

The CATALOG STORAGE ACCESS command creates an alias for accessing remote storage on various cloud providers, including these:

- IBM SoftLayer Object Storage
- Amazon **Simple Storage Service (S3)**

The remote storage access is supported by the INGEST, LOAD, BACKUP DATABASE, or RESTORE DATABASE commands. Setting up a remote storage is a two-step process, as shown below:

Step 1: Catalog storage access (like a catalog database) through CATALOG STORAGE ACCESS command.

Step 2: Use the newly cataloged storage in native DB2 commands using the option DB2REMOTE://<CatalogAlias>/<StorageContainer>/>StorageFullPath>.

The basic command syntax for CATALOG STORAGE ACCESS command is as shown here:

```
CATALOG STORAGE ACCESS ALIAS [AliasName]
VENDOR <SOFTLAYER | S3>
SERVER <DEFAULT | EndPoint]
USER [StorageUserID] PASSWORD [StoragePassword]
CONTAINER [ContainerBucket]
OBJECT [ObjectName]
DBGROUP [GroupID] DBUSER [UserID]
```

Consider the following:

- AliasName: Specifies the name of the external storage location.
- EndPoint: Specifies the authentication endpoint of the remote storage. If it is DEFAULT, it uses the IBM SoftLayer endpoint in the Dallas (TX) data center.
- StorageUserID: Specifies the SoftLayer Username or S3 Access Key ID of the remote storage account.
- StoragePassword: Specifies the SoftLayer API key or S3 Secret Access Key of the remote storage account credentials.
- ContainerBucket: Specifies the SoftLayer storage container or AWS S3 storage bucket.

- `ObjectName`: Specifies the name of the object (file) on the remote storage. If you specify a file name with the OBJECT parameter when you issue the CATALOG STORAGE ALIAS command, then you do not need to specify the file name with the `db2remote://` string when you use the alias in the BACKUP, RESTORE, LOAD, or INGEST command. This is an optional clause.
- `GroupID`: Specifies the user group that may access the alias and, if this is not specified, only users with SYSADM authority may use the alias.
- `UserID`: Specifies the user ID that may access the alias and, if this is not specified, only users with SYSADM authority may use the alias.

If you want to create a storage alias named stoalias_sl, you can create it using the command shown here:

```
CATALOG STORAGE ACCESS ALIAS stoalias_sl
VENDOR SOFTLAYER SERVER
https://mon01.objectstorage.service.networklayer.com/auth/v1.0/
USER SLOS983162-1:SL671212
PASSWORD
ddd8311dbc88bb6da35c25566841c3311c8904319058a94354daa2dba1b6369
CONTAINER sl_container
DBUSER db2inst1
```

You can then use the previously created remote storage using the following format:

```
DB2REMOTE://<CatalogAlias>/<StorageContainer>/>StorageFullPath>
```

For example, if you want to back up the database to the previously created remote storage, you can execute the BACKUP command shown here:

```
BACKUP DATABASE sample TO DB2REMOTE://stoalias_sl/sl_container/
```

When you create a storage access alias, your remote storage account credentials are safely stored in an encrypted key store.

You can use the LIST STORAGE ACCESS command to list all of the storage aliases and, to remove the alias, use the UNCATALOG STORAGE ACCCESS ALIAS <AliasName>.

 Storage access aliases and remote cloud storage are supported under Linux only. The authorization necessary to create and manage the storage access aliases is SYSADM or SYSCTRL.

Other DB2 data movement options

DB2 provides other built-in procedures and features to move data within and between databases. These are as follows:

- SYSPROC.ADMIN_MOVE_TABLE (): Move the data in an active table into a new table object with the same name, while the data remains online and available for access
- SYSPROC.ADMIN_COPY_SCHEMA (): Copy a specific schema and all objects contained in it
- db2move: This data movement tool command facilitates the movement of large numbers of tables between DB2 databases

The SYSPROC.ADMIN_MOVE_TABLE () procedure

This procedure is designed to move data from a source table to a target table with a minimal impact to application access. The changes that can be made using ADMIN_MOVE_TABLE () are as follows:

- The table can be moved from the current data, index and long to a new set of table spaces, which could have a different page size, extent size, or type of table space management (something like moving data from SMS to an automatic storage table space).
- Enabling the compression or changing the compression type from static to adaptive or vice-versa can be implemented during the move.
- MDC clustering can be added or changed using a new ORGANIZE BY DIMENSION clause.
- Alter ITC tables using the ORGANIZE BY INSERT TIME clause.
- The range-partitioning scheme can be added or changed using PARTITION BY RANGE clause.
- Distribution keys can be changed for database-partitioned (MPP) tables using the DISTRIBUTE BY HASH clause.
- New columns can be added, removed, or changed.
- A row-organized table can be converted to a column-organized table.

This multi-phased data movement-processing procedure allows write access to the source table, except for a short outage required to swap access to the target table. You can use this procedure to convert a row-organized table to a column-organized table, as shown here:

```
-- Table and associated index definitions before the move

CREATE TABLE "DEMO"."EMPLOYEE" (
                "EMPNO" CHAR (6 OCTETS) NOT NULL,
                "FIRSTNME" VARCHAR (12 OCTETS) NOT NULL,
                "MIDINIT" CHAR (1 OCTETS),
                "LASTNAME" VARCHAR (15 OCTETS) NOT NULL,
                "WORKDEPT" CHAR (3 OCTETS),
                "PHONENO" CHAR (4 OCTETS),
                "HIREDATE" DATE,
                "JOB" CHAR (8 OCTETS),
                "EDLEVEL" SMALLINT NOT NULL,
                "SEX" CHAR (1 OCTETS),
                "BIRTHDATE" DATE,
                "SALARY" DECIMAL (9, 2),
                "BONUS" DECIMAL (9, 2),
                "COMM" DECIMAL (9, 2))
            IN "USERSPACE1"
            ORGANIZE BY ROW;

ALTER TABLE "DEMO"."EMPLOYEE"
        ADD CONSTRAINT "PK_EMPLOYEE" PRIMARY KEY
                ("EMPNO");

CREATE INDEX "DEMO"."XEMP" ON "DEMO"."EMPLOYEE"
                ("WORKDEPT" ASC)
                COMPRESS NO
                INCLUDE NULL KEYS ALLOW REVERSE SCANS;

  -- Invoking the SYSPROC.ADMIN_MOVE_TABLE () procedure

CALL SYSPROC.ADMIN_MOVE_TABLE
('DEMO','EMPLOYEE','USERSPACE1','USERSPACE1','USERSPACE1', 'ORGANIZE BY
COLUMN', '','','','COPY_USE_LOAD','MOVE');
  Result set 1
  ---------------
```

KEY	VALUE
COPY_TOTAL_ROWS	42
DICTIONARY_CREATION_TOTAL_TIME	1
REPLAY_START	2018-05-22-16.55.23.405657
REPLAY_TOTAL_ROWS	0

```
            SWAP_END                          2018-05-22-16.55.23.903763
            SWAP_RETRIES                      0
            CLEANUP_START                     2018-05-22-16.55.23.943366
            COPY_END                          2018-05-22-16.55.23.405124
            COPY_OPTS                         OVER_INDEX,LOAD,NON_CLUSTER
            COPY_START                        2018-05-22-16.55.20.494424
            INDEX_CREATION_TOTAL_TIME         0
            INIT_END                          2018-05-22-16.55.20.434140
            ORIGINAL_TBLSIZE                  4096
            REPLAY_END                        2018-05-22-16.55.23.875971
            SWAP_START                        2018-05-22-16.55.23.876397
            UTILITY_INVOCATION_ID             00080...16552043546600000000
            AUTHID                            DB2INST1
            CLEANUP_END                       2018-05-22-16.55.23.985374
            INDEXNAME                         PK_EMPLOYEE
            INDEXSCHEMA                       DEMO
            INIT_START                        2018-05-22-16.55.19.405866
            REPLAY_TOTAL_TIME                 0
            STATUS                            COMPLETE
            VERSION                           11.01.0303


    24 record(s) selected.


-- Table and associated index definitions after the move

CREATE TABLE "DEMO"."EMPLOYEE" (
                "EMPNO" CHAR (6 OCTETS) NOT NULL,
                "FIRSTNME" VARCHAR (12 OCTETS) NOT NULL,
                "MIDINIT" CHAR (1 OCTETS),
                "LASTNAME" VARCHAR (15 OCTETS) NOT NULL,
                "WORKDEPT" CHAR (3 OCTETS),
                "PHONENO" CHAR (4 OCTETS),
                "HIREDATE" DATE,
                "JOB" CHAR (8 OCTETS),
                "EDLEVEL" SMALLINT NOT NULL,
                "SEX" CHAR (1 OCTETS),
                "BIRTHDATE" DATE,
                "SALARY" DECIMAL (9, 2),
                "BONUS" DECIMAL (9, 2),
                "COMM" DECIMAL (9, 2))
              IN "USERSPACE1"
              ORGANIZE BY COLUMN;


ALTER TABLE "DEMO"."EMPLOYEE"
        ADD CONSTRAINT "PK_EMPLOYEE" PRIMARY KEY
              ("EMPNO");


CREATE INDEX "DEMO"."XEMP" ON "DEMO"."EMPLOYEE"
```

```
("WORKDEPT" ASC)
COMPRESS NO
INCLUDE NULL KEYS ALLOW REVERSE SCANS;
```

The COPY_USE_LOAD option specified in the previous procedure invocation is to move the data using a LOAD command to generate column dictionaries. Starting with DB2 11.1.3.3, secondary indexes are supported on column-organized tables.

```
DESCRIBE INDEXES FOR TABLE DEMO.EMPLOYEE;
```

Index schema	Index name	Unique rule	Number of columns	Index type	Index partitioning	Null keys
DEMO Y	PK_EMPLOYEE	P	1 RELATIONAL	DATA		-
DEMO Y	XEMP	D	1 RELATIONAL	DATA		-

However, the SYNOPSYS table will only have one CPMA system index, as shown here:

```
SELECT
VARCHAR (INDSCHEMA, 10),
VARCHAR (INDNAME, 50),
VARCHAR (TABNAME, 40),
VARCHAR (COLNAMES, 50),
INDEXTYPE FROM SYSCAT.INDEXES
WHERE TABNAME='SYN180522165523902406_EMPLOYEE';
```

INDSCHEMA	INDNAME	TABNAME	COLNAMES	INDEXTYPE
SYSIBM +SQLNOTAPPLICABLE	SQL180522165519883847 +SQLNOTAPPLICABLE	SYN180522165523902406_EMPLOYEE	SYN180522165523902406_EMPLOYEE	CPMA

There are two new options available within DB2 11.1 for the SYSPROC.ADMIN_MOVE_TABLE () procedure. They are as follows:

- REPORT: This monitors the progress of table moves and focuses mainly on the COPY and REPLAY phase of a running table move.
- TERM: This terminates a failed or an executing table-move operation. When it forces a running table move, it rolls back all open transactions and sets the table move to a well-defined operation status. From this state, the table move can be canceled or continued. You must have SYSADM, SYSCTRL, or SYSMAINT authority to perform TERM.

The SYSPROC.ADMIN_COPY_SCHEMA () procedure

With the SYSPROC.ADMIN_COPY_SCHEMA () procedure, you can copy a specific database schema and associated objects to a new target schema by using the same object names as in the source schema, but with the target schema qualifier. The simple syntax for the copy a schema DEMO into DEMO2 using the copy procedure is as follows:

```
CALL SYSPROC.ADMIN_COPY_SCHEMA ('DEMO', 'DEMO2', 'COPY', NULL, '', ' ',
'ERRORSCHEMA', 'ERRORNAME');

  Value of output parameters
  --------------------------
  Parameter Name  : ERRORTABSCHEMA
  Parameter Value : -
  Parameter Name  : ERRORTABNAME
  Parameter Value : -
  Return Status = 0

-- List of tables in schema DEMO

LIST TABLES FOR SCHEMA DEMO;
```

Table/View	Schema	Type	Creation time
DEPARTMENT 2018-05-22-18.10.42.252085	DEMO	T	
EMPLOYEE 2018-05-22-18.08.30.944491	DEMO	T	

```
-- List of tables in schema DEMO2 (a copy of DEMO schema)

LIST TABLES FOR SCHEMA DEMO2;
```

Table/View	Schema	Type	Creation time
DEPARTMENT 2018-05-22-18.11.26.878441	DEMO2	T	
EMPLOYEE 2018-05-22-18.11.27.364126	DEMO2	T	

Object Copy using the db2move command

The db2move database movement tool command, when used in the EXPORT, IMPORT, or LOAD mode, facilitates the movement of large numbers of tables between DB2 databases. When the db2move command is used in the COPY mode, this tool facilitates a creation of duplicate schema.

The tool command queries the system catalog tables within a particular database, and compiles a list of all user tables based on the command option specified. It then exports these tables in PC/IXF format. The PC/IXF files can then be imported or loaded to another local DB2 database on the same system, or can be transferred to another system and imported or loaded to a DB2 database. Tables with structured type columns are not moved when this tool is used.

The basic syntax for db2move command option is as show here:

```
db2move [DBName] [Action]  -tc [TableDefiners]
                           -tn [TableNames]
                           -sn [SchemaNames]
                           -ts [TableSpaceNames]
                           -tf [FileName]
                           -io [ImportOption]
                           -lo [LoadOption]
                           -co [CopyOption]
                           -l  [LobPaths]
                           -u  [UserID]
                           -p  [Password]
                           -aw
```

Consider the following:

- DBName: Specifies the name of the database the tool command operates on
- Action: Specifies the action to be performed, such as EXPORT, IMPORT, LOAD, and COPY

If you want to export all of the data for schema DEMO from a database, you can execute the following command:

```
db2move sample export -sn DEMO
Application code page not determined, using ANSI codepage 819
*****   DB2MOVE   *****
Action:   EXPORT
Start time:   Tue May 22 19:47:36 2018
All schema names matching:   DEMO;
Connecting to database SAMPLE ... successful!  Server : DB2 Common
```

```
Server V11.1.3
    Binding package automatically ...
/db/home/db2inst1/sqllib/bnd/db2common.bnd ... successful!
    Binding package automatically ...
/db/home/db2inst1/sqllib/bnd/db2move.bnd ... successful!
    EXPORT:      14 rows from table "DEMO      "."DEPARTMENT"
    EXPORT:      42 rows from table "DEMO      "."EMPLOYEE"
    Disconnecting from database ... successful!
    End time:  Tue May 22 19:47:37 2018
```

If you want to copy DEMO schema tables from one database (SAMPLE) to another (TESTDB),
you can execute the command shown here:

```
    db2move sample COPY -sn DEMO -co TARGET_DB testdb USER db2inst1 USING
passw0rd
    Application code page not determined, using ANSI codepage 819
    *****   DB2MOVE   *****
    Action:  COPY
    Start time:  Tue May 22 20:04:44 2018
    All schema names matching:  DEMO;
    Connecting to database SAMPLE ... successful!  Server : DB2 Common
Server V11.1.3
    Copy schema DEMO to DEMO on the target database TESTDB
    Create DMT :  "SYSTOOLS"."DMT_5b04b01c5b069"
    Binding package automatically ...
/db/home/db2inst1/sqllib/bnd/db2move.bnd ... successful!
    Start Load Phase :
    db2move finished successfully
    Files generated:
    ------------------
    COPYSCHEMA.20180522200444.msg
    LOADTABLE.20180522200444.MSG
    Please delete these files when they are no longer needed.
    End time:  Tue May 22 20:04:47 2018
    -- Connect to TESTDB and verify the tables
    CONNECT TO TESTDB
       Database Connection Information
     Database server        = DB2/LINUXX8664 11.1.3.3
     SQL authorization ID    = DB2INST1
     Local database alias    = TESTDB
    LIST TABLES FOR SCHEMA DEMO;
    Table/View                       Schema           Type  Creation time
    -------------------------------- ---------------- ----- ------------------
    ---------
    DEPARTMENT                       DEMO             T
2018-05-22-20.04.44.500776
    EMPLOYEE                         DEMO             T
```

```
2018-05-22-20.04.44.687349
```

If you want to copy DEMO schema from one database (SAMPLE) as DEMO_NEW into another database, use the SCHEMA_MAP option within db2move tool command, as shown here:

```
db2move sample COPY -sn DEMO -co TARGET_DB testdb USER db2inst1 USING
passw0rd SCHEMA_MAP "((DEMO,DEMO_NEW))"
Application code page not determined, using ANSI codepage 819
*****   DB2MOVE   *****
Action:   COPY
Start time:   Tue May 22 20:15:31 2018
All schema names matching:   DEMO;
Connecting to database SAMPLE ... successful!   Server : DB2 Common
Server V11.1.3
Copy schema DEMO to DEMO_NEW on the target database TESTDB
Create DMT :   "SYSTOOLS"."DMT_5b04b2a3bfb84"
Start Load Phase :
db2move finished successfully
Files generated:
------------------
COPYSCHEMA.20180522201531.msg
LOADTABLE.20180522201531.MSG
Please delete these files when they are no longer needed.
End time:   Tue May 22 20:15:34 2018
```

- You can use the SCHEMA_MAP option "((SOURCE_SCHEMA1, TARGET_SCHEMA1), SOURCE_SCHEMA2, TARGET_SCHEMA2))" to rename the schemas on the target copy using the db2move tool command.

- You can use the TABLESPACE_MAP option "((SOURCE_TBSP1, TARGET_TBSP1), (SOURCE_TBSP2, TARGET_TBSP2))" to copy data to a different set of table spaces than that of the source, using the db2move tool command.

- Loading data into tables containing XML columns is only supported for the LOAD and not for the COPY action. The workaround is to manually perform an IMPORT and EXPORT, or use the db2move Export and db2move Import separately. If these tables also contain GENERATED ALWAYS identity columns, data cannot be imported into the tables.

A word about the db2look tool command

The `db2look` tool command generates the data definition language statements for a specific object type. This can be used to reproduce the database objects into another database, for example copying a production database schema into a test system. The basic command syntax is this:

```
db2look -d [DBName] [-e] [-z SchemaName] [-t TableNames] [-v ViewNames]
```

If you want to extract a definition of a database, you can run the following command:

```
db2look -d sample -createdb
-- No userid was specified, db2look tries to use Environment variable
USER
-- USER is: DB2INST1
-- This CLP file was created using DB2LOOK Version "11.1"
-- Timestamp: Wed 23 May 2018 04:38:15 AM EDT
-- Database Name: SAMPLE
-- Database Manager Version: DB2/LINUXX8664 Version 11.1.3.3
-- Database Codepage: 1208
-- Database Collating Sequence is: IDENTITY
-- Alternate collating sequence(alt_collate): null
-- varchar2 compatibility(varchar2_compat): OFF
----------------------------------------------------------
-- Generate CREATE DATABASE command
----------------------------------------------------------
CREATE DATABASE SAMPLE
        AUTOMATIC STORAGE YES
        ON '/db/home/db2inst1'
        DBPATH ON '/db/home/db2inst1/'
        USING CODESET UTF-8 TERRITORY US
        COLLATE USING IDENTITY
        PAGESIZE 32768
        DFT_EXTENT_SZ 32
        CATALOG TABLESPACE MANAGED BY AUTOMATIC STORAGE
         EXTENTSIZE 4
         AUTORESIZE YES
         INITIALSIZE 32 M
         MAXSIZE NONE
        TEMPORARY TABLESPACE MANAGED BY AUTOMATIC STORAGE
         EXTENTSIZE 32
         FILE SYSTEM CACHING
        USER TABLESPACE MANAGED BY AUTOMATIC STORAGE
         EXTENTSIZE 32
         AUTORESIZE YES
         INITIALSIZE 32 M
         MAXSIZE NONE
```

```
;
```

If you want to mimic the system catalog statistics from one database to another, you can extract the statistics using the following command, and then rerun the extracted statistics on the target system:

```
db2look -d sample -z demo -t employee -m -c -r -o statsfile.in
-- No userid was specified, db2look tries to use Environment variable
USER
-- USER is: DB2INST1
-- Specified SCHEMA is: DEMO
-- The db2look utility will consider only the specified tables
-- Schema name is ignored for the Federated Section
-- Running db2look in mimic mode
-- Omitting COMMIT in mimic file
-- Omitting RUNSTATS in mimic file
-- Output is sent to file: statsfile.in
-- COMMIT is omitted. Explicit commit is required after executing the
script.
```

Database maintenance utilities

Some of the data maintenance utilities available within DB2 are these:

```
REORGCHK
REORG
RUNSTATS
REBIND
FLUSH PACKAGE CACHE
ADMIN_CMD
```

The REORGCHK utility

This utility command can use be used to suggest tables and indexes that would benefit from reorganization. The basic command syntax for REORGCHK is this:

```
REORGCHK
<UPDATE STATISTICS | CURRENT STATISTICS>
<ON TABLE USER |
    ON SCHEMA [SchemaName] |
    ON TABLE [USER | SYSTEM | ALL | [TableName]>
```

Consider the following:

- `SchemaName`: Identifies the name to assign to a schema whose objects are to be analyzed to determine whether they must be re-organized
- `TableName`: Identifies the name to assign to a specific table to analyze, to determine whether it must be re-organized

You can invoke the `REORGCHK` command to verify the level of data fragmentation and to decide whether reorganization is necessary, as shown here:

```
REORGCHK CURRENT STATISTICS ON TABLE me.tda_code_master;
```

Take a look at this diagram:

```
Command Output
Table statistics:


F1: 100 * OVERFLOW / CARD < 5
F2: 100 * (Effective Space Utilization of Data Pages) > 70
F3: 100 * (Required Pages / Total Pages) > 80


SCHEMA.NAME              CARD   OV   NP    FP ACTBLK   TSIZE  F1 F2  F3 REORG
------------------------------------------------------------------------------
Table: ME.TAD_CODE_MASTER
                         8434    0   40    41    -    244586   0 83 100 ---
------------------------------------------------------------------------------


Index statistics:


F4: CLUSTERRATIO or normalized CLUSTERFACTOR > 80
F5: 100 * (Space used on leaf pages / Space available on non-empty leaf pages) > MIN(50, (100 - PCTFREE))
F6: (100 - PCTFREE) * (Amount of space available in an index with one less level / Amount of space required for all keys) < 100
F7: 100 * (Number of pseudo-deleted RIDs / Total number of RIDs) < 20
F8: 100 * (Number of pseudo-empty leaf pages / Total number of leaf pages) < 20


SCHEMA.NAME             INDCARD  LEAF ELEAF LVLS  NDEL   KEYS LEAF_RECSIZE NLEAF_RECSIZE LEAF_PAGE_OVERHEAD NLEAF_PAGE_OVERHEAD ...
---------------------------------------------------------------------------------------------------------------------------------
Table: ME.TAD_CODE_MASTER
Index: ME.XPK_AD_CODE_MASTER
                          8434    46    0    2     0    8434          15            15               428                 428 ...
---------------------------------------------------------------------------------------------------------------------------------


CLUSTERRATIO or normalized CLUSTERFACTOR (F4) will indicate REORG is necessary
for indexes that are not in the same sequence as the base table. When multiple
indexes are defined on a table, one or more indexes may be flagged as needing
REORG.  Specify the most important index for REORG sequencing.

Tables defined using the ORGANIZE BY clause and the corresponding dimension
indexes have a '*' suffix to their names. The cardinality of a dimension index
is equal to the Active blocks statistic of the table.
```

You can also use the REORGCHK utility command to collect the statistics using the UPDATE STATISTICS option.

The REORG Utility

This utility command can be used to re-organize tables and indexes either in online or in offline mode to improve storage efficiency, and reduce the I/O access cost. This utility can also be used to implement various compression algorithms for tables and indexes. The basic command syntax for REORG is this:

```
REORG TABLE [TableName]
<INDEX [IndexName]>
<ALLOW READ ACCESS | ALLOW NO ACCESS>
<USE [TmpTSName]>
<INDEXSCAN>
<LONGLOBDATA <USE [LongTSName]>>
<KEEPDICTIONARY | RESETDICTIONARY>
<RECLAIM EXTENTS [ALLOW [WRITE | READ | NO] ACCESS]>
Or

REORG TABLE [TableName]
<INDEX [IndexName]>
INPLACE
[ALLOW READ ACCESS | ALLOW NO ACCESS]
[<TRUNCATE | NOTRUNCATE TABLE> | <CLEANUP OVERFLOWS>]
[START | RESUME] | [STOP | PAUSE]

Or

REORG TABLE [TableName]
<INDEX [IndexName]>
INPLACE
[STOP | PAUSE]

Or

REORG [INDEXES ALL FOR TABLE [SrcTableName] |
       INDEX [SrcIndexName] <FOR TABLE [SrcTableName]>]
<ALLOW READ ACCESS | ALLOW WRITE ACCESS | ALLOW NO ACCESS>
<CLEANUP ONLY ALL | CLEANUP ONLY PAGES | CONVERT>
```

Consider the following:

- `TableName`: Identifies the name of the table whose data is to be re-organized
- `IndexName`: Identifies the name of index to use to order the data stored in the table that is to be re-organized
- `TmpTSName`: Identifies the system temporary table space in which the database manager is to temporarily store a copy of the table to be re-organized
- `LongTSName`: Identifies the temporary table space that the database manager is to use for rebuilding long data, such as LOB and CLOB
- `SrcTableName`: Identifies the name of the table whose associated indexes are to be re-organized
- `SrcIndexName`: Identifies the name of the index whose physical pages are to be re-organized

Online (inplace) table reorganization reorganizes a table and allows full access to data in the table. During an online table `REORG` operation, portions of data are organized sequentially within the current address space, re-establishing the clustering, reclaiming the free space, and eliminate overflow rows (if any) instead of copying it to a temporary table space (this is the behavior in an offline `REORG` operation).

There are four phases in an online table reorganization, and they are as follows:

- **Select a range**:
    - The database manager selects a range of sequential pages based on the extent size for `REORG` operation. The minimum number of pages which it selects is 32.
- **Vacate a range**:
    The database manger performs these steps:
    - The `REORG` process moves all of the pages of selected range to free pages in the table.
    - Each row that is moved leaves behind a `REORG` table pointer (RP) record containing the **record ID (RID)** of the row's new location.
    - The row is placed on a free page in the table as a `REORG` table overflow (RO) record that contains the data.
    - Once it finishes moving a set of rows, it waits until all applications that are accessing data in the table are finished. Any old connection using these rows uses old RIDs (old scanner) when table data is accessed; however, any new connection accessing the same data is accessed via new RIDs (new scanner) to access the data.

- Once all the old scanners are complete, the REORG utility cleans up the moved rows, deleting RP records and converting RO records into regular records.

- **Fill the range**:
    - Once all the rows in a specific range are vacated, the database manager will then write them back in a reorganized format; they are sorted according to any indexes that were used, and obeying any PCTFREE restrictions that were defined.
    - When all of the pages in the range are rewritten, the next sequential pages in the table are selected, and the process is repeated.

- **Truncate the table**:
    - When all of the pages in the table are re-organized, the table is truncated to reclaim space. If the NOTRUNCATE option is specified, the re-organized table is not truncated.
    - If you want to perform an online reorganization on table DB2INST1.EMPLOYEE, you can execute the REORG commands shown here, based on need:

```
REORG TABLE db2inst1.employee INPLACE;
DB20000I  The REORG command completed successfully.
DB21024I  This command is asynchronous and may not be effective
immediately.
REORG TABLE db2inst1.employee INPLACE FULL TRUNCATE TABLE START;
DB20000I  The REORG command completed successfully.
DB21024I  This command is asynchronous and may not be effective
immediately.
REORG TABLE db2inst1.employee INPLACE FULL;
DB20000I  The REORG command completed successfully.
DB21024I  This command is asynchronous and may not be effective
immediately.
REORG TABLE db2inst1.employee INPLACE CLEANUP OVERFLOWS;
DB20000I  The REORG command completed successfully.
DB21024I  This command is asynchronous and may not be effective
immediately.
```

You can use the `RECLAIM EXTENTS` option within the REORG command to re-organize and reclaim extents that are not being used in column-organized BLU Acceleration tables, multidimensional cluster (MDC) tables, and insert time-clustering (ITC) tables, as shown here:
```
REORG TABLE demo.employee RECLAIM EXTENTS;
```

The following are a few `REORG` command tool examples:

If you want to re-organize a table online based on an index order, you can use the following:
```
REORG TABLE [SchemaName.TableName] INDEX [SchemaName.IndexName] INPLACE
ALLOW WRITE ACCESS;
```

If you want to re-organize indexes on a table online and cleanup all pseudo deleted keys and pseudo empty pages, you can use the following:
```
REORG INDEXES ALL FOR TABLE [SchemaName.TableName] ALLOW WRITE ACCESS
CLEANUP;
```

If you want re-organize a partition within a range partition table, you can use the following:
```
REORG TABLE [SchemaName.TableName] INDEX [SchemaName.IndexName] ON DATA
PARTITION [PartitionName];
```

If you want to re-organize a table and associated indexes using a temporary table space and rebuild the compression dictionary, you can use the following:
```
REORG TABLE [SchemaName.TableName] USE [TempTableSpaceName]
RESETDICTIONARY;
```

The RUNSTATS Utility

This utility command can use be used to collect table and index statistics to build efficient access plans. The basic command syntax for `RUNSTATS` is:
```
RUNSTATS ON TABLE [TableName]
USE PROFILE
<UTIL_IMPACT_PRIORITY [Priority]>
```

You could also use this version of the command:
```
RUNSTATS ON TABLE [TableName] FOR
<<SAMPLED> DETAILED>
[INDEXES | INDEX]
```

```
[[IndexNames] | ALL]
<EXCLUDING XML COLUMNS>
<ALLOW READ ACCESS | ALLOW WRITE ACCESS>
<SET PROFILE NONE | SET PROFILE <ONLY> | UPDATE PROFILE
    <ONLY>>
<UTIL_IMPACT_PRIORITY [Priority]>
```

You could also use this version of the command:

```
RUNSTATS ON TABLE [TableName]
<ON ALL COLUMNS |
    ON KEY COLUMNS> |
    ON COLUMNS [ColumnNames] |
    ON ALL COLUMNS AND COLUMNS [ColumnNames] |
    ON KEY COLUMNS AND COLUMNS [ColumnNames]>
<WITH DISTRIBUTION>
<EXCLUDING XML COLUMNS>
<AND <<SAMPLED> DETAILED>
    [INDEXES | INDEX]
    [[IndexNames] | ALL]>
<EXCLUDING XML COLUMNS>
<ALLOW READ ACCESS | ALLOW WRITE ACCESS>
<SET PROFILE NONE | SET PROFILE <ONLY> | UPDATE PROFILE
    <ONLY>>
<UTIL_IMPACT_PRIORITY [Priority]>
```

Consider the following:

- `TableName`: Identifies the name of the table for which to collect statistical information
- `IndexNames`: Identifies the names indexes for which to collect statistical information
- `ColumnName`: Identifies the column names for which to collect statistical information
- `Priority`: Specifies to throttle the `RUNSTATS` utility

`RUNSTATS` command has various options, and a few of them are listed here:

- Can be executed with a specific rate (throttled) using the `UTIL_IMPACT_PRIORITY` setting
- Can collect statistics based on the profile created before
- Can collect statistics for individual columns in a table
- Can collect statistics on all indexes for a table
- Can collect statistics with a table and index sample percentage

If you want to collect statistics on the table DB2INST1.EMPLOYEE and associated indexes based on a 25% sampling rate, you can execute the following command:

```
RUNSTATS ON TABLE db2inst1.employee ON ALL COLUMNS AND INDEXES ALL
TABLESAMPLE SYSTEM (25.000000) INDEXSAMPLE SYSTEM (25.000000);
DB20000I  The RUNSTATS command completed successfully.
```

Similarly, if you want to collect statistics on the table DB2INST1.EMPLOYEE and only two of its indexes, with a sampling rate of 10%, you can execute the following command:

```
RUNSTATS ON TABLE db2inst1.employee AND SAMPLED DETAILED INDEXES
db2inst1.ix1_employee, db2inst1.ix2_employee TABLESAMPLE SYSTEM (10.000000)
INDEXSAMPLE SYSTEM (10.000000);
DB20000I  The RUNSTATS command completed successfully.
```

The REBIND Utility

This utility command can be used to recreate a package stored in the database without the need for a bind file. The basic command syntax for REBIND is this:

```
    REBIND <PACKAGE> [PackageName] <VERSION [VersionID]> <APREUSE [YES |
NO]>
    <RESOLVE [ANY | CONSERVATIVE]>
    <REOPT [NONE | ONCE | ALWAYS] >
```

Consider the following:

- PackageName: Identifies the name to assign to the package to rebind
- VersionID: Identifies a specific version of the package to be rebound

If you want to REBIND the package DEMO.PACKAGE to the database, you can use the following command:

```
REBIND PACKAGE demo.package;
```

If you create any new indexes in a table that the DEMO.PACKAGE relies on, you should rebind the package to make use of the newly created indexes.

Flushing the Package Cache Utility

This utility provides database administrators with the ability to invalidate all cached dynamic SQL statements in the packages cache. The invalidation of a cached dynamic SQL statement package has no effect on currently executing SQL statements. However, any new requests for the statement associated with the invalidated package will cause the DB2 optimizer to reprocess the statement, which in turn will dynamically prepare and compile a new cached package.

The basic syntax for the FLUSH PACKAGE CACHE statement is this:

```
FLUSH PACKAGE CACHE DYNAMIC
```

The ADMIN_CMD () procedure

The ADMIN_CMD () stored procedure is a special system built-in stored procedure that allows applications to run select administrative commands by using the CALL SQL statement. You can invoke the following commands by using the ADMIN_CMD () stored procedure:

- ADD CONTACT
- FORCE APPLICATION
- ADD CONTACTGROUP
- IMPORT
- AUTOCONFIGURE
- INITIALIZE TAPE
- BACKUP (online only)
- LOAD
- DESCRIBE
- PRUNE HISTORY/LOGFILE
- DROP CONTACT
- QUIESCE DATABASE
- DROP CONTACTGROUP
- QUIESCE TABLESPACES FOR TABLE
- EXPORT
- REDISTRIBUTE • REORG INDEXES/TABLE

- RESET ALERT CONFIGURATION
- RESET DB CFG
- RESET DBM CFG
- REWIND TAPE
- RUNSTATS
- SET TAPE POSITION
- UNQUIESCE DATABASE
- UPDATE ALERT CONFIGURATION
- UPDATE CONTACT
- UPDATE CONTACTGROUP
- UPDATE DB CFG
- UPDATE HISTORY
- UPDATE DBM CFG
- UPDATE HEALTH NOTIFICATION CONTACT LIST
- GET STMM TUNING
- UPDATE STMM TUNING

If you want to use the EXPORT command to export a table data, use the following ADMIN_CMD () procedure call:

```
CALL SYSPROC.ADMIN_CMD ('EXPORT to /db/home/db2inst1/employee.ixf OF
ixf MESSAGES ON SERVER SELECT * FROM demo.employee');
    Result set 1
    ---------------
    ROWS_EXPORTED          MSG_RETRIEVAL
MSG_REMOVAL
    --------------------- --------------------------------------------
    42 SELECT SQLCODE, MSG FROM
TABLE(SYSPROC.ADMIN_GET_MSGS('1994780800_1705948006_DB2INST1')) AS MSG
CALL SYSPROC.ADMIN_REMOVE_MSGS('1994780800_1705948006_DB2INST1')
    1 record(s) selected.
```

If you want to re-organize a table online within an application code, you can do so by running the following command:

```
CALL SYSPROC.ADMIN_CMD ('REORG TABLE db2inst1.employee INPLACE')
    Return Status = 0
```

If you want to QUIESCE a database, you can do so by executing the following command:

```
CALL SYSPROC.ADMIN_CMD ('QUIESCE DATABASE IMMEDIATE')
   Return Status = 0
```

If you want to update a database configuration parameter, you can use the following command:

```
CALL SYSPROC.ADMIN_CMD ('UPDATE DB CFG FOR sample USING locklist
AUTOMATIC maxlocks AUTOMATIC')
   Return Status = 0
```

Summary

The objective of this chapter was to provide sufficient knowledge to answer the *DB2 Utilities* chapter questions on the following topics:

- DB2 data movement utilities, file formats, and operations
- DB2 continuous data ingest operations, and their business benefits in data warehouse environments
- The ADMIN_MOVE_TABLE() and ADMIN_COPY_SCHEMA() built-in stored procedures syntax, and their usage
- DB2 database maintenance utilities, such as REORGCHK, REORG, and RUNSTATS, and their usage
- DB2 data movement utilities integration with IBM Softlayer and Amazon web services (AWS) remote storage

Practice questions

Question 1: Which of the following is a best choice to load data in real-time with high concurrency?

1. Load
2. Import
3. Ingest
4. db2move

Question 2: Which of the following is TRUE in the case of the Ingest utility?

1. Client-side utility
2. It supports LOB and XML data types
3. It doesn't support DML operations
4. It allows only read-only workload during ingestion

Question 3: Which `LOAD` command modifier can be used when working with identity column data?

1. `IDENTITYRESET`
2. `IDENTITYOVERRIDE`
3. `IDENTITYSUPRESS`
4. `IDENTITYRETAIN`

Question 4: Which operation cannot be performed on a table that contains a primary key that is referenced by a foreign key in another table?

1. `IMPORT ... INSERT`
2. `IMPORT ... REPLACE`
3. `IMPORT ... INSERT_UPDATE`
4. `IMPORT ... CREATE`

Question 5: Which of the following illustrates the proper order in which to use the DB2 data management utilities?

1. `RUNSTATS`, `REORG` table, `REORG` indexes, `REORGCHK`, `REBIND`
2. `RUNSTATS`, `REORGCHK`, `REORG` table, `REORG` indexes, `RUNSTATS`, `REBIND`
3. `REORGCHK`, `REORG` indexes, `REORG` table, `RUNSTATS`, `REBIND`
4. `RUNSTATS`, `REBIND`, `REORGCHK`, `REORG` table, `REORG` indexes, `RUNSTATS`

Question 6: What does the `FLUSH PACKAGE CACHE` statement do?

1. It invalidates all dynamic SQL statements from the package cache
2. It invalidates only inactive SQL statements from the package cache
3. It saves dynamic SQL statements stored in the package cache to an external file
4. It causes all SQL statements in the package cache that are currently in use to be recompiled

Question 7: Which of the following can be used to move data from one table space to another while the data remains online and available for access?

    1. The `db2move` command

    2. The `db2relocatedb` command

    3. The `ADMIN_MOVE_TABLE ()` procedure

    4. The `ADMIN_MOVE_TABLE_UTIL ()` procedure

Question 8: What is the purpose of specifying the `RESTART CONTINUE` option in an `INGEST` command?

    1. To terminate a failed `INGEST` command

    2. To restart a failed `INGEST` command from the beginning

    3. To clean up the log records of a failed `INGEST` command

    4. To restart a failed `INGEST` command from the last commit point

Question 9: Which two commands can you use to monitor the ingest operation?

    1. `LIST UTILITIES SHOW DETAIL`

    2. `INGEST LIST`

    3. `GET SNAPSHOT FOR INGEST`

    4. `INGEST GET STATS FOR <id>`

    5. `GET SNAPSHOT FOR ALL APPLICATIONS`

Question 10: Which of the following `REORG` commands rebuilds the dictionary?

    1. `REORG TABLE ... REBUILD DICTIONARY`

    2. `REORG TABLE ... ALLOW READ ACCESS RESETDICTIONARY`

    3. `REORG TABLE ... INPLACE REBUILD DICTIONARY`

    4. `REORG TABLE ... INPLACE RECREATE DICTIONARY`

Answers

Question 1: The correct answer is 3. Ingest is the best choice to process and load the data in real-time.

Load: Low: allows read-only operations

Import: High: sometimes escalates to table level lock

Ingest: Very high: row-level locking

`db2move`: This utility is beneficial whenever you want to move data from one database to another. But, it can't be used for real-time processing.

Question 2: The correct answer is 1. Ingest is a client-side utility.

Attribute	Ingest
Speed	Fast: uses parallel insert threads
Concurrency	Very high: row-level locking
Transaction logging	Every record change is logged
Behavior on failure	Rollback, and table is accessible
LOBs and XML data	Unsupported data type
Utility type	Client-side
Triggers activation	Yes
Constraint validation	Yes
Is table space backup necessary?	No
Utility throttling	No impact

Question 3: The correct answer is 2. You use the LOAD command modifiers—IDENTITYIGNORE, IDENTITYMISSING, and IDENTITYOVERRIDE—when loading identity column data. The IDENTITYIGNORE modifier indicates that although data for all identity columns is present in the file being loaded, this data should be ignored, and the Load utility should replace all identity column data found with its own generated values. The IDENTITYMISSING modifier specifies that data for the identity columns is missing from the file being loaded, and that the Load utility should generate an appropriate value for each missing value encountered. The IDENTITYOVERRIDE modifier indicates that the Load utility is to accept explicit, non-NULL data values for all identity columns in the table. This modifier is useful when migrating data from another database system, or when loading a table from data that was recovered by using the ROLLFORWARD DATABASE command's DROPPED TABLE RECOVERY option. Use this modifier only when an identity column that was defined as GENERATED ALWAYS is present in the table that is to be loaded.

Question 4: The correct answer is 2. When you use the Import utility's REPLACE option, any existing data is deleted from the target table (which must already exist), and then the new data is inserted. You cannot use this option if the target table contains a primary key that is referenced by a foreign key in another table.

Question 5: The correct answer is 2. The RUNSTATS utility should be run immediately after any of the following occur:

- A large number of insert, update, or delete operations are performed against a specific table
- An import operation is performed
- A load operation is performed
- One or more columns are added to an existing table
- A new index is created
- A table or index is re-organized

It is also a good idea to run the RUNSTATS utility before running the REORGCHK utility. If the query response is slow because fragmentation and statistics are not current, the REORGCHK utility may report that a table or index reorganization operation is unnecessary when it really is. Upon careful evaluation of the REORGCHK utility's output, you may discover that one or more tables or indexes need to be re-organized. If that is the case, you can re-organize the tables, followed by the indexes, using Db2's REORG utility. After you re-organize data, statistics should be collected again and any packages that are associated with the table should be rebound (using the REBIND utility) so the DB2 Optimizer can generate new data access plans using the new statistics information collected.

Question 6: The correct answer is 1. The FLUSH PACKAGE CACHE statement invalidates all cached dynamic SQL statements in the package cache. This invalidation causes the next request for any SQL statement that matches an invalidated cached dynamic SQL statement to be compiled instead of reused from the package cache.

Question 7: The correct answer is 3. You can use the SYSPROC.ADMIN_MOVE_TABLE () procedure to move the table online, as this example shows:

```
CALL SYSPROC.ADMIN_MOVE_TABLE
('MOHAN',
'EMP_PHOTO',
'TS_SMALL_DATA',
'TS_SMALL_INDEX',
'TS_LOB_DATA',
' ',
' ',
' ',
' ',
' ',
'MOVE');
```

The db2move command creates a copy of the table in the same database or on a different database, but it does not move it. You can use db2relocatedb to perform the following set of actions:

- Change the database name
- Change the database path
- Re-associate the database with another instance
- Change each node database name in a DPF environment
- Change the new log path directory
- Change the container paths
- Change the storage paths
- Change the failarchpath
- Change the logarchmenth1 and logarchmenth2
- Change the mirrorlogpath and overflow log path

The SYSPROC.ADMIN_MOVE_TABLE_UTIL () procedure complements the ADMIN_MOVE_TABLE () procedure by modify the online move table procedure attributes; however, it cannot act on a table on its own.

Question 8: The correct answer is 4. The INGEST command is considered complete only when it reaches the end of the source file or the pipe. Under any other circumstances, the Ingest utility considers the command execution as incomplete, and these conditions include the following ones:

- The utility is unable to read the input file due to an I/O error
- A critical DB2 system error indicates that the job is not functioning as expected
- The INGEST command is killed or terminates abnormally

If an INGEST command fails, you can restart it by reissuing the command with the RESTART CONTINUE clause. The Ingest utility will then start the operation from the last commit point.

Question 9: The correct answers are 2 and 4. The Ingest utility has two simple commands to monitor progress:

- INGEST LIST
- INGEST GET STATS FOR <id>

These commands must be run on the same machine running the Ingest utility. Neither the LIST UTILITIES nor the SNAPSHOTS can capture the progress of the INGEST command.

Question 10: The correct answer 2. You can also force a table-level compression dictionary creation by using the REORG TABLE command with the RESETDICTIONARY clause. This command forces the creation of a compression dictionary if there is at least one row of data in the table. Table re-organization is an offline operation; however, you can let the read workload to select data from the REORG participating table.

7
High Availability

This chapter will introduce you to the backup and recovery tools that are available within Db2. We will cover Db2 high availability features such as HADR with **read on standby (ROS)** and multiple standby databases. You will also be introduced to the Db2 pureScale database cluster and associated components.

In this chapter, we will cover the following topics:

- Understanding the various transaction logging features
- Backing up a database both at the tablespace level and database level
- Restoring a database using tablespace level backup images as well as database level backup images
- Understanding and implementing the HADR features
- Configuring HADR with ROS
- Configuring ACR in an HADR implementation
- Understanding and implementing HADR with multiple standby databases
- Understanding the Db2 pureScale architecture and basic operations
- Understanding the geographically dispersed Db2 pureScale cluster

 Certification test

Number of questions: 8
Percentage in the exam: 13%

Transactions and logging parameters

A **transaction** is a sequence of one or more SQL statements grouped together as a single unit, typically within an application process.

The commands used to complete or end the transaction are as follows:

- COMMIT
- ROLLBACK

Transaction logging is a process to keep track of changes made to a database (by one or more application connections or transactions) as they are made. These changes are recorded in the transaction logs for replay purposes. The following section describes the database configuration parameters related to transaction logging:

- logbufsz: This parameter specifies the amount of memory to use as a buffer for log records before writing these records to disk. The default value is 256 pages, however the Db2 configuration advisor will generally set the size to 2,151 pages (4 K page size).

- logfilsiz: This parameter specifies the size of each primary and secondary log file. The size of these log files limits the number of log records that can be written before the file becomes full and a new log file is required. The default value is 1,000 pages (4 K page size), however the Db2 configuration advisor updates the value based on initial workload statistics. The upper limit for this configuration parameter is 63.99 GB (64 pages short of 64 GB).

- logprimary: This parameter specifies the number of primary log files to be pre-allocated. The default is 3, however the Db2 configuration advisor updates the value based on initial workload statistics. If the logsecond parameter is set to –1, logprimary should be set to <= 256. If the logsecond parameter does not have a value of –1, then (logprimary + logsecond) <=256.

- logsecond: This parameter specifies the number of secondary log files that are created and used for recovery log files. The secondary log files are created only when needed. The default is 10, however the Db2 configuration advisor updates the value based on initial workload statistics. When you set this parameter to –1, it will activate infinite active log space so that there is no limit on the size or the number of in-flight transactions running on the database. The logarchmeth1 configuration parameter must be set to a value other than OFF or LOGRETAIN.

- newlogpath: This parameter specifies a string of up to 242 bytes to specify the location where the active transaction log files are stored. This must always be a fully qualified path name. In both pureScale and ESE environments, the database partition number and a log stream ID are automatically appended to the path, for example, /home/db2inst1/activelog /NODE0000/LOGSTREAM0000/.

- overflowlogpath: This parameter specifies a string of up to 242 bytes to specify the location for Db2 databases to find log files needed for a roll-forward operation, as well as a location to store active log files retrieved from an archive location. This must always be a fully qualified path name. If logsecond is set to −1, this directory will be used to store active transaction log files retrieved from the archive location for rollback operation (if necessary).

- mirrorlogpath: This parameter specifies a string of up to 242 bytes to create a dual copy of active transaction log files. This must always be a fully qualified path name. If logarchmeth2 is set along with mirrorlogpath, then the database manager archives the mirrorlogpath active transaction logs to the logarchmeth2 location.

- blk_log_dsk_ful: This parameter can be set to prevent disk full errors from being generated when the Db2 database system cannot create a new log file in the active log path due to the filesystem full condition. The default is NO. Setting this parameter to YES causes applications to hang when the Db2 database system encounters a log disk full error, thus allowing you to resolve the error and allowing the transaction to complete. Setting this parameter to NO causes transactions to fail and rollback.

- blocknonlogged: This parameter specifies whether the database manager will allow NOT LOGGED operations to be executed on the database. The default is NO. If this parameter is set to YES, then the following statements would fail with an error of SQL0628N:

```
CREATE TABLE ... NOT LOGGED INITIALLY;
ALTER TABLE ... ACTIVATE NOT LOGGED INITIALLY;
```

  Any NOT LOGGED attribute to LOB columns in the CREATE TABLE statement would fail with an error SQL20054N:

```
CREATE TABLE ... (...BLOB (1M) NOT LOGGED);
```

  Any LOAD command with NONRECOVERABLE or without the COPY YES option will fail with an error of SQL2032N.

- `max_log`: This parameter specifies whether there is a limit to the percentage of the primary log space that a transaction can consume, and what that limit is. The default is 0, which means that there is no limit to the percentage of total primary log space that a transaction can consume. If this is set to a non-zero value, then the non-zero value indicates the percentage of total primary log space that a transaction can consume. If an application violates the `max_log` setting, it is forced to disconnect from the database with an error of SQL1224N. The Db2 registry variable `DB2_FORCE_APP_ON_MAX_LOG` controls the behavior of rollback when an application log consumption exceeds the `max_log` setting. If this registry is set to `TRUE` using the command `db2set DB2_FORCE_APP_ON_MAX_LOG=TRUE -immediate`, then the `max_log` violating application is forced off the database and the unit of work is rolled back. If this is set to `FALSE`, the `max_log` violating application can still commit the work completed by previous statements in the unit of work, or it can roll back the work completed to undo the unit of work.

- `num_log_span`: This parameter specifies whether there is a limit to how many log files one transaction can span, and what that limit is. The default is 0, which means that there is no limit to how many log files one single transaction can span. If the value is other than zero, this value would indicate the number of active log files that one active transaction can span. If an application violates this setting, the application is forced to disconnect from the database and the transaction is rolled back.

- `softmax`: This determines the frequency of soft checkpoints and the recovery range during the crash recovery process. This parameter is deprecated and replaced with the new set of parameters, `page_age_trgt_mcr` and `page_age_trgt_gcr`.

- `logarchmeth1`: This parameter specifies the media type of the primary destination for logs that are archived from the current active transaction log path. The default is OFF. If this parameter, along with `logarchmeth2`, are set to `OFF`, the database is configured as a circular logging enabled database, and point in time database recovery is not possible. When this parameter is set to `LOGRETAIN`, the database is configured as archive logging enabled and point in time database recovery is possible using the `ROLLFORWARD` command. When this parameter is set to `USEREXIT`, the database is configured as archive logging enabled and a user exit program is used to archive and retrieve the log files. This is an old way of archiving the logs. When this parameter is set to `DISK`, the database is configured as archive logging enabled and logs get archived to the fully qualified storage path specified. When this parameter is set to `TSM`, the database is configured as archive logging enabled and logs get archived to the **Tivoli Storage Manager** (**TSM**) server. When this parameter is set to `VENDOR`, the database is configured as archive logging enabled and logs get archived to a vendor storage server using the vendor library.

- `logarchcompr1`: This parameter specifies whether the log files written to the primary archive destination are compressed. The default is `OFF`. If this is set to `ON`, the log files written to the primary archive location are compressed. If this is set to `NX842`, the log files written to the primary archive location are compressed using the AIX Power 7 and Power 8 processor's next accelerator algorithm. This option is not available on Intel-based processors. If the `logarchmeth1` configuration parameter is set to anything other than `DISK`, `TSM`, or `VENDOR`, the `logarchcompr1` parameter will have no effect.

- `logarchopt1`: This parameter specifies a string of options which control log archiving behavior when the primary archived log method, `logarchmeth1`, is enabled. For example, if you update the `logarchopt1` database configuration parameter to `-Servername=db2prodclass`, the `TSM` client uses the `db2prodclass` stanza in the `dsm.sys` file to determine the management class to be used for archival.

- `logarchmeth2`: This parameter specifies the media type of the secondary destination for logs that are archived from either the current active transaction log path or the mirror log path. The default is `OFF`. The option supports the `DISK`, `TSM`, and `VENDOR` values. If both `logarchmeth1` and `logarchmeth2` are set, then the transaction logs get archived from the `newlogpath` directory to both archive locations. However, if `mirrorlogpath` is set, the transaction logs are archived from `mirrorlogpath` to the location of `logarchmeth2`.

- `logarchcompr2`: This parameter specifies whether the log files written to the secondary archive destination are for logs that are compressed. The default is `OFF`. If this is set to `ON`, the log files written to the secondary archive location are compressed. If this is set to `NX842`, the log files written to the secondary archive location are compressed using the AIX Power 7 and Power 8 processor's next accelerator algorithm. This option is not available on Intel-based processors. If the `logarchmeth2` configuration parameter is set to anything other than `DISK`, `TSM`, or `VENDOR`, `parameterlogarchcompr2` will have no effect.

- `logarchopt2`: This parameter specifies a string of options which control log archiving behavior when the secondary archived log method, `logarchmeth2`, is enabled.

- `failarchpath`: This parameter specifies a disk location to which the Db2 database will try to archive log files if the log files cannot be archived to either the primary or the secondary (if set) archive destinations because of a storage problem affecting those destinations.

- `numarchretry`: This parameter specifies the number of attempts that the Db2 database must make to archive a log file to the primary or the secondary archive locations specified in `logarchmeth1` or `logarchmeth2` before trying to archive log files to the failover directory. The default is five attempts and this parameter will be ignored if the `failarchpath` database configuration parameter is not set.

- `archretrydelay`: This parameter specifies the number of seconds to wait after a failed archive attempt before trying to archive the log file again from `failarchpath` to `logarchmeth1` or `logarchmeth2` locations. The default is `20` seconds.

- `logindexbuild`: This parameter specifies whether index creation, recreation, or reorganization operations are logged so that indexes can be reconstructed during roll-forward recovery operations or HADR log replay procedures. The default is `OFF` and index objects are marked invalid when the roll-forward operation rolls through index creation, recreation, or reorganization operations. If this parameter is set to `ON`, index creation, recreation, and reorganization operations are logged and are replayed during roll-forward operations.

- `log_ddl_stmts`: This parameter specifies that extra information regarding **Data Definition Language (DDL)** statements will be written to the log. The default is `NO`. If you want to capture the DDL changes such as `CREATE TABLE`, `DROP TABLE`, or `ALTER TABLE` that are to be replayed on the replicated systems like Q replication or **change data capture (CDC)**, set the `log_ddl_stmts` configuration parameter to `YES`.

- `log_appl_info`: This parameter specifies that the application information is written at the start of each update transaction into the transaction log. The default is `NO` and the application user information is written at the end of the transaction. When it is set to `YES`, the application user information is written at the beginning of the transaction and can be used by the replication capture programs to ignore unwanted transactions based on specific user IDs entered in the `IBMQREP_IGNTRAN` table.

- `page_age_trgt_mcr`: This parameter specifies the time in seconds for changed pages to be kept in the local buffer pool before they are persisted to table space storage in a single node ESE database, or to table space storage or to the GBP in a pureScale cluster environment. This is the new parameter that replaces the deprecated parameter `softmax`, which is used to determine the frequency of soft checkpoints. The default is 240 seconds in an ESE environment and 120 seconds in a pureScale environment. This parameter will take effect only when `softmax` is set to 0.

- `page_age_trgt_gcr`: This parameter specifies the time in seconds for changed pages to be kept in the GBP before the pages are persisted to table space storage. This is applicable only to pureScale databases. The default is 240 seconds. This parameter will take effect only when `softmax` is set to 0. The `page_age_trgt_gcr` parameter value must be greater than or equal to the `page_age_trgt_mcr` parameter value.

- `trackmod`: This parameter specifies whether the database manager will track database modifications so that the backup utility can detect which subsets of the database pages must be examined by an incremental or delta backups and potentially included in the backup image. The default is `NO`. This parameter should be set to `YES` to enable the database for incremental and delta backups.

Infinite active log space (`logsecond = -1`) is not supported in pureScale environments. The `ARCHIVE LOG`, `BACKUP DATABASE`, `LOAD`, `REORG`, `RESTORE DATABASE`, and `ROLLFORWARD DATABASE` commands are excluded from the limitation imposed by the `num_log_span` and `max_log` configuration parameters. If you use the `userexit` or `logretain` option for the `logarchmeth1` configuration parameter, the `logarchmeth2` configuration parameter must be set to `OFF`.

Transaction logging strategies

There are the following two transaction logging methods available within Db2:

- **Circular logging**: The transaction log files are rewritten when the available files have filled up with log records and the overwritten log records are not recoverable. To use this transaction logging mode, set `logarchmeth1` to `OFF`. This is the default logging mode. With this type of logging, the only database backup type allowed is offline. This means that an outage to the application is required while performing a backup on the database. In addition, **large binary object (LOB)** and the `LONG VARCHAR` column data changes are not written to the transaction logs. However, these are tracked through shadow paging and are used for a rollback operation (if necessary).
- **Archival logging**: The transaction log files are archived when they fill up with log records. You can activate archival logging by setting the database configuration parameter `logarchmeth1` to `LOGRETAIN`, `USEREXIT`, `DISK`, `TSM`, or `VENDOR`. The database configuration update command to active the archival logging is as follows:

```
UPDATE DB CFG FOR sample USING LOGARCHMETH1 TSM
```

The following table describes the differences between circular logging and archival logging:

Attribute	Circular logging	Archival logging
Database-level backup	Offline only	Online or offline
Database-level restores	Version recovery using offline backup	Version recovery and roll-forward recovery
Crash recovery	Supported	Supported
Point-in-time recovery	Not supported	Supported via the `ROLLFORWARD TO <TIMESTAMP>` command
Recovery to end of logs	Not supported	Supported via the `ROLLFORWARD TO END OF LOGS` command
Table space level backup	Not supported	Online or offline operation is supported
Table space level recovery	Not supported	Online or offline recovery operations are supported
Roll-forward a specific table space	Not supported	Supported point-in-time or to end of logs

Storage requirement	Requires less auxiliary storage space	Requires additional auxiliary storage space to retain the archival logs
Recover an existing database using the RECOVER DATABASE command	Not supported	Supported and can be used to recover an existing database to a point in time or to end of logs
General name for these types of databases	Non-recoverable databases	Recoverable databases

Database recovery methods

There are the following four recovery types supported within Db2:

- **Crash recovery**: Transactions against a database can be interrupted unexpectedly. If a failure, such as power failure, operating system failure, or a hardware failure occurs before all the changes that are part of the transactions are completed and committed, the database is left in an inconsistent state. Crash recovery is the process by which the database is moved back to a consistent state by using transaction logs to undo or redo the changes. The incomplete transactions are rolled back and completed changes are committed that were still in database memory when the crash occurred. The crash recovery will automatically be initiated if there is a problem, however you can also initiate a crash recovery by using the RESTART DATABASE command. The basic syntax for this command is as follows:

```
RESTART [DATABASE | DB] [DatabaseAlias]
<USER [UserName] <USING [Password]>>
<DROP PENDING TABLESPACES ([TbspNames])>
<WRITE RESUME>
```

Let's explore some of the preceding commands here:

- DatabaseAlias: This command identifies the alias assigned to the database that is to be returned to a consistent and usable state
- UserName: This command identifies the name assigned to a specific user who is to perform the crash recovery operation

- `Password`: This command identifies the password that corresponds to the name of the user who is to perform the crash recovery operation
- `TbspName`: This command identifies the name assigned to one or more table spaces to disable and place in Drop Pending state during the crash recovery process

If you want to perform a crash recovery operation on an unusable database named SAMPLE, execute the following RESTART command:

```
RESTART DATABASE sample
```

If you want to perform a crash recovery operation on a database named SAMPLE and place a table space named TS_DATA_4K in the DROP PENDING state, you can do so by executing the following RESTART command:

```
RESTART DATABASE sample DROP PENDING TABLESPACES (TS_DATA_4K)
```

Following are two types of crash recoveries within a Db2 pureScale cluster:

- **Member crash recovery**: Where only a set of members are involved in the crash recovery
- **Group crash recovery**: When the cluster is completely down and recovery is initiated on all the members in the cluster
- **Version recovery**: Version recovery is the restoration of a previous version of the entire database using a backup image that was created. You can use this recovery method with non-recoverable databases as well with recoverable databases by using the WITHOUT ROLLING FORWARD option on the RESTORE command.
  If you want to perform a version recovery, you can use the following RESTORE DATABASE command:

```
RESTORE DATABASE sample FROM /backup TAKEN AT 20180526205844;
```

If the database is a recoverable database, you can use the following command to perform a version recovery:

```
RESTORE DATABASE sample FROM /backup TAKEN AT 20180526210710 WITHOUT
ROLLING FORWARD;
```

- **Roll-forward recovery**: Roll-forward recovery method needs both a database backup image and archived logs. If you restore the database and do not specify the `WITHOUT ROLLING FORWARD` option in the `RESTORE DATABASE` command, the database will be in roll-forward pending state at the end of the restore operation. This state allows roll-forward recovery (applying the transaction logs forward and backward) to take place. The set of commands to perform roll-forward recovery are as follows:
    - Restore the database using a backup image using the `RESTORE` command:

      ```
      RESTORE DATABASE sample FROM /backup TAKEN AT 20180526211541;
      ```

    - Then, check the roll-forward status by executing the `ROLLFORWARD QUERY STATUS` command:

      ```
      ROLLFORWARD DATABASE sample QUERY STATUS;

                                           Rollforward Status

        Input database alias                  = sample
        Number of members have returned status = 1

        Member ID                             = 0
        Rollforward status                    = DB   pending
        Next log file to be read              = S0000014.LOG
        Log files processed                   = -
        Last committed transaction            =
      2018-05-27-01.15.45.000000 UTC
      ```

    - Finally, run the `ROLLFORWARD` command to apply the logs to the end of the logs:

      ```
      ROLLFORWARD DATABASE sample TO END OF LOGS AND COMPLETE
      OVERFLOW LOG
      PATH (/db/overflowpath);

                                           Rollforward Status

        Input database alias                  = testdb
        Number of members have returned status = 1

        Member ID                             = 0
        Rollforward status                    = not pending
        Next log file to be read              =
        Log files processed                   = S0000014.LOG -
      S0000014.LOG
        Last committed transaction            =
      ```

```
2018-05-27-01.15.45.000000 UTC
```

- **Disaster recovery**: Disaster recovery consists of a set of associated processes, policies, and procedures that restore the database to a different site in the event of a natural or human-induced disaster. Db2 provides you with many robust features to enable a smooth disaster recovery process between multiple sites or computers. Two of these features are as follows:
    - HADR data replication
    - SQL, Q, or CDC replication for specific schemas or set of tables

Db2 also supports storage-level mirroring, such as **Peer-to-Peer Remote Copy** (**PPRC**), providing data recovery capability in the event of a disaster. We will discuss HADR in greater detail in the *High Availability and Disaster Recovery (HADR)* section.

Backup and recovery

Following, there are four utilities supported within Db2 to facilitate backing up and restoring a database:

- The backup utility
- The restore utility
- The roll-forward utility
- The recover utility

The Db2 backup utility

The backup utility is used to create images outside the database that can be used to recover the entire database or a portion of it. If the database is an archive logging enabled database, the backup utility can be executed online with multiple concurrent applications connected to the database. The backup utility uses the utility heap to copy the data from the table spaces to the backup image. The utility heap can be controlled via the database configuration parameter UTIL_HEAP_SZ.

The backup utility can write the backup image to storage devices on the database server, to a tape device, or can copy the data directly to the TSM storage devices or another vendor-supplied routine.

Execute the BACKUP command to start the backup process. The basic syntax is as follows:

```
BACKUP [DATABASE | DB] [DatabaseAlias]

<USER [UserName] <USING [Password]>>

<TABLESPACE ([TbspNames]) | NO TABLESPACE>

<ONLINE>

<INCREMENTAL <DELTA>>

<TO [Location] | USE TSM <OPTIONS [TSMOptions]>>

<WITH [NumBuffers] BUFFERS>

<BUFFER [BufferSize]>

<PARALLELISM [ParallelNum]>

<COMPRESS>

<UTIL_IMPACT_PRIORITY [Priority]>

<INCLUDE LOGS | EXCLUDE LOGS>

<WITHOUT PROMPTING>
```

Take a look at the following commands used in the preceding query:

- DatabaseAlias: This command identifies the name assigned to the database from which to create a backup image
- UserName: This command identifies the name assigned to a specific user who is to perform the backup operation
- Password: This command identifies the password that corresponds to the name of the user who is to perform the backup operation
- TbspName: This command identifies the name assigned to one or more specific table spaces to create backup images
- Location: This command identifies the directory or device in which to store the backup image that's been created
- TSMOptions: This command identifies options that the TSM is to use during the backup operation

- `NumBuffers`: This command identifies the number of buffers to use to perform the backup operation
- `BufferSize`: This command identifies the size, in pages, of each buffer used to perform the backup operation
- `ParallelNum`: This command identifies the number of table spaces that can be read in parallel during the backup operation to improve the performance of the operation
- `Priority`: This command is used to throttle the backup utility to control the effects on concurrent database activity; you can assign this parameter a numerical value within the range of 1 to 100, with 100 representing the highest priority and 1 representing the lowest

If you want to back up the entire database SAMPLE online to TSM, use the following command:

```
BACKUP DATABASE sample ONLINE USE TSM WITH BUFFER 8192 PARALLELISM 8
COMPRESS;
```

If you want to back up two table spaces, TS_DATA_4K and TS_INDX_4K, of the database SAMPLE online to TSM, use the following command:

```
BACKUP DATABASE sample TABLESPACE (TS_DATA_4K, TS_INDX_4K) ONLINE USE TSM
WITH BUFFER 8192 PARALLELISM 8 COMPRESS;
```

If you only want to backup the database metadata, such as the history file, without backing up any table spaces, you can use the following command:

```
BACKUP DATABASE sample NO TABLESPACE;

Backup successful. The timestamp for this backup image is: 20180526232357
```

The following command can then be used to restore the metadata backup image:

```
RESTORE DATABASE sample TAKEN AT 20180526232357 REPLACE HISTORY FILE;
```

You can backup and restore from a 32-bit level database to a 64-bit level database without any change to the RESTORE command. If you want to restore a 32-bit database instance's compressed backup image onto a 64-bit instance, you can specify the comprlib libdb2compr.so compression library within the RESTORE DATABASE command. The EXPORT, INSPECT, CREATE INDEX, CREATE TABLE, ALTER TABLE, DROP TABLE, and DROP INDEX commands are compatible with online backups.

`IMPORT` with `REPLACE`, `LOAD` with `COPY NO` and `ALLOW READ ACCESS`, `ALTER TABLESPACE ... AUTORESIZE`, and `REORG TABLE` are not compatible with online backups. There is no difference between an ESE database backup operation and a pureScale database backup operation. In a **database partitioning feature** (**DPF**), also known as a **massively parallel processing** (**MPP**) database, you can use the `DBPARTITIONNUMS` clause within the `BACKUP DATABASE` command to backup multiple partitions at the same time. If no partition is specified, the backup utility runs on all the partitions.

Incremental and delta backups

An incremental backup is a backup image that contains only pages that have been updated since the previous backup image was made. Two types of incremental backup images can be produced: incremental and delta. An incremental backup image is a copy of all database data that has changed since the most recent successful full backup image was created. The predecessor of an incremental backup image is always the most recent successful full backup image of the same object. A delta backup image, however, is a copy of all database data that has changed since the last successful backup (full, incremental, or delta) of the database or table space in question:

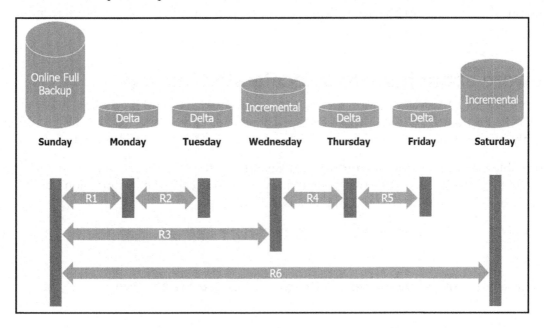

Online full, incremental, and delta backups

The preceding diagram describes an organization's full, incremental, and delta backup policy. For this example, the backup policy is to take an **Online Full Backup** on **Sunday**, **Incremental** backups on **Wednesday** and **Saturday**, and **Delta** backups on the remaining days (as follows) to effectively use the storage on the backup device:

Backup name	Backup description	Day reference	Backup
BKUP1	Online full backup	Sunday	Baseline backup
BKUP2	Delta backup	Monday	BKUP1 (R1)
BKUP3	Delta backup	Tuesday	BKUP2 (R2)
BKUP4	Incremental backup	Wednesday	BKUP1 (R3)
BKUP5	Delta backup	Thursday	BKUP4 (R4)
BKUP6	Delta backup	Friday	BKUP5 (R5)
BKUP7	Incremental backup	Saturday	BKUP1 (R6)

An online full backup consists of a full database image, and Monday's delta backup image constitutes data changes made between Sunday and Monday. Tuesday's delta backup image consists of data changes made between Monday and Tuesday. On Wednesday, the incremental backup image contains data changes made between Sunday and Wednesday because that incremental backup will always be referenced from the last full backup. Thursday's delta backup image consists of data changes made between Wednesday and Thursday.

A word about hardware accelerated backup

You can achieve hardware compression for Db2 backup images and log archive files on AIX POWER 7 and POWER 8 processors by using the nest accelerator NX842. This solution is only supported on AIX versions AIX V7 TL3 SP3 and AIX V6 TL9 SP3 or later.

To enable hardware backup compression by default, set the registry variable `DB2_BCKP_COMPRESSION` to `NX842`, otherwise you must specify the compression library `libdb2nx842.a` in the `BACKUP` command as follows:

```
db2set DB2_BCKP_COMPRESSION=NX842 -immediate

OR

BACKUP DATABASE sample ONLINE COMPRESS comprlib libdb2nx842.a;
```

You can also enable log archive compression by changing the `logarchcompr1` or `logarchcompr2` database configuration to `NX842` as follows:

```
UPDATE DB CFG FOR sample USING LOGARCHCOMPR1 NX842 LOGARCHCOMPR2 NX842;
```

The archive log compression has dependency on the `logarchmeth1` or `logarchmeth2` database configuration parameter settings. If these parameters are set to a value other than `DISK`, `TSM`, or `VENDOR`, the archive logs will not be compressed.

The Db2 restore utility

The Db2 restore utility can be used to restore the database from a backup image taken at the specified date and time. The restore utility uses a separate portion of database global memory called the utility heap to write the data from the backup image to the Db2 table spaces. The Db2 restore utility can be invoked using the `RESTORE DATABASE` command, and the basic syntax for this command is as follows:

```
RESTORE [DATABASE | DB] [DatabaseAlias]

<USER [UserName] <USING [Password]>>

<REBUILD WITH [TABLESPACE ([TbspNames])] |

[ALL TABLESPACES IN [DATABASE | IMAGE]]

<EXCEPT TABLESPACE ([TbspNames])>>

[TABLESPACE ([TbspNames]) <ONLINE> |

HISTORY FILE <ONLINE>> |

COMPRESSION LIBRARY <ONLINE>> |

LOGS <ONLINE>]

<INCREMENTAL <AUTO | AUTOMATIC | ABORT>>

<FROM [SourceLocation] | USE TSM <OPTIONS [TSMOptions]>>

<TAKEN AT [Timestamp]>

<TO [TargetLocation]>

<DBPATH ON [TargetPath]>
```

```
<TRANSPORT [STAGE IN StagingAlias] [USING STOGROUP StoGroupName]]

<INTO [TargetAlias]> <LOGTARGET [LogsLocation]>

<NEWLOGPATH [LogsLocation]>

<WITH [NumBuffers] BUFFERS>

<BUFFER [BufferSize]>

<REPLACE HISTORY FILE>

<REPLACE EXISTING>

<REDIRECT <GENERATE SCRIPT [ScriptFile]>>

<PARALLELISM [ParallelNum]>

<WITHOUT ROLLING FORWARD>

<WITHOUT PROMPTING>
```

Take a look at the following commands mentioned in the preceding example:

- DatabaseAlias: This command identifies the alias assigned to the database associated with the backup image used to perform a version recovery operation
- UserName: This command identifies the name of a specific user who is performing the version recovery operation
- Password: This command identifies the password that corresponds to the name of the user who is performing the version recovery operation
- TbspName: This command identifies the name assigned to one or more specific table spaces to restore from a backup image
- SourceLocation: This command identifies the directory or device in which to store the backup image to be used for version recovery
- TSMOptions: This command identifies options that TSM is to use during the version recovery operation
- Timestamp: This command identifies a timestamp to use as a search criterion when looking for a particular backup image to use for recovery
- TargetLocation: This command identifies the directory in which to store the storage containers for the database that will be created, if the backup image is to be used to create a new database, and automatic storage is used

- `TargetPath`: This command identifies the directory in which to store the metadata for the database that will be created, if the backup image is to be used to create a new database, and automatic storage is used
- `StagingAlias`: This command identifies the temporary staging database for the transport operation
- `StoGroupName`: This command identifies the target storage group for all the automatic storage table spaces being transported
- `TargetAlias`: This command identifies the alias to assign to the new database to be created
- `LogsLocation`: This command identifies the directory or device in which to store log files for the new database
- `NumBuffers`: This command identifies the number of buffers to use to perform the version recovery operation (by default, two buffers are used)
- `BufferSize`: This command identifies the size, in pages, of each buffer used to perform the backup operation
- `ScriptFile`: This command identifies the name of the file to write all commands needed to perform a redirected restore operation
- `ParallelNum`: This command identifies the number of table spaces that can be read in parallel during the version recovery operation

If you want to restore a database SAMPLE from a backup image, execute the following command:

```
RESTORE DATABASE sample FROM /backup TAKEN AT 20180526205844 WITH 4 BUFFERS
BUFFER 2048 PARALLELISM 2;
```

If you want to perform a redirected restore and want to generate a script for the restore, use the REDIRECT GENERATE SCRIPT option of the RESTORE command:

```
RESTORE DATABASE sample FROM /backup TAKEN AT 20180526205844  REDIRECT
GENERATE SCRIPT sample.rst
DB20000I  The RESTORE DATABASE command completed successfully.

-- The above command generates a script file for you to modify and run on
the target system

cat sample.rst

-- ** automatically created redirect restore script
--
************************************************************************
**
```

```
UPDATE COMMAND OPTIONS USING S ON Z ON SAMPLE_NODE0000.out V ON;
SET CLIENT ATTACH_MEMBER   0;
SET CLIENT CONNECT_MEMBER 0;
--
*****************************************************************************
**
-- ** automatically created redirect restore script
--
*****************************************************************************
**
RESTORE DATABASE SAMPLE
-- USER   <username>
-- USING ''<password>''
FROM ''/db/home/db2inst1''
TAKEN AT 20180526205844
-- ON ''/db/home/db2inst1''
-- DBPATH ON ''<target-directory>''
INTO SAMPLE
-- NEWLOGPATH
''/db/home/db2inst1/NODE0000/SQL00001/LOGSTREAM0000/''
-- WITH <num-buff> BUFFERS
-- BUFFER <buffer-size>
-- REPLACE HISTORY FILE
-- REPLACE EXISTING
REDIRECT
-- PARALLELISM <n>
-- COMPRLIB ''<lib-name>''
-- COMPROPTS ''<options-string>''
WITHOUT ROLLING FORWARD
-- WITHOUT PROMPTING
;
--
*****************************************************************************
**
-- ** storage group definition
-- **    Default storage group ID                = 0
-- **    Number of storage groups                = 1
--
*****************************************************************************
**
--
*****************************************************************************
**
-- ** Storage group name                         = IBMSTOGROUP
-- **    Storage group ID                         = 0
-- **    Data tag                                 = None
--
*****************************************************************************
```

```
**
-- SET STOGROUP PATHS FOR IBMSTOGROUP
-- ON ''/ds/data''
-- ;
--
*************************************************************************
**
-- ** table space definition
--
*************************************************************************
**
--
*************************************************************************
**
-- ** Tablespace name                        = SYSCATSPACE
-- **     Tablespace ID                      = 0
-- **     Tablespace Type                    = Database managed space
-- **     Tablespace Content Type            = All permanent data.
Regular table space.
-- **     Tablespace Page size (bytes)       = 32768
-- **     Tablespace Extent size (pages)     = 4
-- **     Using automatic storage            = Yes
-- **     Storage group ID                   = 0
-- **     Source storage group ID            = -1
-- **     Data tag                           = None
-- **     Auto-resize enabled                = Yes
-- **     Total number of pages              = 8192
-- **     Number of usable pages             = 8188
-- **     High water mark (pages)            = 7332
...
...
--
*************************************************************************
**
-- ** start redirected restore
--
*************************************************************************
**
RESTORE DATABASE SAMPLE CONTINUE;
--
*************************************************************************
**
-- ** end of file
--
*************************************************************************
**
```

The restore utility can be used to create a new database with the same or a different name using the RESTORE DATABASE...INTO clause. The restore utility must process a complete backup image for the target database to be operational. Any selected table spaces can be restored from either a database level or table space level backup image. Automatic storage group paths can be redefined during a database restore using the SET STOGROUP command within the RESTORE... REDIRECTED operation. For example, if you want to change the path of a storage group from /ds/data to /ds/newdata, then you can modify STOGROUP using the command: SET STOGROUP PATHS FOR IBMSTOGROUP ON /ds/newdata;. Automatic storage group paths can also be changed using the ON clause of the RESTORE DATABASE command. For example, if you want to change the path of storage group from /ds/data to /ds/newdata, then you can specify: RESTORE DATABASE sample FROM /backup TAKEN AT 20180526205844 ON /ds/newdata. A restore operation in pureScale is no different from a restore operation in an ESE environment.

In an MPP environment, you can use the following RESTORE DATABASE command options to restore a database:

```
db2_all ''<<+0<db2 ""RESTORE DATABASE sample FROM /backup""'' [Restore the
catalog partition]
db2_all ''<<-0<db2 ""RESTORE DATABASE sample FROM /backup""'' [Restore all
except catalog partition]
```

The Db2 roll-forward utility

The Db2 roll-forward utility is used to complete the recovery process started by the restore utility by applying the database changes from the Db2 transaction log files. The restore utility places the database or table spaces in roll-forward pending state when the restore is done without the WITHOUT ROLLING FORWARD option. The Db2 database must be configured for archive logging to use the roll-forward utility for recovery.

You can invoke the Db2 roll-forward utility using the basic ROLLFORWARD DATABASE command, as follows:

```
ROLLFORWARD [DATABASE | DB] [DatabaseAlias]

<USER [UserName] <USING [Password]>>

<TO [PointInTime] <USING [UTC | LOCAL] TIME>

<AND [COMPLETE | STOP]> |

END OF LOGS <AND [COMPLETE | STOP]> |
```

```
COMPLETE |

STOP |

CANCEL |

QUERY STATUS <USING [UTC | LOCAL] TIME>>

<TABLESPACE ONLINE |

TABLESPACE <( [TbspNames])> <ONLINE>>

<OVERFLOW LOG PATH ([LogDirectory])>

<RECOVER DROPPED TABLE [TableID] TO [Location]>
```

Take a look at following from the preceding code:

- `DatabaseAlias`: This command identifies the alias assigned to the database to roll forward
- `UserName`: This command identifies the name assigned to the user who is performing the roll-forward operation
- `Password`: This command identifies the password that corresponds to the user who is performing the roll-forward operation
- `PointInTime`: This command identifies a specific point in time, identified by a timestamp value in the form `yyyy-mm-dd-hh.mm.ss.nnnnnn` to roll forward the database
- `TbspNames`: This command identifies the name assigned to one or more specific table spaces to roll forward
- `LogDirectory`: This command identifies the directory that contains offline archived log files that you can use to perform the roll-forward operation
- `TableID`: This command identifies a specific table (by ID) that was dropped earlier to restore as part of the roll-forward operation
- `Location`: This command identifies the directory to write files containing dropped table data when the table is restored as part of the roll-forward operation

If you want to perform a roll-forward operation to the end of all the logs and then open the database for application connections, you can execute the following command:

```
ROLLFORWARD DATABASE sample TO END OF LOGS AND COMPLETE;
```

If you want to perform a point-in-time recovery operation and then open the database for application connections, you can execute the following command:

```
ROLLFORWARD DATABASE sample TO 2018-05-27-00.00.00.0000 AND STOP OVERFLOW
LOG PATH (/db/overflowpath);
```

If you want to perform a roll-forward operation only on one table space, that is, TS_SMALL_DATA, you can execute the following command:

```
ROLLFORWARD DATABASE sample TO 2018-05-27-00.00.00.0000 USING LOCAL TIME
AND STOP TABLESPACE (TS_SMALL_DATA);
```

When you roll a table space forward to a specific point in time, the time you specify must be greater than the minimum recovery time recorded for the table space. You can obtain this time by executing the following table function:

```
SELECT

VARCHAR (TBSP_NAME, 30) AS TBSP_NAME, TABLESPACE_MIN_RECOVERY_TIME

* FROM TABLE (MON_GET_TABLESPACE ('''',-2)) AS T;
```

The minimum recovery time is updated when DDL statements such as DROP TABLE, CREATE TABLE, ALTER TABLE, ...ADD COLUMN, ALTER TABLE..., DROP COLUMN, and so on are run against a table space or against tables stored in a table space.

When you perform a roll-forward operation in a pureScale environment, all the log streams are merged into one log stream and are applied through the member where you run the ROLLFORWARD command.

In an MPP environment, you can use the DBPARTITIONNUM option within the ROLLFORWARD DATABASE command to roll-forward logs on a specific partition.

The Db2 recover utility

The Db2 recover utility uses the information in the history files to determine the backup image to use for the required point-in-time recovery. If the required backup image is an incremental backup, the recover utility will invoke incremental automatic logic to perform the restore using the db2ckrst command. This utility will only perform a database level recovery; no table space recovery and redirection options are available.

You can invoke the Db2 recover utility using the basic syntax for the RECOVER DATABASE command as follows:

```
RECOVER [DATABASE | DB] [DatabaseAlias]

<TO [PointInTime] <USING [UTC | LOCAL] TIME> |

END OF LOGS>

<USER [UserName] <USING [Password]>>

<USING HISTORY FILE ([HistoryFile])>

<OVERFLOW LOG PATH ([LogDirectory])>

<RESTART>
```

Let's take a look at the following commands from the preceding code:

- DatabaseAlias: This command identifies the alias assigned to the database associated with the backup image which is used to perform a version recovery operation
- PointInTime: This command identifies a specific point in time, identified by a timestamp value in the form yyyy-mm-dd-hh.mm.ss.nnnnnn to roll the database forward
- UserName: This command identifies the name assigned to the user who is performing the recovery operation
- Password: This command identifies the password of the user who is performing the recovery operation
- HistoryFile: This command identifies the name assigned to the recovery history log file that the recovery utility is to use
- LogDirectory: This command identifies the directory that contains offline archived log files which are to be used to perform the roll-forward portion of the recovery operation

If you want to run the recover utility on the database SAMPLE to recover to the end of logs, execute the following RECOVER command:

```
RECOVER DB sample
TO END OF LOGS
USING HISTORY FILE (/db/home/db2inst1/NODE0000/SQL00002/db2rhist.asc);
```

If you want to run the recover utility on the database SAMPLE to recover to a point-in-time, execute the following RECOVER command:

```
RECOVER DB SAMPLE TO 2018-05-27-15.00.00;
```

In an MPP environment, you can execute the RECOVER command for specific partitions, as follows:

```
RECOVER DB SAMPLE TO END OF LOGS ON DBPARTITIONNUMS (0 TO 2, 4, 5)
```

Using the BACKUP command shown in the earlier diagram, to RECOVER the database SAMPLE after the delta backup of **Friday**, the sequence of the RESTORE commands which the recover utility would run internally are as follows:

```
RESTORE DB sample INCREMENTAL TAKEN AT <Friday>; -- Friday''s Delta
RESTORE DB sample INCREMENTAL TAKEN AT <Sunday>; -- Sunday''s Full
RESTORE DB sample INCREMENTAL TAKEN AT <Wednesday>; -- Wednesday''s
Incremental
RESTORE DB sample INCREMENTAL TAKEN AT <Thursday>; -- Thursday''s Delta
RESTORE DB sample INCREMENTAL TAKEN AT <Friday>; -- Friday''s Delta
```

The recover utility performs both the RESTORE and ROLLFORWARD commands using the recovery history file. One single command is used to recover all the partitions in an MPP environment. If no partitions are specified via the DBPARTITIONNUMS clause, all partitions are recovered. The recover utility must run on the catalog partition in an MPP environment.

A word about the db2relocatedb command

The relocate database command (db2relocatedb) is handy for renaming a database or for relocating database table space containers, database log directories, and storage paths. You must deactivate the target database before running the db2relocatedb command to modify the metadata and associated control files.

The command syntax is as follows:

```
db2relocatedb -f [ConfigFileName]
```

Take a look at the following commands from the preceding query:

- `ConfigFileName`: This command specifies the name of the file containing the configuration information required for database relocation
- `db2relocatedb`: This command allows you to change various database characteristics, including:
  - The database name
  - The database path
  - The instance associated with the database
  - Each node database name in a DPF environment
  - The active log path associated with the database (`newlogpath`)
  - The container paths for the table space
  - The storage paths for the database
  - The failure archive log path (`failarchpath`)
  - The archive log paths associated with the database (`logarchmenth1` and `logarchmenth2`)
  - The active mirror log path associated with the database (`mirrorlogpath`)
  - The overflow log path associated with the database (`overflowlogpath`)

The `db2relocatedb` command operates with a control file where you can specify the required changes and perform the necessary relocation. The control file content would look as follows:

```
DB_NAME=oldName,newName

DB_PATH=oldPath,newPath

INSTANCE=oldInst,newInst

NODENUM=nodeNumber

LOG_DIR=oldDirPath,newDirPath

CONT_PATH=oldContPath1,newContpath1

..

STORAGE_PATH=oldStoragePath1,newStoragePath1

..

FAILARCHIVE_PATH=newDirPath
```

```
LOGARCHMETH1=newDirPath

LOGARCHMETH2=newDirPath

MIRRORLOG_PATH=newDirPath

OVERFLOWLOG_PATH=newDirPath
```

If you want to change the storage path for the database SAMPLE from /ds/data to /ds/newdata, you can execute the following steps:

1. Deactivate the SAMPLE database by executing the following command:

    ```
    DEACTIVE DB sample;
    ```

2. Create a control file called stogroupmove.ctrl by executing the following command:

    ```
    DB_NAME=sample
    DB_PATH=/db/db2inst1
    INSTANCE=db2inst1
    STORAGE_PATH=/ds/data,/ds/newdata
    ```

3. Perform the actual relocation by executing the following command:

    ```
    db2relocatedb -f stogroupmove.ctrl
    ```

High availability and disaster recovery

High availability and disaster recovery (HADR) is a Db2 database replication feature that provides a high availability solution for both partial and complete site failures. HADR protects against data loss by replicating data changes from a source database, called the primary database, to one or more target databases, called the multiple standby databases.

In an HADR environment, one database instance acts as the current primary database that is used by the applications. Synchronization with the standby databases occurs by rolling forward transaction log data generated on the primary database which is then shipped to the standby databases.

HADR synchronization modes

With HADR, you can choose different levels of protection for potential data loss by specifying one of the following four synchronization modes:

- SYNC: This mode (synchronous) provides the greatest protection against transaction loss. This option, however, results in the longest transaction response time among the four modes. In this mode, log writes are considered successful only when logs have been written to log files on the primary database and when the primary database has received acknowledgement from the standby database that the logs have also been written to log files on the standby database. The log data is guaranteed to be stored at both sites.

- NEARSYNC: While this mode (near synchronous) has a shorter transaction response time than synchronous mode, it also provides slightly less protection against transaction loss. In this mode, log writes are only considered successful when the log records have been written to the log files on the primary database and when the primary database has received acknowledgement from the standby system that the logs have also been written to main memory on the standby system. Loss of data only occurs if both sites fail simultaneously and if the target site has not transferred all the log data that it has received to volatile storage.

- ASYNC: Compared with the SYNC and NEARSYNC modes, the ASYNC mode (asynchronous) results in shorter transaction response times, but greater transaction losses are possible if the primary database fails. In the ASYNC mode, log writes are only considered successful when the log records have been written to the log files on the primary database and have been delivered to the TCP layer of the primary system's host machine. Because the primary system does not wait for acknowledgement from the standby system, transactions might be considered committed when they are still on their way to the standby database.

- SUPERASYNC: This mode (super asynchronous) has the shortest transaction response time but also has the highest probability of transaction losses in the event that the primary system fails. This mode is useful when you do not want transactions to be blocked or experience elongated response times due to network interruptions or congestion. In this mode, the HADR pair can never be in peer state or disconnected peer state. The log writes are considered successful as soon as the log records have been written to the log files on the primary database. Because the primary database does not wait for acknowledgement from the standby database, transactions are considered committed, irrespective of the state of the replication of the transaction.

The following table showcases the performance and data protection for each synchronization mode:

Mode	Description	Performance	Data protection
SYNC	Log writes on the primary are only considered successful when the log data has been shipped and written to the physical log file on the standby	Compromised	Greatest
NEARSYNC	Log writes on the primary are only considered successful when the log data has been written to the main memory on the standby	Balanced	Balanced
ASYNC	Log writes on the primary are only considered successful when the log data has been delivered to the TCP layer of the primary server	Greater	Compromised
SUPERASYNC	Log writes on the primary have no dependency on the standby	Greatest	Highly compromised

Starting with Db2 10.5, HADR is supported in pureScale environments. The integration of HADR with the pureScale environment provides several advantages, including the following features:

- **Better synchronization**: The SYNC, NEARSYNC, ASYNC, and SUPERASYNC synchronization modes are all supported (SYNC and NEARSYNC were added in Db2 v11.1)
- **DDL support**: HADR replicates the DDL operations
- **Ease of use**: HADR is easy to configure and maintain, just like HADR on an ESE database
- **Native takeover support**: The native TAKEOVER HADR command can be used to perform either a graceful takeover (role switch) or a forced takeover (failover) of the secondary database

HADR-specific parameters

The following section describes the database configuration parameters related to HADR implementation and tuning:

- `hadr_local_host`: This parameter specifies the local host name for **high availability disaster recovery (HADR)** TCP communication.
- `hadr_remote_host`: This parameter specifies the TCP/IP host name or IP address of the remote high availability disaster recovery database server on the HADR primary database, this parameter references the host of the principal standby. In a pureScale HADR environment, it contains a pipe-delimited (|) list of all addresses (hosts and ports) in the standby cluster. For example, in a five member pureScale HADR primary cluster set, `hadr_remote_host` is as follows:

    ```
    (HADR_REMOTE_HOST) = {hadrstandby1:56002| hadrstandby2:56002|
    hadrstandby3:56002| hadrstandby4:56002| hadrstandby5:56002}
    ```

    On the HADR standby database, this parameter references the host of the primary. In a pureScale HADR environment, it contains a pipe-delimited (|) list of all addresses (hosts and ports) in the primary cluster as follows:

    ```
    (HADR_REMOTE_HOST) = {hadrprimary1:56002| hadrprimary2:56002|
    hadrprimary3:56002| hadrprimary4:56002| hadrprimary5:56002}
    ```

- `hadr_local_svc`: This parameter specifies the TCP service name or port number for which the local high availability disaster recovery process accepts connections.
- `hadr_remote_svc`: This parameter specifies the TCP service name or port number that will be used by the remote HADR database server. On HADR primary, this parameter references the port of the principal standby. On a standby, this parameter references the port of the primary. In a pureScale HADR environment, this parameter is always set to `NULL`.
- `hadr_remote_inst`: This parameter specifies the instance name of the remote server. On HADR primary, this parameter references the instance name of the principal standby. On a standby, this parameter references the instance name of the primary.
- `hadr_timeout`: This parameter specifies the time in seconds that the HADR process waits before considering a communication attempt to have failed. The default is 120 seconds.

- `hadr_target_list`: This parameter specifies a list of target hostname and port number (`hostname:port`) pairs that represent HADR standby databases. This is a key parameter in multiple standby HADR and pureScale HADR implementations. On multiple standby HADR primaries, this parameter references the principal standby and auxiliary standby servers in a pipe-delimited (`|`) format. For example, referring back to the configuration shown in the earlier diagram:

  ```
  (HADR_TARGET_LIST) = {HADR2.ibm.com:55002| HADR3.ibm.com:55003|
  HADR4.ibm.com:55004}
  ```

On principal HADR standby, this parameter references the primary and then the remaining auxiliary databases. For example, referring to the configuration as shown in the earlier diagram:

  ```
  (HADR_TARGET_LIST) = {HADR1.ibm.com:55001| HADR3.ibm.com:55003|
  HADR4.ibm.com:55004}
  ```

On the first auxiliary HADR standby, this parameter references the principal standby, then the primary and then the second auxiliary database. For example, referring to the configuration as shown in the earlier diagram:

  ```
  (HADR_TARGET_LIST) = {HADR2.ibm.com:55002| HADR1.ibm.com:55001|
  HADR4.ibm.com:55004}
  ```

On the second auxiliary HADR standby, this parameter references the principal standby, then the primary and then the first auxiliary database. For example, referring to the configuration as shown in the earlier diagram:

  ```
  (HADR_TARGET_LIST) = {HADR2.ibm.com:55002| HADR1.ibm.com:55001|
  HADR3.ibm.com:55003}
  ```

  In a five member pureScale HADR environment, the primary consists of `(HADR_TARGET_LIST) = {hadrsecondary1:56002| hadrsecondary2:56002| hadrsecondary3:56002| hadrsecondary4:56002| hadrsecondary5:56002}`. The pureScale standby cluster consists of `(HADR_TARGET_LIST) = {hadrprimary1:56002| hadrprimary2:56002| hadrprimary3:56002| hadrprimary4:56002| hadrprimary5:56002}`.

- `hadr_syncmode`: This parameter specifies the synchronization mode for the HADR database. The supported modes are `SYNC`, `NEARSYNC`, `ASYNC`, and `SUPERASYNC`.

- `hadr_spool_limit`: This parameter specifies the maximum amount of log data that can be spooled to disk on HADR standby. The default is 0.
- `hadr_replay_delay`: This parameter specifies the number of seconds that must pass from the time that a transaction is committed on the primary database to the time that the transaction is committed on the standby database. The default is 0 seconds.
- `hadr_peer_window`: When this parameter is set to a non-zero time in seconds, the HADR primary-standby database pair continues to behave as though still in peer state, for the configured amount of time, even if the primary database loses connection with the standby database. This helps ensure data consistency. The default is 0 seconds.
- `hadr_ssl_label`: This parameter specifies the label of the SSL certificate which encrypts communication between the primary and standby HADR instances in the key database.

Setting up an HADR multiple standby environment

The process of setting up an HADR environment is straightforward. After ensuring the systems you intend to use as the primary and standby servers are identical and that a TCP/IP connection exists between them, you simply perform the following tasks in order:

1. Determine the host name, host IP address, and the service name or port number for both the primary and the standby database servers.
2. Create the principal standby and auxiliary standby databases by restoring a backup image or initializing a split mirror copy of the database that is to serve as the primary database.
3. Set the HADR configuration parameters on both the primary, principal standby, and auxiliary standby databases.
4. After the standby databases have been created, you must set the HADR configuration parameters which are shown in the *HADR-specific parameters* section.

The following diagram shows the HADR setup, where the host, **HADR1**, is the primary database server, host **HADR2** is the principal standby, and hosts **HADR3** and **HADR4** are auxiliary standbys. This setup also shows virtual IP configuration and automatic management through **Tivoli System Automation for Multi Platforms (TSAMP)**. This setup is only possible between the primary and principal standby with **SYNC** or **NEARSYNC** data synchronization mode:

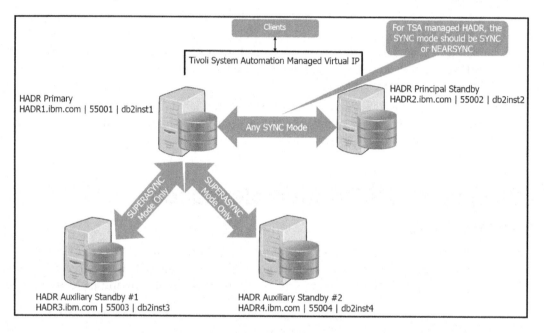

HADR multiple standby databases

Start configuring the standby databases and then the primary database by using the following commands. On the principal standby, the `HADR_TARGET_LIST` command's first entry is always the primary server and associated port number:

```
UPDATE DB CFG FOR sample USING
    HADR_LOCAL_HOST     HADR2.ibm.com
    HADR_LOCAL_SVC      55002
    HADR_REMOTE_HOST    HADR1.ibm.com
    HADR_REMOTE_SVC     55001
    HADR_REMOTE_INST    db2inst1
    HADR_TIMEOUT        120
    HADR_SYNCMODE       NEARSYNC
    HADR_PEER_WINDOW    0
    HADR_TARGET_LIST
HADR1.ibm.com:55001|HADR3.ibm.com:55003|HADR4.ibm.com:55004;
```

On the first auxiliary standby, the `HADR_TARGET_LIST` command's first entry is always the principal standby, then the primary, and then the other auxiliary standby (if there is one):

```
UPDATE DB CFG FOR sample USING
    HADR_LOCAL_HOST HADR3.ibm.com
    HADR_LOCAL_SVC 55003
    HADR_REMOTE_HOST HADR2.ibm.com
    HADR_REMOTE_SVC 55002
    HADR_REMOTE_INST db2inst2
    HADR_TIMEOUT 120
    HADR_SYNCMODE SUPERASYNC
    HADR_PEER_WINDOW 0
    HADR_TARGET_LIST
HADR2.ibm.com:55002|HADR1.ibm.com:55001|HADR4.ibm.com:55004;

UPDATE DB CFG FOR sample USING
    HADR_LOCAL_HOST HADR4.ibm.com
    HADR_LOCAL_SVC 55004
    HADR_REMOTE_HOST HADR2.ibm.com
    HADR_REMOTE_SVC 55002
    HADR_REMOTE_INST db2inst2
    HADR_TIMEOUT 120
    HADR_SYNCMODE SUPERASYNC
    HADR_PEER_WINDOW 0
    HADR_TARGET_LIST
HADR2.ibm.com:55002|HADR1.ibm.com:55001|HADR3.ibm.com:55003;
```

On the primary database, the `HADR_TARGET_LIST` command's first entry is always the principal standby and then the auxiliary standbys:

```
UPDATE DB CFG FOR sample USING
    HADR_LOCAL_HOST     HADR1.ibm.com
    HADR_LOCAL_SVC      55001
    HADR_REMOTE_HOST    HADR2.ibm.com
    HADR_REMOTE_SVC     55002
    HADR_REMOTE_INST    db2inst2
    HADR_TIMEOUT        120
    HADR_SYNCMODE       NEARSYNC
    HADR_PEER_WINDOW    0
    HADR_TARGET_LIST
HADR2.ibm.com:55002|HADR3.ibm.com:55003|HADR4.ibm.com:55004;
```

5. Connect to the standby instances and start HADR on the principal and auxiliary standby databases. To start HADR, you must execute the START HADR command as follows:

```
START HADR ON [DATABASE | DB] [DatabaseAlias]

<USER [UserName] <USING [Password]>>

AS [PRIMARY <BY FORCE> | SECONDARY]
```

Let's explore the following commands from the preceding code:

- DatabaseAlias identifies the alias assigned to the database to start HADR
- UserName identifies the name assigned to the user who is starting HADR
- Password identifies the password of the user who is starting HADR

For example, if you want to start HADR on a database named SAMPLE and indicate that it is to act as a standby database, you could do so by executing a START HADR command that looks as follows:

```
START HADR ON DATABASE sample AS STANDBY;
```

6. Connect to the primary instance and start HADR on the primary database. Execute a START HADR command as follows:

```
START HADR ON DATABASE sample AS PRIMARY;
```

SUPERASYNC is the only supported synchronization mode for auxiliary HADR standby databases. You can use the TAKEOVER HADR ON DATABASE command to perform a role switch between primary and standby HADR databases. After a successful role switch, the HADR_STATE command should be PEER. Multiple standby setup is not supported in the pureScale environment. You can update the value of the hadr_target_list parameter online. However, there are restrictions on modification when HADR is active. You cannot change the principal standby of the primary without first stopping HADR on the primary. You cannot remove a standby from the list if it is connected to the primary. To disconnect a standby, deactivate it. Then, you can remove it from the primary's target list. You cannot dynamically update the hadr_target_list configuration parameter for a standby unless you enabled the HADR reads on the standby feature. You cannot remove the primary database from the target list of a standby if the standby is connected to the primary. The target list must contain IP addresses that are either IPv4 or IPv6, but not a combination of the two. You cannot dynamically update the hadr_target_list configuration parameter in a Db2 pureScale environment.

A word about the Db2 HA instance configuration utility (db2haicu)

The Db2 high availability instance configuration utility (db2haicu) is an interactive, text-based utility you can use to configure and administer highly available databases in a clustered environment. This utility uses the TSA MP Cluster manager to configure a shared database instance.

The utility takes the database instance, cluster environment, and cluster manager as inputs and then configures the instance for high availability failover. The input can be supplied either in interactive mode or by using an XML input file. All the parameters to db2haicu are case-sensitive and must be in lowercase. The basic syntax is as follows:

```
db2haicu [-f XML-input-file]

[-disable]

[-delete [dbpartitionnum dbpartnum-list | hadrdb dbname]]
```

Take a look at the following commands from the preceding code:

- XML-input-file: This command specifies cluster domain details in an input XML file to the db2haicu command.
- -disable: This command ceases high availability on a database manager instance. To reconfigure a ceased database manager instance for high availability, you must rerun the db2haicu utility.
- -delete: This command deletes resource groups in the current database manager instance. To limit the deletion to only a specific partition group in a database-partition-featured instance, use the dbpartnum-list clause. To delete resource groups for an HADR database, use the hadrdb dbname clause.

If you want to use TSA to manage your HADR failover and also the virtual IP, perform the following steps:

1. On an HADR standby database instance, invoke the db2haicu text-based utility as an instance owner:

```
db2haicu
Welcome to the DB2 High Availability Instance Configuration Utility
(db2haicu).

You can find detailed diagnostic information in the DB2 server diagnostic
log file called db2diag.log. Also, you can use the utility called db2pd to
```

query the status of the cluster domains you create.

For more information about configuring your clustered environment using
db2haicu, see the topic called 'DB2 High Availability Instance
Configuration Utility (db2haicu)' in the DB2 Information Center.

db2haicu determined the current DB2 database manager instance is
'db2inst1'. The cluster configuration that follows will apply to this
instance.

db2haicu is collecting information on your current setup. This step may
take some time as db2haicu will need to activate all databases for the
instance to discover all paths ...
When you use db2haicu to configure your clustered environment, you create
cluster domains. For more information, see the topic 'Creating a cluster
domain with db2haicu' in the Db2 Information Center. db2haicu is searching
the current machine for an existing active cluster domain ...
db2haicu did not find a cluster domain on this machine. db2haicu will now
query the system for information about cluster nodes to create a new
cluster domain ...

db2haicu did not find a cluster domain on this machine. To continue
configuring your clustered environment for high availability, you must
create a cluster domain; otherwise, db2haicu will exit.

Create a domain and continue? [1]
1. Yes
2. No
1
Create a unique name for the new domain:
TSA_PROD
Nodes must now be added to the new domain.
How many cluster nodes will the domain 'TSA_PROD' contain?
2
Enter the host name of a machine to add to the domain:
HADR1.ibm.com
Enter the host name of a machine to add to the domain:
HADR2.ibm.com
db2haicu can now create a new domain containing the 2 machines that you
specified. If you choose not to create a domain now, db2haicu will exit.

Create the domain now? [1]
1. Yes
2. No
1
Creating domain 'TSA_PROD' in the cluster ...
Creating domain 'TSA_PROD' in the cluster was successful.
You can now configure a quorum device for the domain. For more information,

see the topic "Quorum devices" in the DB2 Information Center. If you do not configure a quorum device for the domain, then a human operator will have to manually intervene if subsets of machines in the cluster lose connectivity.

Configure a quorum device for the domain called 'TSA_PROD'? [1]
1. Yes
2. No
1
The following is a list of supported quorum device types:
    1. Network Quorum
Enter the number corresponding to the quorum device type to be used: [1]
1
Specify the network address of the quorum device:
10.78.99.254
Configuring quorum device for domain 'TSA_PROD' ...
Configuring quorum device for domain 'TSA_PROD' was successful.
The cluster manager found the following total number of network interface cards on the machines in the cluster domain: '2'. You can add a network to your cluster domain using the db2haicu utility.

Create networks for these network interface cards? [1]
1. Yes
2. No
1
Enter the name of the network for the network interface card: 'eth0' on cluster node: 'HADR1.ibm.com'
1. Create a new public network for this network interface card.
2. Create a new private network for this network interface card.
Enter selection:
1
Are you sure you want to add the network interface card 'eth0' on cluster node 'HADR1.ibm.com' to the network 'db2_public_network_0'? [1]
1. Yes
2. No
1
Adding network interface card 'eth0' on cluster node 'HADR1.ibm.com' to the network 'db2_public_network_0' ...
Adding network interface card 'eth0' on cluster node 'HADR1.ibm.com' to the network 'db2_public_network_0' was successful.
Enter the name of the network for the network interface card: 'eth0' on cluster node: 'HADR2.ibm.com'
1. db2_public_network_0
2. Create a new public network for this network interface card.
3. Create a new private network for this network interface card.
Enter selection:
1
Are you sure you want to add the network interface card 'eth0' on cluster

```
node 'HADR2.ibm.com' to the network 'db2_public_network_0'? [1]
1. Yes
2. No
1
Adding network interface card 'eth0' on cluster node HADR2.ibm.com' to the
network 'db2_public_network_0' ...
Adding network interface card 'eth0' on cluster node 'HADR2.ibm.com' to the
network 'db2_public_network_0' was successful.
Retrieving high availability configuration parameter for instance
'db2inst1' ...
The cluster manager name configuration parameter (high availability
configuration parameter) is not set. For more information, see the topic
"cluster_mgr - Cluster manager name configuration parameter" in the DB2
Information Center. Do you want to set the high availability configuration
parameter?
The following are valid settings for the high availability configuration
parameter:
   1.TSA
   2.Vendor
Enter a value for the high availability configuration parameter: [1]
1
Setting a high availability configuration parameter for instance 'db2inst1'
to 'TSA'.
Adding DB2 database partition '0' to the cluster ...
Adding DB2 database partition '0' to the cluster was successful.
Do you want to validate and automate HADR failover for the HADR database
'SAMPLE'? [1]
1. Yes
2. No
1
Adding HADR database 'SAMPLE' to the domain ...
HADR database 'SAMPLE' has been determined to be valid for high
availability. However, the database cannot be added to the cluster from
this node because db2haicu detected this node is the standby for HADR
database 'SAMPLE'. Run db2haicu on the primary for HADR database 'SAMPLE'
to configure the database for automated failover.
Do you want to validate and automate HADR failover for the HADR database
'SAMPLE'? [1]
1. Yes
2. No
1
Adding HADR database 'SAMPLE' to the domain ...
HADR database 'SAMPLE' has been determined to be valid for high
availability. However, the database cannot be added to the cluster from
this node because db2haicu detected this node is the standby for HADR
database 'SAMPLE'. Run db2haicu on the primary for HADR database 'SAMPLE'
to configure the database for automated failover.
All cluster configurations have been completed successfully. db2haicu
```

```
exiting ...
```

2. Now that you have completed the TSA configuration on standby, connect to the
   HADR primary server as instance owner and execute the db2haicu command:

```
db2haicu
Welcome to the DB2 High Availability Instance Configuration Utility
(db2haicu).

You can find detailed diagnostic information in the DB2 server diagnostic
log file called db2diag.log. Also, you can use the utility called db2pd to
query the status of the cluster domains you create.

For more information about configuring your clustered environment using
db2haicu, see the topic called 'DB2 High Availability Instance
Configuration Utility (db2haicu)' in the DB2 Information Center.

db2haicu determined the current DB2 database manager instance is
'db2inst1'. The cluster configuration that follows will apply to this
instance.

db2haicu is collecting information on your current setup. This step may
take some time as db2haicu will need to activate all databases for the
instance to discover all paths ...
When you use db2haicu to configure your clustered environment, you create
cluster domains. For more information, see the topic 'Creating a cluster
domain with db2haicu' in the DB2 Information Center. db2haicu is searching
the current machine for an existing active cluster domain ...
db2haicu found a cluster domain called 'TSA_PROD' on this machine. The
cluster configuration that follows will apply to this domain.

Retrieving high availability configuration parameter for instance
'db2inst1' ...
The cluster manager name configuration parameter (high availability
configuration parameter) is not set. For more information, see the topic
"cluster_mgr - Cluster manager name configuration parameter" in the DB2
Information Center. Do you want to set the high availability configuration
parameter?
The following are valid settings for the high availability configuration
parameter:
  1.TSA
  2.Vendor
Enter a value for the high availability configuration parameter: [1]
1
Setting a high availability configuration parameter for instance 'db2inst1'
to 'TSA'.
Adding DB2 database partition '0' to the cluster ...
```

```
Adding DB2 database partition '0' to the cluster was successful.
Do you want to validate and automate HADR failover for the HADR database
'SAMPLE'? [1]
1. Yes
2. No
1
Adding HADR database 'SAMPLE' to the domain ...
Adding HADR database 'SAMPLE' to the domain was successful.
Do you want to configure a virtual IP address for the HADR database
'SAMPLE'? [1]
1. Yes
2. No
1
Enter the virtual IP address:
10.0.80.1
Enter the subnet mask for the virtual IP address '10.0.80.1':
[255.255.255.0]
255.255.255.0
Select the network for the virtual IP '10.0.80.1':
1. db2_public_network_0
Enter selection:
1
Adding virtual IP address 10.0.80.1' to the domain ...
Adding virtual IP address '10.0.80.1' to the domain was successful.
All cluster configurations have been completed successfully. db2haicu
exiting ...
```

Activating the RoS feature

You can enable RoS on the HADR standby database by setting the Db2 instance-level registry variable DB2_HADR_ROS to ON and subsequently restarting the standby instance:

```
db2set DB2_HADR_ROS=ON
```

The only isolation level that is supported on the active standby database is **Uncommitted Read (UR)**. Any application requesting more than UR will receive the SQL1773N reason code = 1 error.

You can avoid getting this message by using explicit statement isolation or by setting the Db2 instance-level registry DB2_STANDBY_ISO to UR.

 ROS is not supported on the pureScale standby cluster.

Automatic Client Reroute (ACR) is a Db2 feature that can be used on an HADR database to reroute client applications from a failed database server to a secondary or standby database server previously identified and configured for this purpose. This feature provides an alternative to the automatic HADR failover capability through TSAMP.

The following diagram shows the ACR implementation in an existing HADR environment:

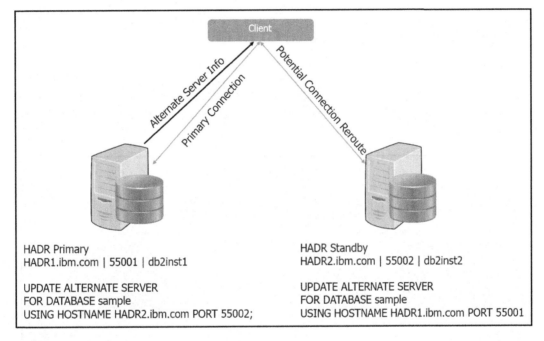

FDb2 automatic client reroute

You can execute the UPDATE ALTERNATE SERVER command to update the alternate server name and the port number. This alternate server information is propagated to the Db2 clients on the first connection. If a communication problem between the client and the primary database occurs, the Db2 client attempts to re-establish the connection to the alternate server using the defined ALTERNATE SERVER information.

You can list the alternate server information using the LIST DATABASE DIRECTORY command, as follows:

```
LIST DB DIRECTORY;

Database alias                  = SAMPLE
 Database name                  = SAMPLE
 Local database directory       = /db/home/db2inst1
```

```
Database release level                  = 14.00
Comment                                 =
Directory entry type                    = Indirect
Catalog database partition number       = 0
Alternate server hostname               = HADR2.ibm.com
Alternate server port number            = 55002
```

Db2 pureScale architecture

The pureScale environment is a Db2 9.8 feature that provides a scalable active-active configuration that transparently delivers high throughput and continuous availability for any business-critical system. From an architectural standpoint, Db2 pureScale leverages the architecture and design principles of the Db2 z/OS sysplex architecture that was introduced in the early 1990s:

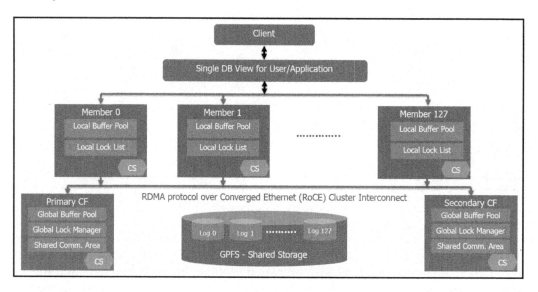

Db2 pureScale architecture

The preceding diagram shows the pureScale components, which are broadly classified as follows:

- Db2 members
- Cluster-caching facility (CF)
- Shared storage
- Cluster services and interconnect

A Db2 member is the core processing engine within the pureScale cluster. A member is similar to a single partition Db2 and contains the following features:

- The system controller process (db2sysc)
- The watch dog process (db2wdog)
- Local buffer pools
- Lock list
- Database heap
- Log buffer
- Sort heap
- Application heap

A set of new **Engine Dispatchable Units** (EDU's) are available within pureScale. They are as follows:

- db2castructevent: This reads the state of the CF links from the following two files:
  - pgrp
  - isOnline

  The preceding files get updates from the db2clstrRscMon EDU.

- db2LLMn1: This processes the information sent by the global lock manager. There are two of these EDUs on each member, one for the primary CF, and another for the secondary CF.
- db2LLMn2: This processes the information sent by the global lock manager for a special type of lock that is used during database activation and deactivation processing. There are two of these EDUs on each member, one for the primary CF, and another for the secondary CF.
- db2LLMng: This ensures that the locks held by this member are released in a timely manner when other members are waiting for these locks.
- db2LLMrl: This processes the release of locks to the global lock manager.
- db2LLMrc: This processes things that occur during database recovery operations and during CF recovery.

You can install pureScale on a physical host, the logical partition of a physical machine (LPAR), or a virtual machine. Each database member has a defined home host and can accept only client connections on the home host. If the home host is not functional, the database member will fail and be started on a guest host (another member host in the cluster) in restart light mode to complete the member crash recovery. This activity completes the rollback of uncommitted changes and deallocates the locks held by the failed member.

A Db2 member can be in one of the following states:

- STARTED: The member is started on the home host and is functioning normally.
- STOPPED: The member has been stopped by the administrator.
- RESTARTING: The member is starting after a crash recovery on the home host or on the guest host.
- WAITING_FOR_FAILBACK: The member is running in restart light mode on a guest host and is waiting to fail back to the home host to function normally. In this state, the member will not accept any client connections.
- ERROR: The member could not be started on the home host or on the guest host, and needs administrator attention to resolve the problem.

A pureScale cluster facilitates data sharing and concurrency control between its multiple database members, using the concept of the cluster-**caching facility** (CF). The CF is a software application managed by Db2 cluster services to facilitate centralized coordination of locking through a **Global Lock Manager** (GLM) and centralized page caching through a **Group Buffer Pool** (GBP). As a minimum, a pureScale environment will require one CF; however, using two CFs configured as primary and secondary databases will eliminate a single point of failure. The GLM's function is to prevent conflicting access to the same object data by multiple members through a physical lock. The Db2 members hold the physical locks and the transaction within a member holds the logical locks.

The **Local Lock Manager** (LLM), the lock manager within each Db2 member, requests the physical lock from the GLM before granting a logical lock to a transaction. The purpose of the **Global Lock List** (GLL) is to track the lock requests made by the LLMs of active database members.

By using the GBP, the Db2 database manager keeps page caching consistent across all members and coordinates the copy of pages that exists across the members' **Local Buffer Pools** (LBP).

A CF can be in one of the following states:

- PRIMARY: The CF is functioning normally as the primary
- PEER: This is the secondary CF, which is ready to assume the primary in case the current primary CF fails
- STOPPED: The CF has been stopped by the administrator
- RESTARTING: The CF is restarting due to a db2start command or after a failure occurred
- BECOMING_PRIMARY: The CF will take over the primary CF role if no other primary CF is running in the cluster
- CATCHUP: The intermediate state of the non-primary CF before the CF can copy all the relevant information, including the GBP and GLL, to reach the PEER state
- ERROR: The CF could not be started on any host on the instance, and needs administrator attention to resolve the problem

The Db2 pureScale cluster operates on a share disk architecture. The disk subsystem is accessed by all members within the pureScale cluster; therefore, this subsystem must allow concurrent read/write operations from all members. To maintain the data files' integrity and consistency, a clustered filesystem called IBM **General Parallel File System (GPFS)** is currently used in the pureScale implementation. This filesystem is also known as IBM Spectrum Storage.

To support fast communication, the Db2 members, CFs, and storage are all connected by using a **Converged Ethernet (RoCE)** high-speed interconnect, which supports **Remote Direct Memory Access (RDMA)** and the **User Direct Access Programming Library (uDAPL)**.

Geographically dispersed Db2 pureScale db2cluster (GDPC)

The **geographically dispersed Db2 pureScale cluster** (GDPC) is a configuration that allows a Db2 pureScale cluster to be distributed, where members of a cluster are at different datacenters serving HA and DR in one solution.

A GDPC typically consists of the following:

- Two or more Db2 pureScale data members
- Two cluster caching (CF) facilities (one in each data center)
- SAN-attached cluster storage running IBM Spectrum Scale (formerly called GPFS)
- A dedicated network channel between Db2 members and CFs

The following diagram shows a simple GDPC setup:

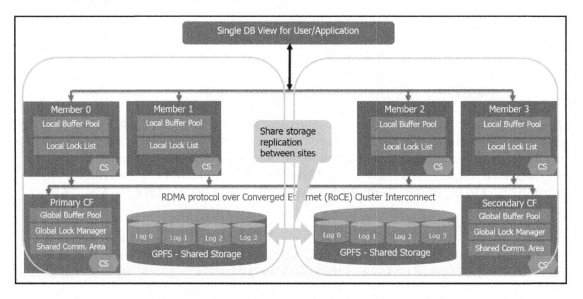

Geographically dispersed Db2 pureScale Cluster architecture

In GDPC setup, half the Db2 pureScale cluster members and CFs will be located at one site and the other half will be at another site. For tie breaking and transparent failover in the event of a site failure, a third site is required. This setup also needs the IBM GPFS (IBM Spectrum Scale) storage to be replicated between the sites to keep all disk write activities such as table space writes and transaction log writes up-to-date across both sites.

Db2 pureScale db2cluster service command options

Db2 provides the db2cluster command to verify the health of a pureScale instance and perform management operations related to cluster services.

You can also use the db2cluster command to verify the health of the members:

```
db2cluster -cm -list -host -state
HOSTNAME STATE
------------------------ ------------
purescale05 ONLINE
purescale04 ONLINE
purescale03 ONLINE
purescale02 ONLINE
purescale01 ONLINE
purescalecf01 ONLINE
purescalecf02 ONLINE
```

You can use the db2instance -list command to check the status of all the members in the cluster:

```
db2instance -list
ID TYPE STATE HOME_HOST CURRENT_HOST ALERT PARTITION_NUMBER LOGICAL_PORT
NETNAME
-- ---- ----- --------- ------------ ----- ---------------- ------------ --
-----
0 MEMBER STARTED purescale01 purescale01 NO 0 0 purescale01-
roce0,purescale01-roce1
1 MEMBER STARTED purescale02 purescale02 NO 0 0 purescale02-
roce0,purescale02-roce1
2 MEMBER STARTED purescale03 purescale03 NO 0 0 purescale03-
roce0,purescale03-roce1
3 MEMBER STARTED purescale04 purescale04 NO 0 0 purescale04-
roce0,purescale04-roce1
4 MEMBER STARTED purescale05 purescale05 NO 0 0 purescale05-
roce0,purescale05-roce1
128 CF PEER purescalecf01 purescalecf01 NO - 0 purescalecf01-
roce0,purescalecf01-roce1
129 CF PRIMARY purescalecf02 purescalecf02 NO - 0 purescalecf02-
roce0,purescalecf02-roce1
HOSTNAME STATE INSTANCE_STOPPED ALERT
-------- ----- ---------------- -----
purescale05 ACTIVE NO NO
purescale04 ACTIVE NO NO
```

```
purescale03 ACTIVE NO NO
purescale02 ACTIVE NO NO
purescale01 ACTIVE NO NO
purescalecf01 ACTIVE NO NO
purescalecf02 ACTIVE NO NO
```

If you want to create a replicated file system for the GDPC implementation, use the db2cluster command with the -create clause:

```
db2cluster -cfs -create -filesystem db2backup
-disk /dev/dm-1, /dev/dm-2 -rdncy_grp_id 1
-disk /dev/dm-2, /dev/dm-4 -rdncy_grp_id 2
-fstiebreaker /dev/tb -host tb_hostname
-mount /db2backup
```

To list the filesystems, use the db2cluster command with the -list clause, as follows:

```
db2cluster -cfs -list -filesystem db2backup
```

If you want to convert a non-replicated file system to a replicated filesystem, use the db2cluster command with the -enablereplication clause. The steps for the conversion are as follows:

1. Enable the replication by executing the following command line:

```
db2cluster -cfs -enablereplication -filesystem <fsname>
```

2. Add disks to redundancy group 2 by executing the following command:

```
db2cluster -cfs -add -filesystem <fsname> -disk <disk1,..diskn> -
rdncy_grp_id 2 -fstiebreaker <tb> -host <tbhost>
```

3. Initiate data replication from redundancy group 1 to 2 by executing the following command:

```
db2cluster -cfs -replicate -filesystem <fsname>
```

Explicit Hierarchical Locking

Explicit Hierarchical Locking (EHL) is designed to eliminate data sharing costs for tables and partitions that are only accessed by a single member in a pureScale cluster. You can activate the EHL feature by running the following UPDATE DATABASE CFG command:

```
UPDATE DB CFG FOR <DBNAME> USING opt_direct_wrkld YES;
```

This parameter, when set to AUTOMATIC, will cause the EHL to only be activated when both cf_gbp_sz and cf_lock_sz are set to AUTOMATIC.

The EHL state changes, based on the table or partition access, are as follows:

- Entering into the NOT_SHARED state:
  - An INSERT, UPDATE, DELETE, and SELECT operation on a table
  - A data partition in a range partition table can enter NOT_SHARED state while the base table is unaffected
  - Index can enter this state when a non-partitioned index is created

- Exiting the NOT_SHARED state:
  - Table access from another member or members
  - Drop table or database deactivation
  - Partition ATTACH or DETACH operation on a partitioned table

It is important to understand the locking behavior during the state change from NOT_SHARED to SHARED. The table lock is held in super exclusive mode (Z) until all the page locks and row locks are registered in the GLM and all the changed pages are written to the GBP.

The EHL monitoring elements are as follows:

- data_sharing_state: The state of the data share. This can be one of the following:
  - SHARED: Fully shared across all the members in the cluster
  - BECOMING_NOT_SHARED: Transitioning from SHARED to NOT_SHARED
  - NOT_SHARED: All access is limited to one member in the cluster
  - BECOMING_SHARED: Transitioning from NOT_SHARED to SHARED

- data_sharing_state_change_time: Timestamp of the last state change.
- data_sharing_remote_lockwait_count: Number of times an application waited on a table transition from NOT_SHARED to SHARED.
- data_sharing_remote_lockwait_time: Application wait time in milliseconds on a table during the transition from NOT_SHARED to SHARED.

If you want to monitor the EHL state, state change time, and the number or duration of lock waits during the state change, use the `SYSPROC.MON_GET_TABLE ()` monitoring table function:

```
SELECT    VARCHAR (TABNAME, 40) AS TABNAME,
          MEMBER,
          DATA_SHARING_STATE AS DS_STATE,
          DATA_SHARING_STATE_CHANGE_TIME AS DSC_TIME,
          DATA_SHARING_REMOTE_LOCKWAIT_COUNT AS DSRL_COUNT,
          DATA_SHARING_REMOTE_LOCKWAIT_TIME AS DSRL_TIME_MS
FROM
TABLE (MON_GET_TABLE (''DEMO'',''EQCMPNT_MEAS'',-2)) ORDER BY MEMBER ASC;
```

Take a look at the following output:

```
TABNAME                        MEMBER DS_STATE         DSC_TIME                    DSRL_COUNT       DSRL_TIME_MS
------------------------------ ------ ---------------- --------------------------- ---------------  ------------
EQCMPNT_MEAS                        0 SHARED           2018-04-13-15.44.33.794652               5           485
EQCMPNT_MEAS                        1 SHARED           2018-04-15-00.05.42.018350              12           865
EQCMPNT_MEAS                        2 NOT_SHARED       2018-04-15-18.14.56.995229              68          6434
```

Summary

The objective of this chapter was to provide sufficient knowledge to answer the Db2 high availability chapter questions on the following topics:

- The Db2 transaction logging parameters
- The Db2 transactions and logging strategies
- Various types of Db2 database backup and recovery features
- HADR feature concepts and implementation procedures
- Implementation techniques for HADR with multiple standby databases
- The Db2 pureScale architecture and basic monitoring through instance commands
- The Db2 geographically dispersed pureScale cluster (GDPC) concepts
- Basic understanding of Db2 pureScale EHL

Practice questions

Question 1

Which command can you use to enable dual logging for a database named SAMPLE?

- **A:** db2set DB2_USE_FAST_LOG_PREALLOCATION=YES
- **B:** UPDATE DB CFG FOR sample USING failarchpath /ds/failarchlogs
- **C:** UPDATE DB CFG FOR sample USING mirrorlogpath /ds/mirrorlogs
- **D:** UPDATE DB CFG FOR sample USING logarchmeth2 TSM

Question 2

What type of recovery operation do you use to reapply transactions that were committed but not externalized to storage, to roll back transactions that were externalized to storage but not committed, and to purge transactions from memory that were neither committed nor externalized to storage?

- **A:** Disaster recovery
- **B:** Crash recovery
- **C:** Version recovery
- **D:** Roll-forward recovery

Question 3

Which command will restore a database by using information found in the recovery history log file?

- **A:** RESTART DATABASE
- **B:** RESTORE DATABASE
- **C:** RECOVER DATABASE
- **D:** REBUILD DATABASE

Question 4

Which statement about roll-forward recovery is FALSE?

- **A:** Table space roll-forward recovery cannot be accomplished while users are connected to the database
- **B:** Recovery must be to a point in time that is greater than the minimum recovery time obtained with the SYSPROC.MON_GET_TABLESPACE() table function

- **C:** Recovery to a specific point in time can only be done on a database that is using archival logging
- **D:** By default, all recovery times specified are interpreted as coordinated universal
- **E:** Time (UTC)-otherwise known as **Greenwich Mean Time (GMT)**-values

Question 5

How do you enable the ROS HADR feature?

- **A:** Set the DB2 registry variable `DB2_HADR_ROS` to `ON`
- **B:** Set the DB2 registry variable `DB2_HADR_SOSNDBUF` to `ON`
- **C:** Set the DB2 registry variable `DB2_HADR_PEER_WAIT_LIMIT` to `ON`
- **D:** Set the DB2 registry variable `DB2_HADR_NO_IP_CHECK` to `ON`

Question 6

Which HADR synchronization mode has the shortest transaction response time, but also the highest probability of transaction losses if the primary system fails?

- **A:** `SYNC`
- **B:** `NEARSYNC`
- **C:** `ASYNC`
- **D:** `SUPERASYNC`

Question 7

Which statement is `FALSE` regarding HADR principal standby functionality in a multiple standby environment?

- **A:** It supports the ROS feature
- **B:** It supports a maximum of two principal standbys
- **C:** It supports both manual and TSA HADR failover
- **D:** It supports all four HADR synchronization modes

Question 8

Which of the following operations changes the minimum recovery time for a table space? (Choose two)

- **A:** INSERT into a table
- **B:** DELETE from a table
- **C:** ALTER TABLE ...ADD COLUMN
- **D:** UPDATE on a table
- **E:** CREATE TABLE

Question 9

What is the page size of a group buffer pool in a pureScale cluster?

- **A:** 4 K
- **B:** 8 K
- **C:** 16 K
- **D:** 32 K

Question 10

How do you enable EHL for the database SAMPLE in a pureScale cluster?

- **A:** UPDATE DB CFG FOR sample USING LOCKLIST AUTOMATIC
- **B:** db2set DB2_DATABASE_CF_MEMORY=AUTO -immediate
- **C:** UPDATE DB CFG FOR sample USING OPT_DIRECT_WRKLD YES
- **D:** UPDATE DB CFG FOR sample USING LOCKLIST AUTOMATIC MAXLOCKS AUTOMATIC

Answers

Question 1

The correct answer is C. To enable log file mirroring, you simply assign the fully qualified name of the mirror log location (path) to the `mirrorlogpath` database configuration parameter.

Question 2

The correct answer is *B*. When a transaction failure occurs, all work done by partially completed transactions that have not yet been externalized to the database is lost. The database might be left in an inconsistent state (and therefore will be unusable). Crash recovery is the process used to return such a database to a consistent and usable state. To perform crash recovery, you must use information stored in the transaction log files to complete any committed transactions that were in memory (but had not yet been externalized to storage) when the transaction failure occurred, roll back any incomplete transactions, and purge any uncommitted transactions from memory.

Question 3

The correct answer is *C*. The recover utility performs the restore and roll-forward operations needed to recover a database to a specific point in time, based on information found in the recovery history file. You can invoke the recover utility by executing the RECOVER DATABASE command.

Question 4

The correct answer is *A*. Table space roll-forward recovery operations can be performed on individual table spaces while a database remains online. However, before a database can be restored, it must first be taken offline. Therefore, roll-forward recovery can be accomplished while users are connected to the database—but only at the table space level.

Question 5

The correct answer is *A*. You can enable the ROS on the HADR standby database by using the Db2 instance-level registry variable DB2_HADR_ROS. The steps involved are as follows:

1. Set the registry variable:

    db2set DB2_HADR_ROS=ON

2. Deactivate the standby database:

    DEACTIVATE DB HADRDB

3. Stop HADR on the standby database:

    STOP HADR ON DATABASE HADRDB

4. Stop and start the standby Db2 instance:

```
db2stop; db2start
```

5. Start HADR on the standby database:

```
START HADR ON DATABASE HADRDB AS STANDBY
```

Question 6

The correct answer is *D*. SUPERASYNC synchronization mode has the shortest transaction response time because primary transaction commits have no dependency on the standby commit. And in the meantime, if a system failure occurs, SUPERASYNC is highly susceptible to data loss.

Question 7

The correct answer is *B*. The HADR multiple standby functionality supports only one principal standby:

Principal standby	Auxiliary standby
Supports ROS feature	Supports ROS feature
Only one standby database can act as the principal standby	Maximum of two standby databases can act as auxiliary standbys
Synchronization is through a TCP/IP direct connection	Synchronization is through a TCP/IP direct connection
Time delayed log shipping is supported	Time delayed log shipping is supported
TSA MP automated failover is supported	Only a manual failover is supported
All four synchronization modes are supported	Only SUPERASYNC synchronization mode is supported

Question 8

The correct answers are *C* and *E*. The minimum recovery time is updated when DDL statements such as DROP TABLE, CREATE TABLE, ALTER TABLE ...ADD COLUMN, ALTER TABLE... DROP COLUMN, and so on, are run against a table space or against tables stored in a table space.

Question 9

The correct answer is *A*. All the cluster caching facility (CF) memory allocation including the GBP, GLM, **Shared Communication Area (SCA)**, and **Smart Arrays** are allocated in 4 K pages.

Question 10

The correct answer is C. EHL takes advantage of the implicit internal locking hierarchy that exists between table locks, row locks, and page locks. EHL functionality helps avoid most communication and data sharing memory usage for tables. Table locks supersede row locks or page locks in the locking hierarchy. When a table lock is held in super exclusive mode, EHL enhances performance for Db2 pureScale instances by not propagating row locks, page locks, or page writes to the caching facility (CF).

To enable EHL, update the database configuration parameter OPT_DIRECT_WRKLD to YES:

```
UPDATE DB CFG FOR sample USING OPT_DIRECT_WRKLD YES;
```

8
Db2 Security

This chapter will introduce you to Db2 security features, including roles, trusted contexts, trusted connections, row and column access control, and Db2 native encryption. You will learn to use Lightweight Directory Access Protocol (LDAP)-based authentication through the LDAP security plugin module. You will also be introduced to the Db2 audit facility to generate and maintain an audit trail for a series of predefined database events.

After the completion of this chapter, you will demonstrate the ability to:

- Understand the authentication and authorization levels used by Db2
- Configure and use transparent LDAP authentication
- Create and use trusted contexts and trusted connections in a three-tier application system
- Implement row or column permissions by using **row and column access control (RCAC)**
- Encrypt data in-transit using SSL, and encrypt data at rest using Db2 native encryption
- Rotate the master key using the `SYSPROC.ADMIN_ROTATE_KEY()` procedure
- Use the `SYSPROC.ADMIN_GET_ENCRYPTION_INFO()` table function to extract database encryption settings
- Configure and use the Db2 audit facility

Certification test:
Number of Questions: 9
Percentage in the Exam: 15%

Authentication and authorization

Authentication is the process of validating the identity of a user before allowing access to perform any operation on database objects. Db2 does not provide native authentication, so a security facility outside the database system, such as the operating system security facility or a security plug-in, is required.

Authorization is the process of evaluating the privileges that have been assigned to a user to determine what operations the user can perform on database objects. This is managed using a set of authorities and privileges within Db2. The following diagram shows an example of authentication and authorization within Db2:

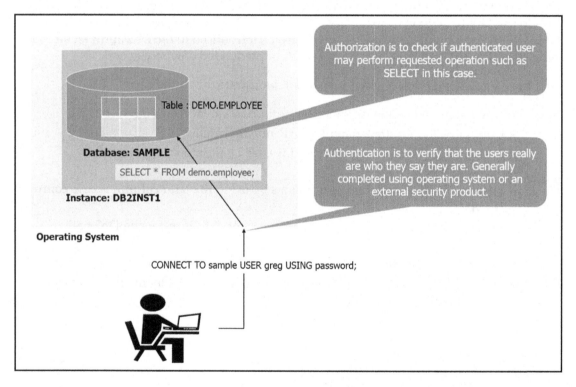

Db2 authentication and authorization example

The authentication database manager configuration parameter specifies how and where the authentication of a user should take place. By default, it is set to SERVER. The authentication types available within Db2 are:

- **SERVER**: Authentication occurs at the server level by using the security facility provided by the server's operating system. The user ID and password combination that the user enters via the client to connect to the database are sent over to the server in a clear text format.
- **CLIENT**: Authentication occurs at the client workstation by using the security facility provided by the client's operating system.
- **SERVER_ENCRYPT**: Authentication occurs at the server by using the security facility provided by the server's operating system. The user ID and password combination that the user enters via the client to connect to the database are sent over to the server in an encrypted format.
- **DATA_ENCRYPT**: Authentication is identical to the SERVER_ENCRYPT authentication method. In addition, all user data is encrypted before it is sent between the client and server.
- **DATA_ENCRYPT_CMP**: Authentication is identical to the DATA_ENCRYPT method. This authentication type also provides compatibility for clients that do not support data encryption. If data encryption is not supported, clients connect using the SERVER_ENCRYPT authentication type.
- **KERBEROS**: Authentication occurs at the server using the security facility that supports the Kerberos security protocol.
- **KRB_SERVER_ENCRYPT**: Authentication occurs at the server using either the KERBEROS or the SERVER_ENCRYPT authentication method. For clients that support the Kerberos security system, the system authentication type is KERBEROS, and for clients that do not support the Kerberos security system, the system authentication type is equivalent to SERVER_ENCRYPT.
- **GSSPLUGIN**: Authentication occurs at the server using a Generic Security Service API plug-in.
- **GSS_SERVER_ENCRYPT**: Authentication occurs at the server by using either the GSSPLUGIN or the SERVER_ENCRYPT authentication methods. For clients that support the GSS plug-in security feature, the system authentication type is GSSPLUGIN. For clients that do not support the GSS plug-in security feature, the system authentication type is equivalent to SERVER_ENCRYPT.

Authorities and privileges

Db2 provides a hierarchy of authorities to assign a set of predefined administrative permissions, to perform database maintenance operations to groups or users. The following diagram showcases a hierarchical view of the authorities and privileges that are available in Db2 11.1.

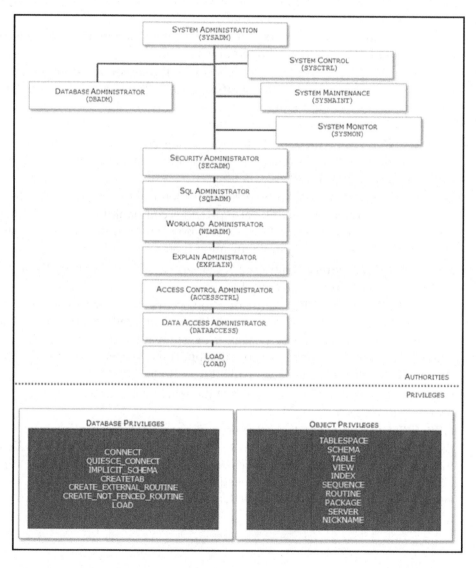

Db2 authorities and privileges

Authorities

Db2 uses 12 different authorities to control how users perform administrative and maintenance tasks against an instance or a database. We will discuss each of these authorities in the following sections.

The system administrative authority (SYSADM)

This is the highest level of administrative authority available within Db2 and it allows the user to perform the following tasks:

- Update database manager configuration parameters
- Grant and revoke table space privileges
- Upgrade and restore databases
- All of the tasks listed in the SYSCTRL, SYSMAINT and SYSMON authorities

You can assign SYSADM authority by updating the database manager configuration parameter, SYSADM_GROUP.

To add an operating system group SYSADMIN to the SYSADM_GROUP use the following command:

```
UPDATE DBM CFG USING SYSADM_GROUP SYSADMIN;
```

To revert to the default setting, execute the following command:

```
UPDATE DBM CFG USING SYSADM_GROUP NULL;
```

The system control authority (SYSCTRL)

This authority allows a user to perform the following maintenance and utility operations at instance and database levels, but does not allow direct access to data:

- Update a database, node, or **distributed connection services** (**DCS**) directory (by cataloging/un-cataloging databases, nodes, or DCS databases)
- Modify the parameter values in one or more database configuration files
- Force users off the system
- Create or drop a database
- Create, alter, or drop a table space
- Make a backup image of a database or a table space

- Restore an existing database by using a backup image
- Restore a table space by using a backup image
- Create a new database from a database backup image
- All of the tasks listed in the SYSMAINT and SYSMON authorities

You can assign SYSCTRL authority by updating the database manager configuration parameter SYSCTRL_GROUP. To add the operating system group CTRLADM to the SYSCTRL_GROUP, use the following command:

```
UPDATE DBM CFG USING SYSCTRL_GROUP CTRLADM;
```

To revert to the default setting, execute the following command:

```
UPDATE DBM CFG USING SYSCTRL_GROUP NULL;
```

The system maintenance authority (SYSMAINT)

This authority allows users to perform the following maintenance and utility operations at instance and database levels, but does not allow direct access to data:

- Make a backup image of a database or a table space
- Restore an existing database by using a backup image
- Restore a table space by using a backup image
- Perform a roll-forward recovery operation on a database
- Start or stop a Db2 database manager instance
- Run a trace on the database operation
- Collect database system monitor snapshots by using monitor table functions for both instance and associated databases
- Quiesce a table space or query the state of a table space
- Reorganize a table
- Collect catalog statistics by using the RUNSTATS utility
- All of the tasks listed in the SYSMON authority

You can assign SYSMAINT authority by updating the database manager configuration parameter SYSMAINT_GROUP. To add the operating system group MAINTADM to SYSMAINT_GROUP, use the following command:

```
UPDATE DBM CFG USING SYSMAINT_GROUP MAINTADM;
```

To revert to the default setting, execute the following command:

```
UPDATE DBM CFG USING SYSMAINT_GROUP NULL;
```

The system monitor authority (SYSMON)

This authority allows users to perform the following monitoring operations at the instance and database levels, but does not allow direct access to data:

- Obtain the current settings of the snapshot monitor switches
- Modify the settings of one or more snapshot monitor switches
- Reset all counters used by the snapshot monitor
- Connect to a database
- Obtain a list of active databases
- Obtain a list of active applications, including DCS applications
- Obtain a list of database partition groups
- Obtain a list of packages, tables, table spaces, and table space containers
- Obtain a list of utilities running on a database
- Collect snapshot monitor data
- Use the snapshot monitor table functions

You can assign SYSMON authority by updating the database manager configuration parameter SYSMON_GROUP. To add the operating system group MONADM to SYSMON_GROUP, use the following command:

```
UPDATE DBM CFG USING SYSMON_GROUP MONADM;
```

To revert to the default setting, execute the following command:

```
UPDATE DBM CFG USING SYSMON_GROUP NULL;
```

The system-level (SYSADM, SYSCTRL, SYSMAINT and SYSMON) authorities can only be granted to operating system level groups in UNIX. Modifications to SYSADM_GROUP, SYSCTRL_GROUP, SYSMAINT_GROUP, and SYSMON_GROUP database manager configuration parameters need an instance restart to take effect.

The database administrator authority (DBADM)

This database-level authority enables a user to perform the following functions within a specific database:

- Create, modify, and drop non-security-related database objects
- Read database transaction log files or query the log manager for current log state information using the db2ReadLog API
- Create, activate, and drop event monitors
- Use a table space, query the state of a table space, or quiesce a table space
- Update the database history file
- Reorganize a table or an index by using the REORG command
- Collect statistics on a table or an index by using the RUNSTATS command
- Perform binding of a package to the database (the BINDADD authority)
- Connect to a database (the CONNECT authority)
- Create tables within a database (the CREATETAB authority)
- Create external fenced functions and routines (the CREATE_EXTERNAL_ROUTINE authority)
- Create a non-fenced function or procedure (the CREATE_NOT_FENCED_ROUTINE authority)
- Create a schema in a database (the IMPLICIT_SCHEMA authority)
- Perform a data load by using the LOAD command (the LOAD authority)
- Connect to a database when it is quiesced (the QUIESCE_CONNECT authority)
- All of the tasks listed in the SQLADM, EXPLAIN, and WLMADM authorities

You can assign DBADM authority on a database called SAMPLE to the user **john** by executing the following statement:

```
CONNECT TO sample;
GRANT DBADM ON DATABASE TO USER john;
```

If you want to revoke DBADM authority on a database called SAMPLE from the user **john**, execute the following statement:

```
CONNECT TO sample;
REVOKE DBADM ON DATABASE FROM USER john;
```

The security administrator authority (SECADM)

This database-level authority allows a user to perform the following functions within a specific database:

- Create, drop, alter and, comment on security-related objects
- Grant and revoke all privileges and authorities, including DBADM, SECADM, DATAACCESS, ACCESSCTRL, EXPLAIN, SQLADM, WLMADM, and LOAD
- Transfer ownership of any object not owned by the SECADM
- Grant or revoke execute privileges on audit system-refined functions and routines
- Create database audits using the Db2 audit facility
- Grant or revoke connect privilege to a database
- Grant or revoke read privileges on system catalog tables and views
- All of the tasks listed in the ACCESSCTRL database-level authority

You can assign SECADM authority on a database called SAMPLE to the user **john** by executing the following statement:

```
CONNECT TO sample;
GRANT SECADM ON DATABASE TO USER john;
```

If you want to revoke SECADM authority on a database called SAMPLE from user **john**, execute the following statement:

```
CONNECT TO sample;
REVOKE SECADM ON DATABASE FROM USER john;
```

The SQL administrator (SQLADM) authority

This database-level authority allows a user to perform following functions within a specific database:

- Create, drop, activate, deactivate, or flush event monitors
- Generate Explain data by using EXPLAIN
- Flush the optimization profile cache
- Perform table and index reorganization
- Perform RUNSTATS on the table and indexes
- Flush the package cache and prepare SQL statements

- Grant or revoke execute privileges on all system-defined routines, except audit procedures
- Grant or revoke select privileges on system catalog tables and views
- All of the tasks listed in the EXPLAIN authority
- SQLADM can execute certain clauses of the following workload management commands:
  - ALTER SERVICE CLASS on collect aggregate activity data, request data, and request metrics
  - ALTER THRESHOLD on collect activity data
  - ALTER WORK ACTION SET on collect activity data and aggregate activity data
  - ALTER WORKLOAD on activity metrics, aggregate activity data, lock timeout, lock wait, and unit of work data

You can assign SQLADM authority on a database called SAMPLE to the user **john** by executing the following statement:

```
CONNECT TO sample;
GRANT SQLADM ON DATABASE TO USER john;
```

If you want to revoke SQLADM authority on a database called SAMPLE from the user **john**, execute the following statement:

```
CONNECT TO sample;
REVOKE SQLADM ON DATABASE FROM USER john;
```

 If the DB2AUTH registry variable is set to SQLADM_NO_RUNSTATS_REORG, users with SQLADM authority will not be able to perform REORG or RUNSTATS operations on tables or indexes

The workload management administrator authority (WLMADM)

Users with WLMADM authority are allowed to perform the following tasks:

- Create, alter, drop, and comment on the following WLM objects:
- Service classes
- Thresholds
- Work action sets

- Work class sets
- Workloads
- Histogram templates
- Grant and revoke workload privileges
- Execute built-in workload management routines

You can assign WLMADM authority on a database called SAMPLE to the user **john**, by executing the following statement:

```
CONNECT TO sample;
GRANT WLMADM ON DATABASE TO USER john;
```

If you want to revoke WLMADM authority on a database called SAMPLE from the user **john**, execute the following statement:

```
CONNECT TO sample;
REVOKE WLMADM ON DATABASE FROM USER john;
```

The Explain administrator authority (EXPLAIN)

Users with EXPLAIN authority can perform the following tasks:

- Generate access plan information for SQL statements
- Prepare SQL statements
- Perform a DESCRIBE on an output of a SELECT statement or of an XQuery statement

You can assign EXPLAIN authority on a database called SAMPLE to the user **john** by executing the following statement:

```
CONNECT TO sample;
GRANT EXPLAIN ON DATABASE TO USER john;
```

If you want to revoke EXPLAIN authority on a database called SAMPLE from the user **john**, execute the following statement:

```
CONNECT TO sample;
REVOKE EXPLAIN ON DATABASE FROM USER john;
```

The Access control administrator authority (ACCESSCTRL)

Users with ACCESSCTRL are allowed to perform the following tasks:

- Grant and revoke SELECT privileges on system catalog tables and views
- Grant and revoke all privileges on table, table space, view, index, nickname, package, routine (except DB2 audit routines), schema, sequence, server, global variables, and XML schema repository (XSR) objects
- Grant and revoke database privileges, including BINDADD, CONNECT, CREATETAB, CREATE_EXTERNAL_ROUTINE, CREATE_NOT_FENCED_ROUTINE, IMPLICIT_SCHEMA, LOAD, and QUIESCE_CONNECT
- Grant and revoke administrative authorities, including EXPLAIN, SQLADM, and WLMADM

You can assign ACCESSCTRL authority on a database called SAMPLE to user **john** by executing the following statement:

```
CONNECT TO sample;
GRANT ACCESSCTRL ON DATABASE TO USER john;
```

If you want to revoke ACCESSCTRL authority on a database called SAMPLE from user **john**, execute the following statement:

```
CONNECT TO sample;
REVOKE ACCESSCTRL ON DATABASE FROM USER john;
```

The data access administrator authority (DATAACCESS)

Users with DATAACCESS are allowed to perform the following tasks:

- Grant or revoke LOAD authority on the database
- Grant or revoke SELECT privileges on tables, including system catalog tables, views, MQTs, and nicknames
- Grant or revoke INSERT privileges on tables, views, MQTs, and nicknames
- Grant or revoke DELETE privileges on tables, views, MQTs, and nicknames

- Grant or revoke UPDATE privileges on tables, views, MQTs, and nicknames
- Grant or revoke EXECUTE privileges on all packages and routines except Db2 audit facility routines
- Grant or revoke usage privilege on all XSR and sequence objects

You can assign DATAACCESS authority on a database called SAMPLE to user **john** by executing the following statement:

```
CONNECT TO sample;
GRANT DATAACCESS ON DATABASE TO USER john;
```

If you want to revoke DATAACCESS authority on a database called SAMPLE from user **john**, execute the following statement:

```
CONNECT TO sample;
REVOKE DATAACCESS ON DATABASE FROM USER john;
```

The data load (LOAD) authority

Users with LOAD authority are allowed to perform the following tasks:

- Quiesce or query the state of a table space
- Perform bulk-load operations by using the LOAD command
- Collect catalog statistics by using the RUNSTATS command

You can assign LOAD authority on a database called SAMPLE to user **john** by executing the following statement:

```
CONNECT TO sample;
GRANT LOAD ON DATABASE TO USER john;
```

If you want to revoke LOAD authority on a database called SAMPLE from user **john**, execute the following statement:

```
CONNECT TO sample;
REVOKE LOAD ON DATABASE FROM USER john;
```

Privileges

Db2 provides two distinct types of privileges to perform certain actions on specific database objects, and these are:

- **Database Privileges**: These privileges apply to a database as a whole and are classified into eight different database privileges:
  - CONNECT: Allows a user to connect to the database
  - QUIESCE_CONNECT: Allows a user to connect to the database while it is in QUIESCE (access restricted state)
  - IMPLICIT_SCHEMA: Allows a user to create a new schema in the database implicitly by creating a fully qualified object
  - CREATETAB: Allows a user to create new tables in the database
  - BINDADD: Allows a user to create packages in the database
  - CREATE_EXTERNAL_ROUTINE: Allows a user to create user-defined functions and procedures
  - CREATE_NOT_FENCED_ROUTINE: Allows a user to create unfenced user-defined functions and procedures
  - LOAD: Allows a user to bulk-load data into one or more existing tables in the database

You can assign one or more database privileges on a database called SAMPLE to user **john** by executing the following statement:

```
CONNECT TO sample;
GRANT CONNECT, QUIESCE_CONNECT, IMPLICIT_SCHEMA, CREATETAB,
BINDADD, CREATE_EXTERNAL_ROUTINE, CREATE_NOT_FENCED_ROUTINE, LOAD
ON DATABASE TO USER john;
```

If you want to revoke one or more database privileges on a database called SAMPLE from user **john**, execute the following statement:

```
CONNECT TO sample;
REVOKE CONNECT, QUIESCE_CONNECT, IMPLICIT_SCHEMA, CREATETAB,
BINDADD, CREATE_EXTERNAL_ROUTINE, CREATE_NOT_FENCED_ROUTINE, LOAD
ON DATABASE FROM USER john;
```

- **Object privileges**: These privileges apply to a specific object within a database:
  - **Tablespace privileges**: Allow a user to use a table space to create database objects

You can grant TABLESPACE privilege to **john** by using the following statement:

```
GRANT USE OF TABLESPACE userspace1 TO USER john;
```

If you want to revoke a TABLESPACE privilege from user **john**, use the following statement:

```
REVOKE USE OF TABLESPACE userspace1 FROM USER john;
```

  - **Schema privileges**: Allow a user to create objects within a schema, change comments, and drop objects within a schema.

You can grant CREATE, DROP object, and COMMENT privileges within the schema DEMO to **john**, using the following statement:

```
GRANT CREATEIN, DROPIN, ALTERIN ON SCHEMA demo TO USER john;
```

To revoke previously granted privileges, execute the following statement:

```
REVOKE CREATEIN, DROPIN, ALTERIN ON SCHEMA demo FROM USER john;
```

  - **Table privileges**: Allow a user to modify the table structure, SELECT, INSERT, UPDATE, DELETE data from a table, CREATE an index on a table, and reference a table in the referential integrity constraint.

If you want to grant a set of table privileges on the DEMO.EMPLOYEE table to **john**, execute the following statement:

```
GRANT ALTER, SELECT, INSERT, UPDATE, DELETE, INDEX, REFERENCES ON
TABLE demo.employee TO USER john;
```

If you want to revoke earlier granted privileges, execute the following statement:

```
REVOKE ALTER, SELECT, INSERT, UPDATE, DELETE, INDEX, REFERENCES ON
TABLE demo.employee FROM USER john;
```

You can also grant CONTROL privilege on a table to a user. This privilege indirectly grants ALTER, SELECT, INSERT, UPDATE, DELETE, INDEX, and REFERENCE privileges to a user.

- **View privileges**: Allows a user to perform SELECT, INSERT, UPDATE, and DELETE on a view.

If you want to grant a set of view privileges on the DEMO.V_EMPLOYEE view to **john**, execute the following statement:

```
GRANT SELECT, INSERT, UPDATE, DELETE ON TABLE demo.v_employee TO
USER john;
```

If you want to revoke earlier granted privileges, execute the following statement:

```
REVOKE SELECT, INSERT, UPDATE, DELETE ON TABLE demo.v_employee FROM
USER john;
```

You can also grant CONTROL privilege on a view to a user. This privilege indirectly grants INSERT, UPDATE, DELETE, and SELECT privileges to a user.

- **Index privileges**: Allow a user to drop an index from a database object.

If you want to grant the index privilege on the DEMO.IX1_EMPLOYEE index to john, execute the following statement:

```
GRANT CONTROL ON INEDX demo.ix1_employee TO USER john;
```

If you want to revoke the earlier granted privilege, execute the following statement:

```
REVOKE CONTROL ON INEDX demo.ix1_employee FROM USER john;
```

- **Sequence privileges**: Allow a user to use and modify a sequence in the database.

If you want to grant use and alter privilege on the DEMO.EMPLOYEE_SEQ sequence to **john**, execute the following statement:

```
GRANT USAGE, ALTER ON SEQUENCE demo.employee_seq TO USER john;
```

If you want to revoke the earlier granted privilege, execute the following statement:

```
REVOKE USAGE, ALTER ON SEQUENCE demo.employee_seq FROM USER john;
```

- **Routine privileges**: Allow a user to execute a user-defined function or a stored procedure in the database.

If you want to grant the EXECUTE privilege on the DEMO.SP_EMP_SALARY_SUM() procedure to **john**, execute the following statement:

```
GRANT EXECUTE ON PROCEDURE demo.sp_emp_salary_sum() TO USER john;
```

If you want to revoke earlier granted privilege, execute the following statement:

```
REVOKE EXECUTE ON PROCEDURE demo.sp_emp_salary_sum() FROM USER
john;
```

- **Package privileges**: Allow a user to bind or execute a package in the database.

If you want to grant bind and execute privileges on the DEMO.EMPLOYEE_PKG package to **john**, execute the following statement:

```
GRANT EXECUTE ON PACKAGE demo.employee_pkg TO USER john;
```

If you want to revoke the earlier granted privilege, execute the following statement:

```
REVOKE EXECUTE ON PACKAGE demo.employee_pkg FROM USER john;
```

You can also grant the CONTROL privilege on a package to a user. This privilege indirectly grants BIND and EXECUTE privileges to a user.

- **Server privileges**: Allow a user to issue DDL and DML SQL statements to a data source through a federated server.

If you want to grant server privilege on an ODS-federated server to **john**, execute the following statement:

```
GRANT PASSTHRU ON SERVER ods TO USER john;
```

If you want to revoke the earlier granted privilege, execute the following statement:

```
REVOKE PASSTHRU ON SERVER ods FROM USER john;
```

- **Nickname privileges**: Allow a user to alter, select, insert, update, delete, and create an index and reference a federated server database object.

If you want to grant ALTER, SELECT, INSERT, UPDATE, DELETE, INDEX, and REFERENCE privileges on the DEMO.EXTN_EXPLOYEE_NN nickname to **john**, execute the following statement:

```
GRANT ALTER, SELECT, INSERT, UPDATE, DELETE, INDEX, REFERENCE ON
TABLE demo_extn_employee_nn TO USER john;
```

If you want to revoke the earlier granted privilege, execute the following statement:

```
REVOKE ALTER, SELECT, INSERT, UPDATE, DELETE, INDEX, REFERENCE ON
TABLE demo_extn_employee_nn FROM USER john;
```

You can also grant the CONTROL privilege on a nickname to a user. This privilege indirectly grants ALTER, SELECT, INSERT, UPDATE, DELETE, INDEX, and REFERENCE privileges to a user.

LDAP-based authentication

Db2 supports LDAP-based authentication and group lookup functionality via two methods:

- The LDAP security plug-in module
- Transparent LDAP

The LDAP security plug-in module allows Db2 to authenticate users defined in an LDAP directory, eliminating the requirement that users and groups be defined locally on the operating system.

When you use LDAP security plug-in modules for authentication, all users associated with the database must be defined on the LDAP server. This includes both the Db2 instance owner ID as well as the fenced user. Commonly, these users are defined in the operating system, but when you use the LDAP security plug-in, these users must also be defined in the LDAP server. In addition, if you use the LDAP group plug-in module, any groups required for authorization such as SYSADM_GROUP, SYSMAINT_GROUP, SYSCTRL_GROUP, and SYSMON_GROUP must be defined on the LDAP server.

You can enable the Db2 security plug-in module for server-side authentication, client-side authentication, or group lookup. You can enable the security plug-in using the following steps:

1. Choose the Db2 security plug-in module to be implemented.

2. Configure the plug-in module's settings, such as `LDAP_HOST`, `ENABLE_SSL`, `SSL_KEYFILE`, `SSL_PW`, `SECURITY_PROTOCOL`, `USER_OBJECTCLASS`, `USER_BASEDN`, `USERID_ATTRIBUTE`, `AUTHID_ATTRIBUTE`, `GROUP_OBJECTCLASS`, `GROUP_BASED`, `GROUPNAME_ATTRIBUTE`, `GROUP_LOOKUP_METHOD`, `GROUP_LOOKUP_ATTRIBUTE`, `NESTED_GROUPS`, `SEARCH_DN`, and `SEARCH_PW` in `$INSTHOME/sqllib/cfg/IBMLDAPSecurity.ini`. You can make use of the `IBMLDAPSecurity.ini.sample` file to create the `IBMLDAPSecurity.ini` file.

3. Enable the plug-in module by setting the appropriate database manager configuration parameters. To enable the security plug-in module using the built-in plug-in modules, execute the following commands:

   ```
   UPDATE DBM CFG USING SRVCON_PW_PLUGIN IBMLDAPauthserver;

   UPDATE DBM CFG USING CLNT_PW_PLUGIN IBMLDAPauthclient;
   UPDATE DBM CFG USING GROUP_PLUGIN IBMLDAPgroups;
   db2 terminate; db2stop; db2start
   ```

4. Test the connection using full or partial LDAP-distinguished names.

The LDAP security plug-in module is supported on the AIX, Linux, Solaris, and Windows operating systems.

Db2 supported transparent LDAP authentication, with effect from version 9.7 fix pack 1. Using transparent LDAP, you can set up the operating system for LDAP authentication against an LDAP directory without having to configure any of the additional security plug-in modules. When you have transparent LDAP set up, Db2 will authenticate the users via the operating system. First, Db2 will issue a call out to the operating system for authentication, and the operating system will authenticate the user. You can enable transparent LDAP authentication by using the following steps:

On Linux operating systems:

1. Ensure the `nss_ldap` and `pam_ldap` packages are installed and verify that the operating system is bound to an LDAP server via the `/etc/ldap.conf` file.

2. Update the PAM configuration file (`/etc/pam.d/db2`) based on the Linux version and the flavor.

3. Configure the operating system to perform group lookup through LDAP, using the /etc/nsswitch.conf file.

4. Update the Db2 registry variable DB2AUTH to OSAUTHDB.

   db2set DB2AUTH=OSAUTHDB

5. Update the database manager configuration parameter authentication to one of the following:

   UPDATE DBM CFG USING AUTHENTICATION SERVER;

   Alternatively, update it to this:

   UPDATE DBM CFG USING AUTHENTICATION SERVER_ENCRYPT;

   Or update it to this:

   UPDATE DBM CFG USING AUTHENTICATION DATA_ENCRYPT;

6. Reset clnt_pw_plugin, group_plugin, and srvcon_pw_plugin to the default factory settings.

7. Restart the Db2 instance.

On AIX operating systems:

1. Ensure that the LDAP client file set has been installed and configured.

2. Update the SYSTEM and REGISTRY attributes within the /etc/security/user file. Db2 supports LDAP and files as the SYSTEM attributes and LDAP, KRB5LDAP, KRB5ALDAP, files, KRB5files, KRB5Afiles as the REGISTRY attributes.

3. Update the Db2 registry variable DB2AUTH to OSAUTHDB:

   db2set DB2AUTH=OSAUTHDB

4. Update the database manager configuration parameter authentication to one of the following:

   UPDATE DBM CFG USING AUTHENTICATION SERVER;

Alternatively, update it to this:

```
UPDATE DBM CFG USING AUTHENTICATION SERVER_ENCRYPT;
```

Or, alternatively, update it to this:

```
UPDATE DBM CFG USING AUTHENTICATION DATA_ENCRYPT;
```

5. Reset `clnt_pw_plugin`, `group_plugin`, and `srvcon_pw_plugin` to the default factory settings.
6. Restart the Db2 instance.

When you have multiple LDAP servers configured in an organization and LDAP-based authentication is set up, you can define the Db2 search scope using the `DB2LDAP_SEARCH_SCOPE` registry variable. The possible values for this variable are LOCAL, DOMAIN, and GLOBAL:

- If this is set to LOCAL, the search scope is limited to the current LDAP server or to the local database catalog
- If this is set to DOMAIN, which is the default setting, the search scope is limited to the directory on which the current LDAP server is defined
- If this is set to GLOBAL, the search is allowed on all the LDAP servers in the entire enterprise

Role-based access control

Role-based access control security mechanisms have emerged as a preferred way to protect an organization's information. With this access control mechanism, you grant the privileges to roles instead of the users' authorization IDs. A role is a database object that groups together one or more privileges and can be assigned to users, groups, PUBLIC, or other roles.

If you want to create a role called `developer`, use the following CREATE ROLE statement:

```
CREATE ROLE developer;
```

All of the Db2 privileges and authorities that you can grant within a database can also be granted to a role. For example, a role can be granted any of the following authorities and privileges:

- Database privileges, including DBADM, SECADM, DATAACCESS, ACCESSCTRL, SQLADM, WLMADM, LOAD, IMPLICIT_SCHEMA, CONNECT, CREATETAB, CREATE_NOT_FENCED, BINDADD, CREATE_EXTERNAL_ROUTINE, and QUIESCE_CONNECT
- Any database object privilege, including SELECT, INSERT, UPDATE, DELETE, CONTROL, EXECUTE, and USE

Once you create a role, you can associate a set of privileges to a role by using the following GRANT statement:

```
GRANT SELECT, INSERT, UPDATE, DELETE ON TABLE demo.employee TO ROLE
developer;
```

If you want to assign the developer role to user **john**, you can execute the following statement:

```
GRANT ROLE developer TO USER john;
```

If you want to revoke the earlier granted privilege, execute the following statement:

```
REVOKE ROLE developer FROM USER john;
```

When privileges are revoked, this can sometimes cause dependent database objects, such as views, packages, or triggers, to become invalid or inoperative. For example:

- The security administrator creates a role called developer, and grants the role to user **john**:

  ```
  CREATE ROLE developer;
  GRANT ROLE developer TO USER john;
  ```

- User BOB creates a new table, DEMO.MEASURE, and the database administrator grants privilege:

  ```
  SELECT on DEMO.MEASURE to role DEVELOPER:
  GRANT SELECT ON TABLE demo.measure TO ROLE developer;
  ```

- User JOHN creates a view, DEMO.V_MEASURE, based on the table DEMO.MEASURE:

  - `CREATE VIEW demo.v_measure AS SELECT * FROM DEMO.MEASURE;`

- If the database administrator revokes SELECT privilege on the table DEMO.MEASURE from the role DEVELOPER, the associated view, DEMO.V_MEASURE, becomes inoperative:

  - `REVOKE SELECT ON TABLE demo.measure FROM ROLE developer;`

- You can verify the validity of the view by running a query on the `SYSCAT.VIEWS` system catalog view, as shown below:

```
SELECT
VARCHAR (VIEWNAME, 10) AS VIEWNAME,
VALID,
VARCHAR (TEXT, 100) AS TEXT FROM SYSCAT.VIEWS WHERE
VIEWNAME='V_MEASURE'"
VIEWNAME VALID TEXT

---------- ----- -----------------------------------------------

V_MEASURE N create view v_measure as select * from demo.measure
```

Trusted context and trusted connections

A trusted context is a database object that defines a trust relationship for a connection between the database and an external entity such as a middle-tier application server (for example, the IBM WebSphere Application Server). The trust relationship is built based on the following set of attributes:

- **Authorization ID**: Identifies the user who establishes a connection to the database
- **IP address or domain name**: Identifies the host name from which a database connection is established to the database server
- **Data stream encryption**: Identifies the data stream's minimum level of encryption between the database server and the client

A person holding `SECADM` authority can create a trusted context by using the `CREATE TRUSTED CONTEXT` statement. The basic syntax is:

```
CREATE TRUSTED CONTEXT <ContextName>

BASED ON CONNECTION USING SYSTEM AUTHID <AuthorizationID>

ATTRIBUTES (ADDRESS <IPAddress> [WITH ENCRYPTION
<EncryptionValue>])

[NO DEFAULT ROLE | DEFAULT ROLE <RoleName> [ENABLE|DISABLE]]

WITH USE FOR [<UseAuthorizationID> | ROLE <UseRoleName>]

[WITH AUTHENTICATION | WITHOUT AUTHENTICATION]
```

To which the following applies:

- **ContextName**: Identifies the name of the trusted context
- **AuthorizationID**: Identifies the system authorization ID to use in establishing a trusted context
- **IPAddress**: Identifies the IP address value to associate with the ADDRESS trust attribute; this must be an IPv4, an IPv6, or a secure domain name
- **EncryptionValue**: Identifies the level of encryption of the data stream or network encryption for a specific IP address; valid values are NONE, LOW, and HIGH
- **RoleName**: Identifies the role name to associate with a trusted connection based on a trusted context
- **UseAuthorizationID**: Identifies the authorization ID that can use the trusted connection
- **UseRoleName**: Identifies the role to use for the user when a trusted connection is using the trusted context

If you want to create a trusted context, TX1, to allow the application user APPUSER to connect to the database `SAMPLE` only from IP address 10.0.96.1, and associate the role developer to it, adhere to the following:

```
CREATE ROLE developer
DB20000I  The SQL command completed successfully.

GRANT SELECT ON TABLE demo.employee TO ROLE developer
DB20000I  The SQL command completed successfully.

CREATE TRUSTED CONTEXT tx1
BASED UPON CONNECTION USING SYSTEM AUTHID appuser
```

```
ATTRIBUTES (ADDRESS '10.0.96.1 ')
DEFAULT ROLE developer ENABLE;
DB20000I  The SQL command completed successfully.
```

If you try to connect to database `SAMPLE` and query the `EMPLOYEE` table from IP address `10.0.96.1`, you will see the following result:

```
CONNECT TO sample USER AppUser
Enter current password for AppUser:

   Database Connection Information

 Database server        = DB2/LINUXX8664 11.1.3.3
 SQL authorization ID    = APPUSER
 Local database alias    = SAMPLE

SELECT COUNT (*) AS COUNT FROM demo.employee;

COUNT
-----------
        42

   1 record(s) selected.
```

Likewise, if you connect from an address than other `10.0.96.1` and run a query on a database called `SAMPLE`, you will get an SQL0551N error.

```
CONNECT TO sample USER AppUser
Enter current password for AppUser:

   Database Connection Information

 Database server        = DB2/LINUXX8664 11.1.3.3
 SQL authorization ID    = APPUSER
 Local database alias    = SAMPLE

SELECT COUNT (*) AS COUNT FROM demo.employee;
SQL0551N  "APPUSER" does not have the required authorization or privilege
to perform operation "SELECT" on object "DEMO.EMPLOYEE".  SQLSTATE=42501
```

By combining the capabilities of trusted contexts and roles, you can control how a user connects to the database to obtain access to database objects.

If you want to create a trusted context to allow user Greg to connect from IP address `10.0.99.1`, and allow the connection to switch from Greg to Bob without authentication and to John with authentication, use the following statement:

```
CREATE TRUSTED CONTEXT tx2
BASED UPON CONNECTION USING SYSTEM AUTHID greg
DEFAULT ROLE developer
ENABLE
ATTRIBUTES (ADDRESS '10.0.99.1')
WITH USE FOR bob WITHOUT AUTHENTICATION,
john WITH AUTHENTICATION;
DB20000I  The SQL command completed successfully.
```

If you want to view information about trusted context objects created in the database, you can query the SYSCAT.CONTEXTS and SYSCAT.CONTEXTATTRIBUTES system catalog views, or, you can use the SYSIBM.SYSCONTEXTS and SYSIBM. SYSCONTEXTATTRIBUTES catalog tables.

```
SELECT VARCHAR (CONTEXTNAME, 20) CONTEXTNAME,
ENABLED FROM SYSCAT.CONTEXTS;

CONTEXTNAME             ENABLED
--------------------    --------
SYSATSCONTEXT           Y
TX1                     Y
TX2                     Y

   3 record(s) selected.

SELECT VARCHAR (CONTEXTNAME, 20) CONTEXTNAME,
VARCHAR (ATTR_NAME, 20) ATTR_NAME,
VARCHAR (ATTR_VALUE, 20) ATTR_VALUE,
VARCHAR (ATTR_OPTIONS, 20) ATTR_OPTIONS
FROM SYSCAT.CONTEXTATTRIBUTES;

CONTEXTNAME             ATTR_NAME             ATTR_VALUE              ATTR_OPTIONS
--------------------    --------------------  ----------------------  -------------
--------
SYSATSCONTEXT           ENCRYPTION            NONE                    -
TX1                     ENCRYPTION            NONE                    -
TX1                     ADDRESS               10.0.96.1               -
TX2                     ENCRYPTION            NONE                    -
TX2                     ADDRESS               10.0.99.1               -

   5 record(s) selected.
```

DDL operations cannot be performed with trusted context privileges that are acquired through roles, but DML operations can.

Row and column access control (RCAC)

RCAC is a data-security feature that limits data access to those users who have a real business need to access the data. This feature is also known as **fine-grained access control (FGAC)**.

You can implement RCAC by using the following database objects:

- **Row permission**: Specifies a row-access control rule for a specific table and describes what set of rows a user has access to, based on an SQL search condition
- **Column mask**: Specifies a column-access control rule for a specific column in a table and describes what column values a user is permitted to see and under what conditions, based on an SQL case statement expression

Row permissions

A user with SECADM authority can create row permissions on a table by using the CREATE PERMISSION statement. The basic syntax is:

```
CREATE <OR REPLACE> PERMISSION [PermissionName] ON [TableName]

FOR ROWS WHERE [SearchCondition] ENFORCED FOR ALL ACCESS

<ENABLE | DISABLE>
```

In the preceding syntax, the following applies:

- **PermissionName**: Identifies the name of the permission, including the explicit or implicit qualifier.
- **TableName**: Identifies the name of the table on which to create the row permission. It must not be: a nickname; a created or declared global temporary table, view, alias, or synonym; a typed table; or a system catalog table.
- **SearchCondition**: Identifies a condition that can be true or false for a row of the table; this follows the same rules used by the search condition in a WHERE clause of a sub-select query.

The following procedures demonstrate how row permission implementation works:

1. Create tables by using the CREATE TABLE statement without an additional security clause.

```
CREATE TABLE hr.employees (
        emp_id          INTEGER NOT NULL,
        f_name          VARCHAR(20),
        l_name          VARCHAR(20),
        gender          CHAR(1),
        hire_date       DATE WITH DEFAULT,
        dept_id         CHAR(5),
        phone           CHAR(14),
        ssn             CHAR(12),
        salary          DECIMAL(12,2),
        bonus           DECIMAL(12,2));
DB20000I  The SQL command completed successfully.

CREATE TABLE hr.department (
        dept_id         CHAR(5),
        dept_name         CHAR(20),
        dept_hr         CHAR(20),
        hr_director     CHAR(20));
DB20000I  The SQL command completed successfully.
```

2. Create roles and row permissions by using the CREATE ROLE and CREATE PERMISSION statements.

   In this example, the HR managers can access an employee's information only from their own department. All HR managers (Jason, Colin) are members of the HRMGR role. The HR director can access all employee information across all departments. All HR directors (Eric) are members of the HRDIRECTOR role. A user with SECADM authority can create the roles and row permissions:

```
CREATE ROLE hrmgr
DB20000I  The SQL command completed successfully.

CREATE ROLE hrdirector
DB20000I  The SQL command completed successfully.

GRANT ROLE hrmgr TO USER jason, colin
DB20000I  The SQL command completed successfully.

GRANT ROLE hrdirector TO USER eric
DB20000I  The SQL command completed successfully.

GRANT SELECT, INSERT, UPDATE, DELETE ON TABLE hr.employees TO ROLE
```

```
hrmgr, hrdirector
DB20000I  The SQL command completed successfully.
```

The business requirement is to allow HR department managers to see their respective department employees' data and to permit the HR director to see all employees' data. The row permissions created for each group of personnel (HR managers and HR directors) in the HR department are as follows:

```
CREATE PERMISSION hr_dept_mgr_access ON hr.employees
 FOR ROWS WHERE VERIFY_ROLE_FOR_USER
 (SESSION_USER,'HRMGR') = 1 AND
       DEPT_ID = (SELECT DEPT_ID FROM HR.DEPARTMENT WHERE
DEPT_HR=SESSION_USER)
ENFORCED FOR ALL ACCESS
ENABLE;
DB20000I  The SQL command completed successfully.

CREATE PERMISSION hr_dept_director_access ON hr.employees
 FOR ROWS WHERE VERIFY_ROLE_FOR_USER (SESSION_USER,'HRDIRECTOR') =
1
 ENFORCED FOR ALL ACCESS
 ENABLE;
DB20000I The SQL command completed successfully.
```

3. Activate row permissions using the ALTER TABLE statement.
   When a row permission is enabled, it is not enforced until you activate row access control at the row level by executing the ALTER TABLE statement:

```
ALTER TABLE hr.employees ACTIVATE ROW ACCESS CONTROL;
DB20000I  The SQL command completed successfully.
```

4. Check the RCAC action by performing the SELECT operation.
   When Jason connects to the database and executes the SELECT statement, he will see only data for DEPT_ID 00001:

```
CONNECT TO SAMPLE USER jason
Enter current password for jason:

   Database Connection Information

 Database server        = DB2/LINUXX8664 11.1.3.3
 SQL authorization ID   = JASON
 Local database alias   = SAMPLE

SELECT emp_id, f_name,dept_id,ssn, salary FROM hr.employees;
```

```
EMP_ID        F_NAME     DEPT_ID SSN           SALARY
-----------   ---------- ------- ------------- ---------------
          1 MOHAN        00001   123-456-7891        17000.00
          2 MILAN        00001   123-456-9810        12000.00
          4 COLIN        00001   123-126-4321        18000.00
          6 HAMDI        00001   123-061-8901        18000.00
    4 record(s) selected.
```

Similarly, Colin will see only data for DEPT_ID 00002:

```
CONNECT TO SAMPLE USER colin
Enter current password for colin:

   Database Connection Information

 Database server        = DB2/LINUXX8664 11.1.3.3
 SQL authorization ID   = COLIN
 Local database alias   = SAMPLE


SELECT emp_id, f_name,dept_id,ssn, salary FROM hr.employees;

EMP_ID        F_NAME     DEPT_ID SSN           SALARY
-----------   ---------- ------- ------------- ---------------
          3 ROBERTS      00002   123-456-0001        18000.00
          5 SIMON        00002   123-561-7898        18000.00

    2 record(s) selected.
```

And, when Eric connects to the database and executes the SELECT statement against HR.EMPLOYEES, he will see all the records:

```
CONNECT TO SAMPLE USER eric
Enter current password for eric:

   Database Connection Information

 Database server        = DB2/LINUXX8664 11.1.3.3
 SQL authorization ID   = ERIC
 Local database alias   = SAMPLE


SELECT emp_id, f_name,dept_id,ssn, salary FROM hr.employees;

EMP_ID        F_NAME     DEPT_ID SSN           SALARY
-----------   ---------- ------- ------------- ---------------
          1 MOHAN        00001   123-456-7891        17000.00
          2 MILAN        00001   123-456-9810        12000.00
          3 ROBERTS      00002   123-456-0001        18000.00
          4 COLIN        00001   123-126-4321        18000.00
```

```
          5 SIMON        00002    123-561-7898        18000.00
          6 HAMDI        00001    123-061-8901        18000.00
    6 record(s) selected.
```

5. If you want to deactivate the row access control, execute the ALTER TABLE statement shown here:

```
ALTER TABLE hr.employees DEACTIVATE ROW ACCESS CONTROL;
DB20000I  The SQL command completed successfully
```

The DML behavior is fairly simple to understand in RCAC. If you cannot read a set of rows, you cannot perform an INSERT of such rows, or cannot perform an UPDATE or DELETE on those rows.

For example, for DEPT_ID 00001, either the HR manager responsible for that department or the HR director can insert a new record into the HR.EMPLOYEES table. In this scenario, either Jason or Eric can perform the insert operations, as follows:

```
CONNECT TO SAMPLE USER jason
Enter current password for jason:
Database Connection Information
Database server = DB2/LINUXX8664 11.1.3.3
SQL authorization ID = JASON
Local database alias = SAMPLE

INSERT INTO hr.employees VALUES (7, 'MARK','HAMILTON','M', CURRENT DATE,
'00001','7804408021','321-001-0001', 19000.00, 38000.00); DB20000I The SQL
command completed successfully.
```

Similarly, when Jason tries to insert a record for DEPT_ID 00002, he receives an SQL20471N error:

```
INSERT INTO hr.employees VALUES (8, 'KAREN','BOUSTEAD','F',CURRENT DATE,
'00002','7801648819','321-001-0002',18000.00,37000.00);
SQL20471N
The INSERT or UPDATE statement failed because a resulting row did not
satisfy row permissions. SQLSTATE=22542
```

No database user is exempted from row and column access control rules, including authorities such as DATAACCESS.

Column masks

If the business requirement is to limit access or mask data at the column level, you can do so by using column masks. A user with SECADM authority can create column masks on a table by using the CREATE MASK statement. The basic syntax is:

```
CREATE &lt;OR REPLACE&gt; MASK [MaskName] ON [TableName]

FOR COLUMN [ColumnName] RETURN [CaseExpression]

&lt;ENABLE | DISABLE&gt;
```

To which the following applies:

- **MaskName**: Identifies the name of the column mask, including the explicit or implicit qualifier.
- **TableName**: Identifies the name of the table on which to create the column mask. It must not be: a nickname; a created or declared global temporary table, view, alias, or synonym; a typed table; or a system catalog table.
- **ColumnName**: Identifies the column to which the mask applies; the column name must be an unqualified name and must not have any existing masks on that column. The column must not be a LOB, XML, or a generated column.
- **CaseExpression**: Identifies the CASE expression to evaluate to determine the value to be returned for the column.

The following procedures illustrate how a column mask is created.

1. Create a column mask using the CREATE MASK statement based on business requirements.
   If the business wants to allow the payroll department to see the **social security number (SSN)** in its entirety, the welfare department to see only the last four digits of SSN, and the communications department to see nothing from the SSN, you can create the appropriate column using the CREATE MASK statement:

```
CREATE MASK hr.emp_ssn_mask ON hr.employees
  FOR COLUMN SSN RETURN
    CASE WHEN (VERIFY_ROLE_FOR_USER (SESSION_USER,'PAYROLL') = 1)
                      THEN SSN
         WHEN (VERIFY_ROLE_FOR_USER (SESSION_USER,'WELFARE') = 1)
                      THEN 'XXX-XX-' || SUBSTR (SSN, 8, 4)
         ELSE NULL
    END
  ENABLE;
DB20000I  The SQL command completed successfully.
```

2. Activate the column mask using the ALTER TABLE statement:

```
ALTER TABLE hr.employees ACTIVATE COLUMN ACCESS CONTROL;
DB20000I  The SQL command completed successfully.
```

3. Verify the column mask behavior.
   When a payroll user runs a SELECT query on HR.EMPLOYEES, he or she will see data similar to the following:

```
CONNECT TO SAMPLE USER hamdi
Enter current password for hamdi:

  Database Connection Information

 Database server        = DB2/LINUXX8664 11.1.3.3
 SQL authorization ID   = HAMDI
 Local database alias   = SAMPLE

SELECT emp_id, f_name, dept_id, ssn, salary FROM hr.employees;

EMP_ID       F_NAME      DEPT_ID SSN            SALARY
----------- ----------- ------- ------------- ---------------
          1 MOHAN       00001   123-456-7891       17000.00
          2 MILAN       00001   123-456-9810       12000.00
          3 ROBERTS     00002   123-456-0001       18000.00
          4 COLIN       00001   123-126-4321       18000.00
          5 SIMON       00002   123-561-7898       18000.00
          6 HAMDI       00001   123-061-8901       18000.00
          7 MARK        00001   321-001-0001       19000.00
          8 KAREN       00002   321-001-0002       18000.00

  8 record(s) selected.
```

When a welfare user runs a SELECT query on HR.EMPLOYEES, he or she will see data similar to the following:

```
CONNECT TO SAMPLE USER jason
Enter current password for jason:

  Database Connection Information

 Database server        = DB2/LINUXX8664 11.1.3.3
 SQL authorization ID   = JASON
 Local database alias   = SAMPLE

SELECT emp_id, f_name, dept_id, ssn, salary FROM hr.employees;
```

```
EMP_ID        F_NAME    DEPT_ID SSN             SALARY
------------  --------- ------- -------------   ---------------
         1 MOHAN        00001   XXX-XX-7891        17000.00
         2 MILAN        00001   XXX-XX-9810        12000.00
         3 ROBERTS      00002   XXX-XX-0001        18000.00
         4 COLIN        00001   XXX-XX-4321        18000.00
         5 SIMON        00002   XXX-XX-7898        18000.00
         6 HAMDI        00001   XXX-XX-8901        18000.00
         7 MARK         00001   XXX-XX-0001        19000.00
         8 KAREN        00002   XXX-XX-0002        18000.00

  8 record(s) selected.
```

Finally, when a communications user runs a SELECT query on HR.EMPLOYEES, he or she will see data similar to the following:

```
CONNECT TO SAMPLE USER eric
Enter current password for eric:

   Database Connection Information

 Database server        = DB2/LINUXX8664 11.1.3.3
 SQL authorization ID    = ERIC
 Local database alias    = SAMPLE

SELECT emp_id, f_name, dept_id, ssn, salary FROM hr.employees;

EMP_ID        F_NAME    DEPT_ID SSN             SALARY
------------  --------- ------- -------------   ---------------
         1 MOHAN        00001   -                  17000.00
         2 MILAN        00001   -                  12000.00
         3 ROBERTS      00002   -                  18000.00
         4 COLIN        00001   -                  18000.00
         5 SIMON        00002   -                  18000.00
         6 HAMDI        00001   -                  18000.00
         7 MARK         00001   -                  19000.00
         8 KAREN        00002   -                  18000.00

  8 record(s) selected.
```

4. Deactivate the column mask, if necessary.

   If you want to deactivate the column mask on a table, execute the `ALTER TABLE` statement:

```
ALTER TABLE hr.employees DEACTIVATE COLUMN ACCESS CONTROL;
DB20000I  The SQL command completed successfully.
```

You can use the listed built-in scalar functions here to express conditions in row permissions and column masks:

- **VERIFY_ROLE_FOR_USER (SESSION_USER, [RoleNameExp])**: Returns a value that indicates whether any of the roles associated with the authorization ID identified by the `SESSION_USER` special register are in (or contain any of) the role names specified by the list of `RoleNameExp` arguments

- **VERIFY_GROUP_FOR_USER(SESSION_USER, [GroupNameExp])**: Returns a value that indicates whether any of the groups associated with the authorization ID identified by the `SESSION_USER` special register are in (or contain any of) the group names specified by the list of `GroupNameExp` arguments

- **VERIFY_TRUSTED_CONTEXT_ROLE_FOR_USER (SESSION_USER, [RoleNameExp])**: Returns a value that indicates that the authorization ID identified by the `SESSION_USER` special register has acquired a role under a trusted connection associated with some trusted context, and that the role is in (or contained in any of) the role names specified by the list of `RoleNameExp` arguments

The Db2 audit facility

The Db2 audit facility provides information to detect any unknown or unanticipated access to data by generating and maintaining an audit trail for a series of predefined database events. The information generated from this facility is kept in an audit log file and analysis of these audit log files can reveal usage patterns that could identify system misuse. Once an unknown or unanticipated access has been identified, actions can be taken to reduce or eliminate such access.

The audit facility provides the ability to audit at both instance and database levels, independently recording all instance- and database-level activities with separate logs for each. Users with `SYSADM` authority can use the `db2audit` tool to configure the audit at instance level as well as to control audit information. You can also use the `db2audit` tool to archive or extract both instance and database audit logs to and from archive locations.

The following table lists the categories of events available for auditing, and for any of these categories you can audit success, failure, or both.

Event	Command Option	Description
Audit	`audit`	Generates records when audit settings are changed or when the audit log is accessed
Authorization checking	`checking`	Generates records during authorization checking of attempts to access or manipulate DB2 database objects or functions
Object maintenance	`objmaint`	Generates records when database objects are created or dropped
Security maintenance	`secmaint`	Generates records when object/database privileges or DBADM authority is granted or revoked; records are also generated when the database manager security configuration parameters sysadm_group, sysctrl_group, or sysmaint_group are modified
System administration	`sysadmin`	Generates records when operations requiring `SYSADM`, `SYSMAINT`, or `SYSCTRL` authority are performed
User validation	`validate`	Generates records when users are authenticated or system security information is retrieved
Operation context	`context`	Generates records to show the context when an instance operation is performed
Execute	`execute`	Generates records during the execution of SQL statements

Categories of events available in the db2audit tool

Db2 provides a set of stored procedures to archive audit logs, locate logs of interest, and extract data into delimited files for analysis. The procedures include:

- `SYSPROC.AUDIT_ARCHIVE()`
- `SYSPROC.AUDIT_LIST_LOGS()`
- `SYSPROC.AUDIT_DELIM_EXTRACT()`

Users with `SECADM` authority can grant `EXECUTE` privileges on these stored procedures to another user, enabling the security administrator to delegate these tasks.

Audit policies

The security administrator can create audit policies to control what is audited within a database. The following objects can have an audit policy defined on them:

- **The entire database**: All auditable events that occur within the database are audited.
- **Tables**: All DML and XQUERY access to the tables, MQTs, and nicknames are audited. The only event category applicable to tables is EXECUTE.
- **Trusted contexts**: All auditable events that happen within a trusted connection defined by the particular trusted context are audited.
- **Authorization IDs representing users, groups, and roles**: All auditable events that are initiated by the specified user are audited.
- **Authorities**: All auditable events that are initiated by a user that holds the specified authority such as SYSADM, SECADM, DBADM, SQLADM, WLMADM, ACCESSCTRL, DATAACCESS, SYSCTRL, SYSMAINT, and SYSMON are audited.

If you want to audit all SQL statements accessing the HR.EMPLOYEES table you can do so by creating a security policy and associating the policy to the respective table:

```
CREATE AUDIT POLICY dataaccess_policy CATEGORIES EXECUTE STATUS BOTH ERROR
TYPE AUDIT;
DB20000I  The SQL command completed successfully.
AUDIT TABLE hr.employees USING POLICY dataaccess_policy;
DB20000I  The SQL command completed successfully.
```

If you want to audit all the activities performed by the SYSADM or DBADM authorities, you can create a policy similar to the following:

```
CREATE AUDIT POLICY admin_policy CATEGORIES EXECUTE STATUS BOTH, SYSADMIN
STATUS BOTH ERROR TYPE AUDIT;
DB20000I  The SQL command completed successfully.

AUDIT SYSADM, DBADM USING POLICY admin_policy;
DB20000I  The SQL command completed successfully.
```

The db2audit tool command

The `db2audit` tool command can be used to perform the following actions within the audit facility:

- Start or stop recording auditable events at database instance level. However, the database level events will always be captured even when recording has been stopped.
- Configure the behavior of the audit facility at the instance level.
- Select the categories of auditable events to be recorded at the instance level.
- Request a description of the current audit configuration for the instance.
- Flush any pending audit records from the instance and write them to the audit log.
- Archive audit records from the current audit log for either the instance or a database under the instance.
- Extract audit records from an archived audit log by formatting and copying them to a flat file or ASCII-delimited file. Extraction is done in preparation for the analysis of log records.

At the instance level, a user with `SYSADM` authority can start or stop the audit facility by using the `db2audit` command:

```
db2audit start
AUD0000I  Operation succeeded.

db2audit stop
AUD0000I  Operation succeeded.
```

To configure the Db2 audit facility, execute the `db2audit` command:

```
db2audit configure scope all status both datapath "/db/home/db2inst1/audit"
```

If you want to view the current instance-level audit settings and status, use the `db2audit` command with the `describe` clause:

```
db2audit describe
DB2 AUDIT SETTINGS:

Audit active: "TRUE "
Log audit events: "BOTH"
Log checking events: "BOTH"
Log object maintenance events: "BOTH"
Log security maintenance events: "BOTH"
```

```
Log system administrator events: "BOTH"
Log validate events: "BOTH"
Log context events: "BOTH"
Return SQLCA on audit error: "FALSE "
Audit Data Path: "/db/home/db2inst1/audit/"
Audit Archive Path: ""

AUD0000I  Operation succeeded.
```

Once the command is executed, you can see audit file at the specified data path location:

```
/db/home/db2inst1/audit
ls -ltr
total 24
-rw------- 1 db2inst1 db2inst1  8911 Jun 15 20:24 db2audit.instance.log.0
-rw------- 1 db2inst1 db2inst1 10944 Jun 15 20:25 db2audit.db.SAMPLE.log.0
```

If you want to archive audit logs, you can do so by executing the db2audit command with an archive command option:

```
db2audit archive database sample to /db/home/db2inst1/auditarchivelogs

Member    DB Partition    AUD      Archived or Interim Log File
Number    Number          Message
--------  --------------  -------- --------------------------------------------
-------
       0                0 AUD0000I db2audit.db.SAMPLE.log.0.20180615205645

AUD0000I  Operation succeeded.
```

If you want to convert the archive audit log to a readable format, use the following command:

```
db2audit extract delasc to /db/home/db2inst1/auditformat from files
/db/home/db2inst1/auditarchivelogs/db2audit.db.SAMPLE.log.0.20180615205645

AUD0000I  Operation succeeded.
```

To see all the converted delimited ASCII files and a sample output file, use the following:

```
/db/home/db2inst1/auditformat
==&gt; ls -ltr
total 16
-rw-rw-rw- 1 db2inst1 db2inst1      0 Jun 15 20:57 secmaint.del
-rw-rw-rw- 1 db2inst1 db2inst1      0 Jun 15 20:57 objmaint.del
-rw-rw-rw- 1 db2inst1 db2inst1      0 Jun 15 20:57 checking.del
-rw-rw-rw- 1 db2inst1 db2inst1      0 Jun 15 20:57 auditlobs
-rw-rw-rw- 1 db2inst1 db2inst1      0 Jun 15 20:57 audit.del
```

```
-rw-rw-rw- 1 db2inst1 db2inst1  464 Jun 15 20:57 validate.del
-rw-rw-rw- 1 db2inst1 db2inst1  194 Jun 15 20:57 sysadmin.del
-rw-rw-rw- 1 db2inst1 db2inst1 2714 Jun 15 20:57 execute.del
-rw-rw-rw- 1 db2inst1 db2inst1  370 Jun 15 20:57 context.del
```

For example, if you look in the sysadmin event file, you will see records pertaining to SYSADM activity, such as initiating the database backup.

```
==&gt; cat sysadmin.del
"2018-06-15-20.54.27.950604","SYSADMIN","BACKUP_DB",3,-2413,"SAMPLE","db2in
st1","DB2INST1",,,"*LOCAL.db2inst1.180616005425","db2bp",,,,,,,,,,,,,,,,,"db
2inst1","db2demo.ibm.com"
```

Using the execute event file, you can see the COMMIT and ROLLBACK statement executions on database SAMPLE.

```
==&gt; cat execute.del
"2018-06-15-20.54.24.709403","EXECUTE","COMMIT",12,0,"SAMPLE","db2inst1","D
B2INST1","DB2INST1",,,"*LOCAL.db2inst1.180616002444","db2bp",,,"
",,,,,"NULLID","SQLC2027",0,,"*z","",,,,,"OTHER",,,,,,,,,,,,"db2inst1","
db2demo.ibm.com "
"2018-06-15-20.54.24.719159","EXECUTE","ROLLBACK",12,0,"SAMPLE","db2inst1",
"DB2INST1","DB2INST1",,,"*LOCAL.db2inst1.180616002444","db2bp",,,"
",,,,,"NULLID","SQLC2027",0,,"*{","",,,,,"OTHER",,,,,,,,,,,,"db2inst1","
db2demo.ibm.com "
```

- For a specific object, there can only be one audit policy in effect at any point in time. For example, you cannot have multiple audit policies associated with the same table at the same time.
- An audit policy cannot be associated with a view or a typed table. Views that access a table that has an associated audit policy are audited according to the underlying table's policy.
- The audit policy that applies to a table does not automatically apply to an MQT based on that table. If you associate an audit policy with a table, associate the same policy with any MQT based on that table.

Secure Socket Layer (SSL) implementation in Db2

Db2 supports the use of Secured Socket Layer (SSL) to enable authentication through digital certificates, and to provide private communication between the client and the server via encryption to encrypt data in-transit. The SSL support is provided through the IBM Global Security Kit (GSKit) libraries that are installed on the Db2 server. The installed images are available in fix central (https://www-945.ibm.com/support/fixcentral/swg/downloadOptions). For more information on the operating system version and the packages that support SSL, read the note at http://www-01.ibm.com/support/docview.wss?uid=swg21577384.

Implement SSL using the following steps:

1. Create a key database:

```
gsk8capicmd_64 -keydb -create -db "KeyDB.kdb" -pw "Passw0rd" -stash
```

The -stash option creates a stash file with an extension of .sth. This stash file will be used by the GSKit to obtain the password during the instance restart

2. Configure digital certificates.

Add a digital certificate for your server to the key database. The server sends this certificate to clients during the SSL handshake to provide authentication for the server.

```
gsk8capicmd_64 -cert -create -db "KeyDB.kdb" -pw "Passw0rd"
    -label "MyKeyDBLabel" -dn "CN=myhost.mycompany.com,O=myOrganization,
        OU=myOrganizationUnit,L=myLocation,ST=ON,C=CA" -size 2048 -sigalg
SHA256_WITH_RSA;
```

3. Configure the necessary Db2 database manager configuration parameters and registry variables for SSL.

   - ssl_svr_keydb: Specifies the key file to be used for SSL setup at server-side. The default is NULL. If this is set to NULL, SSL support is disabled.

     ```
     UPDATE DBM CFG USING SSL_SVR_KEYDB
     /home/db2inst1/sqllib/security/keystore/KeyDB.kdb;
     ```

- `ssl_svr_stash`: Specifies a fully qualified file path for the stash file to be used for SSL setup at the server-side. The default is NULL. If this is set to NULL, SSL support is disabled.

```
UPDATE DBM CFG USING SSL_SVR_STASH
/home/db2inst1/sqllib/security/keystore/mydbserver.sth;
```

- `ssl_svr_label`: Specifies a label of the personal certificate of the server in the key database. The default is NULL. If this set to NULL, the default certificate in the key database is used. If there is no default certificate in the key database, SSL support is disabled.

```
UPDATE DBM CFG USING SSL_SVR_LABEL MyKeyDBLabel;
```

- `ssl_svcename`: Specifies the name of the port that a database server uses to await communications from remote client nodes using SSL protocol.

```
UPDATE DBM CFG USING SSL_SVCENAME db2inst1_ssl_port;
```

- `DB2COMM`: This registry variable specifies communication protocols for the current Db2 instance.

```
db2set DB2COMM=SSL
```

If you want to allow both SSL and TCPIP communications, you can set the `DB2COMM` registry variable to both SSL and TCPIP.

```
db2set DB2COMM=SSL,TCPIP
```

- `ssl_cipherspecs`: Specifies the cipher suites that the server allows for incoming connection requests when using the SSL protocol. The default is NULL. If this is set to NULL, the GSKit will pick the strongest available cipher suite.

```
UPDATE DBM CFG USING SSL_CIPHERSPECS
TLS_ECDHE_ECDSA_WITH_AES_256_CBC_SHA384;
```

4. Restart the database instance:

```
db2stop; db2start
```

If you have the Db2 connect server configured to establish a connection between System i, System z and Db2 Linux, UNIX, and Windows, the connection concentrator must be deactivated to support SSL for both inbound and outbound requests. If it is activated, SSL is supported for outbound requests only.

Db2 native encryption

Db2 native encryption was introduced in version 10.5 FIX PACK 5 to facilitate data encryption at rest without any hardware, software, and application changes. The following diagram showcases the components of Db2 native encryption.

- The data encryption key (DEK): Db2 encrypts data with a data encryption key before the data is written to disk. The data encryption key is stored, and encrypted, in the database or backup image.
- The encrypted master key: A master key is an encryption key that is used to encrypt a data encryption key (DEK). The data encryption key (DEK) is stored and managed within the database. The master key is stored and managed outside the database. Each database has a single master key and the master key for the database is specified by a label.
- The keystore: The master keys are stored outside the database in a keystore. The keystore can be either a local keystore on the same server as the Db2 database server, or a centralized keystore residing on a system other than the Db2 database server, such as a **Public Key Cryptography Standard (PKCS)** #11 keystore.
  You can update keystore information through the keystore_type and keystore_location database manager configuration parameters.

- UPDATE DBM CFG USING KEYSTORE_TYPE PKCS12;
  UPDATE DBM CFG USING KEYSTORE_LOCATION
  /db/home/db2inst1/keystore/;

- The key manager: A key manager is a software tool that can be used to create, update, and securely store a keystore. You can use the IBM Global Security Kit (GSKit) to manage a local keystore or the Key Management Interoperability Protocol (KMIP) to manage a centralized keystore.

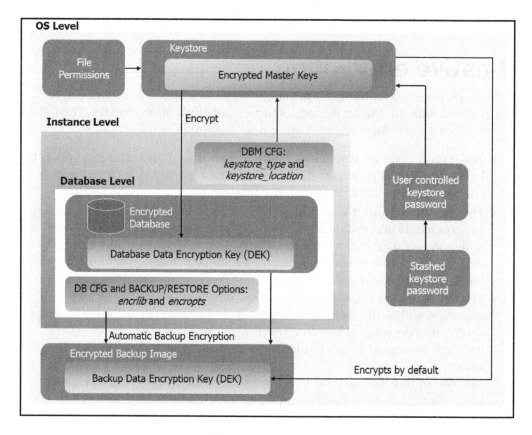

Db2 native encryption components

- Automatic backup encryption: You can use two database configuration parameters, *encrlib* and *encropts*, to automatically encrypt database backup images.
  - `encrlib`: Specifies the absolute path of the encryption library to be used for automatically encrypting backup images. The default is NULL, so backups are not automatically encrypted. To encrypt the backup image, use the ENCRYPT option in the BACKUP DATABASE command.

- `encropts:` Specifies options that are specific to the encryption library to be used for automatically encrypting backup images. The default is NULL. You can also use the COMPROPTS and ENCROPTS options within the `BACKUP DATABASE` command to pass the necessary option string values, such as the cipher name, key length, and master key label.

Once the keystore has been created and registered, you can create a new encrypted database with default settings by using the `ENCRYPT` clause as shown below:

```
CREATE DATABASE sample ENCRYPT;
```

If you want to encrypt an existing database SAMPLE, the database has to be restored from a backup image using the `RESTORE DATABASE` command.

```
RESTORE DATABASE sample FROM /db2/backup TAKEN AT 20180526232357 ENCRYPT;
```

If you want to create an encrypted database using custom settings, you can use the following `CREATE DATABASE` command.

```
CREATE DATABASE sample ENCRYPT CIPHER AES KEY LENGTH 256 MASTER KEY LABEL
masterkey;
```

When you create an encrypted database, it encrypts the following:

- All user data in the database
- All user-defined and system-defined table spaces
- All types of data (LOB, XML, INT, and so on) in the database
- All transaction logs, including the transaction logs in the archive location
- Database backup images
- `LOAD COPY` and `LOAD` staging files

Db2 version v11.1 added support for the Key Management Interoperability Protocol (KMIP) 1.1, the industry standard for centralized key managers. This simplifies the management of encryption master keys at enterprise level by supporting many encrypted databases you will need to manage backup procedures for each local keystore. This also simplifies implementation of HADR by using a common centralized key manager on primary and multiple standbys. You can use the `SYSPROC.ADMIN_ROTATE_MASTER_KEY()` built-in procedure to change a master key for an encrypted database at regular intervals based on the organization's security policies. Although the master key changes, the data stored on disk is not re-encrypted.

If you want to rotate the master key without using a label, you can pass a NULL value to the procedure:

```
CALL ADMIN_ROTATE_MASTER_KEY (NULL)

  Value of output parameters
  --------------------------
  Parameter Name  : LABEL
  Parameter Value : DB2_SYSGEN_db2inst1_SAMPLE_2018-06-17-18.20.29_B26DD222

  Return Status = 0
```

If you want to use a specific label, use the desired label as the input value to the procedure. If a label is specified, it must be associated with a master key at the keystore, or the procedure will fail.

If you want to view the instance's keystore settings, you can use the SYSPROC.ADMIN_GET_ENCRYPTION_INFO table function, as shown here:

```
SELECT
KEYSTORE_NAME,
KEYSTORE_TYPE,
KEYSTORE_HOST,
VARCHAR (MASTER_KEY_LABEL, 100) AS MASTER_KEY_LABEL
FROM TABLE (ADMIN_GET_ENCRYPTION_INFO ());
KEYSTORE_NAME
KEYSTORE_TYPE           KEYSTORE_HOST
MASTER_KEY_LABEL
-------------------------------------------------------------------------
-------------------------------------------------------------------------
-------------------------------------------------------------------------
---------------------------- ---------------------- -----------------------
-------------------------------------------------------------------------
-------------------------------------------------------------------------
-------------------------------------------------------------------------
------- -----------------------------------------------------------------
------------------------------------
/db/home/db2inst1/keystore/ne-keystore.p12
PKCS12              db2demo.ibm.lab
DB2_SYSGEN_db2inst1_SAMPLE_2018-06-17-18.20.29_B26DD222
```

Many of Db2's tools, such as db2cklog, db2flsn, db2LogsForRfwd, db2ckbkp, db2adutl, and db2dart, support encryption. These tools will use the keystore specified in the database manager configuration keystore_location parameter.

The IBM Global Security Kit (GSKit) must be installed and configured before encrypting the database using Db2 native encryption.

Summary

The objective of this chapter was to provide the ability to answer Db2 security chapter questions on the following topics:

- Db2 authentication and authorization concepts
- The LDAP authentication configuration within Db2 using the transparent LDAP feature
- Db2 trusted contexts and trusted connection implementation concepts
- SSL configuration to encrypt data in-flight, and Db2 native encryption to encrypt data at rest
- The Db2 audit facility to implement and monitor unknown or unexpected access to the database

Practice questions

Question 1: Which statement about the SERVER_ENCRYPT authentication setting is true?

1. The user ID and password will be encrypted
2. The user ID will be encrypted
3. The user ID, password, and data will be encrypted
4. The password will be encrypted

Question 2: Which special register is valid in the VERIFY_TRUSTED_CONTEXT_ROLE_FOR_USER built-in function?

1. CURRENT_USER
2. SESSION_USER
3. SYSTEM_USER
4. GROUP_USER

Question 3: Which of these parameters are essential in setting up native encryption? (Choose two.)

1. KMIP_TYPE
2. KEYSTORE_LOCATION
3. KEY_HASH_TYPE
4. KEYSTORE_TYPE
5. KEYSTORE_HOSTNAME

Question 4: Which of the following is NOT a security table function?

1. `SYSIBMADM.PRIVILEGES`
2. `AUTH_LIST_AUTHORITIES_FOR_AUTHID`
3. `AUTH_LIST_GROUPS_FOR_AUTHID`
4. `AUTH_LIST_ROLES_FOR_AUTHID`

Question 5: Which authorities can be audited with the Db2 AUDIT statement?

1. SECADM, DBADM, SYSMAINT, and SYSCTRL can be audited, but SYSADM cannot.
2. SYSADM, DBADM, SYSMAINT, and SYSCTRL can be audited, but SECADM cannot.
3. SYSADM, SECADM, DBADM, SQLADM, ACCESSCTRL, and DATAACCESS can be audited.
4. DBADM, SYSMAINT, ACCESSCTRL, and DATAACCESS can be audited, but SYSADM and SECADM cannot.

Question 6: Which authorities can execute the CREATE ROW PERMISSION and CREATE MASK statements?

1. SYSMON
2. SECADM
3. ACCESSCTRL
4. SQLADM

Question 7: The following statements are run on the database SAMPLE:

```
CREATE MASK HR.EMP_SSN_MASK ON HR.EMPLOYEES

FOR COLUMN SSN RETURN

CASE WHEN (VERIFY_ROLE_FOR_USER (SESSION_USER, 'PAYROLL') = 0)

THEN SSN

ELSE NULL

END

ENABLE;

ALTER TABLE HR.EMPLOYEES ACTIVATE COLUMN ACCESS CONTROL;
```

Which statement about the SSN column is true?

1. Values stored in the SSN column are visible to all users.
2. Values stored in the SSN column are visible to all users except the PAYROLL role users.
3. Values stored in the SSN column are visible only to PAYROLL role users.
4. Values stored in the SSN column are not visible to any users.

Question 8: Which of these is NOT a valid statement about the RCAC feature?

1. Users with SECADM authority cannot be exempt from RCAC rules.
2. You can activate and deactivate RCAC when needed by using the ALTER TABLE statement.
3. RCAC is a more powerful security mechanism than LBAC.
4. When a result set is restricted due to the RCAC rules defined on a table, no warnings or error messages are returned.

Question 9: Which of the following security-label components can you use with LBAC? (Choose two.)

1. Array
2. Tree
3. Forest
4. Range
5. DB2SECURITYLABEL

Question 10: Which statement here about the characteristics of a role is true?

1. Users with SECADM authority create and manage roles
2. Roles can own database objects
3. You can use roles to grant SYSADM, SYSCTRL, SYSMAINT, and SYSMON authorities
4. Privileges and authorities granted to groups are not considered when creating views, MQTs, SQL routines, triggers, and packages containing static SQL

Answers

Question 1: The correct answer is **1**. Authentication occurs at the server by using the OS security facility. However, the user ID and password that the user enters to attach to an instance or connect to a database stored on the server may be encrypted at the client before it is sent to the server for validation.

Question 2: The correct answer is **2**. VERIFY_TRUSTED_CONTEXT_ROLE_FOR_USER (SESSION_USER, [RoleNameExp]) - Returns a value that indicates that the authorization ID identified by the SESSION_USER special register has acquired a role under a trusted connection associated with some trusted context, and that the role is in (or contained in any of) the role names specified by the list of RoleNameExp arguments.

Question 3: The correct answers are **4** and **5**. The database manager configuration parameters `keystore_type` and `keystore_location` are key to implementing the encryption at rest.

- `keystore_type`: Specifies the type of keystore that is used to store encryption keys or remote storage account credentials
- `keystore_location`: Specifies the location of the keystore that is used to store encryption keys or remote storage account credentials

Question 4: The correct answer is **1**. AUTH_LIST_AUTHORITIES_FOR_AUTHID, AUTH_LIST_GROUPS_FOR_AUTHID, and AUTH_LIST_ROLES_FOR_AUTHID are scalar table functions, and SYSIBMADM.PRIVILEGES is an administrative view for security.

Question 5: The correct answer is **3**. The ACCESSCTRL, DATAACCESS, DBADM, SECADM, SQLADM, SYSADM, SYSCTRL, SYSMAINT, SYSMON, and WLMADM authorities can be audited using the AUDIT statement.

Question 6: The correct answer is **2**. Only a user with SECADM authority can execute the CREATE MASK and CREATE ROW PERMISSION statements.

Question 7: The correct answer is **2**. The CREATE MASK statement works in two cases for HR.EMP_SSN_MASK for the column SSN:

- When the session user role is PAYROLL, that user will see a NULL value in SSN column values.
- When the session user role is other than PAYROLL, that user will see the actual SSN values.

Question 8: The correct answer is **2**. LBAC is a more powerful security mechanism compared with RCAC. LBAC is mainly used in defense applications, and RCAC in commercial applications. No database user is inherently exempt from RCAC rules, including DATAACCESS and SECADM authorities. You can easily activate and deactivate RCAC by using this set of statements:

- ALTER TABLE <SCHEMA>.<TABLENAME> ACTIVATE ROW ACCESS CONTROL;
- ALTER TABLE <SCHEMA>.<TABLENAME> DEACTIVATE ROW ACCESS CONTROL;

When a result set is restricted due to the RCAC rules defined on a table, no warnings or errors messages are returned.

Question 9: The correct answers are **1** and **2**. A security-label component represents criteria that you can use to decide whether a user should have access to specific data. Three types of security-label components exist:

- A set is a collection of elements (character string values) where the order in which each element appears is not important.
- An array is an ordered set that can represent a simple hierarchy. In an array, the order in which the elements appear is important. The first element ranks higher than the second, the second ranks higher than the third, and so on.
- A tree represents a more complex hierarchy that can have multiple nodes and branches.

Question 10: The correct answer is **1**. The true characteristics of roles are:

- SECADM users create and manage roles within the database engine.
- Privileges and authorities you grant to roles are considered when creating views, MQTs, SQL routines, triggers, and packages containing static SQL. Roles cannot own database objects.
- Roles cannot grant instance-level authorities such as SYSADM, SYSCTRL, SYSMAINT, and SYSMON.
- You can delegate role maintenance by using the WITH ADMIN OPTION clause in the GRANT ROLE statement.

Other Books You May Enjoy

If you enjoyed this book, you may be interested in these other books by Packt:

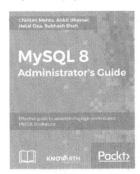

MySQL 8 Administrator's Guide
Chintan Mehta et al.

ISBN: 978-1-78839-519-9

- Understanding different MySQL 8 data types based on type of contents and storage requirements
- Best practices for optimal use of features in MySQL 8
- Explore globalization configuration and caching techniques to improve performance
- Create custom storage engine as per system requirements
- Learn various ways of index implementation for flash memory storages
- Configure and implement replication along with approaches to use replication as solution
- Understand how to make your MySQL 8 solution highly available
- Troubleshoot common issues and identify error codes while using MySQL 8

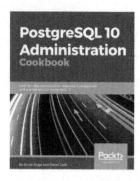

PostgreSQL 10 Administration Cookbook
Simon Riggs, Gianni Ciolli

ISBN: 978-1-78847-492-4

- Get to grips with the newly released PostgreSQL 10 features to improve database performance and reliability
- Manage open source PostgreSQL versions 10 on various platforms.
- Explore best practices for planning and designing live databases
- Select and implement robust backup and recovery techniques in PostgreSQL 10
- Explore concise and clear guidance on replication and high availability
- Discover advanced technical tips for experienced users

Leave a review - let other readers know what you think

Please share your thoughts on this book with others by leaving a review on the site that you bought it from. If you purchased the book from Amazon, please leave us an honest review on this book's Amazon page. This is vital so that other potential readers can see and use your unbiased opinion to make purchasing decisions, we can understand what our customers think about our products, and our authors can see your feedback on the title that they have worked with Packt to create. It will only take a few minutes of your time, but is valuable to other potential customers, our authors, and Packt. Thank you!

Index

316, 319

system administrative authority (SYSADM) 405
system catalog views 199, 201, 204, 207, 209
system control authority (SYSCTRL) 40, 405, 406
system maintenance authority (SYSMAINT) 40, 406
System Managed Space (SMS) 94
system monitor authority (SYSMON) 40, 407

T

table privileges 415
table
  Alter table statement, using 105, 106
  creating 103
  database objects, invalidation 107
  database objects, revalidation 108, 109
  expression-based indexes 106
  Insert Time Clustering (ITC) 124
  Materialized Query Table (MQT) 124
  Multidimensional clustering (MDC) 121, 123
tablespace privileges 415
tablespaces
  about 94
  containers 94, 95
  creating 97, 98, 99
  planning 96
  rebalance operation 100
  reclaimable storage 101
threshold, Db2
  about 72
  activity thresholds 72
  aggregate thresholds 73
  connection thresholds 72
  unit of work thresholds 72
Tivoli Storage Manager (TSM) server 53, 347
Tivoli System Automation (TSA) 138
Tivoli System Automation for Multi Platforms (TSAMP) 376
transaction manager (TM) 36
transaction
  about 343, 345, 347, 349
  logging strategies 350
Transport Layer Security (TLS) 39
triggers

AFTER 195
BEFORE 195
creating 194, 196, 197
INSTEAD OF 195
using 194, 196, 197
trusted connections 423, 425, 426
trusted context 423, 425, 426
types, authentication
  CLIENT 403
  DATA_ENCRYPT 403
  DATA_ENCRYPT_CMP 403
  GSS_SERVER_ENCRYPT 403
  GSSPLUGIN 403
  KERBEROS 403
  KRB_SERVER_ENCRYPT 403
  SERVER 403
  SERVER_ENCRYPT 403
types, crash recovery
  group crash recovery 352
  member crash recovery 352

U

Uncommitted Read (UR) 384
update rule, referential constraints
  about 179
  ON UPDATE NO ACTION 180
  ON UPDATE RESTRICT 179
user defined functions (UDF) 7
User Direct Access Programming Library (uDAPL) 389

V

version recovery 352
view privileges 416
view
  using, with CHECK OPTION 191, 193, 194

W

workload management administrator authority (WLMADM) 410
workload manager (WLM) 13

X

XML compression 149

Made in the USA
Coppell, TX
30 January 2020